Information Assurance Handbook

Effective Computer Security and Risk Management Strategies

Corey Schou
Steven Hernandez

New York   Chicago   San Francisco
Athens   London   Madrid   Mexico City
Milan   New Delhi   Singapore   Sydney   Toronto

Cataloging-in-Publication Data is on file with the Library of Congress

McGraw-Hill Education books are available at special quantity discounts to use as premiums and sales promotions, or for use in corporate training programs. To contact a representative, please visit the Contact Us pages at www.mhprofessional.com.

Information Assurance Handbook: Effective Computer Security and Risk Management Strategies

1234567890   DOC DOC   10987654

ISBN   978-0-07-182165-0
MHID   0-07-182165-1

Sponsoring Editor
Meghan Riley Manfre

Editorial Supervisor
Patty Mon

Project Manager
Ridhi Mathur,
Cenveo® Publisher Services

Acquisitions Coordinator
Mary Demery

Technical Editors
Flemming Faber
Jill Slay

Copy Editor
Kim Wimpsett

Proofreader
Susie Elkind

Indexer
Rebecca Plunkett

Production Supervisor
Jean Bodeaux

Composition
Cenveo Publisher Services

Illustration
Andrew Berg
Jonathan Holmes
Cenveo Publisher Services

Art Director, Cover
Jeff Weeks

For my family—more patient than I deserve; for my mentors, who gave me the lamp to guide me; for my students, who give me constant purpose and challenge.

—*Corey Schou*

For my beloved wife, Michelle; you inspire the very best in me.

—*Steven Hernandez*

About the Authors

Corey Schou, Ph.D., is a Fulbright Scholar, a frequent public speaker, an active researcher, and an author of more than 300 books, papers, articles, and other presentations. His interests include information assurance, risk management, software engineering, developing secure applications, security and privacy, and collaborative decision making.

He has been described in the press as the father of the knowledge base used worldwide to establish computer security and information assurance. He was responsible for compiling and editing computer security training standards for the U.S. government.

In 2003, he was selected as the first University Professor at Idaho State University. He directs the Informatics Research Institute and the National Information Assurance Training and Education Center. His program was recognized by the U.S. government as a Center of Academic Excellence in Information Assurance and is a leading institution in the CyberCorps/Scholarship for Service program.

In addition to his academic accomplishments, he holds a broad spectrum of certifications including Certified Cyber Forensics Professional (CCFP), Certified Secure Software Lifecycle Professional (CSSLP), HealthCare Information Security and Privacy Practitioner (HCISPP), CISSP Information Systems Security Architecture Professional (CISSP-ISSAP), and CISSP Information Systems Security Management Professional (CISSP-ISSMP).

During his career, he has been recognized by many organizations, including the Federal Information Systems Security Educators Association, which selected him as the 1996 Educator of the Year, and his research and center were cited by the Information Systems Security Association for Outstanding Contributions to the Profession. In 1997, he was given the TechLearn award for contributions to distance education.

He was nominated and selected as an honorary Certified Information Systems Security Professional (CISSP) based on his lifetime achievement. In 2001, the International Information Systems Security Certification Consortium (ISC)² selected him as the second recipient of the Tipton award for contribution to the information security profession. In 2007, he was recognized as a Fellow of (ISC)².

Steven Hernandez, MBA, CISSP, CISA, CSSLP, SSCP, CAP, HCISPP, CompTIA Security+, is the chief information security officer for the Office of Inspector General at the U.S. Department of Health and Human Services (HHS). His 16 years of extensive background in information assurance includes work for international heavy manufacturing, large finance organizations, academia, government agencies, nongovernment organizations, and international not-for-profits.

Hernandez is an industry-recognized expert in risk management, information assurance investment performance, privacy in healthcare and commerce, and information assurance management. He guest lectures at Idaho State University as affiliate faculty, the National Information Assurance Training and Education Center as affiliate faculty, George Washington University as a distinguished speaker, and California State University at San Bernardino as an honorary professor. He is the editor and lead author of the third edition of the *Official (ISC)² Guide to the CISSP CBK.* Hernandez is the chair of the (ISC)² HCISPP Common Body of Knowledge Domain committee in addition to editor of the first edition of the Official (ISC)² Guide to the HCISPP CBK.

About the Technical Editors

Flemming Faber is the senior adviser at the Danish Centre for Cyber Security, part of the Danish Defence Intelligence Service. He has been an information security expert since 1994 and was the first Dane to obtain CISSP certification in 1999. Flemming has worked as a security consultant and information security manager in international consultancy companies for a decade. In 2003, he joined the Danish National IT and Telecom Agency, a Danish government agency where he was head of the IT security division until 2009. In the agency, he was in charge of the information security strategy in relation to the general Danish e-government initiatives, the Danish government's information security awareness campaigns, privacy initiatives, and the development of information security standards for Danish government agencies. Since 2006, Flemming has been the Danish government representative on the board of the European Network and Information Security Agency (ENISA). He was the main architect in establishing the Danish GovCERT in 2009, where he is responsible for policy, strategy, and international cooperation. Since 2011, the Danish GovCERT has been part of the Danish Centre for Cyber Security under the Ministry of Defence. He has been active in promoting information security internationally and has been involved with (ISC)² activities since 1999. Flemming was a member of the (ISC)² Board of Directors from 2010 to 2013.

Jill Slay is the director of the new Australian Centre for Cyber Security at UNSW Canberra @ ADFA. With long-term funding allocated, this centre aims to develop critical mass in cross-disciplinary research and teaching in cybersecurity to serve the Australian government and Defence Force and help strengthen the digital economy. She carries out collaborative research in forensic computing, information assurance, and critical infrastructure protection with industry, state, and federal government partners in Australia, South Africa, the United States, and Asia; and she has advised various governments, supporting them in research and process development.

Jill was made a member of the Order of Australia (AM) in the 2011 Australia Day Honours Awards for service to the information technology industry through contributions in the areas of forensic computer science, security, protection of infrastructure, and cyberterrorism. She is a member of the Institute of Electrical and Electronic Engineers and also a fellow of the (ISC)² and the Australian Computer Society. These awards were made for her service to the IT security profession.

Contents

Foreword

Throughout my career in government and private industry, I have seen many approaches to securing information systems and managing risks. One question I get asked repeatedly is, "How do I know when I have enough people, process, or technology to manage risk effectively?" In government and regulated sectors, the response to this question is driven by a complex assortment of standards, mandates, and laws pushing to compliance. In private industry, we often see businesses conforming to "best practices" or "industry standards" as a baseline. While conforming to regulatory or legal requirements is a good start, it really is just the bare minimum if an organization wants to excel and mature in risk management. For years I have said, "One can be compliant but still be insecure, and we need to make sure that by being secure we become compliant."

Schou and Hernandez's book provides a leadership view of information assurance and a practical perspective for both practitioners and aspiring leaders. They take the reader through the international dimensions of risk management for strategic leaders and senior management. Their approach not only guides the reader through the necessary elements of managing risk in today's ever-changing IT environment, but also explains why information assurance is important in creating and maintaining a competitive advantage in today's global economy. They give the reader practical advice for approaching information assurance for emerging technologies, such as the cloud and big data, without getting caught up in the technical details that may confuse or distract leadership.

When I served as vice chair of the President's Critical Infrastructure Protection Board and later as the first Cyber-Security Coordinator of the Obama Administration, I worked with Dr. Schou to improve the responsiveness of academia to both government and industry needs. In the preparation of the *U.S. National Strategy to Secure CyberSpace* and subsequently in the *National Strategy for Trusted Identities in Cyberspace*, the essential linkage between strategic leadership and operations was critical. One of the most difficult challenges I faced was conveying risk; good news needs to travel fast, but bad news needs to travel faster. It is critical to pass the bad news on to senior leaders who may not have an extensive background in information technology or security.

This book functions as a bidirectional guide for leadership and operational personnel alike. For those who are more focused on operational and technical issues, the book provides a guide to why senior leaders insist on specific procedures and visibility. For senior leaders, this book provides information about organizational objectives while explaining some of the limitations and capabilities of today's information assurance risk management tools and professionals. The authors offer real-world examples of applying information assurance in industries such as healthcare, retail, and industrial control systems.

This book takes a broad perspective and is a nexus of information assurance practice, policy, strategy, and implementation applicable to a diverse audience. It provides an up-to-date guide covering some of the best information assurance practices found internationally. System administrators can use the book to understand how risk management operates throughout their organization and why their role is significant. Government leaders can gain new insights into cloud computing concerns and how big data integrates with information assurance and risk management. As the authors state in their introduction, "If you need help, read this book!"

—Howard A. Schmidt, Partner, Ridge Schmidt Cyber LLC,
and former Cyber-Security Coordinator of the Obama Administration

Acknowledgments

We would like to thank those who have contributed to the writing and development of this book, including our colleagues and the project team at McGraw-Hill Education, specifically Meghan Manfre, Mary Demery, Patty Mon, and Jean Bodeaux. We would also like to thank Dr. Larry Leibrock for valuable input about computer forensics and Andrew Berg and Jonathan Holmes for the illustrations you will see in the introduction and throughout this book.

Introduction

Information assurance is not my problem, and it is not your problem. It is an ever-increasing problem for *everyone*—you, home businesses, small enterprises, large businesses, economies, and governments are all at risk. Think of it this way: Information and data in all forms are assets, and you are obliged to protect your assets. Of course, as you run your enterprise, your security efforts do not show up on the bottom line—unless something goes wrong. All information assurance tools and mechanisms required by the largest enterprises are useful at a different scale by the smallest. This book allows you to select from a broad spectrum of information assurance tools to protect assets, manage risk, and provide competitive advantage. While reading, you will see the "juggling leader" as a callout for concepts that warrant special attention for those wearing many hats. She will point out useful subject matter for people juggling several roles.

Read This Book

If you run a one-person enterprise, you must perform a constant balancing act or become a one-man band and keep your focus on the overall success of the enterprise. At a minimum, you must have a plan for what you would do if something destroyed all your records or if a virus took over your computers or if a competitor took your list of prospects or…well, you get the idea. Information assurance must be part of your enterprise planning. You must make yourself do information assurance if you are to remain viable and competitive!

Read This Book

If you run a small to medium enterprise, you may be able to have some specialization among your employees. This is like having a low-budget jazzband or a classic ensemble where the musicians all wait tables in a restaurant on the side (using the same tux for both jobs). If you are lucky, you might have someone who is in charge of information technology. This individual must devote part of their time to information assurance and may provide some leadership, but they also have to support employees and customers. They have help, but you must provide direction and leadership. For example, your accounting staff, your marketing staff, and your production staff will have a role in information assurance, but they must all be going in the same direction. Remember, they will all plead that information assurance is not their job. You as a leader must set the example and the tone from the top. Information assurance must be part of your enterprise planning. You must provide leadership and encourage an information assurance culture. How?

Read This Book

If you run a large enterprise, you have all the challenges of protecting your information assets through a CIO. While the CIO may have good intentions, understanding information assurance and being able to *speak* its language is invaluable when explaining problems, opportunities, and risk to technical professionals. Information assurance must be part of your enterprise planning. It must be central to your information technology strategy. You must provide leadership and encourage an

information assurance culture. In today's competitive and global marketplace, even large enterprises that have existed for years without a formal information assurance function can stumble and fail rapidly because of a breach or cyberattack.

Consider information assurance as a professional symphony orchestra: It has all the attributes of an ensemble and a one-man band. Each group can select more or less complex versions of the music just as you can choose lessons from this book. Take what you need, but read through the book from time to time to see what you might be missing. No matter what, have a plan, execute it, mitigate risk, succeed. Half the battle is choosing the right questions to ask at the right time! This book aims to arm the senior leaders of the organization with the strategic tools to help have constructive discussions around information risk, assurance, and strategy. The conductor of an orchestra doesn't need to understand how to play every instrument. However, she must understand the basic sounds, notes, combinations, and types of music best performed by specific instruments. It is essential that all of this is done in perfect harmony.

This book takes a similar approach with information assurance. Reading it will not make a senior leader a *cyberninja* with deep technical skills. It will, however, create a leader with a strong information assurance strategic understanding who can call in the right combination of skills, experience, and background to meet today's toughest risk management challenges. Remember, the Spartans were amazing soldiers and well-trained in a narrow field. They had numerous amazing battles we remember today; ultimately, though, they were defeated by forces that understood not only warfare but how to mix strategic resources to mitigate risk and deliver results! If you are already experienced with the technology portion of the information assurance profession, reading this book will help you understand what your senior management is trying to do through their strategic planning.

Purpose

Enterprises of all sizes are under increasing competitive pressure to leverage data, information, and communication technology infrastructure to achieve their vision. The well-planned implementation of secure information technology will have a large positive impact on the socio-economic development of an organization and its partners. While information technology (IT) clearly revolutionizes businesses and strengthens governments, it introduces risks.

To make the IT investment pay off, senior management must address and manage risks systematically and economically. Assuring the information assets have integrity, are available, and are confidential presents a significant challenge to even seasoned executives; improvement in this area is a continuous effort. The strategic approach and controls explained provide an executive view of information assurance. The controls and strategic approach are also expected to guide an overall strategy for safeguarding vital information assets and critical functions of an organization.

The essentials of information assurance have been identified and mapped for the senior management and executives of an organization. Our approach to information assurance is broad to ensure that the contents are relevant to organizations of various sizes, complexities, and industries. Assuring information and providing security is an ongoing process; an organization's information assurance policy is an instantiation of a living organizational strategy and helps management establish an organization's risk management strategy.

We have provided best practices and guidelines to assist in preventing, detecting, containing, correcting, and recovering from inevitable security breaches and other information assurance failures. By providing a broad overview of threats, information assurance concepts, and risk management approaches, organizations may use the information presented to strengthen their information assurance risk posture. An organization's mission and objectives are always put first if information assurance is pervasive and not invasive in the organizational culture.

The information presented is designed to reach a broad audience; the content does not provide detailed implementation procedures for security controls nor does it prescribe minimum compliance requirements or penalties for noncompliance. Guidance is provided to management to seek an in-depth solution for their particular challenges. Organizations should seek professional opinions from appropriately certified professionals before implementing security controls that are in accordance with their risk profiles and business objectives.

No matter the size of your enterprise, investing in information assurance controls requires a commitment of limited finances, time, and human resources. It may not be feasible for organizations to invest in all areas of information assurance. The information provided is intended to foster discussion around possible approaches and help organizations prioritize areas for improvement.

The information assurance strategic approach and associated controls provide fundamental information and guidelines for senior management and executives of organizations. The approach outlined provides guidance for protecting information system–based assets (including information, software, and hardware) by describing the interrelationships and provides a comparison analysis of information assurance elements. Executives and senior management who need quick and broad overviews on information assurance–related matters will find this resource useful.

Scope

The material presented is useful to organizations independent of the following:

- Nature of business (telecommunication, education, utility, health, defense)
- Size (small, medium, large)
- Type (commercial, government agencies, nonprofit)

Guidelines are provided for managing information assurance, and we demonstrate a comprehensive approach to identifying, applying, and controlling information assurance initiatives. Common threats and vulnerabilities are discussed as you are guided through a comprehensive list of applicable controls for an organization as a function of its risk profiles.

The approach offered does not go in-depth into implementation procedures. Organizations should view the strategy and controls offered as advisory and use the contents as a starting point to manage its assurance exposures. The strategy and controls are vendor-independent and are not specific to any technology. Every section includes critical thinking questions. These questions are intended to guide you in applying the material discussed to their organization or mission.

Intended Audience

The strategy presented provides a foundation for a broad audience—experienced and inexperienced, technical and nontechnical—who invest in, monitor, administer, support, manage, audit, assess, design, and implement information assurance within their enterprise. These personnel include the following:

- Anyone within an enterprise who wants to know more about information assurance and who is responsible for planning, managing, implementing, operating, and improving the information assurance management system

- Anyone who wants to be able to identify and manage risk

- Business owners and mission owners who rely on information systems but may not have a good understanding of IT risk and how to manage it

- Chief information officer (CIO), who ensures the implementation of information assurance for an organization's information systems

- Chief risk officer (CRO), who needs to be able to identify and manage enterprise risk

- Contract officers, program managers, and acquisition professionals who are responsible for the IT procurement process

- Enterprise owners ranging from single proprietors to small and medium businesses who want to protect their assets and manage risk

- Information assurance program manager or chief security officer (CSO) and the chief information security officer (CISO), who implement the security program

- IT auditors who audit the systems and ensure compliance with the relevant policies and regulations

- New employees who want to understand why their organization has so many rules, policies, and guidelines

- Senior management, executives, or business owners, who plan and approve budget and set business strategy and objectives

- System and information owners, who are entrusted to protect information and information systems in accordance with the protection requirements stipulated

- Technical support personnel (such as application, system, network, and database administrators), who manage and administer security for the information systems

- Anyone who must balance information assurance and their primary job responsibilities

Throughout the book, there are opportunities for you to challenge yourself with critical thinking exercises. The answers to these questions are not right or wrong; they are intended to stimulate your thinking about information assurance. Responses for each question are included in the appendix section of the book.

William Shakespeare told us that "one man in his time plays many parts" and so it is in information assurance. The list of roles appears daunting; however, no matter the size of the organization, someone has to perform the roles.

Overview

We have organized the contents into six parts. Each of these parts is divided into several chapters focused on essentials. Since each chapter is designed to be self-standing, each chapter has a set of critical thinking exercises for self-assessment and a selection of further readings. In general, this structure models an organizational strategy for information assurance (see Figure 1).

Part I: Information Assurance Basics

Part I introduces the essential-to-know matters in information assurance including the need for information assurance, popular concepts, and approaches. Relationships among fundamentals such as assets, threats, vulnerabilities, risks, and controls are discussed. Since there are several interpretations of the terms *information assurance, information security*, and *cybersecurity*, we have developed a model showing the relationship among them. Different types of security professionals and professional organizations will also be discussed. It is important to understand the information assurance management system (IAMS) and how information assurance is a continuous process. This part ends with a discussion of current practices and regulations in the existing competitive market and information technology landscape.

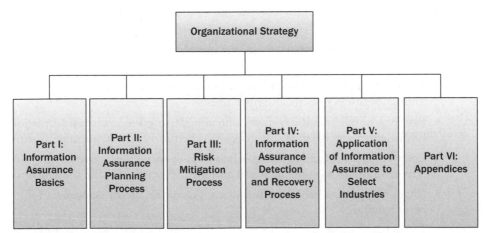

Figure 1 Organization of information

Part II: Information Assurance Planning Process

Part II focuses on important areas for information assurance planning. It describes approaches for implementing information assurance and highlights the importance of an organization's information assurance policy. Once an organization starts to embrace information assurance, it must consider the best framework to implement. This part also explains the importance of asset management, risk management, and human resource security. It concludes with a discussion on why organizations should consider certification and accreditation as part of their information assurance program.

Part III: Risk Mitigation Process

Part III focuses on the prevention process and helps organizations identify processes to be implemented. Following this, the order of execution is explained. Prevention is critical since it avoids information security breaches from the start. The chapters in this part discuss security issues in system development, physical and environmental security, information security awareness, training, and education. This part also discusses preventive tools, techniques, and access controls applicable to those security processes.

Part IV: Information Assurance Detection and Recovery Processes

Part IV focuses on the detection process and explains common tools and methods used to perform detection effectively. It elaborates on security audit, penetration test, and monitoring. Since it is difficult to manage things that are not measured, we highlight the importance of measurement and metrics used by organizations to check and review their information assurance posture. Additional information regarding cloud computing and outsourcing is included in this chapter.

This section also provides information on the steps used to recover from information security incidents. If preventive measures fail, organizations must continue their business and restore. Chapters in this part discuss information security incident handling, computer forensics, business continuity management, backups, and restorations. Additionally, cloud and outsourcing contingency planning will be discussed.

Part V: Application of Information Assurance to Select Industries

Part V applies at a high level the approaches explained to select industries such as healthcare, retail, and industrial control environments. By demonstrating how the information and approaches described are applied, you may adopt and apply the information more quickly to your organization.

Part VI: Appendixes

Part VI includes lists of common threats and vulnerabilities, sample security policy, sample risk analysis table, references used in developing this work, a glossary, and an index.

PART

Information Assurance Basics

Part I provides key concepts, vital components, and definitions fundamental to integrating effective information assurance. Chapter 1 focuses on the development of an information assurance strategy based on the size and complexity of the organization. Chapter 2 discusses the importance and drivers of information assurance, such as why information assurance is important, fundamental principles in information assurance, and the consequence of failure.

Chapter 3 explains the requirements in information assurance, namely, confidentiality, integrity, and availability (CIA); identification, authentication, authorization, and accountability (IAAA); and nonrepudiation and information assurance's association with privacy. Chapter 4 defines the key elements of risks, namely, assets, threats, and vulnerabilities, as well as their interrelationship in managing information assurance. The chapter also provides examples of common threats, vulnerabilities, and controls to manage risks.

Expertise and professionalism are important in the management of information assurance. Chapter 5 provides pointers to organizations with resources for information assurance professionals. In addition, it discusses the code of ethics that information assurance professionals should observe. Chapter 6 discusses the Information Assurance Management System (IAMS) and the Plan-Do-Check-Act (PDCA) implementation model.

Chapter 7 highlights the need to ensure that the implementation of information assurance is done in accordance with existing laws and regulations to ensure compliance. Chapter 7 also provides information about common laws, regulations, standards, and other guidelines in the global enterprise.

Quick Answers

Q: Why is there a need for information assurance?

A: The advancement of technology has caused an increase in vulnerabilities and associated threats. Increased complexity and increased innovation often lead to increased vulnerabilities. This has increased the need to protect the confidentiality, integrity, and availability (CIA) of critical information assets. This minimizes risk. Organizations should comply with relevant laws and regulations, including its own internal policy to increase information assurance.

Q: What are the common concepts in information assurance?

A: Common concepts in information assurance are confidentiality, integrity, and availability (CIA); privacy, nonrepudiation, and authentication; and identification, authentication, authorization, and accountability (IAAA). These concepts are summarized in the internationally recognized Association for Computing Machinery (ACM) Maconachy-Schou-Ragsdale (MSR) model.

Q: There are differing schools of thought on certain concepts in information assurance. How do I know I am following or practicing the right one?

A: True, there are many schools of thought on information assurance. There are no right or wrong choices; the selection of which concept or practice to use depends on the relevant regulations and organizational requirements. One key to success is to have certified security professionals in your organization. They will be able to guide your organization about the right ones to practice. Alternatively, your organization may engage the services of certified security consultants.

Q: What are the differences between the terms *assets, threats, vulnerabilities, risks,* and *controls?*

A: Some *assets* are critical and have high value to organizations that need to be protected. *Threats* can cause harm to these assets, and *vulnerabilities* are items that can allow threats to happen. *Risks* are a combination of exposure (threats and vulnerabilities) together with potential impact. *Controls* are measures, mechanisms, or tools used to protect assets.

Q: In what situations are typical approaches such as the top-down and bottom-up approaches effective in implementing information assurance efforts?

A: A top-down approach is more suitable when organization-wide support is needed and you want to gain management buy-in throughout the information assurance life cycle. A bottom-up approach is appropriate when business functions need immediate action to implement controls. It is a good approach for a decentralized environment.

Q: There are various security organizations offering different courses and certifications. How do I know which one to choose?

A: You should know the professional path you want to embark upon and the business requirements of the organization before deciding to seek particular certification or to attend a preparation course.

For example, the CISSP from (ISC)^2 is for professionals who want to be certified in a broad range of security areas; the CISA from ISSA or CAP is more for professionals who want certified auditing credentials, and the CBCP is for professionals who want to be certified in business continuity or disaster recovery planning. The SANS certification known as Global Information Assurance Certification (GIAC) is a job-specific certification that reflects upon the current practice in lower-level tactical or operational information security. Other certifications from (ISC)^2 include those that focus on computer forensics (CCFP), the software development life cycle (CSSLP), healthcare security and privacy (HCISPP), and cloud security (CCSP).

Q: We often hear security is a continuous improvement process. Is implementing information assurance in a process manner truly the best way?

A: By implementing information assurance in a process manner, you are able to see phases of information assurance improvement efforts systematically, such as planning activities, implementing activities, checking/reviewing activities, and monitoring/tracking activities. A task becomes more manageable when it can be implemented in a systematic way.

Q: What is the difference between a process and a procedure?

A: A *process* is a set of interdependent activities, which are applied to add value. A *procedure* is a systematic method of describing the way in which all or part of that process is to be performed.

Q: How can the Plan-Do-Check-Act (PDCA) cycle be used in the process approach?

A: The PDCA cycle is an established, logical method that can be used to improve a process. This requires the following:

- **P** Planning (figuring out what to do and how to do it)
- **D** Executing the plan (doing what was planned)
- **C** Checking the results (verifying that things happened according to plan)
- **A** Acting to improve the process (figuring out how to improve next time)

1 Developing an Information Assurance Strategy

The information assurance strategy presented is based on ten core principles, as shown in Figure 1-1. The principles fulfill the information assurance requirements and objectives of the majority of organizations. The size, complexity, and organizational environment will drive the relative importance of each of the principles.

Comprehensive

An organization's information assurance strategy and resulting policies and programs should cover topics, areas, and domains needed for modern organizations. Each topic, domain, and area within a policy should contain sufficient breadth and detail to support strategic, tactical, and operational implementation.

Independent

An organization's information assurance strategy should contain independent contents and perspectives related to the defined mission. Organizations are various sizes and use products and services from vendors. To be useful for a heterogeneous community, an organization's information assurance strategy should provide a neutral view of information assurance. Constituent parts within organizations should identify their assurance needs and develop tactical and operational controls in accordance with the strategic plan. Organizations must be cautious not to specify mechanisms, products, or procedural steps to attain organizational information assurance objectives at a strategic level. That level of detail is best left at the tactical and operational level. Organizations should consider vendor-independent strategies while incorporating vendor-specific information into tactical and operational plans.

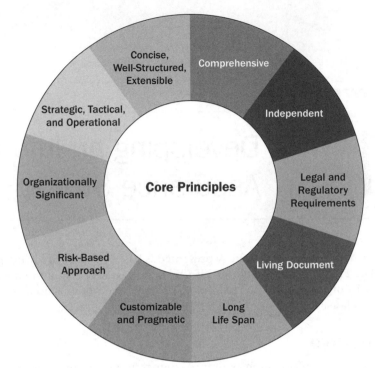

Figure 1-1   Information assurance strategy principles

Legal and Regulatory Requirements

An organization's information assurance strategy must be consistent with existing laws and regulations applicable to but not limited to information assurance, human resources, healthcare, finance, disclosure, internal control, and privacy within the organizational context. Organizations should refer to existing legal frameworks and regulations in their information assurance strategies so leaders understand how to fulfill the regulatory requirements of their industry or environment.

Living Document

An organization's information assurance strategy should be written as a living document comprised of independent components. In smaller organizations with little employee turnover, culture may sustain practices. However, organizations benefit from updated written policies, procedures guidance, and standards to direct operations. Organizations should use the ideas, concepts, and approach outlined in this work to keep their own policies, procedures, standards, and practices up to date.

Long Life Span

Although information assurance is a dynamic, fast-moving, and rapid-changing discipline, it requires a stable strategic foundation. To increase the value and relevance of an organization's information assurance strategy, the strategy must focus on the fundamentals of information assurance that remain constant over time. This is supported by tactical and operational components.

Customizable and Pragmatic

Organizations should develop a flexible information assurance strategy. The strategy should be applicable to a broad spectrum of organization functions independent of size and should consider varied objectives and infrastructure complexity. Organizations should adopt and adapt their tactical and operational plans to reflect identified organizational information assurance requirements and risk profiles. The suggested controls provided throughout this work can serve as guidance.

Risk-Based Approach

In a risk-based approach, organizations identify their risk profiles and prioritize them. Since each organization has a unique risk profile, it must select controls appropriate to its risk tolerance. An organization's information assurance strategy must be broad enough to give guidance to sub-components with diverse risk profiles. This is analogous to risk portfolio approaches in finance. Risk tolerance and profiles are explained later in this work.

Organizationally Significant

Information assurance should be considered significant in an organization's strategy and ongoing operations, and it is a significant investment and area of concern for any organization. Information assurance is part of an organization just like basic accounting. For example, if organizations choose to ignore accounting, they will be subject to possible fines and issues with shareholders, but more importantly, they will be subject to fraud and internal control issues. Information assurance provides controls for an organization's most important assets while bringing visibility into operational and strategic risk.

Strategic, Tactical, and Operational

The organization's information assurance strategy provides a framework to assist senior managers and executives in making strategic (long-term) planning and decisions. It provides information to aid in tactical (midterm) planning and decisions for managers. In addition, an organization's information assurance strategy contains information useful to employees and line managers who make operational (short-term) planning and decisions.

Concise, Well-Structured, and Extensible

Ideally, an organization's information assurance strategy addresses wide-ranging information assurance topics, organized systematically. To help maximize benefits, the structure of a strategy document should facilitate the easy retrieval and use by readers.

The structure and contents of the organization's information assurance strategy should demonstrate high cohesion and low coupling. Each topic should be discussed to the appropriate level completely on its own (high cohesion), and its contents should not be highly dependent (low coupling) on other topics. This approach makes the policy extensible by enabling the easy addition of new information (topics) and by providing a modular approach to information assurance for the user.

Critical Thinking Exercises

1. An organization is considering developing an encryption policy in its organization. The penetration tester from the team starts documenting specific products and configurations to put into the policy. Should the policy contain these details?

2. An organization is considering placing all its policies, procedures, standards, and guidance in a single handbook so executive management has to sign off only once. What are the advantages and disadvantages to this approach?

CHAPTER

2

The Need for Information Assurance

The information assets and infrastructure of organizations are constantly threatened. The dynamic threat environment has increased the need for information assurance. Information assurance is not just a technology issue but is a business and social issue as well. Ultimately, the goal of information assurance is to protect the information and infrastructure that supports the mission and vision of an organization through compliance to regulations, risk management, and organizational policies. A related term, *information technology*, focuses on processing, storing, ensuring the availability of, and sharing information assets.

How does information assurance tackle these problems? *Information assurance* consists of protecting information and services against disclosure, transfer, modification, or destruction (either intentional or unintentional) and ensuring the availability of information in a timely manner. Information assurance also considers the authentication used in a system and how strongly actions can be repudiated. Basically, it ensures only the approved entities receive the accurate information they require when they need it. Securing information by implementing suitable and cost-effective controls ensures critical and sensitive information assets are protected adequately. This chapter focuses on the importance of information assurance, its principles, and the implications of the failure of information assurance.

 To be successful, it is vital for organizations to evaluate the sensitivity and criticality of applications and data as well as the organization's acceptable risk level. As exemplified by the past several years of Verizon Data Breach Investigations Reports, you need only to read the news to see the ongoing assault on organizations' information technology use worldwide. As a fundamental part of doing business, organizations must take inventory of their information assets and evaluate them against threats and vulnerabilities. The evaluation should include customer information, e-mail, financial information, program resources, social media, outsourcing arrangements, and the use of cloud computing technologies. Subsequently, the organization should deploy security controls to protect information assets at an acceptable cost. (For more information, see the 2013 Data Breach Investigations Report at www.verizonenterprise.com/resources/reports/rp_data-breach-investigations-report-2013_en_xg.pdf.)

Protection of Critical and Sensitive Assets

It is a sound business practice to require that critical and sensitive assets be protected. Prior to implementing security controls, an organization must identify the critical business processes and value of the associated assets. The interdependencies between different business processes should be understood for a precise model of the prioritized security control to be implemented.

Compliance to Regulations and Circulars/Laws

Compliance to regulations ensures organizational sustainability. Each day there are new regulatory compliance requirements. Organizations operating in multiple economies or regulatory environments require extra effort to analyze regulatory urgency. Whether requirements stem from international or local laws and regulations, the organization is required to analyze how the requirements can be addressed without compromising the policies and procedures already available within the organization. Understanding how the relevant regulations and standards are in line with one another is the foundation of an effective, efficient, and sustainable compliance.

From a governmental perspective in addition to guidelines and laws, some governments have "enforcement controls" required for public- or private-sector organizations. Examples of these would be *general circulars*, advisories, and directives. The particular terms used for this vary from one nation, economy, and industry to another.

Meeting Audit and Compliance Requirements

From an information assurance point of view, *auditing* is a process that checks and verifies compliance with generally accepted standards, a particular regulation, or a specific requirement. In addition, an audit ensures compliance efforts meet established organizational objectives and follow agreed-upon risk management controls. These different considerations lead to a common goal of compliance through meeting one or more audit requirements and regulations.

Ideally, auditors work with intimate knowledge of the organization to understand the resources subject to audit. Security audits are part of the continuous process of establishing and maintaining practical policies; they are not just something to "put up with." An audit is a sampling process applicable generally to the entire organization. Among other things, a good

Part I

audit should review the effectiveness of the organization's security policies and practices. A complete audit provides a report on the areas of noncompliance and nonconformity regarding the effectiveness of that policy within the context of the organization's objectives, structure, and activities. Certification and Accreditation (C&A), ISO 17799/27001, NIST, COBIT, OCTAVE, and several other standards and guidelines provide information assurance audit frameworks. These are common frameworks used by auditors.

Providing Competitive Advantage

Frequently, individuals fail to recognize that information assurance is a competitive advantage. However, it becomes obvious in the case of a bank. Would you choose to put assets into a bank if it had an inadequate information system? Organizations with proactive controls stay competitive and survive longer. Further, the use of personally identifiable information and personal finance information is now considered commonplace in almost any organization. Breaches of this information not only can be costly from a financial perspective but can also damage an organization's goodwill or public perception.

Viewing information assurance as a differentiator may not be as clear-cut in other markets. For example, one may argue information assurance has no place in a social networking site. However, a social networking site that leaks pictures, message board posts, and user information to the wrong audience will quickly lose its users and therefore possibly its greatest asset (marketing information about its users).

Maintaining a competitive advantage means remaining responsive to current or potential challenges. Successful organizations and those that achieve consistent milestones that exceed the average for its industry have a competitive advantage. A company with strong information assurance practices can build a trusted brand that enhances its business proposition.

There are typically two identified types of competitive advantage. They are cost advantage and differentiation advantage. A competitive advantage exists when the organization is able to give the same benefits as competitors at a lower cost (cost advantage) or to give benefits that outdo those of competing products (differentiation advantage). Having a competitive advantage enables the organization to create value for its customers and make a profit or succeed in its mission. Organizations with strong information assurance are differentiated from their competition as noted in the prior examples of the bank and social media site. Figure 2-1 shows the concept of competitive advantage.

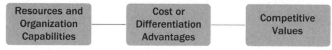

Figure 2-1   Competitive advantage model

Critical Thinking Exercises

1. An organization's board of directors has recently experienced a substantial change in leadership. The new members of the board have demanded an external audit for internal control and information assurance. What should the president or leader of the organization be prepared to provide to ensure the board is comfortable with the audit results?

2. The senior leadership of a large organization has never considered the need for information assurance in the organization's operations. After a series of attacks have crippled similar competitors, senior leadership is now concerned about information assurance. The information technology staff (both in-house and outsourced) has assured senior leadership repeatedly that there is nothing to worry about. Are they right?

3 Information Assurance Principles

Once you understand the importance of information assurance, you need to embrace some fundamental expectations prior to and during the implementation of security, independent of the size or nature of the business. A common model and understanding of information assurance is necessary if an organization is to speak a common risk language and understand common objectives. The information assurance model used throughout this work is the Maconachy-Schou-Ragsdale (MSR) model.

The MSR Model of Information Assurance

In 2001, the Maconachy-Schou-Ragsdale model described three states of information (storage, transmission, and processing); three essential countermeasures (technology, policy, and people); and five basic services (availability, integrity, authentication, confidentiality, and nonrepudiation). The internationally recognized Association for Computing Machinery (ACM) adopted this as an extension of the basic confidentiality, integrity, and availability (CIA) model and an extension of John McCumber's work in the early 1990s.

We have identified fundamental expectations and common beliefs acquired through business practices over the years, and we refer to them here as *information assurance principles*. The seven principles specify that information assurance should do the following:

- Be a business enabler
- Protect the interconnecting element of an organization's systems
- Be cost effective and cost beneficial
- Establish responsibilities and accountability
- Require a robust method
- Be assessed periodically
- Be restricted by social obligations

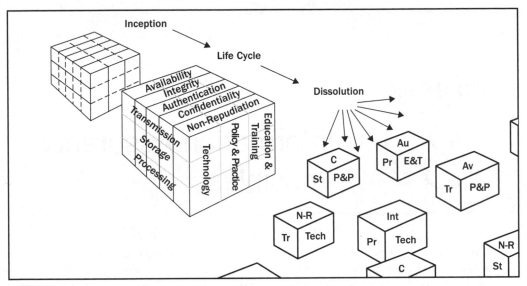

Figure 3-1   MSR model

These seven principles enable you to implement the MSR model shown in Figure 3-1. The MSR model identifies security services, states, and countermeasures, as explained earlier. In addition, the model demonstrates the interlocking relationship among these 45 unique combinations. It reinforces the idea that senior management and senior executives are responsible for the life cycle of the system and an organization's information, from inception to dissolution.

Understanding the distinction between the following terms is crucial for identifying not only the market space but also fundamental concepts in protecting organizations' information assets:

- Information assurance
- Information security
- Information protection
- Cybersecurity

The following sections define each term.

Information Assurance

Information assurance is the overarching approach for identifying, understanding, and managing risk through an organization's use of information and information systems. As noted in the MSR model, information assurance is concerned with the life cycle of information in an organization through the objectives of maintaining the following services or attributes:

- Confidentiality
- Integrity
- Availability
- Nonrepudiation
- Authentication

The following are critical elements to remember about information assurance:

- Information assurance includes all information an organization may process, store, transmit, or disseminate regardless of media. Thus, information on paper, on a hard drive, in the mind of an employee, or in the cloud is considered to be "in scope."
- Information security, information protection, and cybersecurity are subsets of information assurance.

Information Security

Information security is a subdomain of information assurance. As noted in the MSR model, information security focuses on the CIA triad.

- Confidentiality
- Integrity
- Availability

The following are critical elements to remember about information security:

- Like information assurance, information security includes all information an organization may process, store, transmit, or disseminate regardless of media. Thus, information on paper, on a hard drive, in the mind of an employee, or in the cloud is considered in scope.
- Information protection and cybersecurity are subsets of information security.

Information Protection

Information protection is best viewed as a subset of information security. It is often defined in terms of protecting the confidentiality and integrity of information through a variety of means such as policy, standards, physical controls, technical controls, monitoring, and information classification or categorization.

The following are critical elements to remember about information protection:

- Like information security, information protection includes all information an organization may process, store, transmit, or disseminate regardless of media. Thus, information on paper, on a hard drive, in the mind of an employee, or in the cloud is considered in scope.

- Some laws, regulations, and rules specifically cite information protection as a requirement for sensitive information such as personally identifiable information and personal health information.

Cybersecurity

Cybersecurity is a relatively new term that has largely replaced the term *computer security*. This term is often confused with information assurance and information security. Cybersecurity is used to describe the measures taken to protect electronic information systems against unauthorized access or attack. Cybersecurity is primarily concerned with the same objectives of information security within the scope of electronic information systems' CIA.

The following are critical elements to remember about cybersecurity:

- Cybersecurity is primarily focused on the protection of networks and electronic information systems. Other media such as paper, personnel, and in some cases stand-alone systems that rely on physical security are often outside the scope of cybersecurity.

- Cybersecurity often focuses on the vulnerabilities and threats of an information system at the tactical level. System scanning, patching, and secure configuration enforcement are common foci of cybersecurity.

- Intrusion detection and incident response and other functions commonly run from a security operations center (SOC) are often identified as cybersecurity functions.

Figure 3-2 illustrates the relationship among information protection, cybersecurity, information security, and information assurance and their relationship with confidentiality, integrity, availability, and nonrepudiation.

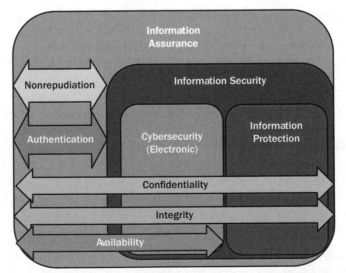

Figure 3-2 Information assurance and subdomains

Information Assurance: Business Enabler

Information assurance is a business enabler and a competitive advantage rather than an obstacle. It allows the organization to achieve its intended objectives. The imposition of disruptive rules and procedures comes from a lack of understanding of business requirements. Frequently, these rules and procedures unnecessarily disrupt normal business operations. Through the implementation and operation of suitable controls, information assurance assists in achieving the organization's vision and mission by protecting its critical assets and resources. Prior to implementation, organizations should identify which controls are to be implemented and weigh the pros and cons associated with each. Security rules or procedures used to protect vital assets while simultaneously supporting the organization's overall vision and mission should be a goal of every senior manager or executive.

When information assurance is properly implemented, it ensures business confidence and competitive advantage; therefore, assurance should be a primary agenda and not a hindrance or an afterthought. Situations exist where a decision may be made not to pursue a new venture or not to adopt a new technology because it cannot be secured appropriately because of unacceptable risk. An example is wireless networking. Some financial organizations have banned the use of IEEE 802.11 (Wi-Fi) networks until enhanced security standards for these networks become available. Thus, information assurance may act as an essential barrier to prevent the adoption of unsafe business practices, rather than as an enabler for business. However, a bank developing a secure mobile application for banking may increase customer satisfaction, reduce personnel costs, and gain customers because of convenience differentiation.

Information Assurance: Protects the Fabric of an Organization's Systems

Information systems provide the interconnecting elements of effective management of organizations. If, however, the information system does not demonstrate the security elements of the MSR model, management cannot make informed decisions. Effective protection from threats requires not only information systems but also information assurance to be an interconnecting, essential part of the entire management system. Security efforts are not silo efforts; they are the essential binding fiber.

Information assurance is a shared responsibility and involves not only the IT organization and other employees. Information assurance should be incorporated into the current management strategy system and requires participation from all functional units. Any information assurance protection program should take into consideration the people, processes, and technology aspects from the MSR model. If one does not do this, the organization will be unable to garner the required support and will not meet its business objectives effectively. Information assurance involves constant review, monitoring, and improvement based on the risk decisions made by management.

Information Assurance: Cost Effective and Cost Beneficial

Information has varying value based on its criticality and sensitivity. Therefore, the protection requirements should be proportional to the value of the information/assets protected and the associated risk. A thorough analysis of the costs and benefits of information assurance may examine either quantitative or qualitative aspects to ensure investment on controls meet expectations. Security investments should take into consideration the cost of designing, implementing, and maintaining the controls; the values of information assets; the degree of dependency on the information systems; and the potential risk and impact the organization is likely to face. Investing in information assurance is both a horizontal and vertical effort.

Information assurance is also a crosscutting program. All information systems and services of an organization have an information assurance requirement. Therefore, an investment should be made in every project for information assurance. This can be thought of as a variable cost. The more services, projects, and information the organization chooses to process, store, or transmit, the greater the information assurance requirements will be.

There is also a fixed-cost aspect to information assurance, which is often the "vertical" aspect of information assurance. Organizations need to have an information assurance program firmly established. This function of an organization is the anchor for the horizontal security efforts and the management area of information assurance for the organization. From this function, common controls and cost-effective security are designed, implemented, and monitored (Figure 3-3).

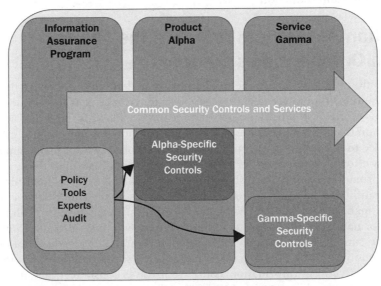

Figure 3-3 Information assurance as a program and service provider

Investments made based on the choice of controls after a risk assessment exercise reduce the impact of information assurance–related losses. For example, by implementing an effective incident-handling process, an organization can avoid losses in terms of unnecessary resources devoted to recovering from a major disruptive incident.

Information Assurance: Shared Responsibilities

System owners, including cloud or outsourced service providers, should share information about planned and implemented security controls so that users can be aware of current efforts and know that the relevant systems are sufficiently secure. Identified critical systems should meet a predefined baseline acceptance level of security. System owners should remember to inform their business users or clients about security controls selected, the nature of the controls implemented, and why the controls are necessary.

Peter Drucker's 1968 book *The Age of Discontinuity* reminds us that knowledge work knows no hierarchy. In addition, information itself knows no individual or organizational boundaries. Information is available to those who need it.

As an information assurance corollary, information can be secured adequately only when all who have access follow established procedures. Thus, information assurance is a team effort that transcends the IT function. The assignment of responsibilities may be to internal or external parties. Clearly defined security responsibilities (both individual and functional level) encourage best practices by users. Refer to Chapter 9 for detailed information assurance roles and responsibilities.

Information Assurance: Robust Approach

Information assurance requires a complete and integrated approach that considers a wide range of processes. This comprehensive approach extends throughout the entire information life cycle. Security controls operate more effectively in concert with the proper functioning of other business process controls. Interdependencies within an information system exist by definition; therefore, a thorough study should be performed before a determination of compatibility and feasibility of controls is made.

Information Assurance: Reassessed Periodically

Information systems and the environments in which they operate are always evolving. Security requirements change rapidly in parallel with emerging technologies, threats, and vulnerabilities. Therefore, there are always new risks. Changing from a centralized to a decentralized IT environment and the increasing amount of information processed in a complex environment make operations challenging and security matters an ongoing priority review.

To assure controls remain relevant, an audit or review should be performed to determine the level of compliance to implemented controls. Increases in complexity or rate of change will necessitate more mature change and configuration management (CM) approaches. Organizations should continuously monitor the performance of controls by conducting regular assessments of their information systems and ensure information assurance is part of any change management and configuration management processes. This will alert management to new risks and the condition of the information systems, data, and networks that may have a negative impact on the mission of the organization.

Information Assurance: Restricted by Social Obligations

Organizations must consider social obligations in the implementation of security controls. Organizations should balance the rights and desires of the organization versus the rights of organizational employees and customers. This involves understanding the security needs of information owners and users.

Expectations and policies may change concerning the suitable use of security controls. Organizations need to balance between security risks they are willing to accept versus human rights or social factors. This can lead to solving issues such as security and the workplace privacy conflict. Employee monitoring and a bring-your-own-device (BYOD) policy are areas where social obligations and information assurance often require extensive analysis.

Implications from Lack of Information Assurance

Despite the rise of information security incidents, organizations are still unaware of the criticality of information assurance. This section discusses the consequences and implications from a lack of information assurance. In general, you must apply both due care and due diligence to ensure a system is operating within acceptable social and legal norms.

Due care is the development and implementation of policies and procedures to aid in performing the ongoing maintenance necessary to keep an information assurance process operating properly to protect assets and people from threats. Systems must be working in accordance with the expectations of a *reasonable person* in a situation. Due care prevents negligence.

Due diligence is the reasonable investigation, research, and understanding of the risks an organization faces before committing to a particular course of action. The organization should do its homework and ensure ongoing monitoring.

Penalties from a Legal/Regulatory Authorities

In the wake of countless corporate scandals and acts of negligence, regulations and laws exist to ensure internal controls are implemented to protect the interests of the public and stakeholders. Common themes from various legal/regulatory authorities are

- **Abuse**   Hacking, theft, password sharing
- **Critical infrastructure protection**   Finance and banking, natural resources, power, water, food, logistics, and military
- **Intellectual property**   Copyright, patent, and trademark
- **Privacy**   Personal information

Together with the laws, acts, or regulations there are associated penalties. Depending on the type of information security breach, the penalty could be, for example, in the form of paying a fine, serving a jail term, or both.

Loss of Information Assets

Organizations regularly suffer loss because of the compromise of information assets. These losses may be caused by the theft of an asset, data corruption, and other threats. In addition to the direct costs involved in replacing assets (for example, the cost of replacing a stolen computer), additional hidden costs are involved. These losses may be in the form of additional time spent to reconstruct the data, disruption to the organization's operation through hacking or other attacks, loss of reputation, financial loss, drop in morale, loss of competitive advantage, or cost of litigation, to name a few.

Operational Losses and Operational Risk Management

Although minimizing operational losses is not always recognized as a component of information assurance, in the final analysis it is the primary objective. Most organizations do not take the need to identify their sources of risk seriously. Despite wide coverage on security-related issues, most organizations are in the dark about the threats and risks to their business and missions. Recall that these risks cover the entire MSR model services/ attributes (availability, integrity, authentication, confidentiality, and nonrepudiation).

The effect of operational or organization-wide risks may not appear to be significant initially, but hidden losses may incur over time. Ignoring small inefficiencies leads to higher costs and can eventually erode revenue and profits. For example, an organization, providing mobile phone services, is at risk of losing its customers if it cannot provide a call when the customer needs it (lack of availability). Unfortunately, ignoring this risk and its implications may be as detrimental to an organization as unplanned downtime of a critical IT system.

Annual computer crime and security surveys, such as the U.S. Federal Bureau of Investigations Internet Crime Report, have shown that organizations suffer millions of dollars in losses because of the poor implementation of security controls. It is easier to determine the action to be taken once the loss sources have been identified. There are books in the market on how to manage operations proactively to avoid unwanted operational losses; however, they often overlook information assurance. Operational risk management should be a priority concern to stakeholders just like those of other corporate risks.

Customer Losses

Organizations lose customers frequently because of poor information assurance practices. One example is software that fails to manage credit card data securely. Poorly implemented or nonexistent security controls lead to the loss of customer information (loss of privacy/ confidentiality). As seen with the December 2013 Target compromise, reports of lost or stolen customer information raise alerts in two areas: poor security practices by the retailers themselves and weaknesses in the software used to process payments through credit card systems.

Major credit card associations have adopted their own cardholder information assurance programs to be compliant with the Payment Card Industry Data Security Standard (PCI-DSS). While compliance with standards such as PCI-DSS does not guarantee an organization will not have incidents, these standards are vital to retaining customer trust and confidence. If a customer fears theft of personal information due to lacking or poor security controls provided by a service or embedded in a product, a considerable loss of customers should be expected. Frequently, major credit card providers offer a zero-liability protection for online purchases. This offer ensures the customer maintains confidence in the credit card provider and that the credit card provider must manage unmitigated fraud risk by accepting a loss due to fraudulent transactions.

Loss of Image and Reputation

Reputation or image is another critical asset. Without a good reputation or image, sales drop, customer complaints increase, and revenue decreases. Reputation is valuable and must be well managed. In safeguarding the respect and good reputation of the organization, it is vital that personnel and business partners follow best-practice information assurance actions to reduce the probability of something bad happening to critical information. All partners share, in common, a risk assumed by one partner.

The following are some of the issues that affect corporate reputations that are addressed through effective and periodic information assurance training or awareness programs:

- Employee misconduct
- Customer complaints
- Security incidents and breaches

Further Reading

- *ACM Computing Curricula Information Technology Volume: Model Curriculum.* ACM, Dec. 12, 2008. http://campus.acm.org/public/comments/it-curriculum-draft-may-2008.pdf.
- *An Introduction to Computer Security: The NIST Handbook (Special Publication 800-100).* NIST, p. 16.
- *An Introduction to Computer Security: The NIST Handbook (Special Publication 800-12).* NIST, 1996.
- Drucker, Peter F. *Management: Tasks, Responsibilities, Practices.* Harper & Row, 1973.
- Drucker, Peter F. "The Age of Discontinuity: Guidelines to Our Changing Society." 1969.
- Herold, R. *Multi-dimensional Enterprise-wide Security: Corporate Reputation and The Definitive Guide to Security Inside the Perimeter.* Realtime Publishers. http://www.bandwidthco.com/whitepapers/itil/The%20Definitive%20Guide%20to%20Security%20Inside%20the%20Perimeter.pdf.

- *Little Inefficiencies Could Lead to Large Operational Losses/Risks in Hi-Tech Security Solutions*, 004., Technews Publishing Ltd., 2006. www.securitysa.com/news. aspx?pklNewsId=14 4&pklIssueId=60&pklCategoryID=106.

- Maconachy, V., et al. "A Model for Information Assurance: An Integrated Approach." Proceedings of the 2nd Annual, IEEE Systems, Man, and Cybernetics Information Assurance Workshop, West Point, New York (June 5–6, pp. 306–310). The MSR Model. 2001.

- Marlin, S. "Customer Data Losses Blamed on Merchants and Software." *Information Week*, 2005. www.informationweek.com/showArticle.jhtml?articleID=161601930.

- McConnell, P. *A Perfect Storm: Why Are Some Operational Losses Larger Than Others?* Portal Publishing Ltd. www.continuitycentral.com/Perfect_Basel.pdf.

- Porter, Michael E. "Competitive Advantage." *Free Press*, 2004. www.12manage.com/ methods_ porter_competitive_advantage.html.

- Schou, Corey D., and D.P. Shoemaker. *Information Assurance for the Enterprise: A Roadmap to Information Security.* McGraw-Hill Education, 2008.

- Conklin, Wm. Arthur, et al. *Introduction to Principles of Computer Security: Security+ and Beyond.* McGraw-Hill Education, March 2004.

- Security Standards Council. *PCI SSC Data Security Standards Overview.* https://www .pcisecuritystandards.org/security_standards/.

- Sullivan, D. *Balancing the Cost and Benefits of Countermeasures.* RealTime Publishers, 2007. http://search security.techtarget.com/general/0, 295582, sid14_ gci1237327, 00.html.

- Swanson, M., and B. Guttman. *Generally Accepted Principles and Practices for Securing Information Technology Systems.* NIST, 1996.

- Tipton, Harold F., and S. Hernandez, ed. *Official (ISC) [2] Guide to the CISSP CBK 3rd edition.* ((ISC)[2]) Press, 2012.

- Verizon. *The 2013 Data Breach Investigations Report.* www.verizonenterprise.com/ resources/reports/rp_data-breach-investigations-report-2013_en_xg.pdf.

Critical Thinking Exercises

1. What assets or services do you think your organization considers critical for success? What is your organization's responsibility for those assets or services, and how are they are currently protected? How do you know an appropriate level of due diligence and due care is being practiced in relation to your organization's use of information systems and data?

2. A member of your team informs you that the organization can purchase insurance for breaches of personally identifiable information (PII) and financial data such as credit card information. The insurance will cost less than the information assurance program proposed by the CISO. Would you purchase the insurance at the expense of an information assurance program?

3. A breach has occurred, and according to the organization's web site privacy policy and terms of service, your customers agreed to whatever level of security the organization deemed sufficient and reasonable. Is the organization protected from retaliation from customers or other entities?

4 Information Assurance Concepts

Information assurance is a broad, interdisciplinary field. Executives and senior management should understand what risk the organization is being protected from. Failure to understand the security requirements means you will not be able to apply the best security protection to the user environment. There are fundamental security concepts that you should know. This chapter discusses three popular concepts in information security: the confidentiality, integrity, and availability (CIA) triad. Additionally, it covers concepts in information assurance such as nonrepudiation and identification, authentication, authorization, and accountability (IAAA). Among the three, the CIA triad (information security) was the earliest and remains the most common assurance concept discussed in the industry. When these concepts are combined with the idea that information assurance must begin with the design of a system and account for all assets through dissolution, they form the Maconachy-Schou-Ragsdale (MSR) model.

Defense in Depth

If the 19th century military strategist Helmuth von Moltke is right, he could discourage even the best planner with his aphorism of "No plan survives contact with the enemy." Once engaged, attackers have the advantage: They know what they are going to do and what their objective is. To provide an effective defense, each layer must be composed of multiple countermeasures of varying complexity, application, and rigor; this is *defense-in-depth*. Defense-in-depth provides an adequate information assurance posture, but it tends to be reactive. Defense must always be planned because it is the *de facto* deployment in response to the escalating sophistication of attack experiences. As former U.S. Defense Secretary Donald H. Rumsfeld stated, "You go to war with the army you have, not the army you might want or wish to have at a later time." A defensive strategy cannot be expected to respond to unknown and potentially urgent risk situations such as last-minute patches and catch-up planning, but it can reduce the impact of such weaknesses. A proper defense-in-depth strategy may mean the difference between a difficult survivability and being put out of business.

A correctly planned, dynamic, information assurance strategy becomes an essential emergent property of the system it protects. To provide defense-in-depth, the strategy and the program it defines cannot be static. Rick Dove, an expert on systems and artificial intelligence, proposes that defense-in-depth must provide parity with the agility of intelligent attacking systems. A defense-in-depth strategy must have six characteristics.

- Self-organizing
- Adapting to unpredictable situations
- Evolving in concert with an ever-changing environment
- Reactively resilient
- Proactively innovative
- Harmonious with system purpose

Defense-in-depth is most appropriately defined as part of an organization's security architecture. Smaller to mid-size organizations may not have the resources to develop fully an information assurance architecture and will therefore often rely on risk assessments to help find weaknesses in their security posture. The security architecture of an organization must develop defenses for every level of an application, system, or workflow using physical, logical, and technical countermeasures to slow the attack of an adversary. To slow the attackers, defenders must present numerous challenges through various dimensions of countermeasures.

Defense-in-depth relies heavily on the application of *segmentation*. Segmentation ensures that a single compromised element of a system cannot compromise the system as a whole. Segmentation also ensures the most efficient use of controls throughout the organization. Information and services require varying degrees of defensive protection depending on their value to the organization. Figure 4-1 illustrates the relationship between assets, impacts, and segmentation.

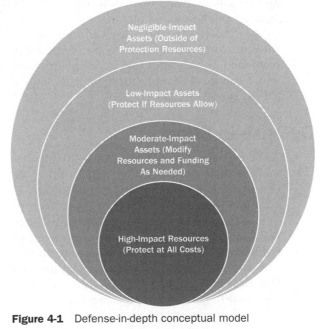

Figure 4-1 Defense-in-depth conceptual model

Confidentiality, Integrity, and Availability

When dealing with information assurance and its subcomponent information security, you should be familiar with three primary security objectives—confidentiality, integrity, and availability—to identify problems and provide proper solutions. This concept is widely known as the *CIA triad*, as shown in Figure 4-2.

Confidentiality

Confidentiality and privacy are related terms but are not synonymous. *Confidentiality* is the assurance of data secrecy where no one is able to read data except for the intended entity. Confidentiality should prevail no

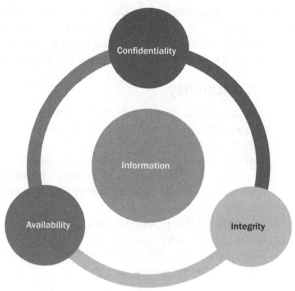

Figure 4-2   CIA triad

matter what the data state is—whether data resides on a system, is being transmitted, or is in a particular location (for example, a file cabinet, a desk drawer, or a safe). *Privacy*, on the other hand, involves personal autonomy and control of information about oneself. Both are discussed in this chapter. The word *classification* merely means categorization in certain industries.

Assign an appropriate sensitivity categorization to information to maintain confidentiality. Different categorizations will address the degree of security controls needed. For example, a range of military classification (categorization in the military) includes unclassified, confidential, secret, and top secret. A military document classified (categorized) as top secret will require control mechanisms to eliminate threats that may expose the location or characteristics of an important asset.

Integrity

People understand integrity in terms of dealing with people. People understand the sentiment "Jill is a woman of integrity" to mean Jill is a person who is truthful, is trustworthy, and can be relied upon to perform as she promises. When considering integrity in an information assurance perspective, organizations will use it not only from a personnel perspective but also from a systems perspective.

In information systems, *integrity* is a service that assures that the information in a system has not been altered except by authorized individuals and processes. It provides assurance of the accuracy of the data and that it has not been corrupted or modified improperly. Integrity may be achieved by applying a mathematical technique whereby the information will later be verified. Examples of integrity controls are watermarks, bar codes, hashing, checksums, and cyclic redundancy check (CRC). A second form of integrity control manages the processes to enter and manipulate information. For example, a physician (and the patient) would want the integrity of medical records. The records should reflect the actual data from the laboratory, and once the data is stored, it should be stored so it is unchangeable outside defined processes.

Availability

Availability is the service that assures data and resources are accessible to authorized subjects or personnel when required. The second component of the availability service is that resources such as systems and networks should provide sufficient capacity to perform in a predictable and acceptable manner. Secure and quick recovery from disruptions is crucial to avoid delays or decreased productivity. Therefore, it is necessary that protection mechanisms should be in place to ensure availability and to protect against internal and external threats.

Availability is also often viewed as a property of an information system or service. Most service level agreements and measures of performance for service providers surround availability above all else. The availability of a system may be one of its most marketable properties.

CIA Balance

The three fundamental security requirements are not equally critical in each application. For example, to one organization, service availability and the integrity of information may be more important than the confidentiality of information. A web site hosting publicly available information is an example. Therefore, you should apply the appropriate combination of CIA in correct portions to support your organization's goals and provide users with a dependable system.

Nonrepudiation and Authentication

As illustrated in the MSR model, the addition of nonrepudiation and authentication complete the concept of information assurance. These concepts relate to providing assurances and trust surrounding the actions of an individual or a system proactively and reactively.

Nonrepudiation

The MSR model of information assurance describes additional services associated with nonrepudiation. Digital transactions are prone to frauds in which participants in the transaction could repudiate (deny) a transaction. A digital signature is evidence that the information originated with the asserted sender of the information and prevents subsequent denial of sending the message.

Digital signatures may provide evidence that the receiver has in fact received the message and that the receiver will not be able to deny this reception. This is commonly known as *nonrepudiation*. In large organizations such as the U.S. government, efforts are in place to implement digital signatures through smartcards, mobile devices, and even biometrics.

The term *nonrepudiation* describes the service that ensures entities are honest in their actions. There are variants of nonrepudiation, but the most often used are as follows:

- Nonrepudiation of source prevents an author from false refusal of ownership to a created or sent message, or the service will prove it otherwise.
- Nonrepudiation of acceptance prevents the receiver from denying having received a message, or else the service will prove it otherwise.

Identification, Authentication, Authorization, and Accountability

Identification, authentication, authorization, and accountability are the essential functions in providing an access management system. This service as described by the MSR model of information assurance is summarized as *authentication* but reflects the entire IAAA process. The overall architecture of an access management system includes the means of identifying its users, authenticating a user's identity and credentials, and setting and controlling the access level of a user's authorization. In addition, it should provide for logging and auditing the trail of a user's activity in search of privilege violations or attempted violations and accounting for system resource usage.

The current industry practice for implementing IAAA security is identity management. Identity management includes, as its first step, the use of logon IDs and passwords. The system verifies that the password entered by a user matches the password linked with the individual's logon ID. A policy should state that the password needs to be changed frequently and must have a minimum strength. Strong passwords must not be guessed easily, such as a mother's maiden name or place of birth, and they must have a combination of characters, symbols, and numbers to increase security. Bear in mind the current threat environment almost renders passwords useless unless combined with other controls or factors to increase the strength of authentication.

In the United States, the Federal Financial Institutions Examination Council (FFIEC) has ruled that a normal username/password authentication is not sufficient for electronic banking purposes that expose users to risks such as identity theft and transaction fraud. In this case, multiple layers of authentication mitigate those risks. Figure 4-3 depicts the steps to access a system and the act of recording a user's actions during system access.

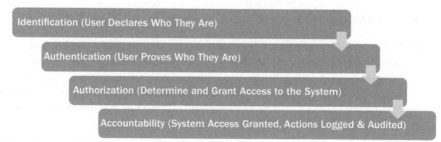

Figure 4-3   Steps of IAAA

Identification

Identification is a method for a user within a system to introduce oneself. In an organization-wide identification requirement, you must address identification issues. An example would be more than one person having the same name. Identifiers must be unique so that a user can be accurately identified across the organization.

Each user should have a unique identifier, even if performing multiple roles within the organization. This simplifies matters for users as well as the management of an information system. It also eases control in that an organization may have a centralized directory or repository for better user management.

A standard interface is crucial for ease of verification process. The same goes for the availability of the verification process itself. This is to ensure that access can be granted only with verification.

Authentication

Authentication validates the identification provided by a user. In other words, it makes sure the entity presenting the identification can further prove to be who they claim. To be authenticated, the entity must produce minimally a second credential. Three basic factors of authentication are available to all types of identities.

- What you should know (a shared secret, such as a password, which both the user and the authenticator know)
- What you should have (a physical identification, such as a smartcard, hardware token, or identification card)
- What you are (a measurable attribute, such as biometrics, a thumbprint, or facial recognition)

In addition, organizations may consider having an implicit factor such as a "where you are" factor.

- Physical location, such as within an organization's office.
- Logical location, such as on an internal network or private network.
- A combination of those factors can be considered to provide different strength levels of authentication. This improves authentication and increases security.

The following are examples of technology used for authentication:

- Public Key Infrastructure (PKI) is a system that provides authentication with certificates based on a public key cryptography method. Public key cryptography provides two independent keys generated together; one key is made public, and another is kept private. Any information protected by one key (public) can be opened only with another key (private). If one key is compromised, a new key pair must be generated.

- Smartcards can store personal information accessible by a personal identification number (PIN). An organization may consider smartcard implementation to provide another identification method via physical identification (physical security) and electronic identification (electronic access).

Authorization

Once a user presents a second credential and is identified, the system checks an access control matrix to determine their associated privileges. If the system allows the user access, the user is *authorized*.

Accountability

The act of being responsible for actions taken within a system is *accountability*. The only way to ensure accountability is to identify the user of a system and record their actions. *Accountability* makes nonrepudiation extremely important.

Privacy's Relationship to Information Assurance

As mentioned earlier, a security concept that is often confused with confidentiality is privacy. *Privacy* describes the control people have to regulate the flow of information about themselves selectively. In contrast, *confidentiality* requires that only an authorized party access information. This makes confidentiality one of the goals in information assurance but with a less personal emphasis. Despite the subtle difference, both concepts are interrelated. For example, identity theft could be a result of lack of privacy or failure in confidentiality.

After several incidents affecting human lives, governments worldwide have taken stronger measures to monitor information about individuals. In some countries, these intelligence and security measures are seen as invading the privacy rights of individuals.

Another issue that gives rise to privacy concern is the proliferation of tools and computing power that could gather personal information at ease. An example of this is the collection of information such as spending pattern, financial standing, and contact information from the web-based applications such as social media. This is often referred to as *big data*. Big data is a vague term, but definitions describe it in terms of size, complexity, and analytics capability. Gartner describes big data as "high-volume, high-velocity, and high-variety information assets that demand cost-effective, innovative forms of information processing for enhanced insight and decision making." While useful for business and research, big data leads to serious privacy and security considerations. Through aggregation, big data and the associated analytics that it enables can predict and uncover patterns about individuals never seen before. *Forbes* reporter Kashmir Hill illustrated this in an article about privacy and predictive analytics.

Hill's article "How Target Figured Out a Teen Girl Was Pregnant Before Her Father Did" explains how Target analyzes and mines data about its customers to try to determine what they may need to buy. Target then markets specific products and services based on the results. In the article, Hill notes Target found a correlation between the purchases of unscented lotion and the third trimester of pregnancy. It also discovered a correlation between pregnancy and the purchase of supplements such as calcium, magnesium, and zinc. Finally, when people buy large quantities of scent-free soap and large bags of cotton balls in addition to hand sanitizers and washcloths, it signals the due date is near. Target was able to use 25 such indicators to not only determine whether a shopper may be pregnant but also predict a due date for the baby!

Countries and economies have laws protecting individual privacy. The European Union, for example, has the Data Protection Act. Organizations that collect personal data must register with the government and take precautions against misuse of that data. In many countries, privacy issues are addressed in criminal law and civil law. In the United States, the Privacy Act of 1974 exists to protect citizens' personally identifiable information from unlawful collection and processing by the government. You can find more information about privacy laws around the world in Appendix F. Several organizations such as the Electronic Privacy Information Center (http://epic.org/) exist not only to help protect the privacy of individuals but also to help organizations understand their duty to protect private information.

Assets, Threats, Vulnerabilities, Risks, and Controls

Information assets have unique vulnerabilities, and they are continuously exposed to new threats. The combination of vulnerabilities and threats contribute to risk. To mitigate and control risks effectively, organizations should be aware of the shortcomings in their information systems and should be prepared to tackle them in case the shortcomings turn into threats to activities or business.

Understanding these entities and their interactions is crucial to ensuring the controls are cost effective and relevant. This chapter provides an overview of threats and vulnerabilities as well as the controls that are implemented to manage their risks.

Figure 4-4 shows the relationships among assets, threats, vulnerabilities, and controls (countermeasures) to risks.

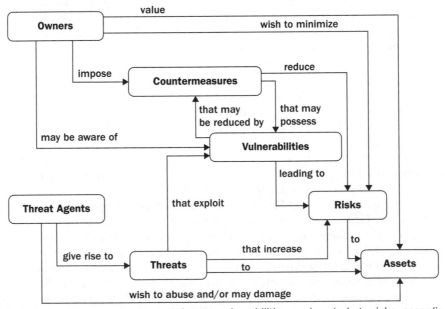

Figure 4-4   Relationships between assets, threats, vulnerabilities, and controls to risks, according to ISO 15408:2005

An *asset* is anything valuable to the organization. An information asset, if compromised, may cause losses should it be disclosed, be altered, or become unavailable. An information asset can be tangible or intangible, such as hardware, software, data, services, and people. The losses can also be tangible or intangible, such as the number of machines or a smeared reputation.

Threats are potential events that may cause the loss of an information asset. A threat may be natural, deliberate, or accidental.

Vulnerabilities are weaknesses exploited by threats. They are threat independent, and if exploited, they allow harm in terms of the CIA triad. Examples of vulnerabilities include software bugs, open ports, poorly trained personnel, and outdated policy. You can find a more complete list of vulnerabilities in Appendix C.

A *risk* expresses the chance of something happening because of a threat successfully exploiting a vulnerability that will eventually affect the organization. Examples of impact are loss of competitive edge, loss of confidential information, systems unavailability, failure to meet a service level agreement, and tarnished reputation.

The probability of a particular risk occurring is known as *likelihood*. To manage risks, controls are established. *Controls* are protective measures or mechanisms that reduce risks.

The types and likelihood of threats vary based on the nature of the business, location, and time. The next section discusses the general threats found in a typical IT environment.

Common Threats

Threats originate with humans, technology, and environmental conditions. Examples are human errors when entering information, misconfigured systems, malicious software, and natural disasters such as floods and earthquakes. When these threats exist and the associated vulnerabilities are not controlled, information could be lost, become unavailable, or become corrupt, hence compromising information assurance.

There are formal organizations that identify and list threat types. According to the German BSI (Bundesamt für Sicherheit in der Informationstechnik), threats can be divided into four categories: force majeure, deliberate acts, human failure, and technical failure (https://www.bsi.bund.de/SharedDocs/Downloads/EN/BSI/Grundschutz/download/it-grundschutz-kataloge_2005_pdf_en_zip.zip?__blob=publicationFile). You can find a suggested list of threats in Appendix B.

An organization planning to perform a threat identification exercise should refer to lists like these. The relevance of the list depends on factors such as geographical location and time. The following sections discuss some common threats and controls.

Errors and Negligence

People are prone to make errors when using computers, especially after long hours of work. Typographical errors can occur when entering data, and if these errors are not checked, validated, and corrected they affect the accuracy and integrity of information. Even the most advanced programs may not detect all input errors or negligence. A thorough awareness program for all employees is beneficial in reducing or eliminating employee error and neglect.

Another source of errors is misconfigured systems and failures to patch software in a timely fashion. While a technical error, a misconfigured system may leave vulnerable services running. These services are ripe for hackers to exploit.

Unfortunately, security concerns are often neglected during product development processes in order to maintain deadlines. In addition, the design phase sometimes omits consideration of full data validation and verification measures prior to live production. Of course, there are always programming errors, also known as *bugs*, that have become threats to organizations and in some cases are causing damage to organizations. A frequently found bug is a buffer overflow that is a programming error that is caused by improper data validation.

Recently, major organizations have incorporated security as a requirement in system design. This has changed what was traditionally known as the software development life cycle (SDLC) into the secure software development life cycle (SSDLC). You can find a further discussion in Chapter 15.

Fraudulent and Theft Activities

Fraud and theft activities are common in the business world. In modern financial systems using IT, fraud involving checks, credit cards, and automatic teller machine (ATM) networks can add up to multimillion-dollar losses. With technical advancement and downloadable materials from the Internet, anyone with basic knowledge of system penetration may successfully trespass sensitive areas of financial information systems. The trespass allows the perpetrator to modify the information. The checklist below provides some tips for avoiding fraud and theft.

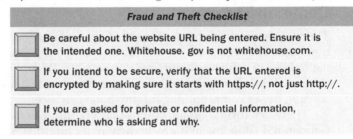

Fraud and Theft Checklist

☐ Be careful about the website URL being entered. Ensure it is the intended one. Whitehouse. gov is not whitehouse.com.

☐ If you intend to be secure, verify that the URL entered is encrypted by making sure it starts with https://, not just http://.

☐ If you are asked for private or confidential information, determine who is asking and why.

An example is transferring large amounts of money into personal accounts online. Someone internal or external to the organization can carry out this type of crime. Internal parties are more familiar with the targeted system. These internal threats are not limited to technical employees. These threats can be exploited by administrative or even suspended employees whose access rights have not been revoked appropriately. As long as the IT infrastructure connects to the outside world, external exploits can come from anywhere including wireless communications.

Loss of Infrastructure

Modern organizations connect through internal and external infrastructures which are not under their direct control. It is crucial to ensure that an organization's physical and virtual infrastructures are well maintained to avoid loss from these communication channels. These services are interdependent; therefore, malfunctions in one area may affect another. Suggested infrastructure support would include communication channels, power lines, and specific peripherals used to support the mission. Infrastructure interruption may cause significant disruption to the organization's usual operations. This leads to losses in terms of money, time, and resource use.

Malware

Malware, or malicious software, penetrates systems resulting in damage to the system. Malware is actually a piece of code or software program that is hostile, intrusive, or at least annoying. Examples of malware are Trojan horses, viruses, worms, and logic bombs.

The costs of eradicating malware may amount to thousands of dollars to repair the affected information systems. In addition to the time and other resources involved in dealing with the problem, malware may affect the overall organization's productivity level. Although the amount is widely debated, the first worm (the Morris worm in 1988) was estimated by industry to have cost between $250,000 and $96 million dollars.

Attackers

Attackers are those who penetrate an organization's system either internally or externally with or without authorization. Internal attackers may be disgruntled employees, and their specialized knowledge potentially makes them a highly capable adversary. Despite this, an external attacker's threat is usually seen as a high-risk threat. Generally, the organization has limited information about the reason of such attacks, whether for fun, for information theft, or simply to cause disruptions to the organization's business process.

Capabilities of Attackers   There are three levels of attacker capabilities. The most dangerous are the elite or expert hackers. These highly technical individuals seek new vulnerabilities in systems and can create scripts and programs to exploit vulnerabilities. These actors are often sponsored by terrorists, nation states, military, or organized crime, or they are engaged in industrial espionage.

Script writers are the next step down on the family tree of attackers. Although less technically qualified in finding vulnerabilities, they are capable of building and executing scripts to exploit known vulnerabilities.

The most numerous attackers are script kiddies who possess neither the expertise to find vulnerabilities nor the skills to exploit them. Their knowledge is limited to downloading and executing scripts and tools that others have developed. These individuals constitute the majority of the threat community. Despite their lack of skills, large numbers of script kiddies constitute a threat. When large numbers of script kiddies are active, they provide sufficient traffic and increased risks for defensive systems by masking activities of the elite hackers. Figure 4-5 illustrates the relationship among attackers, capabilities, and impacts.

Motivation of Attackers   Attackers have diverse motivations. Some are motivated by greed and money; others are motivated by prestige or revenge. Still others are motivated by ideology or patriotism. Most modern militaries employ hackers who make hacking their day job. Hackers' motivations are as complex and interconnected as human relations can be. Understanding people and comprehending the function of an organization can greatly help professionals understand the motivation of hackers.

- **Hackers and hacktivist**   Hackers use technical and social means to gain authorized/unauthorized access to information assets, computer systems, and networks. Some of the technical means include delving deep into the code and protocols used in computer systems and networks.

  Some are *white-hat* hackers who use their skills to determine whether systems are in fact secure. White hats operate within strict rules of engagement and with the

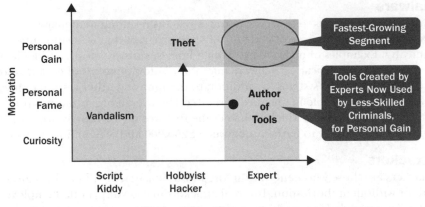

Figure 4-5 Attackers, motivation, and impact

explicit permission of a system's owner. They also often subscribe to professional codes of ethics as part of their professional credentialing. Their opponents are called *black-hat* hackers who are motivated by using their skills to penetrate systems by the path of least resistance without authorization from the system owner. A third type of hacker is called the *gray hat*. The gray hat attempts to walk the line between the black hat and the white hat. White hats will often state there is no "gray"; once a hacker gives up on ethics and the strict rules of engagement, their credibility as a white hat is compromised.

Some hackers, called *hacktivists*, are motivated to use their skills for political purposes. Hacktivists are becoming more common and can take the form of script kiddies, the elite, or anywhere in between. Often, information systems connected with political agendas or national security systems are the targets of hacktivists.

- **Criminal attackers** These attackers view the computer and its contents as the target of a crime—it's something to be stolen or it's used to perpetrate the crime. These individuals are motivated simply by profit and greed. Since most large financial transactions occur on networks, electronic crimes include fraud, extortion, theft, embezzlement, and forgery.

- **Nation states** Nation states are motivated by espionage and economic gain. While nation states spy on each other to gain political information, nation states may also engage in industrial espionage.

- **National warfare, asymmetric warfare, and terrorism** Nations depend on information systems to support the economy, infrastructure, and defense, which are all important assets. They are now targets not only of unfriendly foreign powers that are sources of highly structured threats but also of terrorists who are somewhat less structured. Independent of source, their actions constitute information warfare—warfare conducted against the information and information-processing equipment used by an adversary.

- **Information warfare**   Information warfare is using information technology as a weapon to impact an adversary. Several recent examples have shown how customized malware and computer viruses can dramatically impact the progression of secret nuclear ambitions or severely cripple the command and control infrastructure of an opponent.

Types of Attacks

Since an organization's web site is a purposely exposed asset, attacks may focus on it. For this type of attack, the attacker may create false content or deface the appearance. This may damage the organization's image and reputation in terms of customer confidence and providing reliable services to its clients. To work internationally, worldwide financial institutions are required by law, regulating authorities, or common interest to provide adequate security against threats. The list below provides some common attacks.

Sample Common Attacks		
Technical attacks rely on protocol, configuration, or program weakness within target systems or hardware, which are hacked to gain access.	*Social engineering (SE) attacks* rely on trust. These attacks are performed over the phone after sufficient background information has been obtained concerning the target. Electronic SE attacks seem to be overtaking the phone SE attacks.	*Physical attacks* rely on weaknesses surrounding computer systems. These may take the form of dumpster diving for changed passwords and configuration information, or gaining unauthorized access to a wiring closet and installing a wi-fi bridge to hack from a parking lot outside.

There are several steps commonly used in executing an attack. First, the perpetrator will profile the organization they want to attack. They will do simple things such as Google the organization or use a Whois lookup. Armed with that data, they will try to determine what systems are exposed by using tools such as Nmap or a ping sweep. The third step is finger printing. Using knowledge of the exposed systems, they will use tools such as a banner grab to identify the operating system and the open ports. After intelligence gathering, the attack begins by the attacker searching for vulnerabilities and exploits that match; then, they will systematically execute exploits.

Appropriate countermeasures are discussed later; however, significant protection comes from simple steps such as limiting the amount of information exposed to the outside world. This makes system hardening and patching even more effective.

Employee Sabotage

When considering deliberate human acts, you should consider the motive means, and opportunity of the individual or group. As mentioned earlier, disgruntled employees who know the internal technical details of systems present a continuous threat to the organization. Employees may carry out antisocial or unwanted actions, such as the following:

- Damaging the organization's key infrastructure
- Revealing secret and confidential information to competitors

- Creating tensions and rifts among employees by spreading hoaxes or anonymous rumors
- Threatening the health and safety of others
- Stealing important documents

An employee might resort to sabotage because of the following:

- Belief that management will not treat them fairly
- Desire for revenge because of perceived wrongs against the individual, colleagues, or management
- Need for material gain for themselves or someone they care for

Sabotage is difficult to detect in a timely manner. To improve early detection, establishing a whistleblower policy within the organization is important. This policy allows individuals reporting suspected wrongdoings to remain anonymous. This is a good mechanism to curb sabotage.

Industrial Espionage

Industrial espionage is the act of spying or of using agents to obtain confidential information about business competitors. Industrial espionage attacks have precise motivations, for example, to gain an advantage over the competition by stealing trade secrets and market strategies. Some examples of these illegal methods are bribery, blackmail, and technological surveillance.

Since information is processed and stored on information systems, information assurance can protect against threats related to technology. However, not much can be done to reduce the threat if authorized employees are selling the information. Controls such as restricting the use of flash drives and monitoring employee workstations could be considered as a deterrent, yet they do not eliminate the threat. The users within an organization need to be trusted in order for work to be done.

Industrial espionage focuses on the theft of trade secrets for use by a competitor. The motivation of industrial espionage is often commercial. Research results, manufacturing techniques, chemical formulas, source code, and designs are targets since these assets use significant resources to develop. The attacker hopes to shortcut their research by stealing someone else's. Manufacturing, research, and technology-heavy industries are often the targets of industrial espionage.

Invasion of Privacy

The ubiquitous and widespread use of modern technology and social media has greatly increased the possibility that private and personal information may be leaked. While organizations continue to compile information about their customers, competitors, and employees, they must be concerned with protecting personally identifiable information. The following trends are prevalent and contribute to invasion of privacy:

- Increased surveillance
- More information kept about travelers

- New and existing antiterrorism laws and governmental measures offering powerful search capabilities and increased sharing of information among law enforcement authorities
- Poor management of personal data such as racial origin, health condition, and offenses
- Users unknowingly providing their personal information to "free" services such as social media

Phishing and Spear Phishing

Phishing is an illegal activity, fraud, or swindle carried out by deceiving users into revealing sensitive information for the benefit of the attacker. Phishing can be done via e-mail notification as well as through false links promoted via instant messengers. The usual tactic is to trap the receiver into disclosing personal information for illegal use or manipulation. Personal and account details are often the favorite targets. Figure 4-6 shows an example of a phishing attack.

Spear phishing is similar to phishing except it targets specific individuals with personalized messages and attachments that may appear to be relevant to the user but that contain malware that gives the attacker access to the victim's computer.

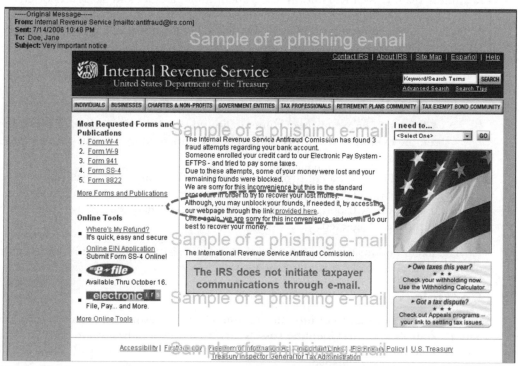

Figure 4-6   Phishing attack, www.irs.gov/pub/irs-utl/phishing_email2.pdf

Spamming

Spamming is the mass sending of e-mail. It causes network traffic jams and junk mails. Spam e-mails generally contain advertising for some products whose reliability is unknown or as a vector for phishing.

Recently, there have been efforts to fight spam by applying technological and legal countermeasures. This approach has had limited success, and it is still impossible to eliminate spam. Consequently, some online service providers have used mechanisms to manage the spamming of their subscribers through regular blacklist updates and filters. An unintended outcome of this approach is that valid mail is blocked inadvertently. More than 37 countries have legislation regarding spam. Organizations must ensure their customer communication and marketing strategy both include safeguards and restrictions to prevent legal exposure from spam.

Vulnerabilities

Vulnerabilities are weaknesses inherent within the information asset that are exploitable by emerging threats. Lack of antivirus software on a workstation, inadequate hiring procedures, and the absence of physical access controls in the server room are examples of vulnerabilities. An exhaustive list of standard vulnerabilities faced by organizations needs to be verified with the business process and asset owners. In the United States, the U.S. Computer Emergency Readiness Team (US-CERT) informs users about vulnerabilities and tackles reported ones. Users can access the US-CERT (www.us-cert.gov/) or other National CERT/CSIRT web pages to learn about the latest vulnerabilities. Generally, there are three ways how users can get information about vulnerabilities.

- **Newsletter** This is for any confirmed vulnerability that has no exploitable characteristic and poses no harm. The parties who discover the vulnerability should inform US-CERT and have the findings published in the newsletter.

- **Advisory** For a confirmed vulnerability, this has low and medium levels of local or remote exploitability. Advice should be accompanied by remedies or workaround solutions.

- **Alert** This is for a confirmed vulnerability that has a high level of local or remote exploitability and poses a definite threat to the information system. Immediate escalation and action needs to be performed depending on the severity of the alert triggered.

The likelihood for the occurrence of threats and existing vulnerabilities would influence the selection of controls needed to manage risk.

Controls

Controls are actions taken or mechanisms established to resolve information assurance issues. Controls to protect identified assets vary from one organization to another because they depend on issues such as an organization's objectives, availability of resources, and risk profiles.

The implementation of controls is driven by the following factors:

- To protect critical and sensitive information assets
- To ensure compliance with regulatory and legislation requirement
- To gain competitive edge
- To mitigate risks and avoid unnecessary operational, financial, and customer losses

Categories of Controls

There are three types of controls used to meet the needs of an organization, namely, management, operational, and technical.

- *Management* controls are security controls that are strategic and suitable for planning and monitoring purposes. Examples of controls in this category are the information assurance policy and information assurance risk management exercises.
- *Operational* controls are controls used in day-to-day operations to ensure the secure execution of business activities. Examples of controls in this category are mechanisms or tools for IT support and operations, physical and environmental security controls, and information security incident-handling processes and procedures.
- *Technical* controls are the possible technical and physical implementation of information assurance solutions and recommendations. Examples of controls in this category are access controls, as well as security audit and monitoring tools.

Parts II, III, and IV will provide more discussion on the various types of controls.

Key Considerations

The implementation of controls is a constant interplay of competing risk models and efficacy of policies, rules, and tools. Controls require organizational resources to install, maintain, and ultimately remove them. The following sections discuss some of the key considerations to be made when implementing a control.

Establish Balance Between Managing Risk and Implementing Controls
Balancing the costs and benefits of countermeasures is a risk management exercise. Risk management identifies assets, threats, the effect of the threat, and, finally, how the organization can mitigate the loss. Refer to Chapter 11 for details on risk management.

Intangible costs such as loss of reputation and image are subjective and difficult to measure. Despite the difficulty, consider all tangible and intangible costs.

Organizations can make a more effective decision about security controls by understanding the risks associated with each asset, the value of each asset, and the cost of protecting the asset. Better decisions can be made about suitable countermeasures after the objectives for information asset protection are understood and documented. Subsequently, policies and procedures are defined to put those decisions into practice.

Ensure the Proper Controls Are Selected and Implemented Organizational considerations should include identifying the following:

- The end users of the controls
- How the security controls act as supporting mechanisms in achieving the organization's mission
- The operational issues such as day-to-day work involved, maintenance, and training on the controls
- The organization's security requirements, with relevance to the higher regulatory requirements and internal policies
- The sensitivity of the data in accordance to information classification

Considerations pertaining to the control itself should include the following:

- Existing vulnerabilities in the control
- Implementation requirements and frequency history for patches
- Interactions with the current infrastructure setup
- Scalability and compatibility requirements
- Test requirements
- Total life-cycle costs (including purchase acquisition, maintenance, and support)
- User friendliness

Assess and Review Controls Once a control has been implemented, it should be assessed and reviewed periodically to determine whether the control is performing as expected. Undertake monitoring, assessing, and reviewing controls to do the following:

- Detect errors in information processing results
- Enable management to determine whether the security activities are performing as intended
- Identify any attempted or successful intrusions into information systems
- Record whether previous actions taken to resolve security breaches were effective

Usually, you can assess the performance of implemented security controls by using information system scans, audit reports, logs, risk assessment reports, or by reviewing security policies. It is vital to benchmark and measure against best practices whether security controls are functioning objectively, as intended, to avoid unwanted security breaches.

The term *continuous monitoring* is often used and touted as a replacement for assessments. Continuous monitoring as an approach is not flawed; however, unless all controls are studied and base lined to determine appropriate frequency and quality of assessment, the approach may give a false sense of security. Continuous monitoring focuses on automating controls such as vulnerability scanning and patching systems. While this automation is desirable, it is largely meaningless unless a vulnerability on one system can be compared against the same vulnerability on other systems in terms of risk and effect on the organization.

Cryptology

Cryptology is a complex topic. This is a high-level presentation of the topic of cryptography intended to provide an overview for senior leaders and managers. *Cryptology* is the study of codes and cyphers and includes *cryptography* (secret writing) and *cryptanalysis* (breaking codes). Cryptography does not attempt to conceal the existence of a message but rather makes the message incomprehensible by transforming the *plain text*, which is the original, clearly intelligible message to be hidden (*cypher text*). Plain text is called *clear text* because it can be read without assistance in a system.

Encryption security is generally adequate if the time required to decrypt and read a message is longer than the time an encrypted file needs to be secure. Security may also be adequate if the cost (in computer time or other resources) required to defeat the encryption is greater than the value of the encrypted file. The caveat here is that the value judgment of an adversary might be different from the organization's, particularly since the adversary can only guess at the content of the file. For more information about asset valuation, see "Assets, Threats, Vulnerabilities, Risks, and Controls".

Codes and Ciphers

A *code* differs from a cipher in that a code consists of letters, whole words, and phrases with code groups (numbers and/or words) that replace the plain text. People desiring to read the encoded message need a codebook to translate the code to plain text. For example, a nine-digit customer account number is a code. On the other hand, a *cipher* uses the individual letters as the basic plain-text units and uses a key (or password), which tells the composition of letters in the cipher alphabet or the pattern of rearranging letters in a message. Messages sent unencoded or unenciphered are in plain language, in the clear, or in clear text.

Types of Encryption

Encryption falls into two broad categories: symmetric and asymmetric. They have different characteristics and strengths.

Symmetric Encryption   *Symmetric encryption* is when the sender and receiver use the same private key to encrypt and decrypt a message. The key and the plain-text (unencrypted) message are combined systematically to yield a cipher text. If the encryption is secure, others cannot recover the message from the cipher text unless they know both the key and the systematic process used (called the *encryption algorithm*). Symmetric encryption is relatively fast.

Historically, one of the most common block cypher symmetric encryption tools was the Data Encryption Standard (DES). The algorithm was an internationally standardized symmetric cipher that performs 16 iterations of the same series of operations. One software instantiation of DES, called Triple DES, uses three applications of DES, one after the other, yielding a total of 48 iterations. DES is now obsolete because of the small key size and has been largely supplanted by the Advanced Encryption Standard (AES).

For example, suppose a CEO wants encrypted, private communication with each of a company's 300 operating managers to ensure privacy among the managers. The CEO must have 300 encryption keys to communicate with all the managers. In addition, the CEO wants managers to have secure communication among them. When a secret key encryption system is used, the first manager must have 299 keys to communicate with the remaining managers; the second must have 298 (299 minus the key shared with the first manager), the third 297, and so on—for a total of 44,850 keys. This is unmanageable particularly if each key must be securely transmitted to each of the parties who will use it. If an unencrypted key is transmitted to one of the managers, how does the CEO know it was not intercepted? Since most algorithms are publicly available and the security of a cipher is in the key, any effort expended selecting an algorithm is wasted if users are careless with the keys. This means each manager must keep secret the 299 keys received from the CEO. If the keys are publicly disclosed or shared, the CEO must issue new keys. Asymmetric encryption was designed to help alleviate these problems.

Asymmetric/Public Key Encryption *Asymmetric encryption* uses two different keys (one is public and the other is kept private) and an algorithm for mathematical functions that would require extensive resources to break. One key, called a *public key*, is used to encrypt a message, and a second key, called a *private key*, is used to decrypt the message (using the mathematical function).

For example, suppose Hord wants to send Nina a message using public key encryption. Hord must possess his own matched private key and public key. Nina must also have her own matched private key and public key. Keys are generated in pairs. Therefore, each key has a mate and will work only with its mate. If a private key is compromised, both keys are discarded for new ones. Nina must ensure Hord can access her public key but doesn't need to worry if other people have it. In fact, she may post her public key on her web site so anyone can get to it. Hord encrypts his message with her public key; Hord cannot decrypt the resulting message with the public key. The message can be decrypted only by using Nina's private key. This is how the keys are matched.

When asymmetric encryption is used in the earlier example, the CEO must produce only 300 key pairs for each of the 300 operating managers. Each manager must store 300 keys, but only that particular manager's own private key must be kept secret. The public keys can be published on a public web site.

Because of their mathematical complexity, asymmetric algorithms are slow and are generally used for encrypting small messages. Examples of these short messages are digital signatures and key exchanges allowing for the faster symmetric encryption. Their use of key exchange allows secure transmission of private (symmetric) keys. The most widely used public key encryption algorithm is RSA, named for its inventors Rivest, Shamir, and Adelman.

Encryption Key Escrow

When individuals use encryption without central mandatory control, the availability of organizational data is threatened. Employees who are fired or die unexpectedly are equally unlikely to return and provide the company with the encryption keys that secure their important files. Senior leaders must ensure the management of encryption is closely monitored. Organizations should implement rules that include termination for unauthorized use of encryption.

The easiest management tool for managing crypto keys is *key escrow*, which is an agreement that describes the rules for storing critical keys in trusted storage. So, if an employee departs the organization, the associated keys are released from escrow to a designated individual or organization. Managers concerned about encryption data security might build an audit program beginning with the following questions. These questions are general and provide only a starting point for identifying encryption security issues.

- What is the cryptography experience and education of the person who selects and approves encryption software?

- How does the person who selects and approves encryption software keep abreast of developments in cryptanalysis (so the person will know when the encryption algorithm is broken)?

- Who decides what information will be encrypted and what will not?

- How is encryption used to secure the transmission of information?

- What use of encryption algorithms is made for each of the following: authentication, secrecy, integrity check, and nonrepudiation?

- How is encryption used to secure stored files, including backup tapes and sensitive information on laptops?

- What, if any, use does the organization make of internal key escrow (to prevent inaccessible data when an employee is discharged or absent)?

- What use does the organization make of private-key algorithms (such as DES) that requires exchanging keys in secret?

- If a block cipher (such as DES) is used, what use is made of block-chaining or feedback (to prevent a block-replay attack)?

- What are the procedures for storing, exchanging, and protecting encryption keys?

- Does the company use encryption software that compresses messages before encryption to eliminate recurring blocks?

- What physical security measures are in place for computers that contain encryption software and/or private keys?

- To what extent are computers that contain encryption software and/or private keys linked to networks of any type?

- How are plain-text files of encrypted or other sensitive information obscured after they are deleted?

- Does the company encrypt all communication to and from a particular server or back up files from a remote location (exposing plain-text files to interception in route)?

- What procedures does the organization use to authenticate each message and the sender of each message to avoid spoofing?

- What reliance is placed on the password security typically offered in word processing, spreadsheet, and other software packages?

- What encryption standards such as FIPS 140-2 must the organization meet?

Further Reading

- *ACM Computing Curricula Information Technology Volume: Model Curriculum.* ACM, Dec. 12, 2008. http://campus.acm.org/public/comments/it-curriculum-draft-may-2008.pdf.

- Armistead, Edwin L. *Information Warfare Separating Hype from Reality.* Potomac Books, 2007.

- Catalogue of Threat 2004 in IT-grundschutz Manual 2004, BSI (Bundesamt für Sicherheit in der Informationstechnik). Federal office for Information Security, Germany, 2004. www.bsi.de/english/gshb/manual/download/threat-catalogue.pdf.

- CERT-SA, Computer Emergency Response Team: Saudi Arabia, 2008. www.cert.gov.sa/.

- Data classification. HDM Clariza Initiatives. June 16, 2007. www.trehb101.com/index.php?/archives/71-DATA-cLASSIFATIoN.html.

- DeCew, Judith W. *In Pursuit of Privacy: Law, Ethics, and the Rise of Technology.* Cornell University Press, 1997.

- Electronic Privacy Information Center. http://epic.org/.

- *Encyclopedia of Applied Ethics.* Academic Press, 1998.

- *FIPS Publication 199, Standards for Security Categorization of Federal Information and Information Systems.* National Institute of Standards and Technology, 2004. http://csrc.nist.gov/publications/fips/fips199/FIPS-PUB-199-final.pdf.

- Friedlob, George T., C. D. Schou, and F.J. Plewa. "An Auditor's Primer on Encryption." *CPA Journal*, 67.11 (1997): 40–46.

- Friedlob, George T., F.J. Plewa, and L.F. Schleifer. "An Auditor's Introduction to Encryption." Institute of Internal Auditors, 1998.

- Frost, J.C., J.M. Springer, and C.D. Schou. Instructor guide and materials to accompany principles of *Introduction to Principles of Computer Security: Security+ and Beyond.* McGraw-Hill Education, 2004.

- Hill, K. "How Target Figured Out A Teen Girl Was Pregnant Before Her Father Did." Forbes, 2014. www.forbes.com/sites/kashmirhill/2012/02/16/how-target-figured-out-a-teen-girl-was-pregnant-before-her-father-did/.

- Holtzman, David H. *Privacy Lost: How Technology Is Endangering Your Privacy.* Jossey-Bass, 2006.

- Howard, M., and S. Lipner. *The Security Development Lifecycle*, Microsoft Press, 2006.

- Hellman, Martin E. "The Mathematics of Public-Key Cryptography." *Scientific American*, August 1979, pp.146–157.

- Malaysian Public Sector Information Security Risk Assessment Methodology (MyRAM)., 2006, Malaysian Administrative Modernisation and Management Planning Unit (MAMPU), Malaysia.

- MyCERT, Malaysia Computer Emergency Response Team. 2013. www.mycert.org.my/en/index.html.

- Nash, A., et al. *PKI: Implementing and Managing E-security.* McGraw-Hill Education, 2001.
- National Institute of Standards and Technology Federal Information Processing Standard 199, Standards for Security Categorization of Federal Information and Information Systems, February 2004.
- National Institute of Standards and Technology. *Special Publication 800-60, Guide for Mapping Types of Information and Information Systems to Security Categories.* NIST, June 2004.
- National Institute of Standards and Technology. *Special Publication 800-12, An Introduction to Computer Security.* NIST, 1996.
- National Institute of Standards and Technology. *Special Publication 800-60 Volume I Revision 1, Guide for Mapping Types of Information and Information Systems to Security Categories.* NIST, 2008. http://csrc.nist .gov/publications/nistpubs/800-60-rev1/SP800-60_Vol1-Rev1.pdf.
- NSTISSI-4011, National Training Standard for Information Systems Security (INFOSEC) Professionals, CNSS, 2004. www.cnss.gov/Assets/pdf/nstissi_4011.pdf.
- Official Journal of the European Communities, Directive 2002/58/EC of the European Parliament and of the Council of 12 July 2000 concerning the processing of personal data and the protection of privacy in the electronic communications sector (Directive on privacy and electronic communications), http://www .planetdata.com/site/uploads/Directive_2002-58-EC_of_the_European_ Parliament_and_of_the_Council_1_Oct_2002.pdfPipkin, D. *Information Security: Protecting the global enterprise.* Hewlett-Packard, 2000.
- Schmidt, Howard A. *Patrolling Cyberspace: Lessons Learned from a Lifetime in Data Security.* Larstan Publishing, 2006.
- Schou, Corey D., and K.J. Trimmer "Information assurance and security," *Journal of Organizational and End User Computing,* vol. 16, no. 3, July/September 2004.
- Schou, Corey D., and D.P. Shoemaker *Information Assurance for the Enterprise: A Roadmap to Information Security.* McGraw-Hill Education, 2007.
- Tipton, Harold F., and S. Hernandez, ed. *Official (ISC)² Guide to the CISSP CBK 3rd edition.* ((ISC)²) Press, 2012.
- Trimmer, Kenneth J., et al. "Enforcing Early Implementation of Information Assurance Precepts throughout the Design Phase." Journal of Informatics Education Research, 2007.
- U.S CERT. United States Computer Emergency Readiness Team, 2013. www.us-cert .gov/.

Critical Thinking Exercises

1. An executive receives an e-mail from a known colleague with an urgent message about the financial state of their organization attached in a PDF. What should the executive do? The executive is unaware of any financial problems with the organization, and the executive didn't request this information.

2. An organization has always kept a "decentralized" information technology infrastructure, which has led to servers under desks, coat closets arbitrarily being turned into wiring closets, and numerous portable hard drives floating around the organization. What could happen if the organization needed to institute a reduction in force because of changing market conditions? What can an organization do to prevent the risk of these changes?

3. An organization's web site has been collecting the actions of users for several years now. The web site was a social media overnight success, and the organization never got around to completing a privacy statement or terms of service. The organization has been selling the demographic information to advertisers and market researchers as part of its core business for more than a year now. The organization receives a legal summons related to privacy concerns of the site. What could have been done in the beginning to prevent the legal exposure?

4. What information does your organization use, and what requirements must be met to ensure the confidentiality, integrity, and availability of the information? What drives these requirements for your organization?

5. Your organization has a web site used for advertising your products or services around the world. The site is used only for disseminating information about your organization and its mission. What requirements (if any) should be in place regarding confidentiality, integrity, and availability?

5 Organizations Providing Resources for Professionals

Because of the eclectic nature of information assurance, you must have some basic structure to guide you. The first step in this process is to define certification and professionalism. They are quickly becoming recognized as critical factors in the success of a corporation as well as a government agency.

Indeed, information assurance and security are often cited as core competencies in industry and government redesign. Prahalad and Hamel referred to corporate core competencies as the *roots of competitiveness*.

Professional certification is a procedure to identify individuals who have a common education and experience, who demonstrate some quantifiable level of knowledge and skills, and who subscribe to a code of professional ethics.

As organizations become more reliant on information systems, information assurance professionals are challenged to put forth formidable efforts to secure information systems against myriad threats. A security professional should be equipped with knowledge in all areas of information assurance and should observe the highest code of professional ethics to assist an organization in protecting information.

Organizations and institutions exist to train and equip security professionals by providing information, security-related information, guidelines, best practices, frameworks, and certification. This chapter presents the background and functions of some of these organizations. In addition, the chapter explores the codes of ethics promoted by organizations for security professionals.

Organizations Providing Resources for Professionals

This section outlines some of the well-known organizations providing professional certifications. Individuals should consider the relevancy to their job requirements and industry recognition before attaining a professional certification.

There are four characteristics of a professional certification standard.

- Agreement on certification criteria specific to ethics, education, and experience and a course of study that meets a prescribed set of standards. This is done by establishing a common body of knowledge that is agreed upon by recognized leaders in the information security field.

- Creation and validation of a testing program that should be professionally supervised by individuals skilled in test development (ISO 17024).

- Definition of an acceptable level of work experience to qualify an individual for certification.

- Examination to demonstrate some quantifiable level of knowledge. Mastery of the common body of knowledge is one indication of competency in this field, while performance testing is another indicator.

Organizations should understand different certification bodies and the drivers of their mission.

(ISC)² International Information System Security Certification Consortium

The International Information System Security Certification Consortium (ISC)² is a nonprofit, vendor-neutral organization known for its guidance of best practices in the areas of information assurance. Established in 1989, (ISC)² provides certification for more than 120,000 professionals. Such certification programs include Certified Information System Security Professionals (CISSP), Systems Security Certified Professional (SSCP), Certified Authorization Professional (CAP), Certified Cyber Forensics Professional (CCFP), HealthCare Information Security and Privacy Practitioner (HCISPP), and Certified Secure Software Lifecycle Professional (CSSLP). For those who have several years' working experience in information assurance or networking and intend to develop a career in this field, CISSP would be the recommended certification to pursue. (ISC)², with more than 120,000 members, is the largest and most senior computer security certifying organization that provides a comprehensive overview of information assurance–related knowledge.

Computing Technology Industry Association

The Computing Technology Industry Association (CompTIA) is a nonprofit trade association that provides a broad spectrum of professional certifications including A+, Network+, and Security+. Additionally, CompTIA provides Cloud+ for implementing secure clouds, Mobile App Security+ for secure mobile deployments, and Social Media Security

Professional for secure social media use. CompTIA's certifications are vendor neutral, and proceeds are directly reinvested into programs. CompTIA has been offering a wide range of certifications for more than 20 years in the United States, Indian, Japan, South Africa, and the United Kingdom.

Information System Audit and Control Association

Since 1967, the Information System Audit and Control Association (ISACA) has been involved in the research and expansion of knowledge in information technology governance. Security and audit experts globally know it for the Certified Information Systems Auditor (CISA) and Certified Information Security Manager (CISM) professional certifications. CISA is generally recommended for information security auditors, whereas CISM is recommended for those who are involved in managerial-related information security tasks. In addition, ISACA publishes the Control Objectives for Information and Related Technology (COBIT) standard, which provides management and business process owners with an IT governance model that helps in delivering value from IT and understanding and managing the risks associated with IT.

Information System Security Association

As a nonprofit organization, the Information System Security Association (ISSA) since 1984 has been organizing and facilitating various information system security initiatives. An example would be conducting forums and knowledge-sharing programs on the information system security environment. These efforts contribute to enhancing the knowledge and skills of practitioners. ISSA's main function is to ensure the confidentiality, integrity, and availability of information resources by promoting good management practices.

SANS Institute

The SysAdmin, Audit, Network and Security (SANS) Institute was established as a privately held training organization involved in cooperative research in 1989. The organization conducts certifications in specialized areas such as forensic analysis, incident handling, and security audits along with the Global Information Assurance Certificate (GIAC). The institute is involved in delivering and maintaining one of the largest collections of research documents on information security. The SANS Institute provides various free resources on information security–related news, vulnerabilities, alerts, and warnings. There are various tracks and certification programs provided by SANS Institute. They are recommended for highly technical professionals who deal with implementing and operating technology.

Disaster Recovery Institute, International

Established in 1988, the Disaster Recovery Institute, International (DRII) focuses on gathering and building contingency planning and risk management knowledge. Educational programs managed by DRII are in the areas of business continuity planning and management. Published standards and industry best practices by DRII are to promote knowledge sharing and act as a common knowledge reference for the business continuity planning/disaster recovery industry.

Business Continuity Institute

The Business Continuity Institute (BCI) was founded in 1994 with the ambition of ensuring that the provision and maintenance of business continuity planning and services are of the highest quality. Business continuity practitioners often refer to BCI for guidance on maintaining high professional competency standards and commercial ethics.

Deciding Among Certifications

Some of the decision criteria that inform an analysis of the value of a certification include the following:

- How long has the certification been in existence?
- Does the certification organization's process conform to established standards?
- How many people hold the certification?
- How widely respected is the certification?
- Does the certification span industry boundaries?
- What is the probability that five or ten years from now the certification will still be useful?
- Does the certification span geographic boundaries?

Answers to each of these questions provide insight into the value of a certification to both the potential employee and the employer.

Codes of Ethics

Different individuals may have different perceptions of ethics. You may have heard of the term *ethical hacker*.

What makes the action of a hacker legitimate and ethical? The action would be legitimate and ethical if consent of the owner is obtained prior to performing an assessment of system security. The consent necessary for ethical hacking is simply the application of one code of ethics among those found in professional security organizations.

Even if an action is not ethical, it may still be legal. Organizations should develop guidelines on computer or business ethics and disseminate this information to their employees through awareness or training sessions.

These ethical guidelines show stakeholders and employees that management is sincere in developing and supporting an ethical environment within the organization. This will limit the occurrence of unethical conduct within the organization eventually.

Certifying organizations may require their certified security professionals to comply fully with their code of ethics. By reference to these guidelines, organizations and the information assurance community can establish ethical guidelines to conform to local custom and in accordance with national laws and regulations in this area.

Table 5-1 summarizes the codes of ethics from organizations such as (ISC)², SANS Institute, ISACA, ISSA, BCI, and Computer Ethics Institute (CEI).

Code	Description
Honesty	• Security professionals should not abuse trust and power entrusted to them. • Security professionals should take only the assignments within their capability. • Security professionals should seek advice when it is required.
Professionalism	• Security professionals must ensure all stakeholders are well informed on the status of assignments and advise cautiously when required. • Security professionals should address the concerns of stakeholders at all levels to gain the broadest acceptance of information security. • Security professionals should not perform any malicious actions that jeopardize organizational or public interest. • Security professionals should observe all contracts and agreements. • Security professionals should protect clients' and employers' interest at all times.
Independence	• Security professionals should discourage any prejudice or conflict when advising and serving clients or employers. • Security professionals should point out any foreseeable conflicts of interest that may arise.
Legal and Ethic	• Security professionals should discourage any misconduct or malpractice that causes unnecessary alarm or fear. • Security professionals should not be involved in any criminal behavior or associate with any criminals. • Security professionals should not serve personal interest through organizational espionage. • Security professionals should report any illegal activities and should cooperate with law enforcement during investigation.
Knowledge	• Security professionals should be committed to enhance and improve knowledge in terms of technical, project, and leadership aspects. • Security professionals should promote information security professionally. • Security professionals should respect intellectual property. • Security professionals should share their knowledge with coworkers and the security community willingly.
Quality	• Security professionals should be familiar with all specifications of work. • Security professionals should oversee all activities and ensure that those activities are well organized to ensure an end product of good quality.
Privacy and Confidentiality	• Security professionals should respect client, employer, supplier, or coworker privacy and should not access any information that is not intended for them. • Security professionals should respect the confidentiality of information accessed even after an assignment. Such information should not be used for personal benefit or be released to inappropriate parties.

Table 5-1   Common Features of Codes of Ethics

Further Reading

- (ISC)². www.isc.org.
- BCI. www.thebci.org/about.htm.
- DRII. www.drii.org.
- *Guide to CISSP.* Information Security Certification, 2007. www.guidetocissp.com.
- ISACA. www.isaca.org/.
- ISSA. www.issa.org/.
- NIATEC training materials web site. http://niatec.info/pdf.aspx?id=169.
- Ryan, D., et al. *On Security Education, Training and Certifications.* Information Systems Audit and Control Association, 2004.
- SANS Institute. www.sans.org/.
- Prahalad, C.K., and G. Hamel. "The Core Competence of the Corporation." *Harvard Business Review,* May–June 1990.
- Schou, Corey D., and D.P. Shoemaker. *Information Assurance for the Enterprise: A Roadmap to Information Security.* McGraw-Hill Education, 2007.
- Tipton, Harold F., and S. Hernandez, ed. *Official (ISC)² Guide to the CISSP CBK 3rd edition.* ((ISC)²) Press, 2012.

Critical Thinking Exercises

1. A chief information security officer (CISO) continuously reports issues of risk to senior management even though they continue to deny requests for resources to mitigate the risk. The CISO holds a CISSP. Why is the CISO continuing to report the risk if the board has not done anything about it in the past?

2. An organization has decided they need a chief security officer to help determine the best way to implement the information assurance strategy of the organization. What certifications might best determine a strategic information assurance individual?

CHAPTER

6

Information Assurance Management System

Information assurance is not dependent on the size of an organization nor is it an once-in-a-lifetime event. It is an ongoing process. The Maconachy-Schou-Ragsdale (MSR) model points out that technology does provide some protection to information assets. However, technology alone is not enough. If an organization does not have a set of well-designed policies and procedures serving as the foundation of information assurance initiatives, deploying even the best technology would be worthless. Organizations of any size can effectively reduce risk exposures by having processes in place that address security.

Implementing and maintaining a high-quality information assurance program requires constant business process engineering and reinvention. However, you must remember that reinvention implies that at some point in the past invention occurred. With the exception of mature organizations (see Chapter 9), processes were never invented; they grew, evolved, and were controlled by bureaucratic rule systems. If they had been invented, there would be some sort of master plan for the system. This plan would include a description of the environment and how it is connected to the organization being reinvented and how to modify itself to contend with a changing environment. If it is true that there is no master plan, you must use a different approach to identify the environment and the organizational processes. If an organization does not establish an information assurance strategy, it must be prepared to implement information assurance through cultural and similar levels of influence.

Organizational processes are changing every day and are frequently distinguished by the formation of autonomous workgroups or teams. Team-based mission-driven organizations are characterized by their reliance on empowerment and knowledge-enabled workers. This transition requires a complete revolution in how individuals interact with their organizational cohorts. To initiate this transition, senior leaders may well use some advice from Peter Drucker in his book *The Age of Discontinuity.*

> *Knowledge is either relevant to a task or irrelevant to the task. The task decides, not the name, the age, or the budget of the discipline or the rank of the individual plying it. Knowledge is to be organized as a team in which the task decides who is in charge, when, for what, and for how long.*

He points out that although modern, knowledge-based workers still require an organizational superior, the knowledge work knows no hierarchy because there is no higher or lower knowledge. Therefore, information assurance programs and the associated management must be prepared to not only lead knowledge-based work teams but also manage the freely flowing nature of knowledge.

The absence of a knowledge hierarchy means that senior leaders must strive to lead information assurance management without forcing a dysfunctional bureaucratic structure. In reengineered organizations, decisions are made on a *just-in-time* (JIT) basis by assembling *ad hoc* decision teams with knowledge particular to the problem at hand. Incident response as described in Chapter 22 and business continuity planning as described in Chapter 24 are excellent examples of *ad hoc* team formation. These teams contain individuals from *all levels* of the organization. In addition, organizations that rely on knowledge workers must recognize that information is an asset to be protected and allocated as a strategic and sometimes scarce resource.

To establish integrated information assurance programs, organizations must break down three traditional barriers. The first is bureaucratic systems, the second is a failure to empower while relying on short-term thinking, and the third is a failure to identify stakeholders correctly. Information assurance management strives to overcome these three challenges through the development of systems incorporating people, processes, and technology to ensure information assurance processes are not viewed as invasive but rather pervade the fabric of the organization.

To manage information assurance effectively and efficiently, there is a need to establish a system. This system is the information assurance management system (IAMS). The IAMS combines the MSR components of people, process, and technology, and it is based on a sound risk management approach to protecting information assets. It stresses the importance of a process-based approach in managing and improving information assurance. The information assurance components of people, process, and technology will be elaborated further in Chapter 9.

Effective IAMSs are described in ISO/IEC 27001 and other related standards published jointly by ISO and IEC. To achieve continuous improvement in managing information assurance, ISO/IEC 27001 incorporates the typical Plan-Do-Check-Act (PDCA) approach that is the central discussion point in this chapter. The PDCA model can be used to drive information assurance initiatives effectively.

This chapter first establishes security considerations made throughout the information asset life cycle. This is followed by a discussion on the PDCA model as found in ISO/IEC 27001.

Security Considerations for the Information Asset Life Cycle

Information has life cycles. The term *information life cycle* means the cyclical stages through which information flows, typically characterized as creation, processing, use or transmission, storage, retention, and eventually disposal.

Organizations constantly acquire data from their environment as well as create information internally. Both data and information are processed and used to meet organizational goals and objectives. The result is stored for retrieval and later use. Information may be archived and retained as part of legal requirements. Finally, when the

organization has no use for it, the
information is disposed.

Figure 6-1 provides a model for the
information asset life cycle. The model shows
the stages that information assets pass
through during their life cycle.

As explained earlier, information assets
are constantly under threat. These threats
may be internal or external sources and can
be caused by accidental or malicious acts.
Using technology to transmit, store, process,
and retrieve information increasingly
exposes organizations to emerging threats.
As information is becoming better
recognized as a valuable business asset,
security considerations should be
incorporated throughout the information
asset life cycle to preserve the confidentiality,
integrity, availability, and usability of
information.

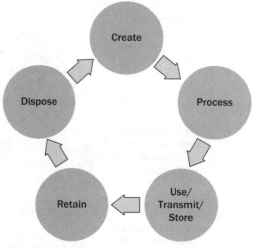

Figure 6-1 Information life cycle model

Since information should be secured throughout its life cycle, securing information
assets against the full spectrum of threats requires a process-oriented approach. The
following section discusses the most commonly used process model, named the PDCA
model from ISO/IEC 27001, which can be used to drive information assurance initiatives
effectively.

Plan-Do-Check-Act Model

The Plan-Do-Check-Act model demonstrates the process of managing security throughout
the life cycle. This includes the implementation of a continuous improvement process
to attain an effective information assurance management system. The IAMS is adaptable to
future changes and developments, business objectives, requirements, and processes; in
addition, it reflects the needs of customers, suppliers, and business partners. The best-known
example of the PDCA specification of IAMS is in the international standard ISO/IEC 27001
and its supporting standards in the ISO/IEC 27000 ISMS family.

The PDCA model highlights the fact that improvement programs initiate thorough
planning, result in effective actions, and progress through planning in a continuous
improvement cycle.

The outcome of each PDCA cycle is a managed information assurance environment in
the organization.

Figure 6-2 depicts how the PDCA steps fit together.

- **Plan** Establish the IAMS.
- **Do** Implement, operate, and maintain the IAMS.
- **Check** Monitor and review the IAMS.
- **Act** Execute, maintain and improve the IAMS.

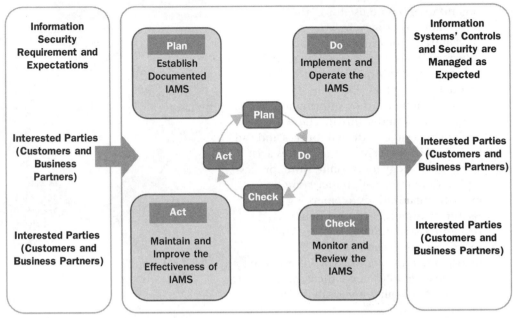

Figure 6-2 PDCA model applied to IAMS process

Based on the PDCA model, the information assurance requirements and expectations from the board members, stockholders, customers, business partners, and regulators are inputs. The output is an information assurance system satisfying the requirements and expectations mapped to the organization's business needs and objectives. The main stages of the PDCA model are described next.

Plan

As the name suggests, this phase is about initial planning for the IAMS. This phase requires meticulous documentation of decisions and the associated criteria. This phase focuses on establishing and documenting the IAMS. The main outcomes of this phase are establishing a documented information assurance policy, defining the scope of the IAMS, and defining a risk management approach (consisting of risk assessment and a risk treatment plan). It is essential that everything related to the planned activities is well documented for management purposes, internal audits, and traceability. This is the planning baseline for implementation.

The parts that make up the Plan phase are as follows:

- Defining the scope of the IAMS. It could be the whole organization or a particular site. This is a management decision.
- Planning and documenting the IAMS policy that sets out basic concepts for information assurance management.

- Determining a systematic approach to risk assessment, that is, clarifying and documenting risk assessment procedures and risk acceptance criteria.

- Identifying the risks by identifying and evaluating information assets, identifying the likelihood of threats, and identifying the loss impact should the threat take place.

- Performing risk assessment (analyzing and evaluating the risks).

- Determining the possible options of the risk treatment that will be adopted that will enable the selection of the control and control objectives.

- Preparing the statement of applicability (SOA). The SOA documentation includes control objectives along with the reason for their selection. It also includes a list of nonapplicable controls with justification for their omission.

Since risks keep changing based on the environmental dynamics, risk management is an ongoing activity. Assess these risks continually to provide protection to exposed assets. The process of reevaluating the risk will be conducted during the Check phase.

Do

The Do phase focuses on implementing and operating the controls selected and planned in the previous phase. The security policy, controls, processes, and procedures are now put into practice. This phase is outlined as follows:

- Defining, implementing, and operating methods to measure control effectiveness.

- Determining the appropriate management actions and priorities for controlling information security risks. This includes the allocation of organizational resources, roles, and responsibilities.

- Developing a risk treatment plan clarifying the activities to be executed to minimize unacceptable risks.

- Developing and implementing procedures for the detection of security incidents to minimize the damages caused if an incident occurs. It is important to check the procedures periodically.

- Implementing and operating the selected controls based on the risk assessment results.

- Implementing and operating training and awareness programs.

- Preparing procedure manuals to govern the operations needed for the controls in place.

Check

This phase assesses the performance of the IAMS process. The primary activity is management review, which is a series of processes in which management observes the effectiveness of the IAMS (in other words, that security controls are in place and achieving their objectives) and makes decisions on improving it. The parts that make up this phase are as follows:

- Executing, monitoring, and reviewing procedures
- Measuring control effectiveness
- Reviewing and re-assessing the risk and residual risk periodically
- Conducting reviews of the effectiveness of the IAMS at regular intervals
- Conducting internal IAMS audits at planned intervals
- Performing a formal periodic review of the IAMS to ensure that the scope remains sufficient and improvements in the IAMS process are identified and implemented
- Recording actions and events that could have an impact on the effectiveness or performance of IAMS

Act

The Act phase focuses on continually improving the effectiveness of the IAMS. Implementing corrective and preventive actions based on the results of the management review is essential. This phase is as follows:

- Implementing and operating the improvements identified in the IAMS
- Implementing corrective and preventive actions
- Communicating the results and actions with all responsible parties
- Ensuring that the improvements accomplish their intended objectives

Ongoing iteration of the PDCA cycle ensures that the organization continues to manage existing, emerging, and new risk issues in the organization and IT environment as they evolve over time. Thus, this guarantees continuous improvement and demonstrates the seriousness of the organization toward information assurance.

For effective and comprehensive implementation, organizations should adopt the PDCA model when developing the process of IAMS. The PDCA requirements are defined and mandated in the internationally accepted information security standard ISO/IEC 27001. This standard defines other mandatory requirements, all of which must be complied with to claim compliance with this international standard.

Boyd's OODA Loop

U.S. Air Force Colonel John Boyd developed the Observe, Orient, Decide, and Act (OODA) loop to help describe strategic military operations. Boyd's intention was to develop a framework that would help soldiers direct their resources toward defeating an enemy. Boyd's loop consists of the following phases:

- **Observe**   Gather raw information about the situation at hand. Be as accurate and thorough as possible.

- **Orient**   This step is designed to weed out bias and includes areas such as genetic heritage, cultural tradition, and previous experiences. Boyd often stated this is the most important phase because these areas inherently influence thoughts. When done properly, this phase can help confuse an adversary because they will make decisions based on the perceived biases.
- **Decide**   Based on the output of the orientation, a decision is made to act.
- **Act**   The action is performed.

Organizations and senior leaders who can complete the OODA loop faster than others hold a distinct competitive advantage in both the marketplace and information assurance situational awareness. Managers frequently rely on the thoughts of American revolutionary Patrick Henry, who said: "I have but one lamp by which my feet are guided and that is the lamp of experience. I have no way of knowing the future but by the past." An important feature of the OODA loop is that the bias of past events and previous experience does not cloud their thinking. Senior leaders must understand a zero-day event may not behave like previous events and the mitigation actions of the past may have already been accounted for by the adversary (they may be performing their own OODA or PDCA process!).

The Kill Chain

Another important concept comes from the U.S. military targeting doctrine that describes the *kill chain* as find, fix, track, target, engage, and assess (F2T2EA). All steps of the process must be successfully performed to produce the desired outcome. In information assurance and cybersecurity industries, many variations of this concept exist. They often involve an adversary studying an organization as a target, developing or acquiring a suitable payload for attack, attacking, and then observing the results before attempting their next move.

If an adversary's kill chain is understood, then efficient and multifaceted disruption methods can be developed to prevent an attack. Through careful restriction of firewall ports and services, it becomes harder to find vulnerable services. Through the use of continuous monitoring and patching, vulnerabilities become harder to target, and hardened systems and intrusion prevention systems lessen the impact of engagement. And careful use of system error messages and reporting discloses little for assessment and observation.

Organizations can merge the PDCA, OODA, and kill chain approaches to help determine the best security architecture for the organization and therefore the best defense-in-depth approach. Organizations that perform continuous risk management and OODA and apply the kill chain analysis will fare substantially better than organizations focusing on a single technology or deep technical solutions for risk mitigation.

Further Reading

- Brehmer, B. "The Dynamic OODA Loop: Amalgamating Boyd's OODA Loop and the Cybernetic Approach to Command and Control." 10th International Command and Control Research and Technology Symposium, 2005. pp. 1–15.

- Dove, R. "Embedding Agile Security in System Architecture." Insight 12, no. 2 (2009): 14–17.

- *International Organization Standardization and the International Electrotechnical Commission 2013 Information Technology – Security Techniques – Code of Practice for Information Security Controls (ISO/IEC 27002).* ISOIEC. www.iso.org/iso/home/store/catalogue_ics/catalogue_detail_ics.htm?csnumber=54533.

- Maconachy, V.C., et al. "A Model for Information Assurance: An Integrated Approach." Proceedings of the 2nd Annual IEEE Systems, Man, and Cybernetics Information Assurance Workshop, West Point, New York. June 5–6, 2001. pp. 306–310.

- Mitropoulos, S., et al. "On Incident Handling and Response: A State-of-the-Art Approach." *Computers & Security*, 25, no. 5 (2006): 351–370.

- Nichols, R. *Defending Your Digital Assets Against Hackers, Crackers, Spies, and Thieves.* McGraw-Hill Education, 2000.

- Schou, Corey D., et al. "Business Process Reengineering: Increasing Empowerment And Enablement." Proceedings Federal Software Technology Conference. Salt Lake, Utah. April 1995.

- Schou, Corey D., et al. *Information Assurance for the Enterprise: A Roadmap to Information Security.* McGraw-Hill Education, 2007.

- Tipton, Harold F., and S. Hernandez, ed. *Official (ISC) [2] Guide to the CISSP CBK 3rd edition.* ((ISC)[2]) Press, 2012.

- Von Lubitz, Dag KJE, et al. "All Hazards Approach to Disaster Management: The Role of Information and Knowledge Management, Boyd's OODA Loop, and Network-Centricity." *Disasters.* 32, no. 4 (2008): 561–585.

Critical Thinking Exercises

1. Why is the planning phase extremely important for an organization?
2. Should all controls be subject to the ongoing Check phase?

CHAPTER 7

Current Practices, Regulations, and Plans for Information Assurance Strategy

This chapter draws an overall picture of how an information assurance strategy and operations fit within the environment of the organization and how the strategy implements existing laws and legislation. The chapter provides an overview of select local and international legislations about information assurance. In addition, an overview is given for some of the more common information assurance best practices and standards available to business and industry.

Understanding these regulations and standards is crucial because this is the source of security requirements.

Due Care and Due Diligence

 The concepts of due care and due diligence are often discussed when evaluating the need for appropriate information assurance controls and risk management. Many areas of law, such as U.S. federal sentencing guidelines (criminal) and tort law (civil), rely on the concepts of due care and due diligence to determine negligence, intent, and severity of damages. Additionally, several safe harbor exceptions to laws require the safe harbor applicant to prove due care and due diligence to a certain standard or test.

Due Care

As adapted from U.S. NIST, *due care* can be defined as the responsibility that managers and their organizations have a duty to provide for information assurance to ensure that the type of control, the cost of control, and the deployment of control are appropriate for the system being managed.

Due Diligence

Due diligence is the continuous activities an organization takes to ensure the efforts established in due care are effective and operating as intended. It is imperative that organizations are aware of the implications of different types of laws around the world. Laws follow similar patterns. The bottommost layer consists of the following laws:

- Criminal laws help identify and prosecute crimes arising from abuses in the use of IT and the Internet. The law defines the crimes, assigns punitive actions for each crime, and identifies the party with the jurisdiction to handle the abuses and enforce punishments.

- Electronic transactions law provides a legal framework for the successful control and regulation of electronic transactions at both local and international levels.

- Intellectual property laws are laws that economies and countries have to protect computer systems software and their contents. Intellectual property is an important right in modern societies.

Specific Laws and Regulations

It is important to understand the relevant legislation and regulations applicable to the organization. They form an important part of the security requirements for establishing protection strategies. They encourage the organization to establish policies and procedures ensuring compliance. This section provides an overview of legislation and regulations supporting information assurance. The summary includes sample legislation and regulations from other countries and regions.

Computer Laws

In the United States, computer laws fall generally into three major categories: criminal, administrative, and civil. Although in specific country laws these may be framed differently, it is important to understand the general principles used worldwide.

- Criminal law
  - Describes the violation of government laws enacted to protect the public. (Criminal law is one of the most established laws in the world.)
  - Deals with crime and how criminal acts are handled. Under this law, punishment comes in the form of a jail sentence, a fine, or other penalties to the offender.
- Administrative law
  - This law is sometimes called regulatory law.
  - It is created with the primary objective of setting standards of performance and conduct for organizations.
  - Violations of this law may result in imprisonment or financial penalties if it is incorporated into a penal law and is described as a crime,
- Civil law
  - One form of this law is known as a tort law, and it deals with the administration of a civil society (property and commercial).
  - There is usually no jail sentence for violations, but there is a financial penalty (compensatory damages, punitive damages, and statutory damages).

Intellectual Property Law

The importance of intellectual property law to the profession of information assurance is obvious since it is directly related to ideas or information. It is concerned with how a company protects what it owns and describes remedies if this law is violated. The protection of intellectual property depends on the type of resource protected. Even where the laws in specific countries are different, understanding the terminology is important. Examples of intellectual property are as follows:

- Patents
  - A patent grants legal ownership of an invention to an individual or organization.
  - The inventor applies formally for a patent, after which ownership, development, and use of the design is limited to the patent holder for a specific period.
  - A patent holder may grant a license to others to use the design information typically for a certain amount.
- Trademarks
  - A trademark is any distinguishing name, symbol, logo, sound, or character that establishes identity for an organization, product, or service.
  - A trademark can be registered and filed in the appropriate jurisdiction.
- Trade secrets
  - A trade secret is proprietary information important for its owner's economic survival and profitability. It requires special skill, ingenuity, expense, and effort to develop and defend proprietary information.
  - Owners of trade secrets should take reasonable steps to protect the information.
- Copyrights
  - A copyright protects the expression of ideas as opposed to the protection of ideas (as for patents).
  - It does not require the author to file for copyright protection because the law comes into effect as soon as the idea is expressed in a tangible form.

Privacy Laws

The principles addressed in privacy and data protection laws of many economies have these four items in common:

- The collection of data should be by lawful means and with the consent of the owner or by the authorized regulatory body. Organizations must always check with existing laws if such activity is allowed or not.
- Data should be accurate, complete, and kept up to date.
- Data should be reasonably protected from possible security breaches.
- Individuals have the right to make corrections to data and to make necessary amendments.

Specific implementations may contain more detail. For example, the Organization for Economic Co-operation and Development (OECD) specifies the principles covered in the following sections (www.oecd.org/internet/ieconomy/oecdguidelinesontheprotectionof privacyandtransborderflowsofpersonaldata.htm#part2).

Collection Limitation Principle

There should be limits to the collection of personal data. Data should be obtained by lawful and fair means and with the knowledge or consent of the data subject, where appropriate.

Data Quality Principle

Personal data should be relevant to the purposes for which it is to be used. To the extent necessary for those purposes, it should be accurate, complete, and kept up to date.

Purpose Specification Principle

Personal data should be collected for purposes specified not later than at the time of data collection. Subsequent use is limited to the fulfillment of the stated purposes. If the data are used after this time for a purpose not stated at the time of collection, then that use must be specified on each occasion.

Use Limitation Principle

Personal data should not be disclosed, made available, or otherwise used for purposes other than those specified in accordance with these principles except with the consent of the data subject or by the authority of law.

Security Safeguards Principle

Personal data should be protected by reasonable security safeguards against such risks as loss or unauthorized access, destruction, use, modification, or disclosure of data.

Openness Principle

There should be a general policy of openness about developments, practices, and policies with respect to personal data. Means should be readily available of establishing the existence and nature of personal data and the main purposes of their use, as well as the identity and usual residence of the data controller.

Individual Participation Principle

An individual should have the right to do the following:

- Obtain from a data controller, or otherwise, confirmation of whether the data controller has data relating to the individual
- Have the data communicated to the individual within a reasonable time; at a charge, if any, that is not excessive; in a reasonable manner; and in a form that is readily intelligible
- Be given reasons if a request made based on the prior two points is denied and be able to challenge such denial
- Challenge data relating to the individual and, if the challenge is successful, have the data erased, rectified, completed, or amended

Accountability Principle

A data controller should be accountable for complying with measures that give effect to the principles stated previously.

Different economies have different privacy and data protection laws. For multinational organizations, this can be a challenge because of transborder data flows. Transborder data flows may be a barrier to the free flow of personal information since acceptable content varies from one country to another. The organization should investigate applicable privacy and data protection laws before deciding how to manage the flow of personal information.

With development in international politics and security, it has become the norm for authorities in some countries to monitor personal information. In some organizations, newly recruited employees sign documents allowing the management to monitor information they are managing, including personal information. In some counties, employees of private organizations have no expectation of privacy while using organizational equipment.

International Laws and Acts

Some multinational companies doing business internationally may also be subject to various international laws and regulations. This section provides an overview of some of the more common laws and regulations existing in other countries. Examples provided are from the United States and Europe. However, current trends show that these laws and regulations are gradually being adopted/adapted worldwide as a guiding principle or reference when dealing with a specific security area. Table 7-1 summarizes these laws.

Law/Regulations	Description
Gramm, Leach Bliley Act (GLBA)	This is a U.S. act requiring financial institutions to implement proper measures to protect customers' personal data. It also mandates the implementation of a risk management framework whereby the board of directors is held accountable for various security issues within the institution.
Sarbanes-Oxley Act (SOX)	The act was passed in the wake of a myriad of corporate scandals. The act specifies new financial reporting responsibilities, including adherence to new internal controls and procedures designed to ensure the validity of financial records.
Basel II Banking Guidelines	This provides a framework and minimum security standard by aligning existing regulatory capital requirements more closely to the underlying risks that banks face. The Basel II framework aims to promote a more forward-looking approach to capital supervision, which encourages banks to identify risks and improve their capabilities in managing those risks.

Table 7-1   Summary of Information Assurance Laws and Regulations

Standards and Best Practices

 Information assurance standards and best practices have been developed over time. These standards and best practices may be referred to as a basis for establishing a security framework for the organization or for personal use. Some of the more common standards and best practices are described in Table 7-2.

Standard/Best Practice	Description
ISO 27000 series	This was previously known as BS7799 (originating from the U.K. Department of Trade and Industry) and later as ISO 17799. The standard comprises two parts. Part I provides a code of practice for information security management, and Part II provides the specifications or requirements for the system. The standard was later adopted at the ISO level. <ul><li>27000: Fundamentals and Vocabulary</li><li>27001: Requirements</li><li>27002: Code of Practice</li><li>27003: Implementation Guidance</li><li>27004: Security Metrics and Measurement</li><li>27005: Risk Management</li><li>27006: Requirements for Bodies Providing Audit and Certification of Information Security Management Systems</li></ul>
ISO/IEC 13335	The standard has five parts and presents the concepts fundamental to a basic understanding of ICT security and addresses general management issues that are essential for successful planning, implementation, and operation of ICT security. The following is the outline of the standard: Part 1: Concepts and Models for Information and Communications Technology Security Management Part 2: Managing and Planning IT Security Part 3: Techniques for the Management of IT security Part 4: Selection of Safeguards Part 5: Management Guidance on Network Security
IT Baseline Protection Manual	The IT Baseline Protection Manual is a manual developed by the Federal Office for Information Security (BSI) in Germany. It contains standard security safeguards, implementation advice, and aids for numerous IT configurations that are typically found in IT systems.
NIST 800-12 The Computer Security Handbook	This is an introduction security book developed by the U.S. National Institute of Science and Technology. It provides an overview of information security issues and recommendations for managerial, operational, and technical controls.

Table 7-2 Summary of Standards/Best Practices (*continued*)

Standard/Best Practice	Description
Payment Card Industry (PCI) Data Security Standard	This is a multifaceted security standard developed by the PCI Security Standards Council (founded by American Express, Discover Financial Services, JCB, MasterCard, and Visa). The standard includes requirements for security management, policies, procedures, network architecture, software design, and other critical protection measures.
ISO TR 13569 Banking and Related Financial Services – Information Security Guidelines	The standard provides guidelines on the development of an information security program for financial institutions. It includes discussions of security controls, policies, and organizational, legal, and regulatory components of such programs. Considerations for the selection and implementation of security control and the elements required to manage information security risks within financial institutions are discussed. Recommendations are given based on consideration of an institution's business environment, practices, and procedures.

Table 7-2   Summary of Standards/Best Practices

Further Reading

- ISO TR 13569. *Banking and Related Financial Services – Information Security Guidelines.*

- ISO/IEC 13335. *Information Technology – Security Techniques – Management of Information and Communications Technology Security.*

- ISO/IEC 27001:2005. *Information Technology – Security Techniques – Information Security Management Systems – Requirements.*

- ISO/IEC 27002:2005. *Information Technology – Security Techniques – Requirements for Bodies Providing Audit and Certification of Information Security Management Systems.*

- ISO/IEC 27003:2010. *Information Technology – Security Techniques – Information Security Management System Implementation Guidance.*

- ISO/IEC 27004:2009. *Information Technology – Security Techniques – Information Security Management – Measurement.*

- ISO/IEC 27005:2011. *Information Technology – Security Techniques – Information Security Risk Management.*

- ISO/IEC 27006:2011. *Information Technology – Security Techniques – Requirements for Bodies Providing Audit and Certification of Information Security Management Systems.*

- ISO/IEC 27007:2011. *Information Technology – Security Techniques – Guidelines for Information Security Management Systems Auditing.*

- ISO/IEC 27010:2012. *Information Technology – Security Techniques – Information Security Management Guidelines for Inter-sector and Inter-organisational Communications.*

- ISO/IEC 27011:2008. *Information Technology – Security Techniques – Information Security Management Guidelines for Telecommunications Organisations Based on ISO/IEC 27002.*

- ISO/IEC TR 27008:2011. *Information Technology – Security Techniques – Guidelines for Auditors on Information Security Controls.*

- Maconachy, V., et al. "A Model for Information Assurance: An Integrated Approach." Proceedings of the 2nd Annual, IEEE Systems, Man, and Cybernetics Information Assurance Workshop, West Point, New York (June 5–6, pp. 306–310). The MSR Model. 2001.

- Schmidt, Howard A. *Larstan's The Black Book on Government Security.* Transition Vendor, 2006.

- Schou, Corey D., and D.P. Shoemaker. *Information Assurance for the Enterprise: A Roadmap to Information Security.* McGraw-Hill Education, 2007.

- Tipton, Harold F., and S. Hernandez, ed. *Official (ISC)² Guide to the CISSP CBK 3rd edition.* ((ISC)²) Press, 2012.

Critical Thinking Exercise

1. What laws, regulations, or standards does your organization need to comply with?

2. An organization's medical information site is tracking individuals and using information about searches and personal information entered to develop individual profiles for marketing. The web site does not inform visitors they are being tracked and their information is being collected. Which OECD principle has been violated, and what can the organization do to remedy the situation?

PART

II

Information Assurance Planning Process

As with any management practice, information assurance starts with comprehensive planning. Part II examines the practical considerations made when planning and establishing an information assurance management program. Central to the management program is establishing an information assurance management system (IAMS), which was discussed in Chapter 2.

Recall that the IAMS combines the components of people, process, and technology. It is a risk-oriented management system stressing the importance of a continuous process-based approach in managing and improving information assurance.

One of the most widely adopted IAMSs is described in ISO/IEC 27001 and achieves continuous improvement in managing information assurance by incorporating the Plan-Do-Check-Act (PDCA) method.

This part begins with Chapter 8, which gives you guidance on the approaches to implementing the IAMS in the contexts of common management practices while recalling that there is also a need to balance information assurance and its cost. Chapter 9 extends the guidance by discussing the possible structures that may be adopted by an organization to implement the IAMS. The discussion includes pertinent issues including staffing, roles, and responsibilities.

Chapter 10 discusses asset management. Asset management is at the core of information assurance management. If an organization can't manage its information assets and know the status of its IT assets in a given moment, the organization will be exposed to risk. Chapter 11 gets into the fundamental processes of risk management and how best to implement it across an organization. The risk management process starts with identification of information assets and their security requirements. This process exposes issues fundamental to performing information asset management. Recall that an information asset has a life cycle throughout which security must be provided. This concept resonates well with the process-based approach of an IAMS in the way that both are continuous processes and constantly needing improvement.

Following this, you'll find an explanation of the information assurance risk management process. Issues such as threats, vulnerabilities, and impact will be analyzed and the identified risks addressed. It is important to realize that risk management should be incorporated as an integral part of an overall information assurance program. Since it is a process, being the risk management itself is continuous. The importance of a successful risk management will be obvious because it provides a sound basis for the objective implementation of controls that are the central themes discussed throughout this book.

Having established the organization's risk profile, policies should be developed to govern the implementation of information assurance so that the identified risks are managed to achieve the stated mission and vision of the organization. Chapter 12 covers organizational information assurance policy. Policy is important in ensuring the organization's leaders clarify their support for information assurance and also their expectations of adherence to sound information assurance principles. Undoubtedly, information assurance policy is the most important element for any successful information assurance management program. The policy is a formal reference point of conduct in the organization. A poorly developed policy is a source of failure in managing information assurance.

The final chapters in Part II reinforce the point that in planning for information assurance, the human resource and quality assurance are also important. It has been the experience of organizations that the weakest link in any security implementation is the one involving people. Chapter 13 focuses on the important decisions to be made before, during, and after employment. Chapter 14 further highlights the importance of quality in both the human resource and security products. This chapter emphasizes certification and accreditation as a means of assurance for security implementation.

Quick Answers

Q: What are the considerations to be made for those who are about to start planning for information assurance?

A: Organizations should first plan how the information assurance management program is to be structured, organized, and then followed by defining the information assurance policies.

Q: **Should information assurance management be retained in-house or outsourced to third parties?**

A: It is a choice for the organization whether to opt for in-house or external management; however, it is not the classic make-vs-buy analysis. The decision to outsource information assurance functions depends on the following:

- The risk tolerance of the organization.
- The cost versus the benefit. The organization needs to conduct a cost-benefit analysis to assess the benefits to be gained from outsourcing against the cost savings from having it done in-house.
- The strategic planning of the organization.
- The capability of the organization's internal audit in dealing with the outsourcing relationship.
- The availability of internal security expertise.

Q: **Which functions of information assurance can be outsourced?**

A: Information assurance functions that can be effectively outsourced include security administration and monitoring. Companies should withhold any activities that require privileged access.

Q: **Considering the breadth of asset classification, are there sufficient resources to implement and support the process?**

A: Determining asset classification for the organization is a lengthy process. Therefore, the organization should consider staggering the exercise over one or two years based on the number of assets and size of the organization. It should be noted that the longer it is left, the riskier the situation. Alternatively, hiring external consultants to speed up the process, which typically includes asset discovery and tagging, is also an appropriate consideration.

Q: **What is the least bureaucratic way of operating the risk management process?**

A: The organization should focus on the more important risks. Embedding risk management into existing processes such as business planning can also help.

Q: **Who will own the risk management process and safeguard it?**

A: The process requires the support of top management, such as the CEO and senior management team—all of whom should actively contribute and participate throughout the process. In some cases, a risk manager will be appointed. This is not a necessity, since the process could be owned by a business planning manager. Internal auditors should be asked to review the process annually, report on its effectiveness, and provide recommendations for improvement.

Q: It is good that a risk assessment exercise identifies real threats and vulnerabilities. Yet how can the organization possibly deal with them with limited resources?

A: The fewer resources the organization has, the more vital the risk assessment process becomes. For example, if funds are scarce, perform a risk assessment to prioritize needs before allocating limited resources. By doing so, risk assessment provides the information needed to address the most pressing needs and increase the effectiveness of resource utilization.

Q: What is the difference between certification and accreditation?

A: The concepts are related. Accreditation is a formal acceptance of risks by management that results from the operation of an information system. Certification assures that a system meets defined requirements and is aligned to specified security controls. The certification is the exercise to support the accreditation decision process. Although the pairing of these two names is tied to specific processes in some economies, the actions, by whatever name, are important for a sound information assurance posture.

Q: Is it possible for an organization to apply information assurance principles without hiring a security officer?

A: Ideally, every organization should have a security officer, but if the organization is small, it may not have the necessary resources for a full-time position. It is important, though, that all employees in the organization play their respective roles in ensuring security policies and procedures are used.

Q: I do not know much about policy-related issues. Should I hire consultants to do the work for me?

A: It is always a good idea to obtain expert opinions. Consultants can give advice of the layout structure and content. Yet, allowing them to do the whole job will not produce the desired outcome. Information assurance is the responsibility of all employees, and they know their organization best. It would be incumbent for employees to shoulder their responsibilities in creating policies. In the final analysis, it is your job.

Q: I am new to the field of information assurance and have to set up an information assurance culture in my organization. Right now, we have good policies. When should I review my organization's information assurance policies?

A: Develop policies based on the organization's information assurance requirements in fulfilling its mission and vision. Any major changes to information assurance requirements, mission, or vision of the organization require a review of policies. The rule of thumb is that reviews should occur twice as frequently as the mistake one is willing to make. Experts agree that policies should be reviewed at least once a year. Policy reviews are effective when they are part of a certification process or an organization's change management process.

CHAPTER 8

Approaches to Implementing Information Assurance

In implementing an information assurance program, the approach taken also plays an important role. Organizations can use a top-down or bottom-up approach to implement and execute information assurance.

Selecting a suitable approach depends on an organization's requirements. Sometimes a hybrid is the right decision. For example, a large multinational organization with branches in different countries might select a top-down approach to match general corporate security requirements, while the bottom-up approach is used at the same time to meet local security requirements within specific economies.

This chapter focuses on the key components of an information assurance implementation followed by a discussion of the levels of organizational controls. It compares the top-down and bottom-up approaches and indicates when a particular approach is more suitable. Of course, organizations should always consider the different views when balancing information assurance against the cost of implementing it.

Key Components of Information Assurance Approaches

Any approach to information assurance should ensure effective interaction of the three key components of information assurance mentioned earlier in Chapter 2.

- People
- Process
- Technology

People are a challenging and crucial resource that need management. By applying the right processes and technology, people add value to organizations. When implementing the technology and operating the processes, an organization should have trained the right employees to maximize the efficient use of the technology. Awareness, training, and education (AT&E) are key to making information assurance work.

Process refers to the use of a formalized sequence of actions to achieve an aim. For example, recruiting new employees has its own process beginning with the advertisement stage and ending with the actual hiring. As an organization matures, processes or procedures should become more efficient and discriminating over time. Legal, regulatory, and contractual requirements and obligations are matters that should be weighed in terms of their impacts to current processes.

The technology component requires examining the hardware, software, and physical facilities to ensure better operations and execution of the computer security processes. Large organizations may spend money for operational problems created by implementing technological solutions without a plan. However, smaller organizations do not have the same resources. Therefore, it becomes riskier when you make an inappropriate selection. An organization should ensure the hardware or software purchased is cost-effective, meaningful, and useful.

Strive to achieve a balance between the three key components of people, process, and technology. Hence, when determining whether a top-down or bottom-up approach is more suitable, you should consider the total cost of ownership (TCO) and associated return on investment (ROI) of either approach with regard to the three components.

A common approach for those beginning to implement an information assurance capability is to focus on technology. This often leads to the purchase of several information assurance tools such as vulnerability scanners, penetration testing systems, and intrusion detection systems. The initial cost of these investments is often substantial, and the technology will require maintenance over the years. What has been achieved? The organization now has freshly installed tools that are already becoming obsolete but no people trained to operate them. The organization has neither built relevant policies/procedures nor determined how these new tools will affect the business. This is an example of a high total cost of ownership with a low return on investment because of a focus on technology over people and process.

Another approach could include hiring information assurance employees, directing them to write policies, standards, and procedures for the secure handling of information, and having them perform a risk assessment. Using the results from the risk assessment, the organization could then determine the best requirements for technology. Purchase technology that meets a specific need of the organization (such as encryption for the banking or healthcare industry) and targets a specific risk. Now the risk of a breach (which can be extensive in terms of monetary and reputation loss) is reduced through procedures and technology. The total cost of ownership is likely similar to the first example, but the return on investment can be measured and is likely quite high in this example.

Implementing information assurance using a top-down or bottom-up approach also depends on management's preference for culture. Before comparing the two approaches, understand the various levels of controls found in an organization. Small and simple organizations often rely on cultural norms to establish behaviors. This approach can be top-down if an organization's leadership is exceptionally strong; however, most often culture is found to be a driving force from the bottom up. Culture can effectively replace policy if used correctly and the same values and strategy have been instilled in every employee. Policies and procedures are often found in organizations that are large, multinational, or complex in their operations. Policies require effort to maintain, create, and negotiate; however, they set an immutable expectation by which the organization is expected to perform. Policies can shape cultures both positive and negative. If policies are not enforced and do not reward those who follow them, the organization's culture and practice will soon be to ignore the policy.

Levels of Controls in Managing Security

An important element of a security program is the collection of controls that an organization needs to have in place. Because each organization is unique, every security program is different. Every organization has its own risk profile (exposure to unique threats and vulnerabilities), business drivers, and compliance requirements. Even though security programs are different, they are composed of the generic elements shown in Figure 8-1.

Strategic management includes security processes such as conducting risk management exercises, security awareness programs, policy development, and compliance efforts with laws and regulations.

Tactical management examines business continuity, data classification, process management, personnel security, and risk management. Operational management includes areas of communication security, security of an information system life cycle, and incident response.

It is important to realize input for the strategic plan should not be merely from the CIO, CISO, or CSO (responsible for an information assurance program). Support for an information assurance program should come from senior management personnel in an organization—the board of directors, CEO, and heads of business or IT functions. Eventually, support should come from all employees in the organization. This support can be stimulated by an effective security awareness program tailored to different groups of employees.

Figure 8-1   Levels of controls in an information assurance program

Top-Down Approach

In a top-down approach, senior management shows that it takes security seriously and is actively involved in spreading information assurance awareness. They should mandate observation of the information assurance policy. This way, security is not just a matter of technology or an antivirus or firewall solution, which is often a result of lack of awareness in the area of information security. Fortunately, that mind-set is changing slowly because of the rise in incidents such as data theft and hacking. By embracing a top-down approach, security is no longer a purely technical matter.

The first step in implementing a formal top-down implementation is developing and presenting an approved, shared, and documented strategic plan. This document becomes a basic reference for continuous efforts. Prior to implementing security controls from the top and going through all organizational layers, senior executives should know priority areas for control. Once there is a clear understanding of threats and risks to critical assets of the organization, the top-down approach should be developed, approved, and distributed as an information assurance policy. This policy should be endorsed and communicated formally by senior leadership and the organization's executives.

External security audits are another security matter via a top-down approach. Audits and information assurance policies are closely related. Audits and policy reviews should be performed regularly to check whether established information assurance policies are effective. There are several standards, guidelines, or procedures related to auditing information assurance in the market such as NIST, COBIT, and ISO/IEC 27001.

A top-down approach is characterized by a high degree of control from the head office. It includes the overall strategy of its approach and phases of implementation. This approach encourages integration. It is easier to combine different elements in an information assurance program when it receives demonstrated support from the highest management level.

A problem with developing a top-down strategy is that it takes a longer time for approval. This creates slower decision making throughout the ranks. Since technology advances rapidly, the slowness may lead to poor technical decisions, and the organization ends up using an out-of-date solution. Avoiding this problem through a rapid enforceable decision-making process such as change management boards makes top-down approaches excel.

The top-down approach is becoming predominant because senior management in organizations has become aware that serious personal consequences (such as large fines or even jail time) may result from lack of attention to regulatory compliance relating to information assurance.

Bottom-Up Approach

A bottom-up approach refers to a situation in which a functional department or unit adopts strategic, operational, or tactical management to develop a security program without senior management support and direction (see Figure 8-1). A bottom-up approach is good for areas in organizations that need immediate security attention because of high risk or available budget. Since this approach focuses fully on technology or operational controls, it is more effective by addressing daily operational requirements.

The bottom-up approach is better when there is clear indication that implementers' resistance to change stems from insecurity such as anxiety about losing jobs because of a potential merger. Linking the elements in a bottom-up approach creates a larger process, part, or system, which is effective for faster integration. In using this approach, the challenge is to gain the support of senior managers to drive process improvement forcefully among subordinates. This poses additional challenges because of managers' fears of losing respect and authority. Despite the fact that a bottom-up approach may be desirable under certain circumstances, management should be informed about progress and decisions made. ISO 27001 embraces the use of a top-down approach where management's involvement and oversight are required throughout the security improvement life cycle.

Outsourcing and the Cloud

When outsourcing or using cloud services, a top-down approach to information assurance is mandatory. Senior leadership must set the tone surrounding security expectations of any business partner, outsource solution, or cloud provider. The senior executives and senior leadership of an organization are ultimately responsible for the performance of security functions of their cloud or outsourcing partners.

Organizations have used frameworks by ISACA, the Cloud Security Alliance (CSA), and the U.S. National Institute of Standards and Technology. These frameworks help ask the important security questions when looking at an outsourced partner or cloud provider. Organizations must remember that their information will be subject to laws and regulations of not only their headquarters but also the laws and regulations of the outsourcing partner and cloud provider.

Balancing Information Assurance and Associated Costs

It is imperative for senior management and security professionals to understand all views on security expenditures. Business and revenue-generating activities motivate senior management; therefore, they focus on productivity and activities related directly to it. The fact that it is not straightforward to calculate a return on security investment (ROSI) makes keeping management support more difficult. Early implementation of controls reduces the probability of high losses because of security incidents. Implement new controls once an organization resolves the situation and cleans up the damage.

Prior to applying a top-down or bottom-up approach, an organization needs to analyze the associated factors and costs of protecting information. Factors such as performance, availability, and coverage are part of the analysis. There is a potential for trade-off analysis here; for example, an organization with a higher level of reliance on availability of information and wider control coverage would require a larger investment.

Ideally, the requirements definition process should start from the top. Drive the process by aligning it with the organization's business objectives. This type of investment is good since it examines the overall information assurance posture of organizations and the immediate controls required. Understanding all business processes is important to ensure that changes in the management or maintenance processes are correctly managed.

Bottom-up investment does not emphasize the prioritized investments for security control. This is certainly the opposite of top-down investment. Making clear decisions based on a bottom-up investment strategy leads to questions about the thoroughness of the review of the organization's needs. This includes becoming familiar with an organization's services, products, financial situation, and evaluation reports on previous efforts related to information assurance.

Ultimately, the manner in which an organization approaches information assurance depends on its appetite for risk. Senior management needs to consider the impact to the organization if they do not adequately mitigate risks. Organizations must avoid giving attention and resources to information assurance deficiencies only after a significant issue such as a breach has occurred; be proactive. From a customer viewpoint, organizations should take full advantage of productivity and opportunity by deploying proper controls to ensure continuity and to increase customer trust and usage.

Finally, organizations should protect not only their own and customers assets but also associated brands, networks, and web sites. All online content, communication, and commerce should be protected within every layer of data transmission and storage proportionate to the value of the data. End-to-end security is not only necessary to preserve customer confidence and encourage online usage, but also to avoid regulatory penalties, financial liabilities, and consequential losses. End-to-end security refers to a situation where information from the sender is being encrypted and secured from the moment it is created, stored, and transmitted, until it is received at the destination.

Further Reading

- Bottom-up Investing in Investopedia.com. Investopedia ULC, 2007. www .investopedia.com/terms/b/bottomupinvesting.asp.

- Cloud Security Alliance. Cloud Controls Matrix, 2012. https://cloudsecurityalliance .org/research/ccm/.

- *ISO 9000:2000 Frequently Asked Questions.* International Standardization for Organization (ISO), 2004. www.iso.org/iso/en/iso9000-14000/explore/transition/ faqs.html?printable=true.

- Rasmussen, Gideon T. *Implementing Information Security: Risks vs. Cost.* 2005. www .gideonrasmussen.com/article-07.html.

- Cloud Computing Synopsis and Recommendations. U.S. National Institute of Standards and Technology, 2012. http://csrc.nist.gov/publications/ nistpubs/800-16/sp800-146.pdf.

- Conklin, Wm. Arthur, et al. *Introduction to Principles of Computer Security: Security+ and Beyond.* McGraw-Hill Education, March 2004.

- Schou, Corey D., and D.P. Shoemaker. *Information Assurance for the Enterprise: A Roadmap to Information Security.* McGraw-Hill Education, 2007.

- Tipton, Harold F., and S. Hernandez, ed. *Official (ISC)*[2] *Guide to the CISSP CBK 3rd edition.* ((ISC)[2]) Press, 2012.

- Tom, P. *Data Protection and Information Lifecycle.* Prentice Hall, 2006.

- "Top-Down Approach for Security." *Network Magazine.* Indian Express Newspapers, June 2003. www.networkmagazineindia.com/20030h6/is15.shtml.

Critical Thinking Exercises

1. An organization has never had a formalized information assurance program. What kind of an approach is most likely currently occurring, and what are the advantages and disadvantages of the approach?

2. An organization operates out of the European Union but wants to use a cloud provider based in the United States to store and process healthcare information about people living in the European Union. What laws, regulations, and rules must the organization be aware of?

3. An organization currently has a web site that processes personally identifiable information (PII) for a client. A network engineer points out a vulnerability in the web site that will cost $125,000 to mitigate. Currently, the system is operating in the United States, and it would be subject to breach notification laws. What is the best approach to ensure return on investment?

CHAPTER

9

Organizational Structure for Managing Information Assurance

Information assurance is an interdisciplinary and multidepartmental issue requiring commitment from the entire organization. Successful implementation of the IAMS depends on the availability of an organizational structure for managing information assurance. As detailed in Chapter 2, defining roles and responsibilities should be started during the Do phase. Experience has shown that ill-defined structures and ambiguous roles contribute to failures in information assurance management. Defining a "right" structure is the cornerstone for successfully implementing an information assurance program. Thus, it should have the highest priority compared with other controls.

Organizations differ in size, complexity, and culture, and there is no single structure to manage information assurance ideally. This chapter describes the common structures that are applicable to most organizations. The discussion also touches on staffing levels and employee roles and responsibilities; of course, smaller organizations may have the same functions spread across a smaller staff.

Importance of Managing Information Assurance as a Program

The popular phrase "information assurance is a process and not a one-off event" is always true. A continuous improvement process adds to an effective information assurance program. This involves activities such as monitoring the program periodically, measuring performance, evaluating the effectiveness of controls, conducting security audits, and performing risk re-assessments. Organizations have discovered that awareness training, and education (AT&E) programs organized at all levels have improved security significantly.

A good information assurance management program is pervasive; it permeates multiple levels of the enterprise and provides benefits to the organizational culture. Every level enhances the entire organizational security profile by using various types of expertise, authority, and resources. A well-planned information assurance management program produces the following positive results:

- It will have continuous support and commitment from the top management to sustain an effective program by ensuring matters such as required resources are available.

- Employees will be directly involved in the planning of local security systems.

- Executives will have a better understanding of the organization and will be able to effectively play their role and use their authority to protect information.

- Information assets will be securely managed by the organization as per information handling categorization.

- Managers within each of the business and operational units will be more aware and familiar with specific security requirements, including technical and procedural requirements, associated challenges, and risks of the IT environment.

- It will implement secured physical and logical access to IT infrastructure.

Based on the strategy of the organization, the list of positive results may be different, but the general outcomes will be similar. For example, in a top-down approach, the first two items in the list will be more obvious. On the other hand, managers who are aware of specific security requirements may be emphasized in a bottom-up approach.

Refer also to Chapter 8 on various approaches for implementing information assurance.

Structure of an Information Assurance Organization

There are three types of structural options available for consideration.

- Centralized structure where an information assurance management program is managed under a centralized unit with ultimate accountability and responsibility for the program

- Distributed structure where roles, responsibilities, and authorities are spread throughout the organization's business units, operations areas, and geographical locations

- Hybrid structure that is a mix of the centralized and distributed structures

In attempting to determine the right structure, the nature of business and the size of the organization are important. Usually, the structure is influenced by the organization's culture, the current business processes, and the IT functions within the organization.

A centralized management program is more suited for smaller organizations that have limited resources and budget. Some examples of activities that should be centralized include the following:

- Defining information assurance roles, responsibilities, and authorities

- Developing IT security architecture

- Developing policies and guidelines

- Organizing an awareness program
- Setting up a computer emergency readiness team (CERT) capability and conducting training for the selected personnel

In contrast, a distributed program management approach may be better suited for complex organizations with multiple locations, international branches, and business units. In a distributed structure, each functional unit (department, division, subsidiary, or business location) is responsible for its own security planning and implementation. In addition, overseas branches may also be subjected to local rules and regulations that would be best managed by the overseas branches themselves. However, some small and medium-sized businesses also operate in a distributed way.

There has been a trend toward the adoption of hybrid structure. The hybrid structure features centralized management of information assurance with decentralized execution of security activities. From a practical perspective, a hybrid structure attempts to avoid redundant tasks and waste of resources. The centralized part promotes uniformity in activities across the organization while the distributed part allows for easier enforcement of policies and internal regulations across the organization.

Information Assurance Staffing

In addition to the basic elements in an information assurance management structure, recruiting and assigning the right personnel to handle information assurance–related jobs are vital tasks. See Chapter 13 on guidelines for recruiting new employees.

Once hired, regularly give all employees appropriate job-related training about IT and information assurance. Competency skill programs are important to nurture talents especially when organizations explore new opportunities in other countries.

Organizations may recruit workers from around the world in accordance with the local labor laws and regulations. However, most laws and regulations do not require newly recruited employees to sign any work ethics or nondisclosure agreements. As a proactive control, new recruits should be required to execute an agreement on ethics and monitoring related to the protection of information during their employment.

Roles and Responsibilities

It is common to find confusion in the organization over responsibility for information assurance. Management should promote awareness that "information assurance is everyone's responsibility." This responsibility lies in the hands of the operational team and cuts across the whole organization with the senior management driving the strategy for information assurance initiatives.

A clearly defined structure of the roles and responsibilities for individuals and teams involved in the information assurance management program is essential to ensure effectiveness and smooth operation of the program. Industry has established a generic list of the main groups that an organization should involve in the information assurance management program structure.

- Senior management
- Information assurance units

- Information security units
- Cyber security units
- Privacy units
- Technology and service providers
- Supporting functions
- Users

Each of these groups is discussed in the subsequent sections.

Senior Management

In addition to accepting risk and setting direction, senior management establishes and enforces the organization information assurance program. They endorse and approve policies and objectives supporting the vision and mission of the organization, define and appoint, or change the roles and responsibilities of the appropriate management representatives and the tactical security team members. As an example, the following roles have been adapted from U.S. NIST role definitions. Note that while an organization may not use these exact titles and divisions of responsibility, the organization should consider where the function is performed. Large organizations may be equipped to have unique individuals assigned to each of the roles.

Chief Executive Officer

The chief executive officer (CEO) has the role of being the head of the organization or business.

The head of an organization is the highest-level senior official or executive within an organization and has the overall responsibility to provide information assurance protections commensurate with the risk and magnitude of harm (that is, affect) to organizational operations and assets, individuals, and other organizations, resulting from the unauthorized access, use, disclosure, disruption, modification, or destruction of information collected or maintained by or on behalf of the organization and information systems used or operated by an organization or by a contractor of an organization or other entity on behalf of an organization. Organization heads are also responsible for the following:

- Ensuring that information assurance management processes are integrated with strategic and operational planning processes
- Ensuring that senior officials within the organization provide information assurance for the information and information systems that support the operations and assets under their control
- Ensuring that the organization has trained personnel sufficient to assist in complying with the information assurance requirements in related legislation, policies, directives, instructions, standards, and guidelines

Through the development and implementation of strong policies, the CEO establishes the organizational commitment to information assurance and the actions required to effectively manage risk and protect the core missions and business functions being carried out by the organization. The CEO establishes appropriate accountability for information assurance and provides active support and oversight of monitoring and improvement for the information assurance program. Senior leadership commitment to information assurance establishes a level of due diligence within the organization that promotes a climate for mission and business success.

Chief Risk Officer

The chief risk officer (CRO) holds the risk executive functional role in an organization.

The risk executive is a functional role established within organizations to provide a more comprehensive, organization-wide approach to risk management. The risk executive (function) serves as the common risk management resource for senior leaders/executives, mission/business owners, chief information officers, chief information security officers, information system owners, common control providers, enterprise architects, information security architects, information systems/security engineers, information system security managers/officers, and any other stakeholders with a vested interest in the mission/business success of organizations. The risk executive (function) coordinates with senior leaders/executives to do the following:

- Establish risk management roles and responsibilities.
- Develop and implement an organization-wide risk management strategy that guides and informs organizational risk decisions (including how risk is framed, assessed, responded to, and monitored over time).
- Manage threat and vulnerability information with regard to organizational information systems and the environments in which the systems operate.
- Establish organization-wide forums to consider all types and sources of risk (including aggregated risk).
- Determine organizational risk based on the aggregated risk from the operation and use of information systems and the respective environments of operation.
- Provide oversight for the risk management activities carried out by organizations to ensure consistent and effective risk-based decisions.
- Develop a greater understanding of risk with regard to the strategic view of organizations and their integrated operations.
- Establish effective vehicles and serve as a focal point for communicating and sharing risk-related information among key stakeholders internally and externally to organizations.
- Specify the degree of autonomy for subordinate organizations permitted by parent organizations with regard to framing, assessing, responding to, and monitoring risk.
- Promote cooperation and collaboration among accrediting officials to include security accreditation actions requiring shared responsibility (such as joint/leveraged accreditations).
- Ensure that security (risk acceptance) decisions consider all factors necessary for mission and business success.

- Ensure shared responsibility for supporting organizational missions and business functions using external providers receives the needed visibility and is elevated to appropriate decision-making authorities.

- The risk executive (function) requires a mix of skills, expertise, and perspectives to understand the strategic goals and objectives of organizations, organizational missions/business functions, technical possibilities and constraints, and key mandates and guidance that shape organizational operations. To provide this needed mixture, the risk executive (function) should be filled by a single individual or office (supported by an expert staff) and supported by designated groups (such as a risk board, executive steering committee, and executive leadership council).

- Designate the CISO and CSO as independent from the CIO if possible.

The risk executive (function) fits into the organizational governance structure in such a way as to facilitate efficiency and to maximize effectiveness. While the organization-wide scope situates the risk executive (function), its role entails ongoing communications with and oversight of the risk management activities of mission/business owners, accrediting officials, information system owners, common control providers, chief information officers, chief information security officers, information system and security engineers, information system security managers/officers, and operational stakeholders.

Chief Information Officer

The chief information officer (CIO) fills the head information systems and information management role in an organization and decides the organization's approach to information technology use, adoption, and operational risk management. The function of the CIO is to do the following:

- Designate a senior information security officer to ensure proper implementation of security controls and continuous information assurance risk monitoring. In some organizations, this may take the role of a CISO; however, organizations must be cautious of this reporting relationship since they must have unbiased risk assessments from the CISO.

- Develop and maintain information security policies, procedures, and controls to address all applicable requirements.

- Oversee personnel with significant responsibilities for information security and ensure the personnel are adequately trained.

- Assist senior organizational officials concerning their information assurance responsibilities,

- In coordination with other senior officials such as the CRO, report at least annually to the CEO or board of directors on the overall effectiveness of the organization's information assurance program, including identified threats and the progress of remedial actions.

The chief information officer, with the support of the CRO and the CISO or CSO, works closely with accrediting officials and their designated representatives to do the following:

- Ensure an organization-wide information assurance program is effectively implemented resulting in adequate assurance for all organizational information systems and environments of operation for those systems.

- Ensure information assurance considerations are integrated into programming/ planning/budgeting cycles, enterprise architectures, and acquisition/system development life cycles.

- Ensure information systems are covered by approved security plans and are accredited.

- Ensure information assurance–related activities required across the organization are accomplished in an efficient, cost-effective, and timely manner.

- Ensure there is centralized reporting of appropriate information assurance–related activities.

The chief information officer and accrediting officials determine, based on organizational priorities, the appropriate allocation of resources dedicated to the protection of information systems supporting the organization's missions and business functions. For selected information systems, designate the chief information officer as an accrediting official or a co-accrediting official with other senior organizational officials.

Chief Information Security Officer

The chief information security officer (CISO) is an organizational official responsible for serving as the primary liaison for the chief information officer to the organization's accreditation officials, information system owners, common control providers, and information system security officers

The chief information security officer does the following:

- Possesses professional qualifications, including training and experience, required to administer the information security program functions (see Chapter 13 for more information about training and education)

- Maintains information assurance duties as a primary responsibility

- Heads an office with the mission and resources to assist the organization in achieving more secure information and information systems in accordance with the requirements of the organization, its industry, and any legal mandates

The CISO (or supporting staff members) may also serve as accreditation official liaisons or security control assessors. The CISO must be cautious to ensure no conflicts of interest exist between the staff and those being assessed.

Chief Security Officer

When instantiated, the chief security officer (CSO) oversees the following:

- The CISO either directly or through an indirect reporting structure for information assurance related to information systems.

- Physical security controls throughout the organization in coordination with the CISO and CRO. You can find more information about physical security in Chapter 16.

- Personnel security throughout the organization in coordination with HR, the CISO, and the CRO. You can find more for information about personnel security in Chapter 13.

Accrediting Official

Although the accrediting model is not universal, it is used by the U.S. government. The process helps organizations assign accountability for information systems in the assurance process. The accrediting official accepts responsibility for unmitigated risks. The U.S. NIST defines the accrediting official (AO) as a senior official or executive with the authority to formally assume responsibility and risk impacts for operating an information system at an acceptable level of risk to organizational operations and assets, individuals, and other organizations. Accrediting officials must have budgetary oversight for an information system or must be responsible for the mission and/or business operations supported by the system. Through the information assurance accreditation process, accrediting officials are accountable for the information assurance risks associated with information system operations. Accordingly, accreditation officials must be in management positions with a level of authority commensurate with understanding and accepting information system–related security risks.

Accrediting officials also approve system security plans, memorandums of agreement or understanding, and plans of action and milestones to determine whether significant changes in the information systems or environments of operation require re-accreditation. Accreditation officials can deny authorization to operate an information system. Or, if the system is operational, they can halt operations if unacceptable risks exist. Accrediting officials coordinate their activities with the CRO, CIO, CSO, CISO, common control providers, information system owners, information system security officers, security control assessors, and other stakeholders during the information assurance accreditation process.

With the increasing complexity of missions/business processes, partnership arrangements, and the use of external/shared services, it is possible that a particular information system may involve multiple accrediting officials. If so, agreements are established among the accrediting officials and documented in the information system's security plan. Accreditation officials are responsible for ensuring that all activities and functions associated with security accreditation are carried out. Accreditation officials often designate a liaison with specific information assurance expertise to assist them in their duties.

Accrediting Official Liaison   The accrediting official liaison (AOL) is an organizational official who acts on behalf of an AO to coordinate and conduct the required day-to-day activities associated with the information assurance accreditation process. AOLs can be empowered by AOs to make limited decisions about the planning and resourcing of the accreditation process, approval of information system security plans, approval and monitoring the implementation of plans of action and milestones, and the assessment of risk. The AOL may also prepare the final accreditation package, obtain the AO's signature on the accreditation decision document, and transmit the accreditation package to appropriate organizational officials. The accreditation decision and signing of the associated accreditation decision document may not be delegated to the AOL. In other words, the acceptance of risk to organizational operations and assets, individuals, and other organizations is exclusively that of the AO.

Information Assurance Units

In large organizations, an information assurance unit directs, coordinates, plans, and organizes information assurance activities organization wide. The unit communicates relevant security matters to both internal and external parties as appropriate. The unit works with a variety of individuals, bringing them together to implement controls in response to current and anticipated information assurance risks.

This unit is also in charge of suggesting strategy and taking steps to implement the controls needed to protect both the organization's information and the information supplied to the organization by external parties. More importantly, it investigates ways that information assurance–related technologies, requirements, processes, and organizational structures are applied to achieve the goals of the organization's strategic plan.

Information Assurance Control Assessor

The information assurance control assessor (IACA) is an individual, group, or organization responsible for conducting a comprehensive assessment of the management, operational, and technical security controls employed within or inherited by an information system to determine the overall effectiveness of the controls. They asses if controls are implemented correctly, operating as intended, and producing the desired outcome with respect to meeting the security requirements for the system.

Information assurance control assessors also report on the severity of weaknesses or deficiencies discovered in the information system and its environment of operation as well as recommend corrective actions to address identified vulnerabilities. In addition to these responsibilities, information assurance control assessors prepare the final security assessment report containing the results and findings from the assessment. Prior to initiating the security control assessment, an assessor conducts an assessment of the information system security plan to help ensure that the plan provides a set of information assurance controls for the information system that meet the stated assurance requirements.

The required level of assessor independence is determined by the specific conditions of the security control assessment. For example, when the assessment is conducted in support of an accreditation decision or ongoing accreditation, the accrediting official makes an explicit determination of the degree of independence required in accordance with organizational policies, directives, standards, and guidelines. The independence of an assessor is an important factor in the following:

- Preserving the impartial and unbiased nature of the assessment process
- Determining the credibility of the security assessment results
- Ensuring that the accrediting official receives objective information possible to make an informed, risk-based, authorization decision

The information system owner and common control provider rely on the security expertise and the technical judgment of the assessor to do the following:

- Assess the information assurance controls employed within and inherited by the information system using assessment procedures specified in the security assessment plan
- Provide specific recommendations on how to correct weaknesses or deficiencies in the controls and address identified vulnerabilities

The information assurance control assessor is also critical in issuing a certification decision. The assessor should review the required information assurance controls and determine whether the system should be certified in accordance with a defined standard.

Information Assurance Engineer

The information assurance engineer (IAE) is an individual, group, or organization responsible for conducting information system assurance engineering activities. Individuals in this role can be certified by organizations such as (ISC)² with its examination for the CISSP-ISSEP. Information system assurance engineering is a process that captures and refines information assurance requirements and ensures that the requirements are effectively integrated into information technology component products and information systems through purposeful information assurance architecting, design, development, and configuration. Information assurance engineers are an integral part of the development team (such as the integrated project team), designing and developing organizational information systems or upgrading legacy systems. (You can find more information about secure development and acquisition in Chapter 15.) Information assurance engineers employ best practices when implementing information assurance controls within an information system, including software engineering methodologies, system/security engineering principles, secure design, secure architecture, and secure coding techniques. Information assurance engineers coordinate their security-related activities with information assurance architects, CISOs, CSOs, CROs, information system owners, common control providers, and information system security officers.

Information Assurance Architect

The information assurance architect (IAA) is an individual, group, or organization responsible for ensuring that the information assurance requirements necessary to protect the organization's core missions and business processes are adequately addressed throughout the enterprise architecture, including reference models, segment and solution architectures, and the resulting information systems supporting those missions and business processes. Individuals in this role can be certified by organizations such as (ISC)² with its examination for the CISSP-ISSAP. The information assurance architect ideally serves as the liaison between the enterprise architect and the information assurance engineer and also coordinates with information system owners, common control providers, and information system security officers on the allocation of information assurance controls as system-specific, hybrid, or common controls. In addition, information assurance architects, in close coordination with information system security officers, advise accrediting officials, chief information officers, CISOs, CSOs, and the CRO on a range of assurance-related issues including, for example, information system boundaries, assessments of the severity of weaknesses and deficiencies in the information system, plans of action and milestones, risk mitigation approaches, security alerts, and potential adverse effects of identified vulnerabilities.

Information System Security Officer

The information systems security officer (ISSO) is an individual responsible for ensuring that the appropriate operational assurance posture is maintained for an information system and as such works in close collaboration with the information system owner. The information system security officer also serves as a principal advisor on all matters, technical and otherwise, involving the assurance of an information system. The information system security officer has the detailed knowledge and expertise required to manage the assurance aspects of an information system and, in many organizations, is assigned responsibility for the day-to-day information assurance operations of a system such as incident response activities and serving as a liaison for investigations.

This responsibility may also include, but is not limited to, physical and environmental protection, personnel security, incident handling, and information assurance training and awareness. The information system security officer may be called upon to assist in the development of the security policies and procedures and to ensure compliance with those policies and procedures. In close coordination with the information system owner, the information system security officer often plays an active role in the monitoring of a system and its environment of operation, which includes developing and updating the system's security plan, managing and controlling changes to the system, and assessing the security impact of those changes.

Technology and Service Providers

Technology and service providers supply information assurance consultancy, services, and products. Table 9-1 describes the security responsibilities of this group based on the experiences gathered by NIST.

A successful implementation of information assurance requires participation from other supporting functions. The important support functions are summarized in Table 9-2.

Technology Providers	Security Responsibilities
Programmer	• Develop systems/software in accordance with specifications set • Ensure that secure programming practices are observed
Help desk	• Act as a first liner in attending to users' complaints and security-related incidents • Escalate the security incidents to the information assurance unit for further review or investigation

Table 9-1   Responsibilities of Technology and Service Providers (*continued*)

Technology Providers	Security Responsibilities
Database administrator	• Implement access control for databases • Take part in user access management such as sanctioning • Implement controls to ensure confidentiality, integrity, and availability of data in the database • Monitor database activities to track potential security violation or performance issues
System/network administrator	• Configure a system and network in accordance with security specifications set by the information assurance unit • Patch and update the system to ensure that it is free from vulnerabilities
Information systems/ business analyst	• Ensure that adequate controls are implemented during the application development life cycle • Ensure that security requirements are incorporated during system design and development • Include suitable controls in all proposed information system solutions

Table 9-1   Responsibilities of Technology and Service Providers

Supporting Function	Security Responsibilities
Physical security/facility management/property management	• Develop and enforce appropriate physical security controls, with input from information assurance management and other relevant parties
Human resource department/unit	• Conduct screening and background investigation for an identified position • Coordinate and provide security training and awareness to employees • Ensure compliance with labor law and relevant legislation • Take part in all personnel-related matters such as definition of terms and conduct of employment, performance evaluation, and career path planning
Audit	• Perform compliance checking and ensure compliance with relevant laws, regulations, or policies • Review effectiveness of internal control and implementation of information assurance
Legal	• Ensure compliance with relevant regulations and legislations • Ensure security requirements are incorporated in contracts and agreements • Provide advice on legal matters

Table 9-2   Responsibilities of Supporting Functions (*continued*)

Supporting Function	Security Responsibilities
Risk management	• Develop a risk mitigation plan • Identify and evaluate risks inherent in the organization including security-related risks • Responsible for contingency planning for the organization • Review effectiveness of internal controls in mitigating identified risks

Table 9-2   Responsibilities of Supporting Functions

Information System Owner

The information system owner (ISO) is an organizational official responsible for the procurement, development, integration, modification, operation, maintenance, and disposal of an information system.

The information system owner is responsible for addressing the operational interests of the user community (that is, users who require access to the information system to satisfy mission, business, or operational requirements) and for ensuring compliance with information assurance requirements. In coordination with the information system security officer, the information system owner is responsible for the development and maintenance of the system security plan and ensures that the system is deployed and operated in accordance with the agreed-upon information assurance controls. In coordination with the information owner/steward, the information system owner is also responsible for deciding who has access to the system (and with what types of privileges or access rights) and ensures that system users and support personnel receive the requisite information assurance training (such as instruction in the rules of behavior).

Based on guidance from the accrediting official, the information system owner informs appropriate organizational officials of the need to conduct the information assurance accreditation, ensures that the necessary resources are available for the effort, and provides the required information system access, information, and documentation to the information assurance control assessor. The information system owner receives the information assurance assessment results from the security control assessor. After taking appropriate steps to reduce or eliminate vulnerabilities, the information system owner assembles the accreditation package and submits the package to the accrediting official for adjudication.

Common Control Provider

The common control provider (CCP) is an individual, group, or organization responsible for the development, implementation, assessment, and monitoring of common controls (that is, information assurance controls inherited by information systems).

Common control providers are responsible for the following:

- Documenting the organization-identified common controls in a system security plan (or equivalent document prescribed by the organization)
- Ensuring that required assessments of common controls are carried out by qualified assessors with an appropriate level of independence defined by the organization

- Documenting assessment findings in an information assurance assessment report and producing a plan of action and milestones for controls having weaknesses or deficiencies

System security plans, information assurance assessment reports, and plans of action and milestones for common controls (or a summary of such information) are made available to information system owners inheriting controls from the common control provider. The control information is released to the information system owners after the information is reviewed and approved by the senior official or executive with oversight responsibility for those controls.

Users

Users play a significant role and a specific responsibility for implementing information assurance. Again, based on the experiences gathered by NIST, the two types of users and their relevant responsibilities are described in Table 9-3.

Information Owner/Steward

The information owner/steward is an organizational official with statutory, management, or operational authority for specified information and the responsibility for establishing the policies and procedures governing its generation, collection, processing, dissemination, and disposal.

In information-sharing environments, the information owner/steward is responsible for establishing the rules for appropriate use and protection of the subject information (that is, the rules of behavior) and retains that responsibility even when the information is shared with or provided to other organizations. The owner/steward of the information processed, stored, or transmitted by an information system may or may not be the same as the system owner. A single information system may contain information from multiple information owners/stewards. Information owners/stewards provide input to information system owners regarding the information assurance requirements and information assurance controls for the systems where the information is processed, stored, or transmitted.

Types of User	Security Responsibilities
Users of information	People, organizations, or other entities that are "consumers" of the services of the information system. Sometimes they directly interact with the information system (for example, to print a report from the system). Otherwise, they may read only information system–generated reports or be briefed on such items. Users of information normally know what their needs are regarding the confidentiality, integrity, or availability of the information.
Users of systems	Individuals who directly use an information system and whose duties are to follow information assurance procedures, attend required information assurance training courses or programs, and report any security problems.

Table 9-3 Responsibilities of Users

Organizational Maturity

Organizational maturity is important in determining an effective information assurance program. Organizational maturity is a reflection of how well an organization manages internal processes, changes, and responses to unexpected events. Several organizational maturity models exist depending on industry. Some of the more common are as follows:

- Information Technology Infrastructure Library (ITIL)
- Capability Maturity Model (CMM)
- Organizational Change Maturity Model (OCMM)

Information Technology Infrastructure Library

Information Technology Infrastructure Library (ITIL) is a service delivery specific model. ITIL was initially developed by the United Kingdom's Central Computer and Telecommunications Agency in the 1980s. It was designed to bring order and control around a growing reliance on information technology in government business. Today, ITIL consists of several volumes covering the following areas of service delivery:

- Service strategy
- Service design
- Service transition
- Service operation
- Continual service improvement

ITIL addresses information assurance through the reference of the ISO 27000 series. ITIL requires information assurance through organizational governance and alignment with organizational goals. Information assurance is included in the Service Design and the Service Operation sections of the ITIL framework. Information assurance should also be part of continual service improvement because information assurance controls can enhance service delivery, transition, and operation. As organizations progress from low levels of maturity, incidents and unplanned events become less, and the ability of the organization to react and learn from unplanned events becomes greater.

Capability Maturity Model

CMM precedes another maturity model called the Capability Maturity Model Integration (CMMI). While CMM looks at organizational maturity, CMMI focuses on software development processes. CMM reviews the processes, practices, and behaviors of an organization and assigns one of the following levels of maturity:

- **Initial**   Most if not all processes are not documented, and there is little if any performance measures and planning. Organizations at this level are often called chaotic or unstable and tend to be reactive in not only general operations but also information assurance.

- **Repeatable**   Organizations at this level of maturity have developed repeatable processes and practices that yield consistent results. Information assurance processes may be some of the processes that are repeatable.

- **Defined**   Processes are documented and defined throughout the organization. Standard processes have been identified and documented and are operating with limited improvement. In times of duress, these procedures are likely to be circumvented.

- **Managed**   The processes of an organization are defined, documented, and measured. Measuring allows the organization to determine whether a process is suitable for a project it may not be currently used in.

- **Optimizing**   Processes are defined, documented, measured, and constantly evaluated for improvements through people, technology, or complementary processes. This stage often uses statistical analysis as part of the process improvement.

CMM does not explicitly mention information assurance or its subdisciplines; however, organizations can use the model to measure the maturity of information assurance programs. Information assurance programs rely on people, processes, and technology. The processes can be subject to a CMM review and progression through maturity.

Organizational Change Maturity Model

The Organizational Change Maturity Model (OCMM) is another derivative of the CMM model. The OCMM focuses on change management throughout an organization. As noted in Chapters 14 and 15, managing change with an integrated information assurance program is crucial for managing risk. One of the few constants an organization has is change. Change can represent opportunities and competitive advantage if managed correctly. It can also represent catastrophic failure and information assurance problems. A vast majority of information assurance–related vulnerabilities result from poorly planned and executed change management efforts. New servers deployed without hardened configurations or entering into cloud agreements without involvement of the information assurance program are examples of changes leading to increased risk.

Outsourcing and Cloud Computing

The previous section discusses some of the areas of concern for the internal management of information assurance.

Outsourcing information assurance management is gradually becoming the norm. This trend is driven by several factors including economic, the rapid increase in the number of information security incidents, and the complexity of information assurance issues. It is important for organizations to understand issues related to outsourcing before actually deciding to engage in such an arrangement. The following are among some of the challenges faced:

- **Loss of control**   An outsourcer would prefer greater control since it makes it harder for organizations to terminate services provided. As a result, an organization may become too reliant on service providers. Of course, without their aid, the organization may suffer from serious failures that affect daily operations.

- **Sensitive information**   The company wants to protect sensitive information from inappropriate misuse and disclosure.

- **Quality of service**   Outsourcers generally work based on the stipulated scope of work and service level agreement. Unlike internal employees, outsourcers would not be responsible for additional or ad hoc job requests unless paid.

- **Viability of service providers to supply the agreed services**   Mismanagement, inadequate funding, merging, and acquisitions are possible factors that could lead to a discontinuation of services.

Outsourcing information assurance is not appropriate for every organization. Some organizations will be better off implementing, managing, and monitoring information assurance management internally. It is important that an organization establish expectations before approaching an information assurance outsourcing arrangement. Basing outsourcing decisions on an analysis of the information assurance risks involved, the required resources and capabilities, current operational capabilities and costs, and the overall business objectives is essential. Remember, the organization outsourced to will never understand the mission or business like an employee will.

An organization deciding to outsource their information assurance should consider the following:

- **Maintain security control**   Organizations should be aware that once an outsourcing service is used, including cloud services, the service provider's employees might have direct access to and control of their information assets. Thus, a service contract and a service level agreement (SLA) should be established that clearly spell out how information assurance is to be managed (ISO/IEC 17799 provides a list of the items to be considered in producing a contract and SLA). These include issues such as what information may be accessed and performing background checks of the provider's employees. In addition, perform regular audits so that the provider is always adhering to the terms of the agreement.

- **Perform due diligence**   Before awarding an outsourcing contract, organizations should have processes in place to perform due diligence checks, such as checking the facts and credentials of the service provider. Do this by checking with current or past clients of the vendors as well as an organization such as Dunn and Bradstreet. In cases where the provider is outside of an organization's home country, organizations should consider hiring legal services in the outsourcing country to check on the status of the provider and examine provisions in the contract to see whether they will be legally enforceable in the provider's jurisdiction.

- **Audit processes and facilities prior to signing an agreement and regularly thereafter**   Trust is undoubtedly important when choosing a service provider. Conduct independent audits on the quality of the provider's information assurance management processes at least twice a year and certainly before agreeing to do business with them. Note that it is easier to establish audits before signing a contract than afterward. Tour the buildings where the work is performed to ensure that they are physically secure, and review existing evidence of security compliance or breaches to ensure risk is acceptable to your organization.

Part II

Further Reading

- *An Introduction to Computer Security: The NIST Handbook (Special Publication 800-12).* NIST, 1996.

- Information Government Toolkit. *Information Security Assurance – Social Care Guidance.* National Health Service (NHS). United Kingdom, June 16, 2007. https://www.igt .connectingforhealth.nhs.uk/guidance/IS_Sc_310_V5%2007-04-27.doc.

- *Information Technology – Security Techniques – Code of Practice for Information Security Management (ISO/IEC 17799)*, ISO/IecIEC.

- Ross, R., et al. *Recommended Security Controls for Federal Information Systems (Special Publication 800-53).* NIST, 2005.

- Schou, Corey D., and D.P. Shoemaker. *Information Assurance for the Enterprise: A Roadmap to Information Security.* McGraw-Hill Education, 2007.

- Tipton, Harold F., and S. Hernandez, ed. *Official (ISC) [2] Guide to the CISSP CBK 3rd edition.* ((ISC)[2]) Press, 2012.

- Wood, Charles C. *Information Security Roles & Responsibilities Made Easy.* PentaSafe Security Technologies, 2002.

Critical Thinking Exercises

1. An organization is thinking about moving its core infrastructure into the cloud. It makes extremely good financial sense. What actions must a prudent executive or senior leader take to ensure the financial windfall isn't caused by security shortcomings?

2. An organization is thinking of collaborating with another to perform some data processing. Your organization has a top-down centralized approach to information assurance while it seems the organization you want to collaborate with has a bottom-up decentralized approach to security. Should you be concerned about this difference in cultures?

CHAPTER 10

Asset Management

The fundamental objective of an information assurance management program is to protect the confidentiality, integrity, and availability of an organization's assets throughout the life cycle in accordance with the MSR model. A best-practice security risk assessment exercise begins with an identification of the assets, followed by an evaluation of the asset sensitivity and criticality. This ensures that asset protection is proportional to the asset value.

In Chapter 2, when discussing the IAMS, we noted that each information asset has its life cycle. At any stage of the life cycle, the asset is constantly at risk. In fact, asset management is among the early activities in the IAMS.

This chapter explores the broad area of information assets. It first explains the types of assets and discusses the various responsibilities associated with them. The rest of the chapter focuses on information classification, handling, and labeling, which are core activities in asset management.

Types of Assets

Assets are tangible or intangible. Tangible assets range from data files to physical assets, such as computer peripherals, while intangible assets include the image and reputation of the organization, general utilities, and skill sets of a workforce. As mentioned in the ISO/IEC 27000 family of standards, assets can be categorized as shown in Table 10-1.

Tangible asset values can be quantified for the organization. For example, a server has a certain monetary replacement cost. This cost is part of its value. Next, the server is critical for providing e-commerce billing services to an organization's web site. If it is down, the organization loses money for every missed sale. This is also a quantifiable value and can be added to the server's total value. Finally, the configuration of the server may be proprietary or an industry trade secret. While the research used to develop the server configuration has a cost, if the proprietary configuration were stolen, the impact to the company because of

Types	Examples
Data/information	Databases, personnel records, proposals, contracts, manuals, statistics, and any data/information in either soft or hard copy
Hardware	Computer/network equipment, tape, removable media
Intangible	Reputation, image, influence, intellectual property
People	Staff with expertise, skill, and knowledge on a subject
Service	Electricity, telecommunication service, lighting
Software	Application software, system software, system utility, development tool

Table 10-1 Types of Assets

increased competition could be immeasurable or extremely hard to quantify and therefore intangible.

Responsibilities for Assets

The objective of assigning responsibilities for assets is to assure adequate levels of protection. The responsibility of controlling an asset should be assigned to an identified individual or entity within an organization. This assignment is both risk management and security responsibilities. Asset responsibility provides accountability for the protection of the assets under the individual's control. Protection includes appropriate information assurance and access control failures resulting in unauthorized access to and use of the assets.

Three controls are required to assign responsibility: inventory of assets, ownership of assets, and acceptable use of assets (see ISO/IEC 27002). Collectively or individually, implementation of these controls allows an organization to establish a suitable asset protection process.

Inventory of Assets

The organization establishes a baseline by identifying and recording important information about assets such as their location, license information, and security classification or categorization. Placing data into categories is the core of the asset management process, which ensures that movement of assets and changes to its information are documented and updated regularly. Following this process ensures that important information about the asset is available readily.

Ownership of Assets

It is important to establish that each asset has an assigned owner. An owner can be an individual or a functional role (for example, the head of finance). Designation as an "owner" means that the individual or party is responsible for the security of the asset and assigns ultimate accountability. The owner ensures that assets are classified properly and asset use authorizations are reviewed periodically. The owner can delegate the implementation of information assurance to someone else; however, the overall accountability remains with the owner.

Acceptable Use of Assets

To protect organizational assets, develop and document policy and guidelines for acceptable asset use. Ensure that the policy is endorsed by senior management. The policy elaborates on the rules and responsibilities of asset usage by internal and external parties in accordance with the security classification of the asset. Groups of assets with similar categorizations may be covered by a similar policy. For example, several different assets categorized as sensitive and mission critical may be covered by the same policies and associated procedures. Additionally, disclosure and release of information should be defined in policies and procedures. The use of nondisclosure agreements and information disclosure processes should be cited in asset use policies. The data owner recommends the parameters of acceptable use for their assets based on the services from the MSR model.

Information Classification and Handling

The rationale behind information classification (categorization) is to organize information according to its sensitivity and criticality of its loss, disclosure, modification, and unavailability. Once information is classified based on its value or impact to the organization, decide on the controls to be implemented to protect it. In addition, information classification is to indicate the level of confidentiality, integrity, and availability required for information protection. Protecting information assets is resource intensive; ensure the investment made is cost-beneficial to the organization. Conducting an information classification exercise ensures that data is protected cost-effectively. To achieve these objectives, two controls should be in place, namely, classification guidelines and information labeling and handling.

Classification Guidelines

Establishing an information classification system in an organization based on information needs and the impact in case of an information security breach or compromise is essential.

When developing and maintaining information, consider security classification and information assurance requirements from the organization perspective. Above all, identify information owners and involve them in providing input about the value or impact of the information. Business, industry, and legal requirements are other important decision criteria that should be supported by professional legal advice. Consider the organizational culture to allow effective implementation of the information classification policies and guidelines.

The originator of the information is responsible for classifying (categorizing) the information and protecting it according to the organization's policy and procedures. There are also cases where the information assurance unit is tasked to classify the information. Information should be made available only to those authorized individuals.

Organizations must perform the classification process on a regular basis to take into account the life cycle of the information and its application. The life cycle shown in Figure 10-1 starts from the creation of information, implementation of the access control, method of processing, and eventually information disposal. The access control associated with the classification should comply with the access control policy of the organization.

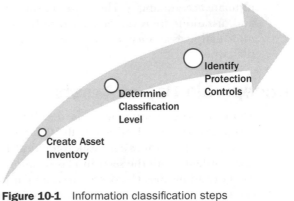

Figure 10-1 Information classification steps

Information Labeling and Handling

The sharing of information among organizations and individuals has become critical for the success of today's businesses. Therefore, a proper and structured labeling scheme and handling mechanism is essential to secure and preserve an organization's information assets. Information may be handled between different organizations, different components within an organization, or even different security levels within a system.

An organization should develop detailed information handling procedures derived from the organization's policy on classification. For confidentiality, most organizations have adopted four levels of information classification: secret, confidential, restricted, and public. Other classifications are used for integrity and availability. The definitions of the classification and methods of processing, transmission, storage, accessibility, and disposal have to be documented by the organization. The procedure should cover physical assets and information kept or transferred in electronic formats such as e-mails and paper documents. Properly labeled assets encourage better handling and management by employees and partners.

In the U.S. government, the importance of information assurance in government operations is described at length in the Federal Information Security Management Act (FISMA). According to the act, measures should be taken to ensure the confidentiality, integrity, and availability of information. These measures are necessary to raise the confidence of the public and to promote usage of IT in industries such as commerce, healthcare, education, and public sector. The following example shows how information classification (categorization) is performed for civilian systems in the U.S. government.

Information Classification (Categorization) Example

It is useful to categorize assets so management can focus on protecting the most important ones. This process of categorization is often called *classification*. One best-practice example comes from the United States, where civilian agencies are required to adhere to the Federal Information Security Management Act. This law directs the U.S. National Institutes of Standards and Technology (NIST) to develop standards and guidelines for U.S. civilian agencies to follow. These standards cover the life cycle of information and the systems that are processing, storing, and transmitting information on behalf of the U.S. government. NIST has standards and guidelines specifically developed for information categorization and control selection. It is important to note that NIST uses the term *categorization* in lieu of *classification*. In the United States, *classification* is usually reserved for systems related to national security. While the terminology differs, the process is the same.

The NIST standards and guidelines are freely available online (http://csrc.nist.gov/publications/PubsFIPS.html). These standards and guidelines may be adopted in whole or partially by any organization at no cost, but they are mandatory for U.S. civilian agencies. The following example will use a sample of fictional information and explain how the categorization system operates.

Assume an information system is being designed for basic human resources (HR) functionality. This system will perform the following HR functions:

- Offboarding (removing employees from system)
- Onboarding (enrolling new employees into system)
- Payroll
- Personnel actions (including discipline)
- Suitability decision retention
- Time and attendance

According to FISMA, U.S. agencies must use Federal Information Processing Standard (FIPS) 199 to determine the categorization of the information. You can find the standard at http://csrc.nist.gov/publications/fips/fips199/FIPS-PUB-199-final.pdf.

In addition, agencies must use NIST Special Publication (SP) 800-60 to categorize their information. SP 800-60 contains numerous types of information and provides provisional impact (value) levels for each type. You can find SP 800-60 at http://csrc.nist.gov/publications/nistpubs/800-60-rev1/SP800-60_Vol1-Rev1.pdf.

Using SP 800-60 Vol. 2: (http://csrc.nist.gov/publications/nistpubs/800-60-rev1/SP800-60_Vol2-Rev1.pdf), the information owner or the information assurance support team determines the following information types are being processed, stored, and transmitted by the information system:

- Compensation management information
- Employee performance management information
- Financial reporting and information
- Organization and position information management
- Separation management information
- Staff acquisition information

When using NIST SP 800-60 and FIPS-199, the information assurance team must understand that the "impact" has been calibrated to the U.S. government. Therefore, a "high" impact means a loss of confidentiality, integrity, or availability would have catastrophic impact to the U.S. government. This means lives are at risk or the government is at risk of failure.

Organizations must understand the impact in terms of their own mission and adjust accordingly. The process is diagramed in Figure 10-2.

NIST SP 800-60 provides provisional impact ratings for confidentiality, integrity, and availability. The impact ratings are provisional because they can be modified depending on special factors. Per NIST's example, "Accounting information may have a provisional impact rating of 'moderate'; however, if the accounting information contains proprietary information about an organization's research and development, it may be adjusted to 'high.'" Table 10-2 explains the impact levels for each security objective based on U.S. law for U.S. civilian agencies.

Once types and impact values have been determined, using the provisional impact ratings for confidentiality, integrity, and availability, the information owner or the information assurance team builds an impact table for the information, as shown in Table 10-3.

The categorization indicates most of the information is of "low" impact to the U.S. government should there be a failure to ensure confidentiality, integrity, or availability. However, note there is a "moderate" impact if the integrity of financial reporting cannot be

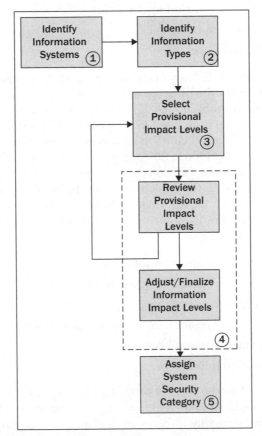

Figure 10-2 NIST SP 800-60 categorization process

Security Objective	Potential Impact		
	Low	**Moderate**	**High**
Confidentiality Preserving authorized restrictions on information access and disclosure, including means for protecting personal privacy and proprietary information (44 U.S.C., Sec. 3542)	The unauthorized disclosure of information could be expected to have a *limited* adverse effect on organizational operations, organizational assets, or individuals.	The unauthorized disclosure of information could be expected to have a *serious* adverse effect on organizational operations, organizational assets, or individuals.	The unauthorized disclosure of information could be expected to have a *severe* or *catastrophic* adverse effect on organizational operations, organizational assets, or individuals.
Integrity Guarding against improper information modification or destruction, and includes ensuring information nonrepudiation and authenticity (44 U.S.C., Sec. 3542)	The unauthorized modification or destruction of information could be expected to have a *limited* adverse effect on organizational operations, organizational assets, or individuals.	The unauthorized modification or destruction of information could be expected to have a *serious* adverse effect on organizational operations, organizational assets, or individuals.	The unauthorized modification or destruction of information could be expected to have a *severe* or *catastrophic* adverse effect on organizational operations, organizational assets, or individuals.
Availability Ensuring timely and reliable access to and use of information (44 U.S.C., Sec. 3542)	The disruption of access to or use of information or an information system could be expected to have a *limited* adverse effect on organizational operations, organizational assets, or individuals.	The disruption of access to or use of information or an information system could be expected to have a *serious* adverse effect on organizational operations, organizational assets, or individuals.	The disruption of access to or use of information or an information system could be expected to have a *severe* or *catastrophic* adverse effect on organizational operations, organizational assets, or individuals.

Table 10-2   Categorization of Information

ensured. Therefore, the overall impact of a system which processes, stores, and transmits this information is "moderate."

This categorization then drives the baseline control selection. This baseline establishes the minimum information assurance control requirements for the information system. Note that the majority of the information has a "low" impact, yet the entire system is being

Information	Confidentiality	Integrity	Availability
Staff acquisition information	Low	Low	Low
Organization and position management information	Low	Low	Low
Compensation management information	Low	Low	Low
Employee performance management information	Low	Low	Low
Financial reporting and information	Low	Moderate	Low
Separation management information	Low	Low	Low
High Water Mark	Low	*Moderate*	Low

Table 10-3 Sample Categorization

designed for moderate impact information. In these cases, the organization may want to determine whether the financial reporting information may be better processed, stored, and transmitted in another system with similar security requirements such as an organization's accounting system. Good enterprise architecture can greatly decrease the cost of information assurance control implementation. Baseline information assurance controls for U.S. civilian agencies and organizations adopting NIST standards are determined using FIPS-200 (http://csrc.nist.gov/publications/fips/fips200/FIPS-200-final-march.pdf) and NIST SP 800-53 (http://csrc.nist.gov/publications/nistpubs/800-53-Rev3/sp800-53-rev3-final_updated-errata_05-01-2010.pdf).

Further Reading

- Federal Information Security Management Act of 2002 (Public Law 107-347, Title III). December 2002.

- International Organization Standardization and the International Electrotechnical Commission. *Information Technology – Security Techniques – Information Security Management Systems –Requirements (ISO/IEC 27001).* International Organization Standardization and the International Electrotechnical Commission, 2005.

- National Institute of Standards and Technology. *Special Publication 800-60, Guide for Mapping Types of Information and Information Systems to Security Categories.* June 2004.

- National Institute of Standards and Technology. *Special Publication 800-53, Revision 4, Recommended Security Controls for Federal Information Systems and Organizations.* DOC, April 2013.

- *NIST FIPS 199, Standards for Security Categorization of Federal Information and Information Systems.* DOC, February 2004.

- *NIST FIPS 200, Minimum Security Requirements for Federal Information and Information Systems.* DOC, March 2006.

- Schou, Corey D., and D.P. Shoemaker. *Information Assurance for the Enterprise: A Roadmap to Information Security.* McGraw-Hill Education, 2007.

- Tipton, Harold F., and S. Hernandez, ed. *Official (ISC)² Guide to the CISSP CBK 3rd edition.* ((ISC)²) Press, 2012.

Critical Thinking Exercises

1. Within your organization, do you use marking methods to determine sensitive information or information critical to business? If so, what automated means do you have to ensure sensitive information is not leaked?

2. Consider the sensitive information in your organization and its life cycle. Where does the data reside at rest? On hard drives? In the cloud? Where does the data reside in transit? Over the mobile phone network? Over the open Internet? Over your network? What protections do you know are in place for each of the mediums you identified to protect sensitive information?

11 Information Assurance Risk Management

Whether government or private, organizations exist to provide value and benefits to their stakeholders. At the same time, they face uncertainty, which can be either a risk or an opportunity. The challenge for management is to decide how much risk it can accept to increase stakeholders' value. Failure to manage risk reduces the benefits to the stakeholders and potentially exposes them to loss and negative effects. To succeed, management should design a strategy that overcomes risk while maximizing opportunities that come with it.

Information assurance risk management is essential for an effective information assurance management program. It is integral to good management practice. As discussed in Chapter 12, risk assessment is one of the activities conducted during the planning stage of establishing the IAMS. It established the foundation for selecting and justifying the implementation of security controls. Initiating new ventures, implementing new services or systems, and changing processes or structure should be preceded by a security risk assessment exercise. This chapter provides an overview of the risk management concept and discusses its key elements.

Benefits of Risk Management

Organizations operate in a dynamic environment. A well-planned and executed risk management plan reduces organizational risk from an ever-changing environment. To manage risk, you must identify it.

Risks are the combination of vulnerabilities that may be exploited by threats together with the potential impact on the asset. In information assurance, risks exist when the result of the previous relationship is positive. Risk management refers to the application of a method that consists of policies, procedures, and practices used to identify these risk events. The objective is to identify, analyze, treat, evaluate, and continue to improve the way the organization manages its risk profile. In short, risk management is a means to identify, manage, and control risk.

Organizations should understand that risk identification and management is a proactive rather than a reactive process. Ignorance or mismanagement of risk results in the loss of asset values, stakeholders' wealth and reputation, and other undesirable consequences. Risk management is not about avoiding risks altogether. It is recognizing the consequences of risks in a deliberate and systematic way, avoiding unnecessary risks and carefully managing the risks taken by accepting residual risk.

Good risk management yields a wide spectrum of benefits. Having proactive risk management evokes a sense of preparedness against unwelcome surprises or incidents. Preparedness boosts confidence and encourages positive behavior within the organizational culture. A well-done risk assessment will identify the real threats and vulnerabilities to organizational assets. If a strategy is based on this assessment, it will be better and usually more reliable. Consequently, limited resources can be focused more effectively to manage prioritized risks.

Risk Management Process

Approaches to risk management have been suggested in standards, guidelines, and reports. You should choose an approach or method that is appropriate to your organization's business environment.

Figure 11-1 shows a model that presents the risk management process as a continuous cycle.

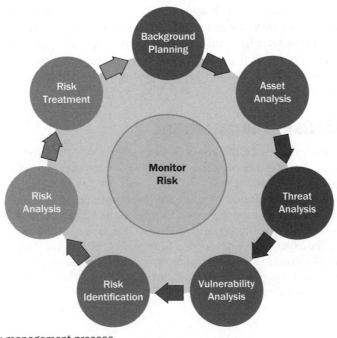

Figure 11-1 Risk management process

The following section shows the main elements of the risk management process, including background planning, asset analysis, threat analysis, vulnerability analysis, risk identification, risk analysis, risk treatment, and risk monitoring.

Background Planning

Establish the strategic and risk management context at the beginning of the process planning process. The following elements should be taken into consideration during the planning phase:

- Establish the aim, scope, and boundary. It is incumbent on management to establish a clear understanding of the aim, goal, and outcomes before the risk management process begins. In this phase, required resources are specified based on the objectives, scope, and boundary of the risk assessment exercise. Defining the scope is an important exercise and can be performed by function or boundary. For example, the assessment may examine all accounting systems that support Sarbanes Oxley [SARBOX] compliance. Or, the assessment may be boundary based such as systems in the marketing and production departments. The scoping method is fundamental in determining the level of the analysis required.

- Establish the risk evaluation criteria. As a good practice, these criteria form the basis for determining whether a risk is acceptable. Acceptability is based on operational, technical, financial, legal, social, humanitarian, and other related criteria. Additional factors will be based on the organization's internal policy, goals, objectives, and the interests of stakeholders. In this case, a standard threat profile (STP) may be used. An STP contains values for different types of typical threats. These threats may be determined by consulting with experts and by observing actual events and incidents. The values may not be precise, but estimates are always helpful. General threat information is widely available through a variety of sources. For example, the Korea Internet & Security Agency (KISAs) has the following mission:

  - Reinforce public information security through the use of security policies and technologies. KISA provides technical experts to assist in vulnerability analysis and incident damage restorations for SCADA systems such as transportation, water purification, energy, healthcare, and railroad.

  - Operate the Privacy Incident Response System (PIRST), which works to detect personal information security breaches on domestic and international web sites.

  - Operate an information security management system dedicated to protecting the intellectual property of businesses and promoting user awareness of information security.

- Another example is in the United States where some businesses participate in the U.S. InfraGuard Program. The program's goals are to do the following:

  - Increase the level of information and reporting between InfraGuard members and the FBI on matters related to counterterrorism, cybercrime, and other major crime programs.

- Increase interaction and information sharing among InfraGuard members and the FBI regarding threats to the critical infrastructures, vulnerabilities, and interdependencies.

- Provide members with value-added threat advisories, alerts, and warnings.

- Promote effective liaison with local, state, and federal agencies, to include the Department of Homeland Security.

- Provide members with a forum for education and training on counterterrorism, counterintelligence cybercrime, and other matters relevant to informed reporting of potential crimes and attacks on the nation and U.S. interests.

- Establish risk management policy. A policy should be established to convey the management's expectation on the risk management program and define roles and responsibilities for successful implementation. Refer to Chapter 12 for details.

Asset Analysis

The process of asset analysis is often conducted in parallel or as part of asset valuation. Organizations identify the significant assets within the scope of assessment and analyze their values in terms of confidentiality, integrity, and availability. These assets will be analyzed based on their types, such as software, hardware, people, service, and platforms.

Determine the owner of each asset and its respective value and impact to the organization. Usually, but not always, the asset owner is the best person to determine the value of assets. Determine the value of the asset in terms of the following:

- Confidentiality (consider the loss or harm that would result from unauthorized disclosure of the asset or of the information handled or protected by the asset).

- Integrity (consider the loss or harm that would result from unauthorized modification of the asset).

- Availability (consider the loss or harm that would result from partial or total unavailability of the asset). An asset value should reflect its replacement cost, its intrinsic value, and the impact of any form of compromise to the asset; this principle should be instilled into every employee.

With more information being processed, stored, and transmitted through the cloud, sometimes the asset owner (in this case, the cloud provider) has little to no idea what information or assets reside in the cloud. In these cases, the business line owner or mission owner must define the value of the information. System owners can enhance the understanding of assets, but the asset's value in terms of the business or mission of the organization must always come first.

Threat Analysis

The goal of this analysis is to identify and examine threats to each asset, respectively. Threats are classified as natural or man-made. Various threat catalogs are available that can be used to examine and estimate associated risks. In practice, you initiate the threat analysis by referring to an established list, such as the one in Appendix B. Although such a list may not be appropriate in all situations, the major and common threats have been included.

The information assurance team then identifies emerging threats (which may not be in the list) or threats that are in the local environment. Other good sources of information about more recent threats are users and employees, vendors, service providers, and business partners as well as online threat advisories.

Threat analysis is the most difficult aspect of risk analysis. Threat information is not limited to merely actors who may want to steal an organization's information but also actors who may want to damage an organization or have a personal vendetta against an organization's employees or partners. Two important categories of threats must be understood: human and natural.

Human threats should be viewed through three dimensions: motives, means, and opportunities. Intentional human actions always have these characteristics:

- **Motive**   Why is a person motivated to perform an act? Common motivations are control, curiosity, duress, fame, monetary gain, nationalism, power, and revenge.

- **Means**   This term describes the ability to actually execute the motivation. A person may deeply desire to "hack" into a banking system, but unless they have an extensive background in technology, system cracking, and cryptography, it is unlikely they will be successful. Some may try to find individuals who have the means to perform the action on their behalf.

- **Opportunities**   These represent the actual moment in time when a motivated actor with means could execute an action. Opportunities may be the physical presence of an individual in a vulnerable location or may be a newly discovered firewall vulnerability.

Accidental actions are another type of human threat. Accidental actions are caused by carelessness, errors, and sometimes inadvertent omissions. While a motivation may not be present, the impact of unintentional actions can have drastic impacts on organizations. Consider the person who unwittingly disposes of a hard drive with sensitive financial information on it because they did not know what was on the drive originally. The drive could then be obtained by a competitor and used to avoid investing years of research and millions of dollars. Well-thought-out policies, procedures, guidelines, training, and technical controls are part of mature organizational processes. Mature processes increase the ability of the organization to avoid or minimize unintentional acts.

Describe human threats in terms of their relationship to the organization. Internal or "insider" threats are individuals within an organization. They are often on the payroll or doing work on behalf of the organization. Insiders can be extremely hard to find and even harder to manage because often they require legitimate access to organizational resources and assets. As noted prior, some insider threats cause unintentional damage to an organization by performing acts through negligence or "trying to do the right thing." Unintentional insider threats are best handled using a combination of training, awareness, rules of behavior, operational controls (such as updated procedures), and technical controls. This combination should help honest insiders do their job without introducing additional risk to the organization.

Intentional human insider threats are another matter entirely. These individuals are intent on causing damage to the organization through either theft or sabotage. Strong technical monitoring controls combined with separation of duties and rotation of duties greatly increase the challenge for a malicious insider threat. Organizations must still focus on holistic information assurance programs because insider threats will often leverage "well-meaning" insiders to do their bidding.

External human threats can be foreign nation states, hackers, former employees, competitors, or industrial espionage spies working for a competitor. The only advantage an organization has against these threats is the ability to keep them out. Unlike internal actors, external human threats have no need for system or facility access. Therefore, training for all users should include external threats. External threats often engage internal actors at public events, conferences, and similar situations where they are less likely to come under suspicion. Additionally, outsiders may pose as repair personnel, janitorial services, or contractors to gain access to facilities and ultimately systems. Organizations must ensure all employees or those doing work on their behalf are familiar with an organization's information assurance program requirements. Employees should feel empowered to report individuals or situations that do not meet the information assurance program's requirements. Organizations should be prepared for a few false alarms. Organizations can weather numerous false alarms, but it may take only one successful outside threat to severely damage a mission!

Examples of natural threats are weather-related phenomenon (such as hurricanes, tornados, and flooding). Other less predictable natural events are volcanic eruptions, sink holes, earthquakes, and mudslides. While organizations may be unable to stop natural events, they can research the local environment and determine common issues such as the following:

- Earthquake frequency and severity
- Flood frequency
- Flood plain location
- Frequency and quantity of rainfall
- Frequency and severity of wind
- Nearby volcanos
- Seismic fault line location

Excellent threat analysis requires a well-rounded team or individual with an understanding of not only technology but the natural world and human psychology.

Vulnerability Analysis

Vulnerability analysis identifies vulnerabilities for which threat events exist. The goal is to identify applicable vulnerabilities (flaws or weaknesses) that can be exploited by the potential threat (identified earlier).

Organizations should refer to an established list of common vulnerabilities. You can find a simple example in Appendix C. A process to discover vulnerabilities should be used and updated continuously; if not, lists will never be completely accurate. A vulnerability management team should identify new vulnerabilities and constantly update the new vulnerability list. As with the threat identification, users and employees, vendors, service providers, and business partners as well as online vulnerability advisories are good sources of information for more recent vulnerabilities.

Technical vulnerabilities are often the easiest to identify since several products automate the technical vulnerability scanning process. Operational and managerial vulnerabilities are substantially more difficult to identify and are often identified only through independent assessment teams and audits with proper scoping. Organizations should ensure that vulnerability analysis programs include operational, technical, and managerial vulnerability identification.

Risk Identification

Risks should be identified as early as possible. While "perceived" risks may appear to be initially true, this does not mean the identified findings will be accurate or valid subsequent to further analysis or assessment. There is no single method that will guarantee complete risk identification, especially if the approach or mechanism has flaws or is limited in scope.

A best practice for risk identification is by using a structured brainstorming session that draws on the experience of the project team. If the team lacks knowledge or experience in risk management, then bring in outside help.

Risk Analysis

During risk analysis, the sources of the risks are revisited, followed by an estimate of the likelihood of occurrence. As stated earlier, an organization should determine asset values, the probability of the threats being able to exploit the vulnerabilities, and the impacts. This allows the organization to calculate the best estimate for its exposure to risks. Mathematical techniques can also be employed to calculate the risk. A simple rule of thumb is that risk is the product of the impact and likelihood of occurrence.

Risk is estimated by considering the potential impact, as well as the likelihood of the threats being able to exploit the vulnerabilities when using current control measures. The goal of this is to derive an overall likelihood rating, which gives an estimate of the vulnerability being exploited within the associated threat environment. In contrast, consequences determine adverse impacts resulting from a successful threat exercise of vulnerability.

The last step in risk analysis is to identify existing mechanisms that control the risk, followed by an assessment of the strengths and weaknesses of the system. Once the existing controls have been identified, you can identify the consequences and likelihood of the risk occurring. Values for likelihood can be determined based on historical data or statistical analysis. Figure 11-2 shows a more detailed explanation of risk as described by the U.S. National Institute of Standards and Technology in Special Publication 800-30, Revision 1: Guide for Conducting Risk Assessments.

A practical but subjective qualitative approach to this is to use simple quadrants called a *risk matrix*, as shown in Figure 11-3. An event with high impact and high likelihood of a happening is consequently high risk. Consequently, all activities that fall into this category should be reduced if not eliminated.

Risks in the medium or low cells may be accepted with minimal treatment. Nevertheless, even low accepted risks should still be monitored and periodically reviewed to ensure they remain acceptable.

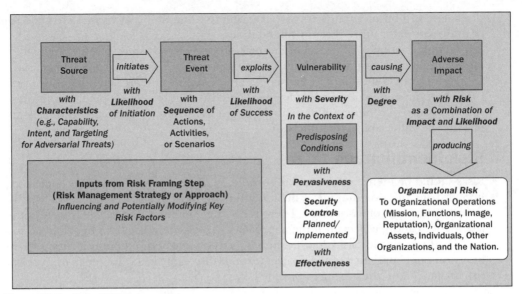

Figure 11-2 U.S. NIST risk analysis process

Risk Treatment

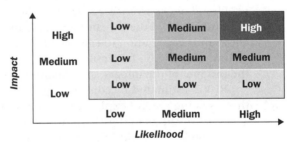

Figure 11-3 Risk matrix

Based on the gap analysis results and the risk assessment, appropriate and justified options or controls for treating risks will be identified, selected, and documented in a risk treatment plan. The options and controls selected for risk reduction to an acceptable level are decided by the organization's management. Owners of the treatment plan will be responsible for the implementation of the plan.

The following are some of the options for the treatment of risks based on the Standard Associations of Australia (www.dtic.mil/dtic/tr/fulltext/u2/a434592.pdf):

- **Avoid risk**   Do not proceed with the activity likely to generate risk.
- **Reduce likelihood of occurrence**   Implement audit and compliance programs, formal reviews, inspection and process controls, and preventive maintenance.
- **Reduce the consequences**   Reduce the consequences by contingency planning, business continuity planning, or reducing the interdependence of activities.
- **Transfer risk**   Use insurance, partnerships, and joint ventures.
- **Accept risk**   Some risks cannot be eliminated or reduced. The management needs to decide what level of risk can be accepted as residual risk.

When treating risk, senior leaders must be wary of ignoring risk. Ignoring risk is simply choosing to reject the reality of risk and the potential impacts that may follow. An example of ignoring risk is the Chernobyl Blindness. Frost and Schou observed:

> *An even greater danger to the individual empowerment and organizational growth is the effect known as Chernobyl Blindness. Chernobyl Blindness is characterized by going through the motions of a process, but only accomplishing the motions, not reacting to anything new or different. It was originally used to describe the reactions of a senior Soviet technician at the Chernobyl nuclear facility during its meltdown and reactor explosion.*

> *When the instrumentation indicated a problem with the reactor, the technician walked over to a window that overlooked what was formerly the nuclear reactor area. Now there was a hole instead of a structure and black graphite covered the area. However, the technician looked, but saw nothing new; he was blind to the fact a nuclear accident had occurred because that was impossible. His self-imposed blinders prevented him from reacting to an actual event because it was not standard operating procedure. Too often, opportunities or threats are ignored in the business environment because that is out of the "acceptable operating conditions/procedures." This condition is sometimes referred to as paradigm paralysis.*

Senior leaders must exercise caution when understanding and accepting risk. They must also be willing to accept the fact that previously secure systems may now be vulnerable in a matter of milliseconds. The worst approach a senior manager can take is to ignore risk. This position accepts risk by default without fully understanding mitigation options or impacts to the organization.

Monitoring Risk

Monitoring risk ensures all controls are monitored at a frequency commensurate with their significance to the organization. Some policies may need to be reviewed only yearly or during a major change, while vulnerability scanning should occur every week or when a new vulnerability is released.

In addition to periodical risk assessment, risk reviews should be triggered whenever there are changes to the business environment and in the IT infrastructure. Such changes may challenge the integrity and validity of the risk priorities set previously. The controls should be evaluated based on effectiveness and whether they meet the risk reduction and acceptance targets. It is good practice to maintain and update the risk register so it is possible to check the organization's risk status at any given time.

Organizations are developing *risk dashboards*. Caution must be exercised when understanding what these dashboards contain and what they more importantly do not. Often, they show a network security vulnerability perspective and miss several other critical areas of the organization. Relying on only network vulnerabilities distracts from other critical business or mission areas. Organizations should determine whether the entire risk formula (impact and likelihood equals risk) is represented in the dashboard or simply a single variable such as vulnerabilities or threats.

Integration with Other Management Practices

Risk management can be linked to four other areas of management practice.

- **Budgeting** Risk management addresses the need to mitigate identified risks. The treatment plan or actions require time and resources; therefore, a link to the budgeting process is useful.

- **Business planning** The organization should develop business planning that is aligned to the organization's objectives. The organization may already have carried out SWOT (strength, weakness, opportunity, and threat) and PEST (political, economic, socio-cultural, and technological) exercises in other areas, and these could be expanded into a more detailed information assurance risk analysis.

- **Internal audit** Organizations should use information from information assurance risk management to contribute to the organization's internal audit and internal control reviews.

- **Periodic reporting** A periodic report is a tool that the management can use to monitor key risks. Controls should be ranked according to how critical they are to a system and the overall organization. The frequency of the reporting should be based on the impact of the control. Existing reporting lines can often be improved to cover a wider range of risks without a major overhaul.

Further Reading

- Baker, Dixie B. *Assessing Controlled Access Protection.* The National Computer Security Center, Dec. 1, 2006. www.fas.org/irp/nsa/rainbow/tg028.htm.

- Frost, James, and Schou, C.D. "Looking Inward for Competitive Strength in the International Arena." Presented at the Mountain Plains Management Association Meetings. October 1993.

- Gross, I., and P. Greaves. *Risk Management: A Guide to Good Practice for Higher Education Institutions.* HEFCE, 2001. www.hefce.ac.uk/pubs/hefce/2001/01_28/01_28.pdf.

- Korea Internet Security Agency (KISA). www.kisa.or.kr/eng/main.jsp.

- National Institute of Standards and Technology. *Special Publication 800-12, An Introduction to Computer Security: The NIST Handbook. 1996.*

- National Institute of Standards and Technology. *Special Publication 800-18, Revision 1, Guide for Developing Security Plans for Federal Information Systems.* February 2006.

- National Institute of Standards and Technology. *Special Publication 800-30, Revision 1, Guide for Conducting Risk Assessments.* September 2012.

- National Institute of Standards and Technology. *Special Publication 800-37, Revision 1, Guide for Applying the Risk Management Framework to Federal Information Systems: A Security Life Cycle Approach.* February 2010.

- National Institute of Standards and Technology. *Special Publication 800-53, Revision 3, Recommended Security Controls for Federal Information Systems and Organizations.* August 2009.

- National Institute of Standards and Technology. *Special Publication 800-53A, Revision 1, Guide for Assessing the Security Controls in Federal Information Systems and Organizations: Building Effective Security Assessment Plans.* June 2010.

- National Institute of Standards and Technology. *Special Publication 800-137, Initial Public Draft, Information Security Continuous Monitoring for Federal Information Systems and Organizations.* December 2010.

- National Institute of Standards and Technology. *Special Publication 800-53, Revision 4, Recommended Security Controls for Federal Information Systems and Organizations.* DOC, April 2013.

- Nichols, R., et al. *Defending Your Digital Assets Against Hackers, Crackers, Spies, and Thieves.* McGraw-Hill, 2000.

- Risk Management AS/NZS 4360:1999, 1999. Standards Association of Australia, Australia. www.google.com/search?sourceid=navclient&ie=UTF-8&rlz=1T4GGIH_enUS242US242&q=AS%2fNZS+4360%3a1999.

- Schou, Corey D., and D.P. Shoemaker. *Information Assurance for the Enterprise: A Roadmap to Information Security.* McGraw-Hill Education, 2007.

- Tipton, Harold F., and S. Hernandez, ed. *Official (ISC)² Guide to the CISSP CBK 3rd edition.* ((ISC)²) Press, 2012.

Critical Thinking Exercises

1. A CIO has just implemented a new dashboard for the organization. As part of the dashboard, the IT employees and senior management can review the vulnerability status of all IT network assets. Is this dashboard giving a holistic view of risk for the organization?

2. An organization has approximately 20,000 workstations and 5,000 servers around the world. A new zero-day vulnerability has been published that affects 90 percent of the systems, including servers. "Zero-day" vulnerabilities are recently discovered previously unknown system or software weaknesses. How should the organization go about prioritizing mitigation efforts?

12 Information Assurance Policy

The information assurance policy is undoubtedly the most important element for a successful information assurance management program. In the same way that it is unthinkable that a country could function without laws and legislations, it is unthinkable that an organization could operate without information assurance policies.

Establishing the IAMS starts with identifying information assets and associated life cycles. This is followed by a risk identification and assessment exercise on the assets that provides a sound basis to develop and implement controls to manage the risks. A successful risk assessment exercise is also important in that it gives the correct foundation to formulate the information assurance policy of the organization.

Policy is a formal rule of conduct, controlled by some authority. This chapter provides guidance to information assurance units and related stakeholders about the necessary information to develop a comprehensive information assurance policy document.

Importance of Policy

The following outlines why an organization needs a policy document:

- To establish a foundation for an effective information assurance management program. Good management control makes good business sense. Failure to implement controls may lead to financial penalties, loss of customer confidence, and loss of competitive advantage. An information assurance policy is the cornerstone of any effective information assurance management program.

- An effective information assurance management program covers a management framework for information assurance and the implementation of information assurance controls. The most critical component in the information assurance management framework is a policy document.

- The policy must establish and define appropriate security conduct. No one likes cumbersome or inefficient security controls, particularly if they affect business processes. Despite an increase in the number of security risks, most information assurance organizations still find it difficult to enforce information assurance and obtain necessary employee support. Policies convey senior management's information assurance commitment and expectations. Once policies are approved and endorsed by senior management, information assurance becomes an important agenda item within the organization. Employees should then be encouraged to support senior leadership with their own information assurance efforts.

- To support regulatory and governance requirements and fiduciary duties. With the emergence of various legislation and regulatory requirements, the management needs to demonstrate to stakeholders that sufficient internal controls have been implemented. Policy is a management control and demonstrates management commitment to improving and enforcing information assurance.

- To ensure consistent implementation of security controls. Security is as strong as its weakest link. Any mishap in the information assurance chain may jeopardize the entire security effort. Thus, it is important that everyone subscribe to the required minimum level of security. This is possible only when policy rules are clearly documented and understood by all.

- To support the coordination of activities of internal and external groups. In today's business environment in which outsourcing and business partnerships are becoming the norm, there is a need to have a policy document to manage and monitor the activities of the various parties who have access to information assets.

Policy and Other Governance Functions

Policies provide direction to an organization's intents and objectives that meet its requirements in various areas. Guidelines and procedures are developed and aligned to these policies. They are distributed to the employees to create awareness and better understanding of the organization's processes. This ensures effective implementation of them.

Figure 12-1 illustrates the hierarchy of security documents usually found in an organization.

The next section defines and discusses the differences between policy, procedures, standards, and guidelines.

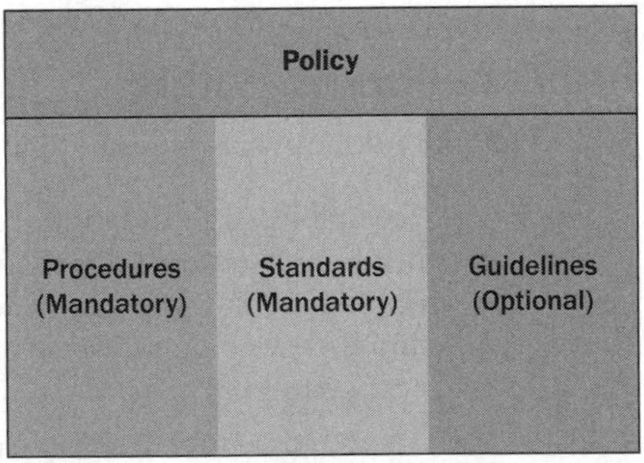

Figure 12-1 Framework of security documents

Policy in Relation to Standards

Standards are mandatory rules, regulations, activities, or actions designed as supporting documents to provide policies with direction and specificity. They ensure policies developed are meaningful and practical. Policies without enough specificity are difficult to endorse

Policy	All personally identifiable information sent via a public network must be encrypted.
Standard	The encryption algorithm must at a minimum use a 1,024-bit key and be AES compliant.

Table 12-1   Examples of Policy and Standard Statements

and also do not convey accurate meaning. Standards and procedures provide the necessary specificity regarding the "what" and "how" of a policy. Policies and standards are generally mandatory as well as being compliance documents.

While related to each other, policies and standards differ significantly. Policies are high-level requirement statements and address a broad audience. Standards may be both high- and low-level requirement documents. For example, some standards may focus on information assurance management issues, while others focus on specific technical requirements and specifications. They target a specific audience. Policies and information assurance management standards as well as international technical standards are developed to be relevant for several years. On the other hand, industry standards are usually developed and updated to reflect rapid changes in technology.

Table 12-1 illustrates the difference between policy and standard.

Policy in Relation to Guidelines

Guidelines provide advice designed to achieve a policy's objectives and standards.

Guidelines are useful in situations where employees need to comply with a local policy because of the nature of the business and its operations. For example, a company with multiple subsidiaries may introduce guidelines on business continuity management. It provides room for subsidiaries to develop business continuity plans reflecting the parent company's business objectives. Each subsidiary may develop a local policy on business continuity management, guided by the recommendations provided in the guidelines issued by the parent company. Table 12-2 shows examples of policies, standards, and guidelines.

Policy	All information-processing facilities and personnel shall be adequately protected.
Standard	The data center and secured areas should have the following features: • Dual power supplies with feed from an existing substation and diesel power generator. • Fire sensor systems should include smoke or temperature sensors located under raised floors, in ceilings or dropped ceilings, and in air conditioning ventilations. • Fireproof ceilings.
Guideline	• Where applicable, a biometrics authentication system should be installed. • Employees are advised not to bring personal belongings into secured areas.

Table 12-2   Examples of Policy, Standard, and Guideline Statements

Policy	All sensitive information must be handled with care and in accordance with its impact categorization.
Standard	Information is categorized into three impact categories. • Low • Moderate • High
Guideline	Where appropriate, an external document shall be categorized to indicate its impact.
Procedure	For information categorized as "moderate," the following items need to be observed: • Label the document "Confidential." • Dispose of the document by shredding. • Encrypt the document during storage or transmission. • The owner's authorization is required for copying.

Table 12-3 Examples of Policy, Standard, Guideline, and Procedure Statements

Policy in Relation to Procedures

Procedures define the specifics of how the policy and supporting standards and guidelines should be deployed and used in an operational environment. A policy statement provides high-level direction for addressing a particular problem, while procedures provide systematic instructions, guidance, and/or methods that employees need to use. Procedures are typically mandatory.

For example, to avoid data loss or corruption, a policy {XE "policy"} can describe the need for backups, for offsite storage, and for safeguarding backup media. A procedure can describe how to use backup software and when to make backups. Table 12-3 illustrates the differences between policy, standard, guideline, and procedure statements.

Policy Development Steps

This section details the policy development steps starting from gathering key reference materials, defining a framework for policies, developing a policy, and reviewing and approving the policy, as well as the enforcement processes. Figure 12-2 shows the relationship among these steps.

Figure 12-2 Policy development steps

Information Gathering

Information gathering is essential to policy development. This ensures that developed policies are consistent with the organization's culture, vision, and mission.

An important reason to expend resources on background research is that it ensures that a policy developed is in line with the strategic direction of the organization. For example, it would not be sensible to develop a group wide information assurance policy for a company with multiple subsidiaries when it has been decided to decentralize information assurance management.

The following documents should be studied and/or reviewed during the information gathering step:

- An overview of IT infrastructure and a list of IT systems used as background reference
- Current policies, standards, guidelines, or procedures
- Risk assessment (refer to Chapter 11 for details on risk assessment) or audit reports as references; they indicate the organization's current and future information assurance needs
- Security incidents or other loss-related historical information and any information that might help in identifying areas that need further attention

It is normal for information systems to change frequently; therefore, related documentation becomes outdated and introduce new risks. You should interview relevant parties to learn background information prior to policy development. Some organizations do practice oral policies or informal culture-based policies. Such policies are ones that the employees practice on a daily basis without formal documentation. Interview sessions can uncover undocumented policies practiced by organizations. Oral policies should be discouraged because they are rarely enforceable and are subject to conflicting interpretation.

Policy Framework Definition

After the relevant information collection, compile a list containing the topics covered. Organizations may want to prioritize policy coverage based on the urgency of issues to be addressed.

Next, the organization should define how it intends to present the information assurance policies. For example, issue some policies in the form of a manual. Alternatively, the information assurance department may issue memos summarizing the policies periodically or post them on the Intranet.

As there may be several topics addressed in the policy document, it is crucial that information is conveyed to the right parties. It may be useful for the organization to identify the target audience group that the policy will address.

Policy Development

Before developing the policy document, the organization should understand the style of existing policies, the documentation format, and the system for numbering policies. The message should be kept brief, with words such as *shall* (imperative form) applied to indicate that an item in a policy statement is mandatory and such words should be used consistently throughout the policy. Most organizations will not have a single policy

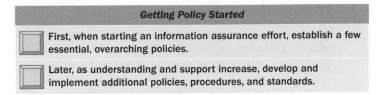

Getting Policy Started

First, when starting an information assurance effort, establish a few essential, overarching policies.

Later, as understanding and support increase, develop and implement additional policies, procedures, and standards.

to cover all of information assurance needs. Large organizations may have a single master policy supported by subpolicies, with each subpolicy being pertinent to particular aspects of the organization. Standards, procedures, and guidelines may be referenced in the policies.

Review and Approval

Several review cycles are recommended to gain support from the key players. As more feedback is received, the policy has greater chances to be accepted later. At a minimum, it should be a three-step process peer review; review by internal parties such as internal audit, IT, human resources, or legal department; and finally, review by senior management.

☑ Ensure policy is aligned to organizational objectives and mission

☑ Check your grammar and spelling to maintain credibility

☑ Streamline the language and keep message focused

☑ Make sure policy is realistic and practical

☑ Identify the target audience and select vocabulary appropriately

The final step in the review process is endorsement by senior management. A notice to all employees informing them that compliance is mandatory as a condition of continued employment should be stated on the first page of the document or on the main page of an organization's web site if the policy is posted on the intranet. This conveys to readers that the policy is indeed supported by top management and that they have given their serious commitment to it.

Enforcement

Policy enforcement is the final crucial step to ensure the success of an organization's information assurance management program. Suitable actions should be taken to detect and respond to noncompliance. It is appropriate to discuss noncompliance

Automating Policy Enforcement

• In some cases policy enforcement could be automated too.

• A good example of an automated tool to enforce a network access policy is a firewall.

issues with all parties involved and the human resource department. This discussion encourages proper execution of existing disciplinary processes for noncompliance. To avoid future disputes, the organization should clearly document activities that violate the policy and associated penalties.

Prior to enforcement, employees should understand why a policy is being introduced. Communicate expectations through an information security awareness program to ensure an effective policy development exercise. Refer to Chapter 16 for more details on information security awareness. Additionally, organizations may choose to have employees sign the rules of behavior document. This document signifies employees have read and understand expectations regarding their behavior when using information systems.

Policy Layout

The actual layout of a policy document varies from organization to organization. However, a policy document should consider the following components as a starting point:

- **Objectives**   This section will define the goals of the policy and the issues to be addressed.

- **Scope**   The scope establishes which resources of the organization are covered by the policy. This can include all electronically stored, processed, transmitted, printed, faxed, or verbal information.

- **Definitions**   This section will define important terms and definitions to be used throughout the policy document to establish a common ground of understanding among all readers.

- **Responsibilities**   This section will establish who is responsible for the review, maintenance, and implementation of the policy.

- **Compliance**   This section will detail the consequences if the policy is violated.

- **References**   This section will list materials referred to in the policy document such as specific regulations, decrees, mandates, standards, and other policies.

- **Related documents**   This section will list relevant documents that are created in relation to the policy document.

- **Effective date**   This section will specify the effective date of the policy.

- **Signature**   The document should have a signature of approval by senior management.

Further Reading

- Code of Federal Regulations, Part 5 Administrative Personnel, Subpart C- Employees Responsible for the Management or Use of Federal Computer Systems, Section 930.301 through 930.305 (5 C.F.R 930.301-305).

- Frost, J.C., J.M. Springer, and C.D. Schou. Instructor guide and materials to accompany principles of *Introduction to Principles of Computer Security: Security+ and Beyond*. McGraw-Hill Education, 2004.

- Nash, A., et al. *PKI: Implementing and Managing E-security*. McGraw-Hill Education, 2001.

- Nichols, R., et al. *Defending Your Digital Assets Against Hackers, Crackers, Spies, and Thieves*. McGraw-Hill, 2000.

- National Institute of Standards and Technology. *Special Publication 800-100, Information Security Handbook: A Guide for Managers*. October 2006.

- National Institute of Standards and Technology. *Special Publication 800-53, Revision 4, Recommended Security Controls for Federal Information Systems and Organizations.* DOC, April 2013.

- Office of Management and Budget. Memorandum M-04-26, "Personal Use Policies and File Sharing Technology." September 2004.

- Office of Management and Budget. Circular A-130, "Appendix III, Transmittal Memorandum #4, Management of Federal Information Resources." November 2000.

- Schmidt, Howard A. *Patrolling Cyberspace: Lessons Learned from a Lifetime in Data Security.* Larstan Publishing, 2006.

- Schou, Corey D., and K.J. Trimmer. "Information Assurance and Security," *Journal of Organizational and End User Computing,* vol. 16, no. 3, July–September 2004.

- Conklin, Wm. Arthur. *Introduction to Principles of Computer Security: Security+ and Beyond.* McGraw-Hill Education, 2004.

- Schou, Corey D., and D.P. Shoemaker. *Information Assurance for the Enterprise: A Roadmap to Information Security.* McGraw-Hill Education, 2007.

- Tipton, Harold F., and S. Hernandez, ed. *Official (ISC)^2 Guide to the CISSP CBK 3rd edition.* ((ISC)^2) Press, 2012.

- Wood, Charles C. *Information Security Roles & Responsibilities Made Easy.* PentaSafe Security Technologies, 2002.

Critical Thinking Exercises

1. An organization has had more than a dozen personal health information (PHI) breaches in the past year. The organization has a policy in place that stipulates sensitive information is not to be e-mailed or transmitted outside of the organization. The human resources department has just enabled a new "work from home" telework policy. However, individuals have complained ever since the start of the telework program because they are unable to take information with them to work on at remote locations. How can the organization address this issue with policies, standards, procedures, and guidelines?

2. An organization has a clear policy creation mechanism, and the organization's information assurance team has ensured every specification and requirement is incorporated into the organization's policy. The organization routinely evaluates the policy every six months to determine whether updates are needed. A breach just occurred, and the encryption policy needs to be updated to include a new standard; however, the next update window isn't for another five months. Additionally, the policy review process is cumbersome and time-consuming because every department in the organization must review and approve of the policies being created. What could the organization do to help streamline this process?

CHAPTER 13

Human Resource Assurance

Even though society has evolved and become dependent upon technology, human resources still determine organizational success. It is undeniable that people are often the weakest link in maintaining the information assurance chain.

Within any organization, the people who have direct or indirect interaction with information systems are the internal users, such as office employees, system operators, implementers, administrators, designers, and managers.

There are also external users such as vendors, service providers, business partners, and unregistered users who may have access to the system. There is a wide range of information assurance issues relating to how individuals gain authorization and access to the system to perform their duties. To ensure a well-managed information assurance program, highlight these issues accordingly.

Since it is difficult to predict individual behavior, this chapter discusses controls that can be implemented to minimize human risks. Examples of these controls include hiring the most qualified individuals, performing background screening, using detailed job scope and descriptions, enforcing strict access control, providing awareness and training programs, and defining a clear disciplinary process.

Recruitment

It is essential to control the recruitment process while having information assurance objectives in mind before proceeding with any recruitment exercise. There are four key areas of focus applicable to the recruitment process.

- Inclusion of information assurance aspects in the job scope and description
- Defined level of confidentiality or sensitivity required
- Filling the vacant positions with suitable candidates
- Use of legal documents to enforce information assurance

Of course, the prudent manager will apply these four areas according to the sensitivity of the position and the associated risk.

Include Security in Job Scope/Description

A well-managed organization should document the policy implications and potential personal sanctions within all job descriptions. Not all organizations have reached this level of maturity; the information assurance team could be an exemplary starting point. Chapter 9 explains organizational maturity. In the case of an effective information assurance management program, it supports the organizational structure in place. The job scope and description should give a clear explanation about employees' roles, responsibilities, and authorities in the organization. It is crucial to state the access level during the employee's tenure. A defined job scope and description eliminates "gray" areas about employee responsibilities and how to respond in different situations.

Every employee has some responsibility for information assurance. It is important, therefore, to ensure that each job description in the organization emphasizes the information assurance components: its scope and the tasks, roles, and responsibilities to be fulfilled. This indicates to employees the importance of information assurance in the workplace. Furthermore, it is crucial to include a section on the sanctions to be imposed on employees if they fail to adhere to the information assurance scope of their work. The job scope/descriptions should state the responsibility to comply with the overall information assurance structure, and it should define specific information assets, information assurance processes, or activities attached to the position. Minimally, all employees should execute an acceptable use policy document to demonstrate the importance of information assurance.

Organizations may consider using an information assurance workforce framework such as the United States National Initiative for Cybersecurity Education (NICE). NICE provides organizations with a common understanding and lexicon for information assurance workforces. The framework features knowledge, skills, and abilities for the following information assurance areas:

- Operate and Maintain
- Protect and Defend
- Investigate
- Collect and Operate
- Analyze
- Securely Provision
- Oversight and Development

You can find more information regarding NICE in the "Further Reading" section later in this chapter. Human resource and capital divisions should reach out and establish relationships with the information assurance program to ensure that suitable descriptions of information assurance responsibilities and penalties are included in job descriptions.

Defined Level of Confidentiality or Sensitivity

The responsible supervisor should work with the information assurance program to determine the level of information access required for the position once a post has been identified. Employees should have only sufficient access to perform their duties and to avoid disclosure of information to unauthorized personnel. There are two general principles that apply when granting access: job division and employee rights restriction.

Examples of internationally defined standards for separation of duties or job division include the following:

- Generally Acceptable Accounting Principles (GAAP)
- Sarbanes-Oxley
- OECD principles
- U.S. National Institute of Standards and Technology Minimum Security Controls
- EU internal controls
- Monetary Authority of Singapore Internal Controls

Separation of duties relates to an act of creating distinct and separate responsibilities among the employees of a critical process to prevent compromise, breaches, or fraud. It is the responsibility of the top management to define clearly each role and responsibility. The practice of job division may minimize collusion as a component of fraud, sabotage, misuse of information, theft, and other information assurance compromises. Collusion means more than one individual working together to cause some malicious act or fraud.

Access restrictions define what level of access to information and services are appropriate for individuals to carry out their official tasks. An organization should limit reliance on key employees. When such a situation is unavoidable, the organization should include it in the information assurance policy and plan for an unexpected illness, absence, or departure.

Filling the Position

The placement of individuals in a specific position in an organization should be based on the position's confidentiality level, suitable screening, and selection methods. Place the right candidate in the right position. Consider the following during the screening and selection process:

- Aptitude testing
- Certifications and related ethics oaths
- Employment history
- Financial checks
- Qualification of academic record and professional experience
- References from previous employment and education
- Security background check

The organization should ensure that the screening and selection process is not contrary to regulations on collection and use of personal information as well as any legislation regarding labor, credit worthiness, and employment. If personnel recruitment agencies are involved, the organization's standard outsourcing procedures should be in place to avoid any setbacks during the process. The organization must clearly define applicant privacy protection requirements to any personnel recruitment agencies.

Use of Legal Documents to Protect Information

Acceptable use policies and other binding documents and agreements should be used to remind employees of their responsibilities and commitment to the organization. Relate this to information assurance. Two documents used frequently as legally binding in organizations: employment contract and nondisclosure agreements (NDAs).

An employment contract is an agreement between the organization and the employee defining all the terms and conditions of employment. Hence, from the point of view of information assurance, the employee's information assurance roles and responsibilities should be defined pertaining, but not limited to, copyright, data protection rights, information ownership, information management, and information classification.

Legal counsel should help frame contracts that state that the information assurance terms and conditions are applicable beyond working hours and outside the organization's premises. The contract should emphasize that the information assurance terms and conditions apply to all organizational information and data independent of the media or system that processes, stores, or transmits it. The contract should include a provision that the terms remain in force for a specified period after termination of service or so long as the individual holds organizational information after termination. Moreover, the contract should clearly specify the legal remedies available upon noncompliance. Prior to signing the contract, the employee and employer should ensure there is a "meeting of the minds" about the contents.

An NDA defines the identity of the organization and the employee, the level of confidentiality of the information covered, and to whom information may not be divulged. Hence, an employee should sign an NDA before they have access to the organization's information systems or facilities. Furthermore, an NDA agreement should be reviewed whenever terms and conditions of employment change.

Employment

Organizations should define and enforce information assurance controls during the course of employment to prevent personnel from misusing information facilities and to protect information systems from human error, theft, fraud, or other breaches. This section provides some of the applicable controls that an organization may consider.

Employee Monitoring Guidelines
☐ Monitor all e-mail messages, incoming and outgoing to or from a work e-mail address.
☐ Record and monitor all instant messaging conducted on organizational systems.
☐ Record and monitor all internet usage performed using organizational computers and infrastructure.
☐ Personal telephone calls are not monitored longer than necessary to determine that the calls are personal.
☐ Monitoring is for a reasonable business purpose.
☐ Scope and manner of monitoring are not unreasonable.
☐ Use of GPS devices in organization cars and cell phones to track location, driving speed, and other work-related activities is for routine matters such as enhancing performance through data analytics.
☐ Use of keystrocke, computer screen, and hard-drive monitoring techniques is restricted to organizational system.
☐ Voice mail is on organizational voice mail systems.

Supervisory Controls

Use appropriate supervisory skills and controls to ensure that operations run smoothly. Upon employment, managers should observe new and inexperienced employees from various aspects within the limits of the law. This observation should range from activities such as patterns of accessing the information system and facilities or personal and financial problems that may affect the employee's performance as part of a personnel evaluation. Although laws differ among economies, in the United States, private organizations may monitor employees' communications consistent with the prior checklist.

Organizations should always consult with legal professionals to determine the legality of all employee monitoring. Of course, employers practicing workplace monitoring should have clear policies about which activities they monitor. If during monitoring, criminal activity is suspected or identified, organizations should contact their legal counsel and appropriate law enforcement.

Rotation of Duties

The National Computer Network Emergency Response Technical Team – Coordination Center of China (CNCERT/CC) points out that rotation of duties is a form of control that minimizes fraud. It may also keep an individual from staying in a job position for long periods; it helps manage their level of motivation. These controls may not be feasible in all cases, for example, in terms of the amount of time taken to train the employee for specific tasks. However, keeping an employee in one job position for extended periods may lead the employee to having too much control over certain business functions. Such employee control may lead to fraud, can lead to misuse of resources, or may even jeopardize data integrity.

The CNCERT/CC further cites (ISC)[2] documents that recommend employees holding sensitive positions should be directed to consume their annual leave. With this mandatory annual leave policy, any error or fraud can be detected during the period of employee absence. As mentioned earlier, other variations that might be considered are separation of duties to ensure split knowledge and/or dual control. For split knowledge control, no one person has all the information to perform a task; thus, teamwork is crucial to complete the task. Dual control refers to two or more individuals being required to perform a task at any one time. There are times when having two individuals perform the task together is important; this is known as the two-person rule.

Monitoring and Privacy Expectations

Personal privacy is an important aspect of an employee's life. Employees have an expectation of privacy in certain communications such as with their doctors or with their banks. Organizations are blurring the lines between work and personal life with aggressive telework programs and the use of bring-your-own-device (BYOD) programs. Organizations must ensure they clearly delineate the expectations of the employee in terms of privacy when it comes to employee-owned devices or employees using organizational equipment for personal use.

Organizations may offer a *de minimus* policy for employees that states an employee may use organizational information systems and resources for personal use during a break or lunch period as long as there is no material cost to the organization. *de minimus* is Latin for "minimal things," and in risk assessment it refers to a level of risk too low to be concerned with. These policies are often put in place to help employee morale and bring about work-life balance. Issues arise when an employee is put under surveillance and the monitoring captures information about their personal lives where they may have an expectation of privacy. For example, an organization monitoring an employee for an allegation of misconduct may capture sensitive restricted medical information of the employee if the employee is using the *de minimus* policy during his lunch break with an encrypted SSL connection to his healthcare provider. If the organization is intercepting the connection and decrypting the information, it may be wading into the waters of a privacy violation. Organizations must work carefully with their legal departments to determine appropriate policies for work-life balance that ensure proper scoped monitoring can be performed when needed.

BYOD brings more privacy issues to the table. As noted in prior chapters, an organization's information assurance requirements should follow the organization's information onto any media or platform. Therefore, when an organization allows its information to be processed, stored, or transmitted on an employee's personal device, it may inadvertently give up control of the information and also expose its information through the BYOD device. Should an organization decide to pursue a BYOD approach, it must ensure it has an agreement with the employee that clearly stipulates at a minimum the security requirements of the device:

- The organization may access or seize the device and all its contents for monitoring, disciplinary, legal, or information assurance reasons.

- The employee has no expectation of privacy from the organization on any device that processes, stores, or transmits the organization's information.

While *containerization* software and other mobile device technologies may greatly enhance the ability of organizations to monitor BYOD devices, organizations should assume at some point the system may fail or there may be leakage from the secure container into the personal device. At that point, the organization must ensure the previous criteria have been met.

There are emerging trends toward bringing your own software (BYOS). BYOS is characterized by employees bringing their own productivity tools to the workplace. It may increase innovation and productivity; however, it introduces unmanaged vulnerabilities and makes baseline and configuration management more complicated. Information assurance professionals should make the increased risk clear to management. Additionally, in some governments there are legal implications related to licensing and also budget augmentation. For example, in the United States, it is often illegal for anyone to give the government a gift (including software) exceeding a certain value.

Periodic Monitoring

As detailed in the earlier "Supervisory Controls" section, an organization may perform periodic monitoring of employees' activities to detect potential fraud. Clearly, this must be consistent with local laws; however, it is important for employees to know that such monitoring may take place. Security threats may be spontaneous. If a possible threat source knows his activities and access are logged, then the controls may discourage and deter such actions.

The organization should be cautioned against routine and undisclosed monitoring because this may trigger employees' uneasiness: feelings that they are not being trusted and are being spied upon. In some countries, there are laws that protect both employer and employee regarding monitoring. As noted prior, organizations must always confirm the legality of any monitoring. In the European Union, for example, organizations are not allowed to monitor employees without notification.

Employee Training and Awareness

The recruitment process does not stop once an employee is hired. The new employee will be trained to perform job-specific tasks including information assurance duties and responsibilities. As an example, a data entry clerk should not have the same level of training as a database administrator; however, both need to know about information assurance in general. Nevertheless, a successful information assurance training or awareness program should be tailored to specific groups. It should meet organizational security objectives and achieve specific results.

Disciplinary Processes
Obtain evidence prior to initiating an investigation.
Outline a proper investigation process, including roles and responsibilities, evidence collection procedures, and chain of custody of evidence.
Define disciplinary controls, consistent with legislation and regulatory requirements.
Make a list of evidentiary standards to determine omission and avoid mistreatment.
Take into consideration the nature, impact, and significance of the breach. For example, consider whether it is a first time or repeated offense, whether due to negligence or intent.

Awareness, training, and education (AT&E) is an iterative process in which employees are required to update their information assurance knowledge constantly because of changes to their positions, duties, and the overall threat/risk environment. To minimize possible information assurance risks, grant employees minimal or restricted access to the information system prior to the awareness and training program being conducted. You can find more discussion on training and awareness in Chapter 16.

Disciplinary Process

Establish and explain a formal disciplinary process for all employees specific to security breaches. The disciplinary process should ensure that employees suspected of committing any security breach are treated correctly and fairly. The impact and actions to be taken, severity of the breaches, relevant legislation, business contracts, and other relevant factors should be taken into consideration when outlining the disciplinary process.

To assure due process, use a disciplinary process based on this checklist; it should be adapted by management to ensure that all actions are in accordance not only with organization policy but also local laws and customs.

Termination or Change of Employment

Employees leave jobs or are suspended for various reasons and under voluntary or involuntary circumstances. Voluntary circumstances include study leave, vacations, family, or personal matters. Involuntary circumstances include dismissal, death, or medical incapacity.

Organizations should establish policy and procedures for secure offboarding by defining actions to be taken to handle absence and departure. The actions should include temporary or permanent closing of accounts, steps for forwarding e-mails, change of critical passwords and phone numbers, and disabling access to all systems.

Termination and suspension happen for many reasons. The employees involved have different reactions. Although termination is usually conducted in a professional manner among all parties involved, organizations may face risks when termination is adversarial. Organizations should have specific procedures to follow with each termination.

Here are some examples:

- The employee will leave the premises immediately, escorted by a security guard or manager.
- The employee will return all company assets and items of identification such as access cards or any keys that belong to the organization. If identification cannot be recovered, the employee will be added to a "No Entry Granted" list for physical security.
- The employee will receive specific instructions on whether to format the computer.
- The user account will be restricted immediately by disabling it or removing it.
- Any logs of activity and access for the employee will be archived for 90 days minimum.

Independent of the circumstances, terminated employees need to know the following:

- Their ongoing security requirements and legal responsibilities within any confidentiality agreement, employee contract, or rules of behavior
- Their terms and conditions of employment
- The effective period of those terms, conditions, and agreements

Further Reading

- AICPA. GAAP Codification. https://asc.fasb.org/imageRoot/47/49128947.pdf.
- Directive Administrative Controls. China Education and Research Network Computer Emergency Response Team (CCERT). https://www.cccure.org/Documents/HISM/015-019.html (Citing (ISC)²).
- Code of Federal Regulations, Part 5 Administrative Personnel, Subpart C—Employees Responsible for the Management or Use of Federal Computer Systems, Section 930.301 through 930.305 (5 C.F.R 930.301-305).
- Data classification. HDM Clariza Initiatives, June 16, 2007. www.trehb101.com/index.php?/archives/71-data-classifation.html.
- Financial Accounting Standards Board. GAAP Report. www.fasb.org.
- Homeland Security Presidential Directive 12. Policy for a Common Identification.
- Intelligence Community Directive Number 704. "Personnel Security Standards and Procedures Governing Eligibility for Access to Sensitive Compartmented Information and Other Controlled Access Program Information." October 2008.
- National Institute of Standards and Technology. *Special Publication 800-12, An Introduction to Computer Security: The NIST Handbook.* 1996.
- National Institute of Standards and Technology Federal Information Processing Standards Publication 201-1. Personal Identity Verification (PIV) of Federal Employees and Contractors. March 2006.

- Office of Management and Budget Memorandum M-01-05, Guidance on Inter-Agency Sharing of Personal Data—Protecting Personal Privacy. December 2000.

- Office of Management and Budget Memorandum M-03-22, OMB Guidance for Implementing the Privacy Provisions of the E-Government Act of 2002. September 2003.

- Office of Management and Budget Memorandum M-04-26, Personal Use Policies and File Sharing Technology. September 2004.

- Privacy Act of 1974 (P.L. 93-579).

- Sadowsky, G., et al. *Information Technology Security Handbook, The International Bank for Reconstruction and Development.* www.infodev-security.net/book/.

- Schou, Corey D., and D.P. Shoemaker. *Information Assurance for the Enterprise: A Roadmap to Information Security.* McGraw-Hill Education, 2007.

- Standard for Federal Employees and Contractors. August 2004.

- United States National Initiative for Cybersecurity Education (NICE). National Cybersecurity Workforce Framework. http://csrc.nist.gov/nice/framework/.

Critical Thinking Exercises

1. Consider an organization with several different levels of management and a decentralized information technology infrastructure. Marketing has its own information technology as does manufacturing and finance. What is the best approach when hiring new employees in any area to ensure they understand their information assurance responsibilities?

2. An EU-based organization operating in the United States has knowingly allowed its employees to use personal information technology to process, store, and transmit organizational information. The organization is now being sued in a U.S. court, and all information of the organization is subject to legal hold. What must be done with the information on an employee's personal devices?

3. Recent malware attacks encrypt the storage of computers and devices for ransom. How would an organization handle this situation with information on an employee personal (BYOD) device?

CHAPTER 14

Advantages of Certification, Accreditation, and Assurance

In general, *certification* refers to a thorough assessment of a process, while *accreditation* is a formal declaration about the status of a process. In information assurance, certification and accreditation (C&A) are complex topics. In some economies, it is associated with government rules and regulations; however, the concept is much broader. It spans everything from compliance with an internationally recognized standard such as ISO 27001 to a more specifically focused audit to assure that management acknowledges and accepts the inherent risk in a system. In today's fast-changing environment, where every new day brings new threats and vulnerabilities, information assurance is required for both technical as well as nontechnical operations.

Certification and accreditation (and its analogs) have long been staples in the U.S. government and other *high assurance* industries. When performed properly, C&A provides a level of assurance and due diligence with management and stakeholders. It provides a baseline of information assurance organization-wide and provides a focused baseline for the organization to identify areas for improvement or enhanced efficiency. C&A is ultimately about mature processes and policies being enacted by a capable workforce throughout the organization.

Certification and accreditation support information assurance. Certification, accreditation, and assurance are crucial elements to evaluate if security controls are implemented correctly, they are operated as expected, and residual risk is visible. C&A is a risk management tool that examines and reports on the effectiveness of controls in managing risks, as discussed in Chapters 11 and this chapter.

Providing assurance is never a one-time event; it is an ongoing exercise. Temporal, environmental, and organizationally defined events trigger a review and update of the C&A. Recalling the discussion in Chapter 6 about IAMS, managing security is a process that requires continuous review and improvement. In the context of the PDCA model, which is the most commonly used model in IAMS, perform this review during the Check phase.

The improvement is identified in the Act phase. This chapter offers guidelines for a generalized process of certification and accreditation and discusses how these processes contribute to the assurance of the information system.

C&A of information systems supports senior management risk awareness, mitigation, avoidance, and acceptance. Certification and accreditation help achieve more secure information systems within an organization by doing the following:

- Enabling more consistent, comparable, and repeatable assessments of security controls in information systems

- Promoting a better understanding of organization-related mission risks resulting from the operation of information systems

- Creating more complete, reliable, and trustworthy information for accrediting officials—to facilitate more informed security accreditation decisions

Certification and accreditation are important activities that support a risk management process and are an integral part of an agency's information assurance program. Accreditation is a risk-based decision made by senior management to authorize the operation of an information system and to accept the explicit risk based on the implemented security controls.

C&A of a system is a form of quality control and challenges the organization to implement the most effective security controls possible. A difficult task is made more complex since it is an analysis of not just a single system. Information assurance is a system of systems that must interoperate reliably while minimizing risk.

Concepts and Definitions

Certification evaluates a system against a set of criteria that demonstrates that the system is secure enough to be operated in a target environment. The objective of certification is the evaluation of the controls present within a system to ensure compliance with predefined functional and security requirements. The results of certification activity are the input for the accreditation process, which is the formal approval by management. Certification uses various techniques for evaluation purposes, such as risk analysis, validation, testing, control evaluation, and audit.

Accreditation, also known as authorization, is the official decision by management to operate a system (or system of systems). It is a formal acceptance of the adequacy of a system's security to conform to operational requirements within an acceptable risk level. An accreditation exercise considers the following within an existing or proposed system:

- Acceptable risk level
- Defined interconnections to other systems
- Defined period of time and conditions
- Mechanism to counter identified threats and vulnerabilities with current or planned controls

- Operating with a set mode of security
- Prescribed set of security controls

Factors affecting the target system in its unique environment such as installed applications, operational security mode, sensitivity of the stored information, system setup, site location, and interconnections with other systems should be carefully considered.

Certification and accreditation are also closely related to risk management. The objective of risk management is to identify specific areas where safeguards are needed against security threats. Specific controls are applied to mitigate, eliminate, or acceptably reduce the identified risk. The results of this exercise provide critical information for making an accreditation decision.

The process of certification and accreditation is an ongoing one in line with the IAMS discussed in Chapter 6. Clearly, it should be a formal continuous process. Formal re-certification and re-accreditation should be mandatory when there are major changes to the system, when a major application is introduced, when the threat/risk environment changes, or when there are significant technological upgrades.

Purpose of Certification and Accreditation

There are many reasons for having management commit to a certification and accreditation exercise. In some cases, laws (U.S. government) require certification and accreditation; however, in the absence of law, there are other advantages to the organization.

- Certification and accreditation promote the importance of risk management in operating a system with appropriate management review and monitoring.

- Implementing and practicing a formal certification and accreditation process assist the organization in providing evidence that it has exercised due diligence if a security problem or incident arises.

- Management of an organization can obtain a higher level of assurance that its security systems are in fact configured and operated properly to secure assets instead of being victims of or unwitting contributors to their compromise. It is important that an organization has an appropriate level of security and trust of the system being used to safeguard its assets.

Primary Roles for Supporting Certification and Accreditation

Many roles are involved in the certification and accreditation exercise. The number of people involved in the exercise depends on the complexity of the system assessed. However, the functions remain the same. For the exercise to be effective, all parties need to work as a team to ensure success of the program. Table 14-1 provides an overview of the roles and associated responsibilities for supporting the certification and accreditation exercise.

Role	Responsibility
Authorizing authority	Responsible for approving the system formally to operate within an acceptable level of risk. This should be a senior leader in the organization with a deep understanding of the mission or business the information system supports. This individual is responsible for understanding and accepting ongoing residual risk for the organization.
Certifier	Responsible for evaluating and assessing the system in accordance with predetermined security requirements. The certifier should ideally be operationally independent from the system they are certifying.
Information system security officer	Responsible for ensuring the security of the system.
Program manager	Responsible for the overall funding, procurement, development, integration, operation, management, and maintenance of the system. This person is often responsible for the information in the system.
System manager	Responsible for ensuring that the security controls are adequately implemented and monitored.
User	Responsible for protecting the system using established rules. (A *user* is a person or process that uses and accesses the system.)

Table 14-1 Roles for Supporting Certification and Accreditation Exercise

Certification and Accreditation Process

The security certification and accreditation process consists of four phases. Figure 14-1 provides brief descriptions of the activities in each phase.

Certification Baselines

Certification is commonly derived from baselines. Organizations can save time and resources by determining standard information assurance baselines for their information systems based on the classification or categorization of the system. These baselines become the foundation for certification activities. In the United States, cloud service providers that are providing services to civilian departments and agencies must comply with FedRAMP baselines. The FedRAMP baselines provide minimum information assurance requirements that systems must comply with if they are to receive the FedRAMP certification called a *provisional ATO*. Figure 14-2 summarizes the baseline control requirements.

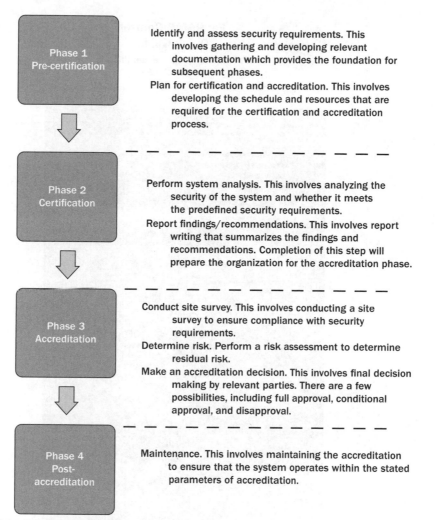

Figure 14-1   Certification and accreditation process flow

Considerations for Product Evaluation, Certification, and Accreditation

To decide whether to embark on certification and accreditation exercises, an organization should take into account several factors. Since accreditation is about the acceptance and management of risk, organizations should weigh the appropriate factors and decide to

FedRAMP Control
Quick Guide

Control requirements are identified in the
FedRAMP SSP

ID	Family	Class	Low Count	Moderate Count
AC	Access Control	Technical	11	17 (24)
AT	Awareness and Training	Operational	4	4
AU	Audit and Accountability	Technical	10	12 (9)
CA	Certification, Accreditation, and Security Assessment	Management	6 (1)	6 (2)
CM	Configuration Management	Operational	6	9 (12)
CP	Contingency Planning	Operational	6	9 (15)
IA	Identification and Authentication	Technical	7 (2)	8 (10)
IR	Incident Response	Operational	7	8 (4)
MA	Maintenance	Operational	4	6 (6)
MP	Media Protection	Operational	3	6 (5)
PE	Physical and Environmental Protection	Operational	11	18 (5)
PL	Planning	Management	4	5
PS	Personnel Security	Operational	8	8
RA	Risk Assessment	Management	4	4 (5)
SA	System and Services Acquisition	Management	8	12 (7)
SC	System and Communications Protection	Technical	8 (1)	24 (16)
SI	System and Information Integrity	Operational	5	12 (9)

Legend:

Count = # of controls (#of enhancements)
Impact Level: L = Low/**M** = Moderate
Enhancements: (#, #)
Additional FedRAMP Requirements = ★
FedRAMP Guidance = G

Note: Controls and Enhancements added by FedRAMP are in **Bold**.

Figure 14-2 Sample baseline summary

either accept or reject the risk. To ensure that credible, risk-based decisions are made, the following points should be considered during the security certification and accreditation process:

- **Effectiveness of security controls**   Do the security controls provide the appropriate and desired level of protection as required?

- **Reasonable and acceptable risk**   Prior to the certification, are the risks established in the risk analysis real and reasonable? Would these risks be acceptable?

- **Relevancy and benefits**   In what way would the certification be relevant and beneficial to the organization?

- **Risk mitigation and control**   Are there any steps being taken or do any plans exist to rectify weaknesses or to remove known vulnerabilities arising in the security controls?

Security requirements that apply to a system differ considerably from one system to another. Every system's security requirements are interpretations of generic requirements within the context of the system's purpose, operational concept, and threat environment. Tailor certification and accreditation activities to address a system's specific security requirements. In addition, evaluate the complexity and sensitivity of the system. For example, the depth of technical analysis required for a stand-alone computer that handles routine work is less when compared to a mission-critical system that handles multimillion-dollar transactions.

Further Reading

- National Institute of Standards and Technology. *Special Publication 800-37, Revision 1, Guide for Applying the Risk Management Framework to Federal Information Systems: A Security Life Cycle Approach.* February 2010.

- National Institute of Standards and Technology. *Special Publication 800-39, Managing Information Security Risk: Organization, Mission, and Information System View.* March 2011.

- Nichols, R., D. Ryan, and J. Ryan. Defending *Your Digital Assets Against Hackers, Crackers, Spies, and Thieves,* McGraw-Hill Education, 2000.

- Risk Management AS/NZS 4360:1999. Standards Association of Australia.

- Ross, R., et al. *Guide for Assessing the Security Controls in Federal Information Systems, (Special Publication 800-53 Rev 1).* NIST, 2008.

- Ross, R., et al. *Recommended Security Controls for Federal Information Systems (Special Publication 800-53 Rev 1).* NIST, 2006.

- Ross, R., M. Swanson, et al. *Guide for the Security Certification and Accreditation of Federal Information Systems (Special Publication 800 37).* NIST, 2007.

- Schmidt, Howard A. *Larstan's The Black Book on Government Security.* Transition Vendor, 2006.

- Schou, Corey D., and D.P. Shoemaker. *Information Assurance for the Enterprise: A Roadmap to Information Security.* McGraw-Hill Education, 2007.
- The Common Criteria Evaluation and Validation Scheme. www.niap-ccevs.org/cc-scheme/.
- Tipton, Harold F., and S. Hernandez, ed. *Official (ISC)² Guide to the CISSP CBK 3rd edition.* ((ISC)²) Press, 2012.

Critical Thinking Exercises

1. An organization chooses to have its CIO be the accreditation official for all its information systems. What are the strengths and weaknesses of this approach?

2. Within an organization, who is best suited to determine the independence of the certifier?

PART

Risk Mitigation Process

Logically, the first strategy in managing risk is to try to prevent threats from exploiting existing vulnerabilities. Although we cannot reduce all risk, there is no doubt a well-implemented risk management strategy will reduce the probability of most of the risks occurring.

Part III discusses preventive controls that an organization should consider when developing protection strategies to minimize risks. It begins with Chapter 15, which highlights the importance of incorporating security considerations in system development and how this could be achieved. Chapter 16 discusses the more often trivialized issue of physical and environmental security controls and their importance as the first layer of defense.

A successful information assurance program can be achieved by the correct emphasis on people, process, and technology.

Chapter 17 highlights the importance of awareness, training, and education as a proactive strategy in trying to prevent a security incident. Finally, Chapters 18 and 19 discuss the technical aspects of preventive tools and techniques with special focus on access control.

Quick Answers

Q: How do I make sure that the access control implemented in my organization a year ago still meets my current requirements?

A: In today's world of changing technology, nothing is perfect. The best way to deal with this situation is to conduct an information security access control audit. An audit is an effective way to determine the level of compliance that the organization has with its access control policies and procedures. Taking into consideration the imperfect world we live in, organizations are encouraged to prepare for preventing information security incidents rather than reacting to them. An information security access control audit is a good method to ensure organizations comply with its access control policies and procedures. Furthermore, it is a relatively inexpensive method and far more cost effective compared to recovering from damages of an information security incident. Moreover, it provides an objective assessment to evaluate how secure an organization actually is.

Q: What should one bear in mind when developing awareness or training materials?

A: Training should always be customized to the needs of the organization and the type of industry the organization is in. Thus, it is crucial that the training materials be developed in a customized manner, taking into consideration the organization, the industry, and, most importantly, the type of audience attending the training.

Q: What should be the contents of awareness programs and training programs?

A: Any development program should be targeted to improve behavior, skills, and knowledge. Awareness contents for the targeted improvisation and changes in behavior of the participant should focus on elements such as password usage and management, protection from viruses, web usage, and laptop information assurance practices, whereas training program contents should be based on what skills the trainer wants the audience to learn and apply, such as how to conduct an information assurance audit.

Q: Usually, awareness sessions tend to be so boring; how can I make awareness sessions more fun?

A: It is a common perception that awareness sessions can be uninteresting; thus, there is a need to ensure the training materials are interesting. In addition, the trainer should be someone who is capable of captivating the audience not only with knowledge and materials but also by communicating in a clear and interesting manner. Training materials should be interactive and require participation from the learners. Thus, video, multimedia presentation, role-playing, and case studies are often used to make the training materials more appealing to the audience.

Q: **Rather than just encrypting important files, why don't I encrypt all information on my computer?**

A: Whole drive and whole device encryption is the best approach; however, the processes of encryption and decryption are time consuming and can cause incompatibility with software. Careful testing is necessary to ensure software remains operational and performance is not impacted by the encryption.

Q: **Which is of more importance: network information security or physical and environmental security?**

A: Physical and environmental security is as important as network information security. Physically securing information resources should be an organization's first line of defense in securing its business. If physical security is not properly addressed, all the other information assurance controls would be void. Thousands of dollars can be spent on implementing the most current information assurance technologies on company servers, but if the servers are not physically secured, this may prove to be a costly lesson. Physical and environmental security safeguards organizations against physical damage, physical theft, unauthorized disclosure of information, and other threats.

Q: **Why do I need to practice proper media disposal?**

A: Proper disposal of media is essential to ensure that the security of sensitive information, such as personnel records, financial data, and proposals, is not compromised. It is a false impression that deleting a file or a record deletes it forever. Unfortunately, such deletion does not permanently destroy information. Media should be properly sanitized using multiple erasure techniques before disposal to prevent unauthorized retrieval and use of information. Merely formatting a disk does not protect you.

CHAPTER 15

Information Assurance in System Development and Acquisition

An emerging trend in software engineering is the consideration of the information assurance requirements during system design and development. Integrate secure design into all stages of system development to ensure appropriate protection. As with other aspects of system development, countermeasures are most effective when planned and managed from the initial planning phase up to the disposal phase. This was introduced in Chapter 2 as part of the MSR model.

This chapter provides an overview of how to integrate information assurance requirements into each stage of the system development life cycle (SDLC) to ensure producing a secure system. This chapter also explains the role of information assurance planning in a system development context to ensure that information assurance issues are addressed at the earliest stages of a software project. Although agile, scrum, waterfall, XP, and Kanban differ in detail, the discussion in this chapter also applies in general to application development.

Frequently, software systems projects are designed and implemented by programmers without adequate consideration for information assurance, architectural, and software engineering principles. One view of system development is that software engineers have the imagination to see how something can be created, while other engineers imagine how things might fail. In the middle are programmers who just build things and worry little about either problem. Just make it run. They create software to function and skip the security portion. The secure software development life cycle (SSDLC) is more than programming. For managers, the SSDLC requires establishing mechanisms that direct or restrain the actions of the program stakeholders and to those enumerated in the requirements and specifications. Information assurance and associated security measures must be early binding functions; build these in from the beginning to produce hack-resistant and resilient software.

Internationally recognized software engineer and computer scientist Fred Brooks realized that functionality frequently supplants design. In his classic work, *The Mythical Man Month*, he suggests that only one-sixth of the effort be devoted to coding, while one-third be devoted to planning and design. The remaining half of the effort is focused on the component and system tests.

Benefits of Incorporating Security Considerations

Organizations that develop their own systems benefit when integrating information assurance and security into their development methods. Since adding information assurance at a later stage may introduce disruptions to current operations and incur additional costs, information assurance is managed best if planned at the beginning of system development.

Even though it is advisable to integrate information assurance at the beginning of system development, it also needs to be examined and integrated throughout the life cycle to ensure that information assurance keeps up with changes in the threat/risk environment. Adding new information assurance controls to a system after a security event or incident happens is more expensive. Since it is impossible to anticipate problems that may arise during a system's lifetime, update the system security plan at the end of each phase in the system development and regularly throughout its use. For most organizations, the system security plan should be updated twice as frequently as the period in which you are willing to accept unauthorized changes to the system.

To ensure that information assurance is covered comprehensively and that related issues can be traced and managed, you should document decisions made about information assurance in all phases of system development. This documentation is useful to both technical personnel and auditors. Auditors can use the documentation as evidence that adequate information assurance has been incorporated into the system.

Overview of the System Development Life Cycle

The system development life cycle is the overall process of creating, implementing, and decommissioning information systems through a multistep process from initiation, analysis, design, implementation, and maintenance to disposal. Figure 15-1 is an overview of the system development life cycle, while Table 15-1 summarizes the information assurance activities in each phase of the system development life cycle. Other system development approaches that also apply the phases in Figure 15-1 are process model, model-driven, and component-based.

The five phases of the system development life cycle can be used to develop either a new or an upgraded system or module. Table 15-1 describes activities performed for each respective phase in the system development life cycle.

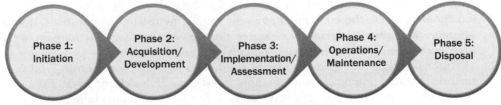

Figure 15-1 Overview of the system development life cycle (SDLC)

Initiation	In this phase, the need for a system is established, and the requirement capabilities of the system are stated.
Acquisition/development	In this phase, a system based on the user's input, time, and financial constraints is purchased, outsourced, or developed. This phase often consists of other defined cycles, such as the system development cycle or the acquisition cycle.
Implementation	This phase involves vigorous initial testing. Once satisfactory results are obtained, the system is installed or integrated.
Operation/maintenance	During this phase, the system is made to perform the intended task and maintained. The system is also modified by adding new hardware and software when needed.
Disposal	This stage occurs when the system fails to cater to new expectations or requirements. Here, the system is disposed of and usually replaced by a new system.

Table 15-1   Activities in a System Development Life Cycle

Information Assurance in the System Development Life Cycle

Integrate information assurance activities into the system development life cycle to ensure proper identification, design, integration, and maintenance of applicable information assurance controls throughout an information system's life cycle. The information assurance team should actively participate in each stage of the life cycle to ensure that information assurance is examined and integrated during system development. Table 15-2 summarizes the activities in all phases of the system development life cycle.

System Development Activities	Security Activities and Definitions
A. Initiation Phase	
Need establishment	• Identify the purpose of and need of having a system. • Conduct interviews to estimate the user requirements and needs. • Document the needs gaps and findings. • Ensure that the information assurance team is involved.
Security categorization	• Determine the categories or classification of the information that will be processed or handled by the system. • Establish the security requirements based on the sensitivity and categorization (classification) of information.

Table 15-2   Secure System Development Life Cycle (SSDLC) in Information Assurance (*continued*)

System Development Activities	Security Activities and Definitions
Initial risk assessment	<ul><li>Conduct initial risk assessment. Refer to Chapter 11 on risk assessment.</li><li>Identify threats and vulnerabilities in which the system or product will operate.</li><li>If required, select the appropriate minimum information assurance control baseline.</li><li>Define and tailor the basic minimal security requirements of the system.</li></ul>
B. Development/Acquisition Phase	
Requirement analysis/ development	<ul><li>Conduct more in-depth study of the security requirements and incorporate them with user requirements.</li><li>Develop security specifications needed for the system.</li><li>Analyze the security functional requirements.</li><li>Analyze assurance requirements.</li></ul>
Risk assessment	<ul><li>Conduct formal risk assessment in greater depth than the initial risk assessment.</li><li>Identify additional system protection requirements.</li><li>Document priority list of which risks to address first.</li></ul>
Budgeting	<ul><li>Determine the budget.</li><li>Include all the costs of hardware, software, personnel, and training. Ensure that information assurance costs are included.</li></ul>
Security planning	<ul><li>Document the final security controls either planned or in place in a system security plan.</li><li>Refine the system security plan. Make sure it is comprehensive enough.</li><li>Develop other supporting documents (for example, contingency plan, incident response plan, risk assessment, awareness, and training plan).</li><li>Develop a user/operational manual for the system.</li></ul>

Table 15-2 Secure System Development Life Cycle (SSDLC) in Information Assurance

System Development Activities	Security Activities and Definitions
Security control development	• Put the plans into practice by implementing security controls as described in the respective security plans.
Security test and evaluation	• Test security controls developed for a new information system or product for proper and effective operation. • Ensure the independence of the assessor (tester) is understood by all parties. • Develop technical test cases.
C. Implementation Phase	
Security test and evaluation	• Develop test data (a copy of some parts of real data can be used). • Try to simulate the environment and test unit, subsystem, and entire system. • Evaluate whether the system conforms to technical aspects and to regulations, policies, guidelines, and standards.
Inspection and acceptance	• Check that the functionality is exactly as specified in the system and can be used to its optimum level.
System integration/installation	• Ensure that after system testing and employee training, the system may be integrated at the operational site. • Make sure the relevant prescribed security control settings are implemented.
Security accreditation	• This process should aim to determine to what level the information processed, stored, or transmitted through the system is free from vulnerabilities and risks. Authorization can be granted by a senior official through verification of the effectiveness of the security controls to some desired level. The senior official is also responsible for accepting residual risk on behalf of the organization.

Table 15-2   Secure System Development Life Cycle (SSDLC) in Information Assurance (*continued*)

Part III

System Development Activities	Security Activities and Definitions
D. Operation/Maintenance Phase	
Configuration management and control	• Refine the configuration management plan and baselines. • Ensure that the potential security impacts because of specific changes to an information system or its surrounding environment are taken into consideration. • Schedule proper audits.
Continuous monitoring and continuous accreditation (authorization)	• Monitor to ensure that security controls continue to be effective and function as expected. • Perform independent security audits or other assessments periodically. Make sure the audits are comprehensive. • Monitor the system and/or users. It can be done by reviewing logs and reports using automated tools. • Ensure residual risk is reported to the senior management team on a regular basis. Risk information should be updated commensurate with the criticality of the system. The most critical systems should have near-real-time reporting available if possible.
E. Disposal Phase	
Information preservation	• Make sure the vital information is retained to conform to current legal requirements (if any) or to accommodate future technological changes. • Determine the archiving method. • Make sure there is written approval from the senior management to destroy information.
Media sanitization	• Delete, erase, and overwrite data as necessary. • It is a good idea to have observers oversee the process.
Hardware and software disposal	• Dispose of hardware and software as directed by the existing policy.

Table 15-2   Secure System Development Life Cycle (SSDLC) in Information Assurance

Information Assurance in the System or Service Acquisition Life Cycle

Integrating information assurance into business processes and development or acquisition life cycles can be a challenging, yet necessary, business function. System developers and system owners are most interested in ensuring their system is up and operational at the lowest cost and the greatest performance. System developers and owners must know about information assurance requirements and the risks of not implementing them as part of their life cycles. Information assurance teams must work hard to integrate information assurance into change management and configuration management processes within their organizations, or they will constantly be playing "catch up!"

System Development

As noted earlier, system development relies on stakeholders to establish requirements for the developers. Information assurance teams must be represented at the table, and they must deliver accurate and concise information assurance requirements for the development process. This is often the most overlooked step in ensuring information assurance is included in the system development process. Information assurance teams should perform the following to ensure they are part of any system development process:

- Gain management buy-in for mandatory involvement of the information assurance team during the requirements gathering phase of system development. The lead information technology professional must require developers to consult and get the information assurance team's sign-off on any new requirements.

- Develop and use standard information assurance enterprise architectures that explain commonly available security services and controls throughout the organization. These baselines can then aid the system development team in understand what existing services and controls can be adopted or inherited into new development processes.

- Information assurance teams must be able to provide solutions. Stating an application cannot be developed because of security concerns is largely seen as obstructionist; development teams may try to circumvent information assurance processes. If the information assurance team is requiring a control, they must be able to offer realistic implementation options or considerations.

System Acquisition

More systems are being procured in the cloud as Software as a Service (SaaS) than ever before. While these solutions provide "turn-key" access to information systems, the organization and senior management must be aware of the limitations and restrictions these providers may entail. The information assurance team is a vital member of the acquisition team. To ensure information assurance risk is uncovered and treated as part of a system acquisition, the information assurance team should do the following:

- Ensure the team is involved in the budget authorization process for all information technology and service acquisitions. If the information assurance function of an organization must "sign off" on budgets that involve information technology, it gives the team leverage to ensure risk is managed as part of the process.

Part III

- Develop standard contract and procurement language with the aid of legal counsel. These contract standards should include information assurance requirements for not only information systems but also personnel and legal jurisdictions. Remember, an organization's information is subject to the legal jurisdictions of all countries in which it is processed, stored, or transmitted.

- Review contract proposals and provide input into the information assurance advantages and deficiencies of providers.

- Participate in negotiations with vendors to ensure information assurance requirements are initially met and are continuously monitored for compliance.

- If needed, assess, audit, or independently verify and validate the provider to ensure it has met the requirements of the contract and the organization.

Change Management

Organizational change management often separates chaotic low-performing organizations for nimble high-performing organizations. Change management is the process of ensuring changes to the organization are communicated to all relevant stakeholders and impacts are understood prior to changes being implemented. Configuration management is a subprocess of change management for information systems and services. Information assurance teams must be involved in change management to ensure changes to organizational systems, people, and processes do not have undesired impacts to the organization. Information assurance teams should do the following:

- Ensure a change management process exists and ensure they are part of the voting process. Information assurance team members often have a "veto" vote for projects that are not fully information assurance compliant. Thus, their vote does not count for anything specifically, but they can demand a change be put on hold or canceled because of associated risks.

- Collaborate with business lines and stakeholders to understand which changes are on the horizon and what direction the organization is headed. Is the organization moving toward more outsourcing? Is a merger or acquisition in the future? Does a mission area want to adopt a new mode of working like telework? Are services or systems out of maintenance because of age or a lack of renewal? These are all questions that can have a substantial information assurance impact if not managed correctly.

- Clearly communicate the risk of a change through a formal assurance impact assessment process. This assessment process should review the change in light of the organization's risk posture and risk tolerance. The information assurance team should ensure clear explanations of impact are reported and the senior management officials involved in the decision are aware of the impact and approve of the residual risk.

Configuration Management

Configuration management is a more specific subset of change management. Configuration management specifically focuses on the information systems and services used by an organization. Configuration management ensures consistent secure baselines are applied to information services and systems. To ensure configuration management does not introduce information assurance risk, the information assurance team should do the following:

- Ensure they are involved in any configuration development or modification processes. This includes the development of new system or services configuration baselines and the updating of baselines already in development.

- Assess and test new configuration baselines and proposed changes to configuration baselines. An information assurance impact assessment can be used to test changes and ensure they are not introducing risk to the information system.

- Monitor patches and vendors to ensure new security and information assurance–related patches are acquired, tested, added to the baseline, and propagated as quickly as possible.

- Scan and monitor the organization's networks and information systems to determine whether all systems are in compliance with the approved configurations. Deviations should be identified and assessed to determine whether the baseline should be updated or a new baseline should be created for the deviation.

Further Reading

- *An Introduction to Computer Security: The NIST Handbook (Special Publication 800-12).* NIST, 1996.

- Bowen, P., et al. *Information Security: A Guide for Managers (Special Publication 800-100).* NIST, 2006.

- Brooks, Frederick P. *The mythical man-month.* Vol. 1995. Addison-Wesley, 1975.

- Howard, M., and S. Lipner. *The Security Development Lifecycle.* Microsoft Press, 2006.

- Schou, Corey D., and K.J. Trimmer. "Information Assurance and Security." *Journal of Organizational and End User Computing,* vol. 16, no. 3, July–September 2004.

- Schou, Corey D., and D.P. Shoemaker. *Information Assurance for the Enterprise: A Roadmap to Information Security.* McGraw-Hill Education, 2007.

- Tipton, Harold F., and S. Hernandez, ed. *Official (ISC)² Guide to the CISSP CBK 3rd edition.* ((ISC)²) Press, 2012.

- Trimmer, K.J., C.D. Schou, and K. Parker. "Enforcing Early Implementation of Information Assurance Precepts Throughout the Design Phase." *Journal of Informatics Education Research,* 2007.

Critical Thinking Exercises

1. A cloud CRM provider verbally promises state-of-the-art security and protection of all organizational information. What can the organization do to ensure the cloud provider is keeping its word? What other concerns should the organization have?

Part III

2. An organization currently allows employees to use their personal devices for organizational work. Because of the openness of this policy, the organization now has almost every modern operating system and every mobile device imaginable operating on its network. Network utilization is extremely high, the help desk is unable to provide effective resolution of support calls because of the variation of platforms, and information assurance incidents are on the rise. What can the organization do to help reign in this environment?

3. An organization wants to develop a new information system that will process and store personally identifiable information and some health-related information about individuals. The organization works primarily in the United Kingdom and the United States. In a general sense, what requirements should an information assurance team be focusing on during the requirements gathering phase?

CHAPTER 16

Physical and Environmental Security Controls

Since information is frequently in electronic form, organizations seldom recognize the importance of physical and environmental security. Some organizations have the misperception that they have adequately safeguarded their environment by simply placing security guards at the main door or using electronic key badges at the entrances. This is a good start; however, with other threats on the rise, physical and environmental security should be treated as important as other information assurance threats. Implementation of physical and environmental security is part of the fundamental capability an organization should establish in any business continuity management (BCM) initiative. Refer to Chapter 24 for further details on BCM.

Physical and environmental security protects an organization's physical infrastructure, its equipment, and its facilities, as well as its employees, from physical events, threats, or incidents. The main threats for physical and environmental security are

- Energy, for example, electricity
- Equipment, for example, mechanical or electronic component failure
- Fire and Chemical, for example, explosion, smoke, or industrial pollution
- Human, for example, riot, war, terrorist attack, or bombing
- Natural Disaster, for example, earthquake, volcano, landslide, or tornado
- Pandemic disease, for example, bacteria or virus
- Radiation, for example, electromagnetic pulse
- Weather, for example, sandstorm, humidity, flood, or lightning

This chapter explains physical and environmental security controls, media handling controls, and benefits of physical security controls.

Benefits

Organizations benefit by establishing physical and environmental security controls/ countermeasures to protect information in storage, transit, and processing. These countermeasures help protect information-processing systems from the following events:

- **Environmental disruption**   Natural disasters and man-made environmental problems are regarded as some of the most prevalent threats today. For example, fire can destroy buildings. Floods can cause damage to infrastructure, assets, and data.

- **Interruptions to service**   Serious business interruption may cause business disaster. If an organization faces services disruptions because of breaches of physical security, the organization's reputation will be at stake. This may lead to loss of public confidence.

- **Loss of system integrity**   If intruders are able to gain physical access to hardware components, they may be able to bypass logical access controls. With this access, they may perform malicious acts on systems and components. These activities can cause loss of information system availability, confidentiality, and integrity.

- **Physical damage**   The acts of sabotage or vandalism can impair hardware components. Damaged media may raise concerns on data confidentiality, integrity, and availability.

- **Physical theft**   In the event of loss of hardware components because of physical theft (or robbery), organizational functions may be interrupted particularly if the organization does not have backup or fails to replace stolen components in a timely manner.

- **Unauthorized disclosure of information**   Insufficient physical security controls may enable intruders to obtain easy access to an organization's information assets. This will place the security of classified information at risk.

Physical and Environmental Security Controls

Precede the implementation of physical and environmental security controls with a risk assessment to identify vulnerabilities and sources of threats that place organizations' operations and individuals' lives and safety at stake. Refer also to Chapter 11 on risk assessment.

Physical and environmental security is best managed using a layered defense approach. The concept of a layered defense approach (also known as defense-in-depth approach) is that if an intruder successfully manages to penetrate one control layer, there will be other control layers in his way before he can access the organization's assets. Note that layered defense should be adopted for all aspects of information assurance, not just physical assets. The layered defense approaches for physical and environmental security are divided into two broad areas:

- Physical security of premises and offices
- Physical security of equipment

Physical Security of Premises and Offices

Premises, which hold critical information or systems, require special protection. The following controls deal with physical security of premises. One establishes the security perimeter as the outer boundary. That perimeter should contain all your critical assets. Within that perimeter, there may also be more secure areas or enclaves.

Physical Security of Premises

The first line of defense in safeguarding employees, information resources, and property is the security perimeter.

Examples of ways to provide physical protection are fences and creating layered physical barriers around the premises and information-processing facilities, including a manned reception area, security guards, or intrusion alarm systems. Perimeter protection also includes deploying lockable doors and windows, grills for windows, and fire escapes. The impact or value of the assets and the results of a targeted risk assessment are the factors that determine the placement and strength of each physical security perimeter location and related controls.

Physical Entry Controls   Physical entry controls restrict access to information-processing resources by allowing only authorized individuals in the area. They control the entry and exit of employees, equipment, and media from an area, such as an office building, data center, and areas that contain critical information-processing resources.

Minimal physical entry controls should include the positive identification of all employees, vendors, and visitors at each point of entry. Unauthorized individuals in the facility should be easily identifiable. It should be difficult to confuse them with employees, vendors, and authorized visitors. People who are unable to show proof of identity and area authorization are a physical security risk. They should not be allowed to remain in secured spaces.

The following provides further explanation about access controls for employees and visitors:

- **Employee access**   Restriction of employee access depends on the need for access, job function, and responsibilities. Positive identification and access control are mandatory; therefore, all employees should be required to wear some form of visible identification (ID badge) at all times whenever they are on the premises. Since the badge may disclose the employee's identity, role, employer, and access levels of the individual, employees should not display the badge when offsite.

  Employees who work in a restricted area are important participants in physical security. If they notice either strangers or long-time employees behaving suspiciously in the area, they should stop and challenge them or immediately report their presence to their supervisor or security personnel.

- **Visitor access**   Visitors include vendors, consultants, maintenance personnel, contractors, and other nonemployees. Permit visitor access only to those areas where they have specific and official purposes. A record of visitors who enter the premises should be maintained. Before a visitor can access a restricted area, the visitor should be required to present appropriate credentials and register at a reception area or security guard station. In most cases, they should also be escorted at all times and informed of the physical security requirements of the area and emergency procedures. The dates and times of their admissions and departures should be logged. This recording may be accomplished with a card access control system, a sign-in log, or other mechanisms.

Organizations must periodically assess the effectiveness of physical entry controls in each area to determine whether improvements should be made. Assess the controls' effectiveness during both normal office hours and when an area is unoccupied. Several factors affect the effectiveness of physical entry controls. These factors include the type of control devices used, the implementation, and the operational use. Organizations should determine the effectiveness of the control procedures and whether intruders can bypass the controls in place. Physical penetration tests are often used to test the resiliency of human, technology, and procedural controls. Based on these assessments, enhance the physical entry controls.

Securing Offices, Rooms, and Facilities   Secure areas are frequently called *enclaves*. Organizations must select the location of the enclaves within the security perimeter carefully. Locked offices or rooms located inside the perimeter may be considered as enclaves. For example, network and communications equipment rooms or human resources offices are enclaves that may require additional controls.

Different risks such as natural or man-made disasters should also be considered in the planning process. When man-made events occur, access to the restricted areas may be compromised during a panic. In some circumstances, the secure area should not be publicized in any manner. Boards, banners, or signs indicating the presence of important facilities or activities should be concealed.

By policy, organizational telephone directories are for internal use only; exceptions can be made for specific purposes. Disclosure of the directory may attract unnecessary attention or expose confidential information about the organizational structure. This is an ideal tool for social engineers to begin their reconnaissance.

To control exfiltration of data on paper, organizations should ensure that equipment such as photocopier machines, printers, scanners, and fax machines are located within secure areas or configured to work only when a password or token is used.

Physical security is an ideal tool for compartmenting information; consider using badge readers or cipher locks that require a unique code, key, and/or badge for entry. This helps ensure that only authorized individuals can gain access, and in the event an incident occurs, these technologies provide logs that can help locate the attacker. By combining a badge with a key code, the organization has a two-factor physical access system.

Working in Secure Areas   The physical security should accommodate third parties working in the area. A secure work area may include closed circuit television (CCTV) and card-controlled doors. The personnel working in this area should have adequate training about device operation, as well as awareness of the importance of the physical security controls. Carefully screen personnel working in the secure work areas prior to employment or engagement to ensure the employees and third parties are honest, competent, and aware of their responsibilities. The use of any photographic, audio, video, mobile devices, or other recording equipment in secure areas should be restricted. Exceptions may be authorized based on a demonstrated need and a risk review.

Public Access Delivery and Loading Areas   Frequently, there is continuous movement of incoming and outgoing items at several portals on premises. For example, it is important that access to areas such as entry, delivery, and loading areas is limited to authorized individuals. If possible, separate these entrance and exit areas from secure areas to minimize threats.

Establish appropriate physical and inventory controls to ensure that all items are loaded and unloaded at the loading areas only. Prohibit access to other parts of the premises, and before incoming items are allowed within the premises, they should be registered or inventoried and examined for potential threats.

Duress   In high-risk environments, organizations should establish a duress alarm or code that gives a covert alert about a increased risk situations. A person can use it secretly to indicate that a serious information or physical security event has occurred or is in progress. For example, a physical security alarm causes the security operations center to call a guard station. The operations personnel asks the guard if everything is okay. The guard responds, "Everything is fine; the zebra system is down again." The operation center immediately dispatches law enforcement to the guard's location. What happened? The term "zebra system is down" is a predesignated signal to indicate the guard was under duress. Perhaps someone was threatening the guard and telling him he must tell the operations center "everything is fine" while thieves attempted to rob the organization. To be effective, duress codes must be maintained confidentially within the organization, and their implementation must be practiced by those who routinely use them. A duress alarm response procedure should be in place to ensure that every alarm is handled properly and immediately.

Physical Security of Equipment

Organizations should physically protect information-processing equipment to minimize the risk of unauthorized access to information, as well as to safeguard against loss or damage. For example, if someone has physical access to your network equipment, it is easier for them to modify the security profile of the equipment than by trying to do it electronically from offsite. Offsite computing systems for reconstitution or contingency operations should also be addressed in a physical security plan. This is particularly important with cold sites that may be overlooked until they are needed. The following section explains controls that deal with equipment issues concerning physical security.

Equipment Placement and Protection   Organizations should secure equipment from environmental threats, hazards, and opportunities for unauthorized access. Organizational assets face destruction from exposure to fire, smoke, water, and other hazards, so information and information processing resources should be protected with a diverse set of countermeasures:

- **Fire**   Information processing equipment may be damaged in fires. Installing fire sensors, heat sensors, smoke sensors, fire extinguishers, or sprinkler systems can reduce risks from fire hazards.

  Fire alarms should have the feature of both manual and automatic operation, since a person may notice a fire before an automatic smoke alarm. Automatic sensors should be able to detect both visible smoke and ionized particles. Deploy fire sensors and firefighting systems not only in the room but also in the plenum spaces both above and below the room.

Fire extinguishers should be located in visible locations and near fire exits. They should be easily accessible and readily available at all times for immediate use. To assure optimal operation, inspect and certify the extinguishers periodically; for example, a certified professional or the fire department should do this at least twice a year. It is essential to provide adequate training and appropriate instructions to the employees regarding the use of these devices.

- **Sprinklers**   Water-based sprinklers should be dry pipe systems that do not have water in normal conditions. In the equipment rooms, avoid water. There are fire-fighting systems that use special gasses to stop fires. They work by displacing the oxygen in the room. However, the gasses may be dangerous to personnel, and special training is necessary. The systems should sound an alarm for the fire, as well as alert personnel to leave the area before the fire-fighting material is deployed.

> ## Life and Safety
>
> - Life and safety should be the ultimate consideration in any physical security control effort or implementation.
> - For example, barring a door to prevent unauthorized physical intrusion may prevent individuals from being able to escape for safety in the event of a fire.

Consider using an automated emergency notification system that alerts the police and fire departments of an emergency automatically. Not only can this save lives, but also valuable equipment and facilities may be spared if emergency responders arrive quickly. Notification systems should be tested regularly, and agreements should be worked out with the fire and emergency responders so they understand where people have been instructed to shelter and who they need to meet with in case they need access to restricted locations.

- **Smoke**   Smoke is hazardous to both personnel and equipment. Smoke may originate from malfunctioning computer systems or electrical fires, such as those caused by power transformers. Video monitors and electronics release an acrid smoke that may be fatal to humans and impair other equipment. Install smoke detectors both inside computer rooms and directly outside; ensure the smoke detectors work in the plenum areas above and below the room. As noted earlier, there are two types of smoke detectors: photoelectric (visible smoke) and ionization (invisible particulate byproducts) detectors. Smoke alarms use one or both methods. In addition, some use a heat detector to warn of a fire. These alarms provide people with critical seconds to escape a burning building by sounding an alarm in the presence of smoke or fire. Another significant danger is smoke that comes from cigarettes. Forbid employees from smoking in computer rooms. Not only can the smoke damage sensitive equipment, but it may also cause a false alarm and set off fire suppression systems.

- **Water**   Water can damage power supply facilities and information-processing equipment. It may render these devices unserviceable through short-circuits or mechanical damage. There are two types of sprinkler systems: wet and dry. In wet systems, the pipes are always charged with water, while dry systems fill with water only if there is evidence of a fire. A "wet" pipe sprinkler system may cause damage by simple leakage or breakage from natural disasters.

Disruption of water supply and sewage systems could also contribute to an uncontrolled flow of water. Natural disasters such as rain or floods may also allow uncontrolled flow of water into facilities.

To mitigate water damage, do not install systems in basements that are prone to flooding. Install water sensors on the floor or under a raised floor near computer equipment. They should be set up so in the event of a flood, they sound an alarm and cut off power automatically.

Supporting Utilities   Organizations require supporting utilities such as electric power, heating and air conditioning, and telecommunications equipment, which if disrupted lead to a loss of availability.

- **Electric power**   Information processing systems fail without a continuous supply of stable power. Thus, they require redundancy in electric power system availability. If electrical power to the building in which information systems are hosted gets cut off, a backup device needs to be ready to take over and keep those systems powered. This can be accomplished using three approaches and combinations thereof: dual main power, a uninterruptible power supply (UPS), or a backup generator.

  The least expensive first line of defense is to have the facility connected to two separate sources of power from the grid. Ideally, the feeds would be able to operate the entire facility even if one failed. Minimally, they should come from two separate branches of the power grid and, if possible, they should come from two separate providers on different power supply grids.

- **Backup generators**   If a system's requirements demand uninterrupted processing in the event of a prolonged outage, a backup generator should be considered. Backup generators should be tested on a regular basis in accordance with the manufacturer's specifications. This will ensure that they will function successfully during an outage. To ensure that generators can sustain operation over a prolonged period, make sure that generators have sufficient supply of fuel. Organizations enter into fuel supply contracts with local fuel wholesalers; however, during an emergency or outage, fuel suppliers are often restricted by a prioritization of customers to deliver whatever fuel they may have. Make sure your contract provides you with priority service. Remember, generators often require fuel tanks that are subject to inspection for safety and environmental regulations.

- **UPS**   A UPS can be used to support critical business operations. It is designed to protect against a short power outage, and it provides enough time for system administrators to shut down systems and equipment in a systematic manner. Contingency plans should include the action to be taken upon failure of the UPS. All UPS equipment should undergo regular maintenance to ensure it is in good operational condition at all times. Batteries have a finite life and cycle count that must be managed.

- **Heating, ventilation, and air conditioning (HVAC)** Computer systems that manage critical information should have air-conditioning units that provide continuous monitoring and recording of temperature and humidity. To avoid computer damage because of temperature fluctuations, maintain all computer equipment in a designated computer room. After determining the temperature and humidity ranges tolerated by the equipment, maintain that temperature and humidity. Humidity must be managed to minimize static electricity from low humidity and equipment damage from condensation from high humidity. Install heat sensors inside the computers, in the computer rooms, and directly outside the rooms to warn of any noticeable rise in temperature, through either an audible or a visible alarm. When designing HVAC systems, it is important to remember they will need power during an outage or emergency. Therefore, the electrical capacity of generators or UPS must consider not only the computer equipment but also the associated HVAC equipment.

Organizations should build all systems with redundancy to provide a resilient information infrastructure. Planning for low-impact systems is typically *N-1*. This means a system should see no impact for failure of one substantive asset where failure is credible. This planning is part of long-term growth plan. It is a deterministic approach. *N-1* criteria cover most creditable asset failures. It depends on the ability to install temporary fixes for damaged assets. Operational processes and practices should be used for restoring the electrical grid on a "business as usual" basis. Critical systems or those that have a history of tight supply should be designed to meet "N-2 plus" requirements. This system would still be able to operate if a major asset failed. Organizations must be careful not to outgrow planning; this requires that the physical security plans and contingency plans be tested and reevaluated often. Compliancy is the enemy of successfully surviving an outage or emergency.

Equipment Maintenance Organizations should perform maintenance of information-processing equipment based on the manufacturer's recommended service intervals and specifications. The task of fixing and servicing the equipment should be done only by authorized personnel. Record all faults noticed, documented, and maintained. All maintenance services to the equipment either onsite or sent off the premises also need to be recorded and tracked. Consider statistical process control (SPC) techniques to forecast failures. For example, track the failure rate of disk drives. Based on the analysis, it is sometimes less expensive to perform prospective maintenance by replacing all drives at one time.

Physical Security of Equipment Off-Premises Information-processing equipment policies must include personal computers and laptops used for working in an office or home. The organization should apply appropriate information assurance controls to secure equipment off-premises. Use of any equipment outside an organization's premises should be authorized by management. Prior to granting authorizations, management should carefully consider the risks of working outside the organization. Users should also be educated about the approved methods of handling equipment off-premises, for example, using procedures to respond to locking down, damage, loss, and theft of equipment.

Do not allow personnel to use personal software or data on organization-owned equipment except as provided in BYOD and BYOS policies. All data on the computer should be encrypted and protected to the same level as if it were on an internal system. No encryption should be allowed unless the key is held or escrowed by the organization. No company information should be stored on the system if it is not also backed up internally. The loss of the system should not compromise operations.

Remind employees they are bound by the same rules when using portable, BYOD, BYOS, and off-premises systems as they are when at their desk in the office. Employees forget that portable systems are not theirs and sometimes adopt undesirable habits. Explicitly prohibit the following activities on organization-owned systems, even if off-premises:

- Becoming involved in partisan politics
- Causing alteration, congestion, disablement, disruption, or impairment of organization networks or systems
- Defeating or attempting to defeat security restrictions on company systems and applications
- Engaging in malicious activities
- Engaging in personal business
- Engaging in private activities
- Engaging in unlawful activities
- Misrepresenting oneself
- Misrepresenting the company
- Sending, receiving, distributing, or accessing pornographic materials
- Using abusive, profane, threatening, racist, sexist, or otherwise objectionable language in either public or private messages
- Using recreational games

Secure Disposal and Reuse of Equipment

Careless disposal, disposition, or recycling of equipment can put information at risk. Storage devices have long-term memory, so simple or mere file deletion is insufficient. Destroy them! Recovering overwritten data on hard drives, removable disks, and tapes is not impossible. There are software tools that can be downloaded freely from the Internet that may recover the data easily. Proper protection and disposal of sensitive or confidential information is important. This is the dissolution of the system.

Properly sanitized, obsolete equipment may be donated to charities or for environmental reasons, disposed of by third parties. Take proper precautions to ensure that all information stored in the equipment is eradicated prior to donation or disposal. Prior to disposal, a thorough check should be made to verify that any sensitive information and licensed software are completely erased or overwritten. It is advisable that equipment with hard disks containing sensitive information should not be passed on. If the data is valuable, it is less expensive to buy a new drive for any machine you donate.

Part III

Equipment sent for repair is equally prone to unauthorized reading of data from *deleted* storage devices. Therefore, the device should undergo thorough erasing and overwriting to wipe out the data instead of via the standard delete function. If this is not practical, ship it for repair without the disk drive.

Clear Desk and Clear Screen Policy

On another physical security front, the implementation of a clear desk and clear screen policy is an effective control for organization information assets. Not only information-processing resources, but also printed papers or media containing confidential information will be protected. When developing the policy, the organization should consider such matters as information assurance classifications and the organization's risk assessment results.

Apply the following guidelines:

- Lock away classified material when not in the area.
- Do not leave classified information on unattended printers.
- Log off sessions or protect the system with a key lock whenever personal computers or computer terminals are left unattended; use passwords and protected screensavers to provide protection.
- Secure incoming and outgoing mail boxes and unattended fax machines to avoid unauthorized access.
- Use a suitable storage place (ideally in a cabinet or fire-resistant safe) when paper or electronic storage media that holds sensitive information is not needed.

Handling of Media

Protect all media used to store information. In addition to data storage media, remember other devices that create processes or transmit the information may also store information. Apply a method appropriate to the sensitivity and value of the information to safeguard it from the time of creation to the time of disposal and dissolution of the system.

Employ suitable procedures to protect all media from physical damage, theft, loss, unauthorized access, or other attacks. To preserve the confidentiality of information stored in media, exercise methods to remove the data completely prior to discarding media or any other devices. The following sections discuss the physical security controls to protect media.

Management of Removable Media

Removable media is the most common form of storage devices today. A few examples of commonly used removable media are USB flash drives, memory cards, mobile phones, digital cameras, and MP3 players. Since these devices are cheap, they are the obvious way to store information such as business proposals, accounts, clients' details, and marketing plans.

Current popular media, such as iPods, USB flash drives, mobile phones with a removable SD cards, and even digital cameras with flash memory, can be used to transport confidential information away from an organization's network (exfiltration). Another potential danger of portable media storage devices is that they can completely bypass perimeter defenses such as firewalls and antivirus software on a mail server and introduce malicious software such as Trojan horse or viruses onto organizations' networks. In late 2008 and early 2009, these attacks became more effective.

Organizations should ensure that the correct physical and information assurance controls are implemented to manage the use of removable media devices securely. This will aid in minimizing damage from malicious code and loss of proprietary information or intellectual property and consequently avoid lawsuits and loss of reputation.

Inform employees about policies about removable media. With policies and procedures in place, restrictions or prohibition of removable media usage from critical activities can be enforced. As mentioned earlier, encryption and key escrow for authorized copying of corporate information to removable media are mandatory. Aligning this policy and procedure with other corporate policies and procedures will assist in enforcing controls.

Disposal of Media

Disposal of media means the same procedures as mentioned in the section "Secure Disposal and Reuse of Equipment" earlier in the chapter. To guard against exposing and damaging an organization's image and reputation, the organization should practice proper methods for disposing of media. Management should establish procedures for disposing of and destroying media containing sensitive information. These procedures should be risk-based relative to the sensitivity of information and the types of media used to store it. Disposal procedures should acknowledge that records kept on media such as tapes and disk drives could cause disposal problems because residual data can remain on the media even after erasure. Since such data can be retrieved, additional disposal techniques should be applied to remove sensitive information entirely.

The following are some guidelines of proper media disposal:

- Electronic media containing sensitive customer information should be degaussed prior to disposal. *Degaussing* completely erases the information stored on the magnetic surface.

- Printed materials, which hold confidential and restricted data, should be destroyed in a secure way, such as by shredding or burning.

Further Reading

- Bowen, P., et al. *Information Security: A Guide for Managers (Special Publication 800-100).* NIST, 2006.

- International Organization Standardization and the International Electrotechnical Commission. Information Technology – Security Techniques – Information Security Management Systems – Requirements (ISO/IEC 27001). ISO/IEC, 2005.

- NSTISSI-4011, National Training Standard for Information Systems Security (INFOSEC) Professionals, CNSS, 2004. https://www.cnss.gov/CNSS/issuances/Instructions.cfm.

- Nichols, R., D. Ryan, and J. Ryan. *Defending Your Digital Assets Against Hackers, Crackers, Spies, and Thieves.* McGraw-Hill Education, 2000.

- Physical and Environmental Security Guideline. Information Technology at Emory University, Atlanta. http://it.emory.edu/showdoc.cfm?docid=1860.

- Ross, R., et al. *Guide for Assessing the Security Controls in Federal Information Systems, (Special Publication 800-53 Rev 1)*. NIST, 2008.

- Schou, Corey D., and D.P. Shoemaker. *Information Assurance for the Enterprise: A Roadmap to Information Security*. McGraw-Hill Education, 2007.

- Tipton, Harold F., and M. Krause. Information Security Management Handbook, 5th edition. Auerbach, United States, 2006.

- Tipton, Harold F., and S. Hernandez, ed. *Official (ISC)² Guide to the CISSP CBK 3rd edition*. ((ISC)²) Press, 2012.

Critical Thinking Exercises

1. An organization is renting office space and has noticed several new building maintenance personnel requesting access above and below the organization's server room. An employee thinks she saw one of them plugging a cable into a "box" in the server room when she was in the room trying to get a system to restart. What should the organization do?

2. An organization has just finished implementing its contingency plan. It has a large data center and has installed several generators, fuel tanks, two power supplies from MEGA Power Company, and UPS devices. After installing the new UPS devices, the organization also noted it needed to update its chillers because the UPS systems were generating more heat than the chillers could cool. Once the chillers were finished being installed, the senior leadership of the organization announced they were prepared for the worst! Are they correct?

Information Assurance Awareness, Training, and Education (AT&E)

Organizations invest millions to secure their systems as new threats and information risks emerge. Most fail to realize a common "weakest link" in securing systems and networks is the human, especially an organization's employees. Frequently, employees do not understand their role in the information assurance plan. They do not see the big picture described in Chapter 2. They see only parts and do not see how they fit into cybersecurity, information protection, information security, and finally information assurance. This lack

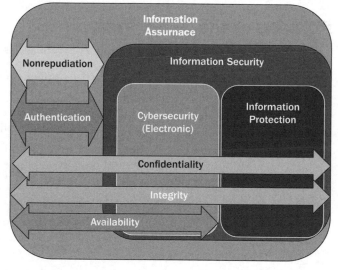

of awareness means employees do not effectively apply appropriate countermeasures from the MSR model. Some examples of information assurance risks attributed to employees include the following:

- Using weak passwords
- Downloading malware
- Using of out-of-date antivirus signatures and software
- Being unaware of becoming targets of social engineering attacks

However, with a proper information assurance AT&E development program, users become the organization's strongest information assurance asset. Users are the front line of any organization. They handle information and have access to sensitive systems, and often they are "just trying to do the right thing." An enterprise-wide AT&E program is essential to ensure employees are equipped to handle modern threats and those who would take advantage of their willingness to help!

The AT&E program ensures that employees understand personal responsibility and organizational policies. It allows them to better use and protect information system resources entrusted to them. This chapter discusses various types of AT&E programs and makes suggestions about program implementation.

An effective AT&E program has four stages: literacy, awareness, training, and education (LATE). Not all employees will progress through the entire program to education nor is progression of all employees to education necessary for effectiveness. However, the AT&E program will not succeed if literacy is not established. Employees must have a common vocabulary to be able to communicate about information assurance.

Purpose of the AT&E Program

The purposes of information assurance AT&E are as follows:

- To circulate and ensure effective implementation of the organization's information assurance policies, procedures, and guidelines

- To cultivate a strong information assurance culture by making employees aware of their responsibilities with regard to information assurance

- To emphasize the fact that the organization is taking information assurance seriously and therefore will train its employees about the importance of protecting the organization's information assets

- To encourage employees to seek additional education about information assurance

- To encourage employees to be more information assurance–conscious in their daily tasks, for example, by considering information assurance risks when making business decisions

- To highlight management's support for and commitment to information assurance

- To inform employees about information assurance risks and controls in a general sense and provide more specific information and guidance where necessary

Employees should understand how their actions affect the overall information assurance posture of the organization. They must understand not only how to protect the organization's information but also why this protection is important. Making them aware of their information assurance responsibilities and training them about proper practices makes it easier for them to understand the impact they have and do the right things in risky situations.

Benefits of the AT&E Program

 The following are the benefits introduced by awareness, training, and education programs:

- An AT&E program raises an organization's reputation and brand. An organization's reputation and brand are enhanced if their customers perceive the organization as an entity that protects the availability, integrity, sensitivity, and confidentiality of their customers' data.

- An AT&E program minimizes the severity and number of information assurance incidents. Early detection of information assurance incidents reduces impacts to an organization. This reduction decreases direct costs such as data recovery and customer notification. A significant reduction in crucial indirect costs such as loss of reputation, customers, and productivity is an additional benefit.

- An AT&E program provides better protection for assets. An organization's information and information assets can be better protected by training employees to recognize and respond proactively to real or potential information assurance concerns.

- An AT&E program reduces the risk of lawsuits against the organization. Organizations should exhibit a genuine corporate concern for information assurance. They should implement processes to ensure its workforce will provide adequate protection for information assets.

Design, Development, and Assessment of Programs

Organizations may kick off information assurance initiatives with literacy exercises followed by both awareness and training programs. To ensure that an information assurance plan is introduced effectively, it needs to be designed and customized to the needs of the organization. One size does not fit all.

Before organizations embark on any information security awareness or training programs, take steps to ensure proper information assurance processes and information assurance roles and responsibilities have been established. This ensures that questions such as "Who should I contact?" and "What reporting process do I need to use?" as well as issues raised by the employees during the programs are answered and discussed. This will reveal that the organization is ready and committed to pursue the information assurance initiatives with the employees' support.

A well-designed AT&E program begins with a needs analysis. This analysis indicates the literacy level of the audience on the subject and allows needs-based prioritization. Organizations should develop an AT&E strategy based on the results of this assessment. They should focus the strategy on developing, implementing, and maintaining information assurance AT&E programs. Reflect the strategy in the plan, which is a working document containing the strategic elements and how they relate to the overall information assurance strategy.

Develop awareness and training materials to support the plan in the next phase. Security awareness and training materials are widely available on the Web and can be customized to any particular organization's culture and strategic needs. It is always a good idea to look for feedback once an awareness or training program has been conducted because it will help improve future endeavors on training and awareness. Survey forms, evaluation forms, and independent observations can always be used as input.

Types of Learning Programs

The types of programs usually consist of awareness, training, and education. These are explained in the following subsections. There is also a subtle difference between *training* and *education*. The former emphasizes more on skill development especially in using the information system. The latter is more general in the sense that it imparts general knowledge, preparing the audience for a more mature life in managing security of information.

Information Assurance Awareness

After you have established the literacy level of your employees, awareness programs explain to employees their roles in the areas of information assurance. The objective is to provide insight to employees on how they play an important part in the protection of confidentiality, integrity, availability, nonrepudiation, and authentication of the organization's information assets. Awareness programs serve to motivate a sense of responsibility and encourage employees to be more cautious about their work environment. Because people tend to forget, awareness also reminds people of basic information assurance practices, such as changing passwords at predetermined intervals.

Most organizations focus their awareness efforts on the information security subdomain of information assurance. This targeted approach means all employees will be exposed to how their behavior and role intersect with the confidentiality, integrity, and availability of an organization's data and services. Organizations should then focus training on the additional responsibilities associated with nonrepudiation and authentication based on their role in the organization.

Implementing a successful information assurance awareness program is often a difficult but rewarding task. The following guidelines can help organizations develop an effective information assurance awareness program:

- **Obtain management commitment**   Management's commitment should be clearly stated in the information assurance policy. As with all information assurance initiatives, an awareness program will never reach its goals without strong management support. Unless the organization's management team is on board, leading and creating awareness for any organization's awareness program is going to be useless. Funding, employee attendance at awareness sessions and employee perception of the importance of information assurance all depend on support at all layers of management.

  Organizations should write the policy in a comprehensive but concise manner. Policies are scoped for numerous years and therefore should convey senior leadership's high-level commitment to information assurance. Once the policy is produced, employees should be made aware of the policy's contents and existence. Formal information assurance policies, no matter how carefully they are written, are less valuable unless employees know about them, understand their responsibility within the context of the policy, and comply with them.

- **Appoint personnel to lead the planning process**   Organizations should assemble a team or taskforce to begin the process of planning an awareness program. Dedicate at least one accountable individual to lead information security awareness training across the organization. The task force helps create and approve training materials and determines suitable delivery methods.

- **Ensure establishment of an information assurance program and associated policy**   An information assurance policy is the basis of an effective information assurance program. Organizations in consultation with their information assurance team should begin with documenting all of the high-level goals, requirements, and objectives of the information assurance program in an information assurance policy prior to developing an information security awareness program.

- **Get their attention**   To ensure that the awareness initiatives reach everyone in the organization, introducing information assurance as a fun and interesting topic is the most practical approach. In general, people are afraid of information assurance, while others may find it a boring subject. To garner the employees' attention, the awareness program should be proactive, fresh, and current. Messages need to be made in a variety of ways to accommodate the audience, for example, through presentations and posters. To be influential, awareness presentations should have credible trainers or speakers. They should use creative ways to deliver the message. In addition, the content of the programs should be compelling. Without a high degree of credibility, the integrity and clarity of the message will be lost, and the whole communication process will be a waste of resources.

- **Make it applicable to the employee**   As more information is being stored online and more people are using online services for banking, health, travel, and personal matters, people are interested in protecting themselves online. The organization's awareness program is an opportunity to help employees learn how to protect their private lives in addition to the organization's information.

- **Measure the effectiveness**   The effectiveness of an awareness program and its ability to improve information assurance can be measured. The need for information security awareness is broadly recognized, but not many organizations have tried to quantify the value of awareness programs. Evaluation of an awareness program is essential to understand its effectiveness, as well as to use the data gathered as a reference to fine-tune the initiatives to make it even more successful.

- **Test the awareness level**   An awareness program is an agent to create change. Its purpose is not just to convey information but also to change behavior. It should change behavior by persuading employees to take action toward the organization's objectives. To determine whether an organization has successfully promoted an information assurance–conscious culture within the organization, questions can be asked about whether any information security breaches have happened and employees understand how to report the breaches.

To acquire and maintain management support, the effectiveness of the program should be measured. Improvement activities should be based on these measurements and the results forwarded to upper management. Additionally, organizations may use friendly competition between constituent parts to spur on higher completion rates and lower rates of incidents.

Stimulation	Focus	Attention	Decisions
Security-only colors	Change locks	Bulletin boards	Read security regulations
Security-only music theme	Reminders	Flyers	Read magazines
Assimilation			
Key ring with message Short seminars		Short demonstrations Video tape programs	

Table 17-1 Awareness Characteristics

Recall that awareness is at the lowest level of the AT&E solution to information assurance. It is designed to affect short-term memory. It is composed of stimulation, focus, attention, decision, and assimilation. A successful AT&E program will begin by meeting the five requirements listed in Table 17-1.

In addition to training, literacy is also important. Information assurance literacy places fundamental working knowledge of information assurance into the minds and into the actions of a workforce. This working knowledge should involve both definitions and distinctions; Table 17-2 shows some examples of literacy.

A literate employee will be able to define appropriate terms, and if well-trained, the employee should be able to make distinctions among the terms.

Information Assurance Training

The distinction between training and awareness is that training aims to teach or improve an individual's skill, knowledge, or attitude, which allows a person to carry out a specific function, while awareness aims to focus an individual's attention on an issue or a set of issues.

There is a gray zone between awareness and training. A distinction between them is that in awareness activities the learner is a passive recipient of information, while in the training environment the learner has a more active role in the learning process (see Table 17-3). In other words, awareness explains "what" needs to be done and training explains "how" it should be done. A primary role of awareness programs is to motivate employees/learners to move into a training mode and actively seek more knowledge. A fundamental goal of training programs is to motivate learners to move knowledge and skills from short-term memory to long-term memory. Often, knowledge and skills become chained sequences of behavior that require little higher-level mental processing.

The objective of any information assurance training is to equip personnel with skills that facilitate their security-related job performance. This includes teaching people what is

Definitions	Distinctions
Virus, Trojan horse, worm	Authentication versus passwords
Insider threat	Certification versus accreditation

Table 17-2 Examples of Literacy

Active Knowledge Seeker	Long-Term Memory
Self-paced course On-the-job training (OJT) Conferences	Computer-based instruction Multisession seminar

Table 17-3   Training Characteristics

required and the methods and procedures required to do their work. Information assurance training can be categorized from basic information assurance practices to more advanced certification-based programs. It is flexible since it caters either to a unique computer system or to more generic systems. Through training, the organization is on track to produce relevant and required information assurance skills with its related competencies. Refer to Chapter 5 for various certification programs for information assurance professionals. Certification programs are often targeted at the training and experience of an individual.

Information Assurance Education

The distinction between training and education can be made by examining the intent and scope of the instruction. In a training environment, the employee is taught to use specific skills as part of specific job performance. In an education context, the employee would be encouraged to examine and evaluate not only skills and methods of work but fundamental operating principles and tenants upon which job skills are based. The employee is using internalized concepts and skills to perform operations such as analyzing, evaluating, and judging to reach higher cognitive-level decisions that lead to the accommodation of newly integrated knowledge and skill (see Table 17-4). Accommodation is an end process in which the learner makes a conscious decision to modify existing ways of thinking and responding to satisfy new experiences and knowledge.

Through information assurance education, professionals are better able to integrate their information assurance skills and competencies into daily practices. A formal education program allows for acquisition of knowledge, skills, and proper understanding of their role at the holistic level. This will cultivate development of right behaviors, values, and wisdom. People who are in charge of information assurance of the organization should be encouraged to pursue higher education relevant to their job scope. Globalized usage of IT will establish their credibility and give them a fair idea of where they stand at an international level. They can also validate their education by seeking external independent certifications as discussed in Chapter 5.

Internalization	Accommodation
Point papers	Long-term training
Study groups	Research and briefings

Table 17-4   Education Characteristics

Further Reading

- *ACM Computing Curricula Information Technology Volume: Model Curriculum.* ACM, Dec. 12, 2008. http://campus.acm.org/public/comments/it-curriculum-draft-may-2008 .pdf.

- *An Introduction to Computer Security: The NIST Handbook (Special Publication 800-100).* NIST, p. 16.

- CNSSI-4012, National Information Assurance Training Standard for Senior Systems Managers. June 2004. Supersedes NSTISSI No. 4012, August 1997.

- CNSSI-4013, National Information Assurance Training Standard for System Administrators (SA). March 2004.

- CNSSI-4014, Information Assurance Training Standard for Information Systems Security Officers. April 2004. Supersedes NSTISSI No. 4014, August 1997.

- CNSSI-4016, National Information Assurance Training Standard For Risk Analysts. November 2005.

- National Institute of Standards and Technology. *Special Publication 800-16, A Role-Based Model for Federal Information Technology/Cyber Security Training.* NIST. http://csrc.nist .gov/publications/drafts/800-16-rev1/draft_sp800_16_rev1_2nd-draft.pdf.

- NIATEC training materials web site. http://niatec.info/pdf.aspx?id=169.

- NSTISSI-1000, National Information Assurance Certification and Accreditation Process. CNSS, 2004. www.cnss.gov/Assets/pdf/nstissi_1000.pdf.

- NSTISSI-4011 National Training Standard for Information Systems Security (INFOSEC) Professionals. CNSS, June 1994.

- NSTISSI-4015, National Training Standard for Systems Certifiers. November 2000.

- Rusell, C. "Security Awareness – Implementing an Effective Strategy." SANS Institute, 2002. www.sansorg/reading_room/whitepapers/awareness/416.php.

- Ryan, D., J.C.H. Julie, and C.D. Schou. "On Security Education, Training, and Certifications." Information Systems Audit and Control Association, 2004.

- Schou, Corey D., et al. "Defining Information Security Education, Training, and Awareness Needs Using Electronic Meeting Space. In *Enabling Technologies for Law Enforcement and Security* (pp. 356–367). International Society for Optics and Photonics, January 1999.

- Schou, Corey D., and K.J. Trimmer. "Information Assurance and Security," *Journal of Organizational and End User Computing,* vol. 16, no. 3, July/September 2004.

- Schou, Corey D., W.V. Maconacy, and J. Frost. *Developing Awareness, Training and Education: A Cost Effective Tool for Maintaining System Integrity.* SEC 1993:53–63.

- Schou, Corey D., and D.P. Shoemaker. *Information Assurance for the Enterprise: A Roadmap to Information Security.* McGraw-Hill Education, 2008.

- Tipton, Harold F., and S. Hernandez, ed. *Official (ISC)² Guide to the CISSP CBK 3rd edition.* ((ISC)²) Press, 2012.
- User's Guide: How to Raise Information Security Awareness. European Network and Information Security Agency, Dec. 1, 2006. www.enisa.europa.eu/doc/pdf/deliverables/enisa_a_users_guide_how_to_raise_IS_awareness.pdf.

Critical Thinking Exercises

1. An organization wishes to instill a culture of information assurance throughout its operations. What is the best AT&E level to focus on for all employees?

2. An organization has spent significant resources on several tools and technologies designed to prevent spear phishing attacks. While the number of successful attacks has certainly decreased, the organization is still unhappy with the number of successful attacks. It seems to take only one attack to take down a significant portion of the network for a day or longer. Worse, when the antiphishing technology is configured for aggressive detection, legitimate business information is falsely captured and must be manually reviewed before release. The operations manager is suggesting buying more hardware and technology to further inspect e-mail as it comes into the organization, and the CISO is suggesting a targeted awareness and training campaign focused on spear phishing. Which is the best approach?

Part III

CHAPTER

18

Preventive Tools and Techniques

The aphorism "An ounce of prevention is worth a pound of cure" points out that preventive effort may bring larger benefits when compared to fixing a broken or compromised system. Prevention is clearly better than cure if there are demonstrable benefits in choosing a preventive effort and the implementation is cost justified. Frequently, it is more cost and time effective to implement prevention steps against a computer virus infection rather than spending time recovering from (or curing) the virus attacks.

In information assurance management, this aphorism is not always true. Following a risk assessment (refer to Chapter 11), an organization may decide to choose neither prevention nor cure. This is feasible since an organization may decide to avoid or transfer the risk.

This chapter discusses the tools and techniques for cases in which an organization chooses to prevent undesirable impact. Recall that preventive mechanisms are not entirely technical. Some of the choices are managerial or at least a combination of technical and managerial approaches. For example, to reduce the risk of an insider threat stealing corporate information, an organization may choose to implement credit and suitability background checks prior to hiring and throughout an employee's tenure. (Refer to Chapter 13.)

Preventive Information Assurance Tools

In the global information environment, communications and network security seem to dominate management concerns. Some solutions may have privacy concerns in some legal systems. For example, in the United States, monitoring of employees by companies is acceptable in most jurisdictions, while monitoring by the government is more closely regulated. It is advisable to notify everyone connected to a network that monitoring may be used. Notify individuals by warning banners at login and using signed acceptable use and behavior agreements. The following sections discuss tools used to establish preventive controls.

Content Filters

Content filters control the access of end users to portions of the Internet. These tools allow network administrators to block access selectively to certain types of web sites based on predefined local policy. Content filters may be used to change employees' productivity and to increase an organization's information assurance profile by reducing user access to web sites that have no organizational value, improper content, or malicious code. Content filters not only block access to web sites but also are capable of monitoring activity and generating reports on usage. This feature is useful for following trends for employee network usage or for detecting suspicious behavior of employees. Content filters may control bandwidth use. For example, video streaming sites can be blocked to conserve bandwidth. Content filters are implemented by several industries with differing levels of success and acceptance. In some areas, this practice has been controversial. Typically, the benefit of blocking malicious web sites outweighs the social cost of restricting browsing. The most successful implementations of content filters contain a process through which users can request web sites be unblocked after it has been analyzed to determine whether it should be opened for use.

Cryptographic Protocols and Tools

Cryptography is a technique for hiding information by transforming it so that only authorized individuals can access it in its original form. All others are denied access since they cannot decrypt the information. Cryptographic tools also provide confidentiality, integrity, and nonrepudiation protection as defined by the MSR model discussed earlier.

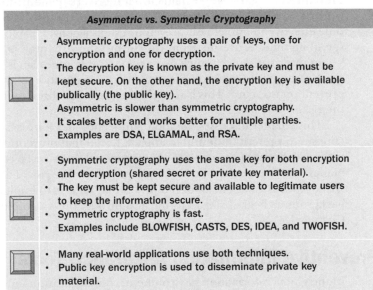

Asymmetric vs. Symmetric Cryptography

- Asymmetric cryptography uses a pair of keys, one for encryption and one for decryption.
- The decryption key is known as the private key and must be kept secure. On the other hand, the encryption key is available publically (the public key).
- Asymmetric is slower than symmetric cryptography.
- It scales better and works better for multiple parties.
- Examples are DSA, ELGAMAL, and RSA.

- Symmetric cryptography uses the same key for both encryption and decryption (shared secret or private key material).
- The key must be kept secure and available to legitimate users to keep the information secure.
- Symmetric cryptography is fast.
- Examples include BLOWFISH, CASTS, DES, IDEA, and TWOFISH.

- Many real-world applications use both techniques.
- Public key encryption is used to disseminate private key material.

Encryption techniques for hosts range from encryption of the entire hard disk, database encryption, selective folder (group of files) encryption, or individual file encryption.

Specially designed secure network protocols are used to secure data traveling over networks such as the Internet. Examples of protocols that implement network services include Secure Sockets Layer (SSL), Transport Layer Security (TLS), and IP Security (IPSec) protocols. SSL and TLS are preferred information security protocols in web environments, while IPSec protocols are preferred for implementing virtual private networks (VPNs).

As noted in Chapter 16, if the employee is allowed to encrypt data, then the key must be controlled by management or held in an appropriate key escrow system.

Firewalls

Firewalls act as a primary control for information assurance technology. They may be implemented as hardware, software, or a combination of both. They exist at the host (desktop, user level) and the network or server level. They enforce access control policies for network segments. They are not a panacea; they do not solve all problems. Access control policies may be implemented in the firewall and are important for controlling information traffic and movement from public accessible networks to private networks. Traffic movement from source to destination may be managed by a firewall using filtering rules to verify, permit, or obstruct data movement. Network protocol types can also be determined by and included in these rules.

Firewalls are widely used throughout organizations; however, recently there has been an increase in the usage of personal firewalls. Note that there are limitations in firewalls because they can only inspect and filter the traffic that flows through them; they cannot protect from internal threats unless appropriately implemented. Additionally, firewalls are often multifunction devices that may also contain solutions for remote users to connect to an organization's intranet and web content filtering.

Network Intrusion Prevention System

A network intrusion prevention system (NIPS) inspects network traffic based on organizational information assurance policy and configuration. It may reduce the exploitation of a network with its capability to manage network packets and identify attacks. This system uses application content, behavior, and context, and not IP addresses or ports, to formulate decisions on access control.

There are two types of network intrusion prevention systems: content based and anomaly based. To detect attacks, the contents of the network packets are checked for distinctive sequences called *signatures*. An anomaly-based NIPS may be used to prevent denial of service (DOS) attacks by monitoring and learning normal network behavior. It uses a statistical approach to determine whether the network behavior is deviating from the normal traffic. Of course the real trick is to define normal.

NIPS can be problematic if they are configured incorrectly or if they are unable to detect legitimate changes to an organization's network. As noted, they are preventive devices and can often automatically shut off traffic or redirect it based on the rules provided to it. This can cause unplanned outages and confusion if NIPS configuration and modification is not part of an organization's change management and configuration management process. Organizations may choose to use network intrusion detection systems (NIDSs) instead of NIPS because of the disruptions NIPS may create.

Proxy Servers

Proxy servers act as an intermediary between clients and the Internet by allowing clients to make indirect connections to other network services through them. Proxy servers can be

Part III

configured to require authentication of the end user, restricting communication to a defined set of protocols, applying access control restrictions, and carrying out auditing and logging. Care should be used with proxy servers since they can be used to disguise sources of traffic (anonymized). The simplest form of a proxy server is called a *gateway*. They can also be used to cache web content.

Public Key Infrastructure

The use of public key infrastructure (PKI) implementation is growing worldwide. PKI enables a secure method for exchanging confidential information over unsecured networks and is the *de facto* standard for implementing trust online. PKI provides a secure electronic business environment. With faster growth of e-commerce, e-business, and e-government applications, the adoption of PKI has increased in recent years. The implementation of PKI combines software, hardware, policy, and procedure to support business needs.

PKI uses technology known as *public key cryptography* (also known as *asymmetric cryptography*). Public key cryptography scales better (works well on large systems) than a private key cryptography (also known as *symmetric cryptography*). The use of public key cryptography reduces the key distribution problem associated with symmetric systems. By associating a unique private key and unique public key with each participant, public key cryptography provides a way for secure protocols to link actions to individuals. It enables digital signatures and nonrepudiation information assurance services noted in the MSR model.

A common way of associating public keys with their owners is to use digital certificates. In PKI, user credentials take the form of a digital certificate, think of it as an electronic passport. Digital certificates may contain names, e-mail addresses, the dates the certificates were issued, and the names of certificate authorities that issued them, among other things. A digital certificate is an electronic message that links a public key to the name of the owner in a secure way by using a trusted third party, known as a *certificate authority* (CA), that guarantees the relationship. Authentication using PKI technology means proving one's identity by proving knowledge of the associated private key (as indeed *the owner of that private key*).

Figure 18-1 illustrates the components of a PKI and how they work together. Most PKI implementations include a CA component, a registration authority (RA) component, and a directory component, e.g., lightweight directory access protocol (LDAP).

Since the CA signs certificates and revokes information, it is the most important and essential component. It is customary to deploy or establish a root CA, since the root CA is the server that forms the foundation for the PKI infrastructure. The root CA has a self-signed certificate, and the public key is published in multiple available public directories. In some situations, the public key is issued (made public) only where necessary. Subscriber certificates, which are signed by other signing CAs, are at first signed by the root CA.

Certificates may be published and stored in public directories such as an LDAP server. The function of the directory component in PKI infrastructure is to publish certificates and revoke invalid access and signatures. Protocols such as LDAP retrieve certificate information from the directory. In addition to LDAP, there are other ways to make certificates available to applications. For example, SSL/TLS allows the server to send an X.509 certificate to the client, binding a name to a public key value certificate to the client and requesting a certificate from

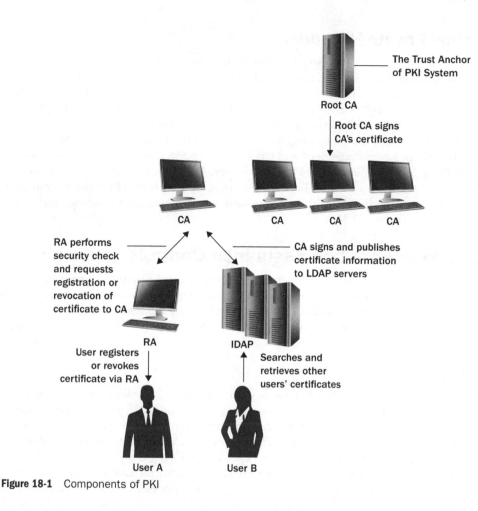

Figure 18-1   Components of PKI

the client. IPSec uses the Internet Key Exchange (IKE) protocol to exchange certificates as part of the key exchange procedure.

One of the most egregious attacks on PKI occurred in the spring of 2014. This attack was called the *heartbleed* attack and focused on the implementation of PKI called OPEN Secure Sockets Layer or OpenSSL. OpenSSL is used by two-thirds of the secure web traffic on the Web. The protocol is used whenever a web browser needs an HTTPS connection for activities, such as secure banking and other sensitive transactions. If the server was running OpenSSL, it would follow instructions very closely, and because of the way OpenSSL was written, a simple flaw allowed an attacker to arbitrarily read the memory of a server far beyond what they should have had access to. This meant if a user's password or other sensitive information was sitting in memory at the time of an attacker "bleeding" it out, it was subject to compromise. Numerous web site owners and vendors had to contact their customers and request they change their passwords.

Virtual Private Networks

A virtual private network is a secure network that uses a public network (usually the Internet) to allow users to interconnect. It uses cryptographic means (encryption) to provide secure communications on public networks. Various types of VPN protocols are IPSec, SSL, Point-to-Point Tunneling Protocol (PPTP), and others. A VPN provides cost-effective solutions to organizations spread over wide areas. Various out-of-the-box VPN solutions are readily available. Organizations should be vigilant and do pre-implementation research about key management and types of encryption algorithms used and their strengths before employing any VPN technology. The strongest VPN solutions use multifactor authentication and have their cryptography certified by independent parties such as the U.S. National Institute of Standards and Technology's Cryptographic Module Validation Program (CVMP).

Preventive Information Assurance Controls

 Network and computing environments constantly change. Organizations need to ensure that proper mechanisms exist to complement the use of technology. Although a firewall protects network assets, organizational systems will be at a higher risk of compromise if patch management is implemented inappropriately. The full suite of preventive information assurance mechanisms that can be used follows.

Backups

A backup is a copy of information assets: data, software, or hardware. It is an essential preventive process for information assurance; it mitigates risks and helps to ensure business continuity. A backup makes restoration (restitution) possible when needed, ensuring that data can be recovered when needed, software can be recovered during application corruption, and hardware is replaceable during disaster.

An organization should have a policy on what to back up (data, software, and hardware), when to back up (depending on the frequency of changes that occur), and how to back up (the process of backup). The backup process should be fully supported by the baseline process.

There are also different types of backup, such as full backup, differential backup, incremental backup, and mirror backup, which can be conducted at different times. Frequency and type of backups to be performed in any organization should be determined by the organization, depending on the risk tolerance and objectives of the organization.

Backing up systems is important, but more important is the correct restoration of the backup. It is thus critical that restoration and integrity tests are performed frequently. Another good practice is to document each restoration step. Refer to Chapter 25 for more information on backup and related matters.

Change Management and Configuration Management

If an organization is to remain competitive, it should be prepared to change continuously since the environment is not static. Change comes from a variety of sources. The following are sources of change drivers that should be addressed and managed effectively in the business and IT environment:

- Alliances and partnerships
- Business market demands
- Competitive markets
- Operational issues
- Regulations changes

Change management is a disciplined process that organizations apply to ensure standardized methods and procedures are employed when implementing changes to their organization, information systems, and IT environments. The change management processes sustain and improve organizational operations while minimizing risks involved in making changes. It ensures all changes (permanent, temporary, new, or modified) to the IT infrastructure are assessed, approved, implemented, and reviewed in a controlled manner. This activity may eliminate or minimize disruptions to business or mission.

Configuration management controls hardware, software, and their associated documentation. Organizations should track all changes to configuration items throughout the life cycle of the components and system with tracking records. Configuration management is closely related to asset management (refer also to Chapter 10); it represents the detailed configuration information for each identified asset. Configuration is also closely related to contingency planning (refer to Chapters 24 and 25) because restored systems must comply with configuration baseline standards.

Change management and configuration management work hand-in-hand. Organizations should not implement configuration management without having a change management process in place. The result will be wasted resources.

The change management system defines and controls a configuration. For example, maintaining accurate configuration information for all the constituent parts of the IT service and infrastructure involves identifying, recording, and tracking all IT components. In addition, it includes versions, constituent components, and relationships of configurations. This tracking ensures that all necessary steps are taken so that changes to the IT components do not adversely affect system performance, reliability, or availability. Accountability and nonrepudiation are also included in change management since all changes must be authorized and assigned to a change agent. The assigned change agent is responsible for the implementation of the change and accountable for the results. Individuals making changes without authorization should be warned and later disciplined if the process is not followed.

Implementation of change and configuration management ensures that a *clear and complete picture* of the IT environment is always available, thus together serving as a strong preventive control to counter risk. Guide both change and configuration management with a properly documented set of policies. Refer also to Chapter 12 for details on policy.

IT Support

During day-to-day operations, the IT support or help-desk employees encounter myriad problems. Information technology support should be able to identify the nature of the problem and determine whether the problem should be raised to a higher level.

Well trained IT support technicians should respond to IT security problems, inform appropriate individuals, and prevent an actual security incident or breach. IT support employees should focus their attention when IT security complaints come repeatedly from the same user or system. If the problem is an information assurance problem, then the manager of this area should take the necessary policy-based action. On the other hand, the problem may represent AT&E failure. Maintenance of logs and appropriate SPC activities may narrow down the problem.

Media Controls and Documentation

Ensuring information confidentiality, integrity, and availability is limited not only to server-based information. Organizations must safeguard all media, including tapes, disks, and printouts. They are equally important and should be properly secured. Remember, the requirement for protection follows the data, not the media. Operational controls addressing media protection may include the following:

- Environmental protection against problems relating to fires, air conditioning, and humidity
- Logging of usage (for example, users should check in and check out the media)
- Maintenance of the media including overwriting or erasing of data and disposal of media
- Prevention of unauthorized access
- Proper labeling of media providing information such as the owner's name, date of creation, version, and classification
- Storage considerations, such as off-site locations or in locked server rooms

Documentation is an effective means of mitigating information assurance risks. The availability of documentation is vital. It allows assigned personnel to understand the architecture of information system functions and associated controls. Documentation should be written such that individuals have a good idea about things to be done or avoided. It reduces the probability that information assurance is not compromised. Information assurance documentation should be customized to user needs. Keep documentation current to ensure business processes are operated as expected and agreed upon. The certification and accreditation (C&A) process requires thorough documentation and is one of the best approaches to ensuring an organization has comprehensive documentation for its systems and practices. You can find more information regarding C&A in Chapter 14.

Patch Management

Patch management requires performing planned and timely system patches to maintain operational efficiency and effectiveness, mitigate information security vulnerabilities, and maintain the stability of IT systems. It is part of configuration management. From this perspective, patch management can also be viewed as part of change management. This is so important that in 2013 the European Union Agency for Network and Information Security

(ENISA) published a report regarding patching in industrial control systems and other critical network components. A successful and effective patch management program combines well-defined processes, effective software, and training into a strategic program for assessing, obtaining, testing, and deploying patches. Common practices for an effective patch management include the following: standardized patch management policies, procedures, and tools. Employees of organizations have to be made aware of the availability of a patch management policy. This ensures that patch management requirements are understood by all. Organizations without standardized policies and procedures in place may allow each subgroup within an entity to implement patch management differently or not at all. A good patch management policy should contain provisions for patch deployment, describing how and when new patches should be applied to the organization and an acceptable "discovery-to-patch" timeframe. Examine tools to assist, facilitate, and automate the patch management process.

- **Establishing dedicated resources**   One of the most important items in a patch management process is to ensure that roles and responsibilities are identified and defined for those involved in maintaining an organization's systems and applications. Their task would be to ensure that these systems and applications are updated with the current released patches. This group of people will also be looking into related information assurance issues. Some organizations may establish a dedicated patch management team. Others may assign responsibility based on related duties.

- **Monitoring and identifying relevant vulnerabilities and patches**   Currently, vulnerabilities and patches appear on a daily basis. Organizations must identify and monitor vulnerabilities proactively. Associate the vulnerabilities with their respective patches using various tools and services available in the market. Use free services only after vetting the quality, reliability, and integrity. Ensure software in use is supported by the vendor and the vendor is contractually required to address security issues discovered.

- **Identifying risk in applying a patch**   Apart from considering the criticality of vulnerability, an organization should consider the importance of the system in question to operations and the risk of applying a patch. The organization has the option not to follow the vendor's advice. This is to ensure that the patch management process does not disrupt the systems' operations. Mission owners and business owners should always have representatives available to test patches. They should test functionality in a test environment and provide feedback before going live. Organizations should also consider a phased patching approach. If the patch fails or causes undesired results, systems of less importance can be impacted first. Organizations should also consider what compensating controls are available for a particular vulnerability. If vulnerabilities can be blocked completely at a firewall, the organization would be wise to consider blocking it and taking extra time testing and deploying the patch.

- **Testing a patch before installing**   Implementing the patch management process assures the information of the IT infrastructure; however, organizations should first assess the patches in a test environment. This is to determine the impact of installing the patch and making certain that it does not disrupt the IT operations.

Such testing will help determine whether a patch functions as intended and does not have an adverse effect on the existing system. If a test environment is not available, the organization should consider a phased roll-out. Doing so ensures a patch won't disable an entire organization. Test environments should mirror production environments as closely as possible. While this may not always be possible because of cost and complexity, organizations must be aware of testing limitations of nonparity systems. Organizations should receive patches only from known and trusted sources. Organizations should demand patches be digitally signed and hashed for verification prior to deployment.

Further Reading

- Aiello, B. "How to Implement CM and Traceability in a Practical Way." September 2013. www.cmcrossroads.com/article/how-implement-cm-and-traceability-practical-way.

- Do's and Don'ts for Effective Configuration Management, TechTarget. http://blogs.pinkelephant.com/images/uploads/pinklink/Dos_Donts_For_Effective_Configuration_Management.pdf.

- Friedlob, T., et al. *An Auditor's Introduction to Encryption*. A monograph published by the Institute of Internal auditors, 1998.

- G Data Development. G Data TechPaper #0271, 2013, G Data, Germany, Patch Management Best Practices, www.cpni.gov.uk/Documents/Publications/2006/2006029-GPG_Patch_management.pdf.

- Good Practice Guide Patch Management. NISCC National Infrastructure Security Co-ordination Center, 2006. www.docstoc.com/docs/7277421/Good-Practice-Guide-Patch-Management.

- NIST FIPS 140 Series. http://csrc.nist.gov/groups/STM/cmvp/documents/140-1/140val-all.htm.

- NIST FIPS 140-1. http://csrc.nist.gov/publications/fips/fips1401.htm.

- NIST FIPS 140-2. http://csrc.nist.gov/publications/fips/fips140-2/fips1402.pdf.

- Pauna, Adrian, and K. Moulinos. "Window of Exposure…A Real Problem for SCADA Systems?" ENISA, December 2013. www.enisa.europa.eu/activities/Resilience-and-CIIP/critical-infrastructure-and-services/scada-industrial-control-systems/window-of-exposure-a-real-problem-for-scada-systems.

- Schmidt, Howard A. *Patrolling Cyberspace: Lessons Learned from a Lifetime in Data Security*. Larstan Publishing, December 15, 2006.

- Conklin, Wm. Arthur, et al. *Introduction to Principles of Computer Security: Security+ and Beyond*. McGraw-Hill Education, March 2004.

- Schou, Corey D., and D.P. Shoemaker. *Information Assurance for the Enterprise: A Roadmap to Information Security*. McGraw-Hill Education, 2007.

- Security Tools to Administer Windows Server 2012. Microsoft, October 2012 http://technet.microsoft.com/en-us/library/jj730960.aspx.

- Stamp, M. *Information Security Principles and Practice.* Wiley-Interscience, 2005.

- Tipton, Harold F., and S. Hernandez, ed. *Official (ISC)[2] Guide to the CISSP CBK 3rd edition.* ((ISC)[2]) Press, 2012.

- U.S. General Accounting Office. "Report to the Ranking Minority Member, Subcommittee on 21st Century Competitiveness, Committee on Education and the Workforce, House of Representatives, EMPLOYEE PRIVACY – Computer-Use, Monitoring Practices, and Policies of Selected Companies." www.gao.gov/new.items/d02717.pdf. GAO-02-717, 2002.

- Wen, J., D. Schwieger, and P. Gershuny. "Internet Usage Monitoring in the Workplace: Its Legal Challenges and Implementation Strategies." Information Systems Management Archive, January 2007)., Volume 24, Issue 2. pp. 185–196.

Critical Thinking Exercises

1. An organization is changing the way it works. For the past ten years, the organization has operated out of a downtown office, and all employees were expected to report onsite for work. Because of the increased costs of real estate, the executive management has identified substantial savings if all employees worked remotely from their homes and the organization maintained only a small office for meetings and executives downtown. The organization has never allowed outside access to its networks and has never allowed equipment off-premises prior to this change. Now employees are being issued laptops, tablets, and smartphones to do their work. What preventive information assurance controls and tools should the organization be concerned with as part of this change?

2. In addition to a near 100 percent remote working situation, the organization decides it is also going to outsource several business functions to "cloud" Software as a Service (SaaS) providers. One function the organization wants to move first is e-mail. The organization has a statutory requirement to ensure all e-mail is encrypted with a U.S. FIPS 140-2 validated encryption process. What precautions should the organization take prior to committing to an e-mail cloud provider?

Part III

CHAPTER 19

Access Control

An access control system prevents actions on an object by unauthorized individuals (subjects). To permit or deny access to an information asset correctly, an organization must manage identification, authentication, authorization, audit, and eventually accountability (refer also to Chapter 2).

A few key concepts are essential for understanding access control. A *subject* is the party or system seeking access. Since a subject can be a user, a program, or simply a machine, sometimes the word *party* is used because it is more generic. An *object* is the target to be accessed by the subject. The object is one of information assets, as discussed in Chapter 10. The subject will execute actions on objects through a controlled access.

As a principle, access to an information asset should be granted for a specific need to fulfill a specific purpose and suspended once the need is no longer there. With these expectations, access control is never trivial. This chapter presents a discussion about the importance and the techniques commonly used for access control.

Access Control: The Benefits

In today's global business, an authorized user should have access to required resources at any time and from anywhere (availability). Organizations may work around the clock (24/7) to provide customers with "anytime, anywhere, any device" access. For some organizations, provision of access itself is core to their business. E-commerce organizations are a perfect example of this. You should consider that although access to resources is critical for running the business, a single breach might cost an organization its entire reputation or tangible assets. Access breaches today have grown from mere annoyances to causing enormous financial losses (confidentiality).

Access control should protect vital resources not only from unauthorized external access but also from internal attacks. Since an internal attacker knows exactly what to look for and how to find it, internal access breaches are sometimes more damaging than external ones. Access control is the first line of defense to protect the system from unauthorized modification (integrity). A benefit of access control is that it serves as an auditing tool. You can use auditing tools to trace information security breaches, incidents, and events.

Access Control Types

There are two broad types of access control: physical and logical. Organizations usually manage physical access with human, technological, or mechanical controls. A physical control might be biometric identification technology used to restrict entry to a property, a building, or a room to authorized persons. Logical access controls manage access based on processes such as identification, authentication, authorization, and accountability. Examples of logical access controls are digital signatures and hashing.

Access Control Models

An access control model defines how subjects access objects. There are three types of access control models: discretionary, mandatory, and nondiscretionary (also known as role based). An organization's mission or business requirements will drive the type of model used. An organization can opt for one of the following mentioned models or a combination of them. Organizations should also consider their culture and the nature of business to decide which model to use.

Discretionary Access Control Model

In a discretionary access control (DAC) model, the owner of the object determines the access policy. The owner decides which subjects may access the object and what privileges the subject has. For example, the file owner on a network defines which subjects (who) can access files and what privileges a subject can have over those files, such as reading, deletion, or modification. Windows, Apple, and various Linux systems adopt the DAC model.

DAC Example

- It is through the discretionary model that Sean can share his hard drive with Michelle so that Michelle can copy all of Sean's presentations.

- Sean can also block access to his hard drive from his manager since the manager may not approve of his sharing presentations with other divisions.

- A further weakness of DAC systems is that if Sean receives malicious code, it executes at Sean's privilege level.

- Finally, if Sean doesn't know what every person is involved in, he may inadvertently give access to the wrong person for the wrong reason. This necessitates a strong need for information assurance AT&E programs in organizations using DAC.

Role-Based Access Control Model

A problem with the DAC model is that as the number of subjects and objects grows, subjects are bound to gain unnecessary privileges, which may be unhealthy for system information security. The role-Based Access Control (RBAC) model uses a centrally managed set of rules, which grants access to objects based on the roles of the subject.

Since subjects are not assigned permission directly like with other models, they acquire it through their role (or roles), and the management of access becomes relatively easier.

One of the biggest challenges of RBAC is establishing it. Ensuring that the design and implementation meets the company's business model is challenging, but once implemented, it scales for growth and requires less maintenance.

Do not confuse RBAC with access control lists (ACLs) used in discretionary access control systems. ACLs assign permissions to operations defined by the organization chart or systems design rather than to low-level data objects.

Mandatory Access Control Model

A mandatory access control (MAC) is a more sophisticated model commonly used to control access to sensitive or controlled data in systems with multiple levels of classification. In MAC systems, the owner does not establish the access policy. In fact, the system decides on the access control based on the information security classification and policy rules.

Here subjects have labels reflecting their category or classification (e.g., secret, top secret, and confidential), and objects are similarly categorized or classified. Therefore, when a subject wants to access an object, the system checks the labels for the subject and the classification of the object as well as the policy rules. The information security officers define policy rules. In general, higher-level subjects dominate lower-level subjects; a subject may access (read) any object at its level or lower (Bell-LaPadula rule). A corollary is the Biba rule, which is designed to protect the integrity of data by not allowing a subject to access (write) only to an object at its level or higher. Refer to Chapter 10 for more information regarding categorization, classification, and more information regarding labeling.

MAC Example

- Gereon has a clearance for documents classified secret, but the document he has requested has the classification of top secret.

- His access in this case will be denied because his clearance is not equal to, or higher than, the classification of the object.

- Gereon may also have a secret document that he wants to post to the top-secret file system.

- In this case, he will be denied because the label of the object he wants to post is not equal to, or higher than, the file system he wants to use (based on the Biba rule).

SELinux is a security enhancement to Linux developed by NSA to allow users and administrators to implement MAC and other tools to control access. System policies determine how SELinux grants access independent of the application or user. Several Android mobile phone manufacturers are implementing SELinux. Trusted Solaris is another good example of an operating system using the MAC model.

Access Control Techniques

Selecting an access control model needs to complement the selection of proper access control techniques. The following section sheds light on the techniques that can be used based on the model that has been selected.

Rule-Based Access Control

A rule-based access control uses simple rules to determine the result of privileges, which a subject can have over an object. This just determines what can and cannot be allowed. It is simply an "if A, then B" rule. These rules are general in nature and are not identity-based as is the case with DAC. Access properties are stored in ACLs associated with each resource object in the same way they are with discretionary access control. Rule-based access control is often confused with role-based access control. Rule-based access control uses sets of rules such as access control lists to determine access between subjects and objects. Role-based access control uses the role of the subject to determine access to an object.

The configuration rules of routers are another good example of rule-based access controls, which are the same for all, rather than specific to an individual. When a particular account or group attempts to access a resource, the operating system checks the rules contained in the ACL for that object.

Access Control Matrix

An access control matrix or access matrix is usually a static, abstract, formal computer protection and information assurance model used in computer systems. When implemented, it characterizes the relationship of each subject to every object in the system. An access control matrix represents the relationship of subjects and objects in a tabulated form. Each cell (intersection of the subject and object) defines the privileges for the "right to use" the object by the subject.

Access Control Lists

An ACL is another technique used to represent accessibility. An ACL is a list containing information about the individual or group permission given to an object; the ACL specifies the access level and functions allowed onto the object. There are two types of ACLs. Network ACLs are implemented on servers and routers (layer 3). File system ACLs implement file access by tracking subjects' access to objects. Clearly, an ACL should be well protected from unauthorized modification.

Capability Tables

A capability table is an authorization table that identifies a subject and specifies the access right allowed to that subject. The rows of the table list the capabilities that the subject can have with respect to all of the objects. A capability table is bound to a subject, whereas an ACL is bound to an object. Capability tables are frequently used to implement the RBAC model.

Constrained User Interfaces

A constrained user interface is a way to limit access of subjects to a resource or information by presenting them with only the information, function, or access to the resource for which they have privileges.

For example, the operating system of an ATM is capable of all kinds of commands, but a user is presented with the constrained/limited options to do personal banking. Similarly, a limited user in Windows 8 is not presented with certain administrative options. Another example is an online academic result system, which restricts the display to view results only, despite the fact that the system is capable of doing much more than mere display of results.

Content-Dependent Access Control

This technique is used in databases. As the name suggests, access to objects is dependent on the content of the objects themselves. This access control technique aims at controlling the availability of information by means of views.

Example of a Content-Dependent Access Control

- Jack and Jill are two customer service employees of a bank.
- When Jack logs on to the client complaints system, he can just see the pending complaint details handled by him but will not be able to see the pending complaint details handled by Jill.

Context-Dependent Access Control

Context-dependent access control defines the access controls of a subject on objects based on a context or situation.

A firewall is a good example of context dependent access control because it understands the necessary steps of communication pertaining to specific protocols. For example, in a TCP connection, the sender sends a SYN packet, the receiver sends a SYN/ACK, and then the sender acknowledges that packet with an ACK packet. A firewall reviews this communication to check whether anything is out of order. However, it should be noted that not all firewalls are capable of tracking TCP connections.

Access Control Administration

The administration of access controls is critical to implementing access controls. Access control administration can be centralized or decentralized. The following section discusses the two modes of access control administration.

Centralized Access Control Administration

The central administration may be contained in a department, unit, or information security administrator. This management approach ensures uniformity across the organization. Centralized access control is a simplified method of managing access controls and is thus cost effective. However, this approach can be slow because all changes are processed by a single entity. Examples of centralized access control protocols are Remote Authentication Dial-in User Service (RADIUS), Terminal Access Controller Access Control Systems (TACACS), and DIAMETER.

Decentralized Access Control Administration

Decentralized management gives control to people who are closer to the objects. This mode is usually faster since changes are made to a function rather than to the whole organization. It does not have the organizational momentum caused by just one entity making all the changes. However, decentralized access control does not ensure uniformity. Decentralized access control is more relaxed compared to centralized access control. This becomes more complicated if an employee is a member of more than one function and enjoys more privileges than they should.

Further Reading

- Hu, Vincent, D.F. Ferraiolo, and D.R. Kuhn. Interagency Report 7316, "Assessment of Access Control Systems." NIST, September 2006. http://csrc.nist.gov/publications/nistir/7316/NISTIR-7316.pdf.

- Hu, Vincent, and K. Scarfone. Interagency Report 7874, "Guidelines for Access Control System Evaluation Metrics." U.S. National Institute of Standards and Technology, September 2012. http://csrc.nist.gov/publications/nistir/ir7874/nistir7874.pdf.

- Information Security Media Group. "NIST Issues Access-Control Guidance." Bank Info Security, Sept. 23, 2012. www.bankinfosecurity.com/nist-issues-access-control-guidance-a-5134.

- International Organization Standardisation and the International Electrotechnical Commission 2005. *Information Technology – Security Techniques – Code of Practice for Information Security Management (ISO/IEC 17799)*. ISO/IecIEC, 2005.

- *NASA IT Security Handbook: Access Control*. U.S. National Aeronautics and Space Administration, Dec. 21, 2011. www.nasa.gov/pdf/613762main_ITS-HBK-2810.15-01_%5BAC%5D.pdf.

- Nichols, R., D. Ryan, and J. Ryan. *Defending Your Digital Assets Against Hackers, Crackers, Spies, and Thieves*. McGraw-Hill Education, 2000.

- Schou, Corey D., and D.P. Shoemaker. *Information Assurance for the Enterprise: A Roadmap to Information Security*. McGraw-Hill Education, 2007.

- Tipton, Harold F., and S. Hernandez, ed. *Official (ISC)² Guide to the CISSP CBK 3rd edition*. ((ISC)²) Press, 2012.

Critical Thinking Exercises

1. An organization has recently acquired a contract that involves processing and storing sensitive information for a government client. The organization uses a decentralized approach to information technology, often letting employees purchase whatever systems they like and connect them to the organization's network. Given the new contract, what access control changes, if any, should the organization consider?

2. Given the cost and resources involved in mandatory access control, why would an organization consider implementing it instead or other less expensive options?

PART

IV

Information Assurance Detection and Recovery Processes

In addition to the preventive controls, organizations should establish capabilities to detect security incidents and anomalies as they occur. Part IV discusses the various controls that organizations could consider. Specifically, Chapter 20 discusses the monitoring tools and methods employed in achieving the objectives.

The maxim that information assurance is a continuous process should be emphasized and made known that it is critical. As such, another important aspect of a successful information assurance program is the ability of the organization to measure the performance and effectiveness of the implemented controls over time. Without measurement and metrics, it would be impossible to evaluate weaknesses and make improvements. Chapter 21 discusses the importance of measuring its implementation.

When preventive controls fail, reactive controls must engage to minimize risk. Chapter 22 describes the incident-handling process and reporting. Chapter 23 covers the forensics aspect of information assurance in an incident response. Forensics is deployed to help determine root causes of information assurance failures with a high degree of certainly. Forensics is often used in legal matters when information technology will be submitted as evidence.

Business continuity helps ensure an organization can remain viable and operational in dire circumstances. Chapter 24 discusses business continuity and related aspects such as disaster recovery, contingency plans, and crisis management. While Chapter 24 primarily focuses on organizational processes, Chapter 25 focuses on the technical aspects of information technology backup and restoration.

Quick Answers

Q: **What is the prime difference between IPS and IDS?**

A: The main difference between an intrusion prevention system (IPS) and an intrusion detection system (IDS) is that an IDS focuses on detection only while an IPS focuses on detection and prevention. IDS products inform users that something is penetrating your system and it monitors potential intrusions. An IPS, on the other hand, attempts to prevent access, ensuring it identifies and blocks attacking traffic.

Q: **I have an IPS already. Is that all I need?**

A: An IPS is an important control and adds considerable value to a defense-in-depth posture. However, IPS is not a complete information security solution. It is no alternative to a soundly managed system of well-established solutions including firewalls, IDS, and antivirus programs.

Q: **I have a firewall and an IDS, and I think I am totally secured now. Why should I need information assurance professionals?**

A: Having a firewall and an IDS does not guarantee total information assurance. These provide only one aspect of information security. Unless implemented within a framework of appropriate process and personnel, these technologies cannot provide appropriate information assurance in any given situation. Recall that information assurance components should be properly configured and actively managed to maintain a secure environment. A bank vault that is never monitored or maintained will not provide an appropriate level of protection for the valuables inside.

Q: **Why is intrusion detection required in an organization?**

A: With the advancement of technology and evolution of the Internet, it is impossible for an organization to keep up with current and potential threats and vulnerabilities. In addition, these threats and vulnerabilities constantly evolve. Intrusion detection is a mechanism to assist an organization in managing these rising threats and vulnerabilities.

Q: How does an IDS differ from a firewall?

A: A firewall normally functions as a barrier between an authorized network and an unauthorized network. It is not able to detect all intrusions since the firewall will not be able to differentiate between "good" and "bad" traffic. This is where IDS becomes helpful because it is able to detect suspected intrusions as soon as it takes place and sends out alarm signals. Both firewalls and an IDS should be used in a complementary way by organizations to ensure information assurance.

Q: What should an organization do after deploying an IDS?

A: An IDS should be a technology that is part of a total integrated information assurance system. Once an IDS is deployed onto the system, it should be monitored, and any alerts triggered should be resolved. An IDS may have false positives (it sounds an alarm; however, no intrusion has been attempted. The information assurance team must tune the system to minimize false positives while not allowing true intrusion attempts to succeed. If there are too many false positives, no one will believe the system; on the other hand, if the IDS lets too many real attacks through, your system fails. To aid in this tuning, develop a set of documented monitoring guidelines and alert criteria so an organization can respond effectively and efficiently to incidents.

Q: What is malware?

A: *Malware* is short for malicious software. Malware is developed with the intention of causing harm or damage to information, processing equipment or facilities. Examples of software classified as malware are viruses, worms, and Trojans.

Q: Why is a penetration test good for an organization?

A: Well-structured penetration testing helps protect an organization by identifying vulnerabilities in the system, applications, networks, or processes before a real attack occurs. Organizations should consider conducting a penetration test at least twice a year or when there is a major change in the infrastructure or the operational environment. It is important for an organization to consider implementing recommendations given after the test results are presented and evaluated. This will reduce risks to the overall organization's information assurance posture.

Q: Can an organization monitor its employees' e-mail and Internet usage?

A: Privacy rights vary from economy to economy and compliance is important. At a minimum, the organization should review local laws and regulations to ensure compliance when monitoring employees' activities in information systems. Although tools are available to monitor employee activities (e-mail reading and Internet browsing), some may violate local laws. Using such tools enables an organization to monitor just about every computer-based activity undertaken by an employee. Establish a policy and supporting rules on the use of communication resources. To prevent issues about a breach of an employee's privacy rights, make sure you communicate the policy to employees and include it in your AT&E program. Make sure your use of monitoring tools and techniques does not violate any laws or regulations.

Q: **What are the factors to consider when selecting a vulnerability scanner to assess a server?**

A: Many vulnerability scanners are available, they range from commercial to open source scanners. Select a vulnerability scanner that meets your specific needs. Here are some points to think about while selecting a scanner:

- Can the scanner be used for compliance checking such as against Payment Card Industry (PCI) or Sarbanes-Oxley Act (SOX)?
- Does the scanner have a user-friendly interface?
- Does the scanner use Common Vulnerability Enumeration (CVE) as its standard?
- How frequent does the scanner update its database signature?
- What type of report can be produced by the scanner?

Q: **In what situations are typical approaches such as the top-down and bottom-up approach effective in implementing information assurance efforts?**

A: A top-down approach is more suitable when organization-wide support is needed and to gain management buy-in throughout the information assurance life cycle. A bottom-up approach is appropriate when business functions need immediate action to implement controls. It is also a good approach for a decentralized environment.

Q: **Why is a business impact analysis (BIA) important?**

A: A BIA is the preliminary and most critical phase of any BCM program. The purpose of a BIA is to identify and prioritize critical business functions and supporting resources for an organization during the BCM program. BIA helps to identify vulnerabilities and threats and to calculate risks.

Q: **How do you ensure a successful implementation of a business continuity management (BCM) program?**

A: The critical success factors for BCM are

- Adoption of proven methodology and standards
- Experience in recovery process
- Full support from top management
- Integration of BCM into the organization's information assurance management program
- Well-defined roles and responsibilities for BCM committee members

Q: Should an organization outsource or develop the BCP in-house?

A: This is not a simple make vs buy decision. Most recovery strategies combine both options. An organization may not completely outsource BCP because most resources for planning and testing have to come from within the organization itself. Moreover, the decision to outsource BCP requires the management to weigh all the pros and cons of each option by balancing the speed, risks, skills, strategies, and costs.

Q: What are the considerations to be made when choosing a hot-site vendor?

A: Before beginning the selection process, the planner should ensure that vendors are thoroughly evaluated. The following are some of the key considerations:

- Compatibility of the technical environment
- Complementary services
- Cost
- Experience in recovery process
- Facilities at recovery center
- Geographical location of the recovery center
- Personnel support
- Responsiveness and flexibility
- Testing capabilities

Q: What is information security incident handling?

A: An information security incident handling is the activity of managing actions or plans targeted for resolving information assurance–related events. Information security incident is crucial in business continuity management because it shows how an organization can contain and recover from information security incidents.

Q: What is the relationship between information security incident handling and computer forensics?

A: Computer forensics should work hand-in-hand with information security incident handling. Computer forensics should act together or be embedded in incident-handling procedures to achieve maximum results.

Q: What is the meaning of *chain of custody*?

A: A chain of custody is the historical record of how evidence is collected, analyzed, transported, and preserved with the goal of ensuring its admissibility in court. The chain of custody states that all evidence should be tagged with information to indicate the individuals who secured and validated the evidence.

Q: Why is backup required?

Backup is important for business continuity when there is a need to resume normal operations after an incident or disaster. Without backup of critical data, it may not be possible for organizations to restore business functions and its survival is at stake. In addition to backup data, you should make sure your critical software is backed up and that a backup plan exists for hardware.

Q: What should be taken into consideration when designing and planning backup strategies?

A: When designing and planning backup strategies, criticality of data, data size, and volume, frequency of backup, application requirements, and storage media requirements should be taken into consideration.

Information Assurance Monitoring Tools and Methods

Independent of the investments made by an organization to implement security controls, its information is still vulnerable because there is no guarantee that all controls function perfectly at all times. To complement this effort, an organization should employ a continuous vigilant surveillance of its environment. Additionally, a model that addresses critical systems using overlapping countermeasures should be implemented. This provides yet one more form of defense in depth.

Information assurance monitoring surveys a system 24 hours a day 7 days a week to ensure that the information assurance posture (that is, confidentiality, integrity, and availability from the MSR model) is not compromised and that breaches to the system are reported in a timely manner. Effective monitoring of an environment requires being aware of its state by observing all changes occurring over time.

This chapter focuses on the methods and tools employed to monitor an organization's information assurance risk posture. Monitoring covers surveillance not only over the network and on machines, but also over personnel (human behavior).

Intrusion Detection Systems

An intrusion detection system is an information assurance management system (IAMS) that detects inappropriate, incorrect, or anomalous activities (remember, you cannot be sure as behavior is anomalous unless you have a reliable baseline). An intrusion detection system (IDS) detects malicious activities not ordinarily detected by conventional firewalls. Detectible malicious activities include network-based attacks such as SYN flooding, as well as host-based attacks such as privilege escalation.

There are two broad classes of IDS: host IDS and network IDS. A host IDS operates on a host to detect malicious activity upon that host, while a network IDS operates on network data flows.

Host Intrusion Detection System

A host intrusion detection system (HIDS) is one of the first lines of defense for electronic information systems against attackers. An HIDS detects unauthorized access attempts on computers and generates warning alerts (via pager, e-mail, or SMS) or takes corrective actions. An HIDS looks for events in the system logs for evidence of malicious code activities in real time. Other features of an HIDS include checking the critical system file changes and accesses for attempts to tamper with information or evidence of modifying users' privileges.

Network Intrusion Detection System

A network intrusion detection system (NIDS) operates at the ISO network layer (layer 2) and protects a wide range of targeted platforms. An NIDS detects intrusions by monitoring network traffic and monitoring multiple hosts via a network switch with port mirroring capabilities, through the connection to a hub or a network tap.

In addition, an NIDS may detect the network vulnerabilities and provide recommendations to protect the network. When malicious activities are identified, the response generated from an NIDS system may be a notification to the network engineer's monitor screen, generation of e-mail alerts, or SMS alerts to the network administrator.

Log Management Tools

Logs are the records maintained by systems. Depending on the budget, resources, and level of interest, almost any action can be recorded. The log can contain information ranging from when an individual logged in and which resources were used to failed attempts to access resources. The more details kept, the more resources used. Log only the activities that represent potential threats, and store only those that one might reasonably address.

Log management tools provide access control to log information and enable system administrators to trace attacks or suspicious activities. Gaining valuable information from audit logs in organizations is difficult. One of the problems encountered when trying to obtain information from log files is the volume of data to be analyzed (frequently in the range of multiple terabytes).

Log management tools have filters that reflect sets of rules. They select a subset of data from the data pool. However, using filters may cause important data to be accidentally *filtered out.* This may interrupt the ability to detect and recognize important attack patterns and valuable information.

Security Information and Event Management (SIEM)

Security Information and Event Management (SIEM, also known as security information management [SIM]) is software designed to import information from security systems logs and correlate events among systems (NIST-SP800-94). SIEM analyzes logs collected from log management tools and IDS. Normalization converts the log data into standard fields and values common to the SIEM. Without normalization, matching relevant information is extremely difficult. A field titled *logonTime* may mean the same thing as *successFullLogonTime*, but if the SIEM isn't programmed to treat them the same, it may process them as different events. Logs are collected over secure channels and normalized.

Correlation is a process of identifying relationships among two or more security events. Events are correlated in various ways, such as rule based, statistical, and visualization. If automatic correlation is used, it generates an alert for further investigation. Correlation

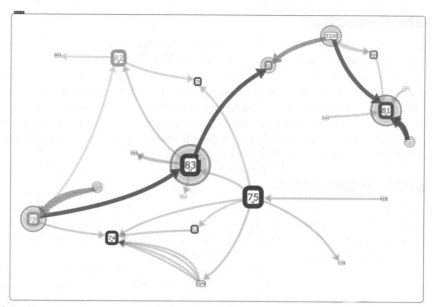

Figure 20-1   Network visualization

reduces the number of events to be investigated by eliminating the number of irrelevant events (false positives).

SIEM includes a report generator to produce summaries of activities over a period of time or ad hoc reports based on certain events. Organizations should consider training information assurance personnel in statistics, data science, and data visualization to get the most out of SIEM solutions. An example of network model is shown in Figure 20-1.

Honeypot/Honeynet

A honeypot is a computer system set up with intentional/known vulnerabilities. The main purpose is to study hackers' behavior, motivation, strategy, and tools used. The honeypot has no production value; any attempt or connection to a honeypot is potentially suspicious or malicious.

There are two types of honeypot: low interaction and high interaction. A low-interaction honeypot simulates only limited services of any operating system or application. It is useful to gather information at a higher level such as to learn about behavior of worm, botnet, or spammer. A high-interaction honeypot simulates the behavior of an entire operating system. It can be used to study hacker behavior and to identify new methods of attack.

When used, a honeypot gives an organization another layer of detection, but extra precautions are still needed so that the honeypot will not be used as a platform to launch attacks on other organizations. The Honeynet Project, a nonprofit research organization dedicated to computer security and information sharing, actively promotes the deployment of honeypot.

Part IV

Malware Detection

Malicious software, often referred to as *malware*, is software designed to break into or damage a computer system without the owner's consent. Hostile or intrusive code is malware. Malware includes all software programs (including macros and scripts) intentionally coded to cause an unwanted event or problem on the target system. Table 20-1 gives examples of malware.

Removing malware from a computer can be difficult, even for experts. As a precautionary measure, it is essential to detect malware and simultaneously prevent the system from becoming infected. There are three commonly used methods for detecting malware, as discussed next.

Signature Detection

One of the most widely used detection methods is *signature detection*. It detects the patterns or signatures in a particular program that may be malware. When malware is suspected, it is verified against the database of known bad code fragments. To be effective, this database must be updated constantly with current threats.

There are advantages and disadvantages of the signature detection method. It is most effective for known malware represented in the database. An additional advantage is that users and administrators can perform a simple precautionary measure keeping signature files up to date and periodically scanning for viruses. However, the signature files may be quite large, which makes scanning slow. Regardless of this condition, keeping the signature files up to date should be performed frequently for them to be effective. Since there are not signatures for new malware, these systems are vulnerable to zero-day attacks.

Change Detection

Finding files that have been changed is called *change detection*. A file that changes unexpectedly may be due to a virus infection. One of the advantages of change detection is that if a file has been infected, a change can be detected. An unknown malware, one not previously identified (zero-day), can be detected through change detection.

There is a possibility of false positives resulting from frequent changes of the files in the system. This is not convenient for users and administrators. If a virus is inserted into a

Type	Description
Logic bomb	Piece of code in a computer program that will set off a malicious function when specified conditions are met
Spyware	Computer program that is installed secretly to intercept and collect information without user realizing it
Trojan horse	Computer program that appears to perform legitimate function but, in fact, performs others, usually with malicious intent
Virus	Computer program that can copy itself and infect a computer and cause harm
Worm	Computer program that can replicate itself without the need to attach to an existing program and cause harm

Table 20-1 Types of Malware

file that changes often, it will may slip through a change detection procedure—masked by the normal high volume of activity. Therefore, careful analysis of the log files is recommended, and an organization may have to fall back on a signature scan method. In this case, the reliability of the change detection system is uncertain. This approach also requires constant maintenance of baseline data so changes can be detected.

State Detection

State detection aims to detect unusual/anomalous behavior. It relies on an expert system that determines if a state change is anomalous. These state changes includes malicious behavior; by extension, anomaly detection is the ability to identify potentially malicious activity. Clearly, the challenge in using this technique is to determine what is normal and what is unusual and to be able to distinguish between the two. Having current system baselines is essential.

Vulnerability Scanners

A vulnerability scanner is software that detects vulnerabilities by analyzing networks or host systems. The results from scanning networks or host systems are presented as reports. Based on these reports, the personnel in charge may respond to mitigate or resolve the vulnerabilities discovered. Several types of scanners address different types of vulnerabilities. They are host-based scanners, network-based scanners, database vulnerability scanners, and distributed network scanners.

Vulnerability Scanner Standards

Vulnerability scanners take technical results from a scan and try to present the vulnerability as human-readable and understandable information. Vendors have varying professional opinions as to the severity and reporting of weaknesses. To help address the discrepancy between scanners, the U.S. National Institute of Standards and Technology, in coordination with MITRE, has developed the Common Vulnerabilities and Exposures program. The following is from the program's web site (https://cve.mitre.org):

> *Common Vulnerabilities and Exposures (CVE®) is a dictionary of common names (i.e., CVE Identifiers) for publicly known information security vulnerabilities. CVE's common identifiers make it easier to share data across separate network security databases and tools, and provide a baseline for evaluating the coverage of an organization's security tools. If a report from one of your security tools incorporates CVE Identifiers, you may then quickly and accurately access fix information in one or more separate CVE-compatible databases to remediate the problem. CVE is:*
>
> *One name for one vulnerability or exposure*
> *One standardized description for each vulnerability or exposure*
> *A dictionary rather than a database*
> *How disparate databases and tools can "speak" the same language*
> *The way to interoperability and better security coverage*
> *A basis for evaluation among tools and databases*
> *Free for public download and use*
> *Industry-endorsed via the CVE Editorial Board and CVE-Compatible Products*

Part IV

CVE works with several other programs to form a comprehensive and standardized method to convey configuration, vulnerability, and weakness information between scanners and reporting methods. Standards related to CVE include the following:

NVD	U.S. NIST's National Vulnerability Database
SCAP	U.S. NIST's Security Content Automation Protocol
CWE	MITRE's Common Weakness Enumeration
OVAL	MITRE's Open Vulnerability and Assessment Language
XCCDF	U.S. NIST's Extensible Configuration Checklist Description Format
CVSS	U.S. NIST's Common Vulnerability Scoring System
CCE	U.S. NIST's Common Configuration Enumeration
CPE	U.S. NIST's Common Platform Enumeration

These standards provide a framework which organizations can use to standardize vulnerability, configuration, and platform vulnerability severity and reporting. Organizations should consider adopting only the vulnerability scanning technology that supports full integration with the standards noted prior.

Host-Based Scanner

Host-based scanners retrieve detailed information from operating systems and other hosts' services and configurations. A host-based scanner seeks potentially high-risk activities involving users' passwords, for example. This type of scanner is ideal for verifying the integrity of file systems for signs of unauthorized modifications.

Network-Based Scanner

Network-based scanners scrutinize the network looking for vulnerabilities. Network scanners can provide a map of what devices are alive on the network by using simple probes, such as the echo request command (ping command), performing port mapping, and identifying which network services are running on each host on the network. For example, if a machine is not a web server, it would be unusual for it to have port 80 open. Advanced network scanners also include databases containing information on known vulnerabilities.

Database Vulnerability Scanner

Database vulnerability scanners perform information security analysis of database systems. Database vulnerability scanners examine authorization, authentication, and integrity. It identifies potential vulnerabilities in areas such as password strength, information security configurations, cross-site scripting, and injection vulnerabilities.

Distributed Network Scanner

Distributed network scanners perform information security analysis for distributed networks in large organizations spanning geographic locations. It consists of remote scanning agents, which are updated using a plug-in update mechanism and controlled by a centralized management console.

Penetration Test

A penetration test (pen test) involves conducting reconnaissance scans against an organization's perimeter defenses such as routers, switches, firewalls, servers, and workstations to allow the organization to determine the overall network topology. Pen tests are performed at two levels, external as well as internal to the organization. This activity is the same sort of approach the adversary might take.

The information gathered can identify the attack vector in an attempt to penetrate targeted systems to see whether they can be compromised using known vulnerability scans and exploits. The overall plan is to map the entire network and perform an assessment to make sure any vulnerable devices are identified and patched frequently.

External Penetration Test

An external penetration test concentrates on external threats (mainly hackers) attempting to break into an organization's network. There are two methods for an external penetration test: a black-box test and a white-box test.

Black-box testing assumes that a hacker has no prior knowledge of the target organization, network, or systems. The objective of this testing is to discover how information can leak from an organization. White-box testing, on the other hand, assumes that a hacker has complete knowledge of the organization's network. The focus of white-box testing is to determine the potential for exploitation and not discovery.

Internal Penetration Test

Most successful attacks originate within the organization's perimeter. Organizations need to conduct testing from different network access segments, both logical and physical. However, today organizations may focus more on the external threat and pay less attention to securing their systems from internal threats.

Internal penetration testing identifies vulnerable resources within an organization's network and assists the system administrator in addressing these vulnerabilities. Internal information assurance controls not only protect an organization from internal threats but also help provide an additional layer of protection from external attackers who attempt to penetrate the perimeter defenses. Access to internal systems can be obtained through physical access to the organization or by remotely exploiting a vulnerable system. An internal penetration test assumes a successful bypass of perimeter controls such as firewalls and intrusion detection systems (IDSs), making it possible to access resources and services not accessible outside of the perimeter, such as RCP, NetBIOS, FTP, and Telnet services.

Wireless Penetration Test

Wireless penetration test is important. It helps organizations understand the overall information assurance infrastructure through the eyes of an attacker. A wireless penetration test evaluates how vulnerable a network is to wireless attackers. Wireless penetration test should be organized and well planned and should simulate the action of a highly skilled attacker determined to break into the network.

Basic wireless penetration test tasks may be limited to the ability to connect to the access point (a layer 1 device, a hub for wireless LAN) and get free bandwidth to the Internet. An advanced wireless penetration test involves packet analysis to find valuable data, collecting and cracking passwords, attempting to gain root or administrator privileges on vulnerable hosts in a range, connecting to external hosts, and finally hiding their tracks.

War driving is the act of gaining (potentially) illegal access to a network resulting from an individual's continuous exploring of the Wi-Fi wireless networks via a laptop with a Wi-Fi feature enabled. There are free and downloadable tools on the Internet to gain access to unsecured wireless networks.

Figure 20-2 shows an example of using an open source tool to crack Wired Equivalency Privacy (WEP) keys of wireless networks.

A WEP key can be extracted from wireless communication within seconds or minutes. Leaving wireless networks unattended is asking for trouble. Designing a network with information assurance in mind from the beginning mitigates wireless security problems.

In most cases, the human factor again proves to be the weakest link. Because of improper network design, an attacker associated with a wireless network may find himself connected directly to a wired LAN behind a corporate firewall with unsecured and unpatched services exposed to an unexpected attack.

The security of a wireless network can be improved by adopting the followings:

- **Network segregation** Provide proper network segregation between wireless and LAN with a firewall and appropriate routing.

- **Change the default settings** Access points are vulnerable when using a default configuration. Changing the access point name and administrator password should be done to ensure that the wireless network is harder to penetrate.

- **IEEE 802.1X** The IEEE 802.1X is an IEEE standard that when implemented provides a certificate-based authentication mechanism. The standard can also be implemented in a wireless network to ensure stronger security in terms of encryption.

```
CH  9 ][ Elapsed: 1 min][ 2007-04-26 17:41 ][ WPA handshake: 00:14:6C:7E:40:80

BSSID               PWR RXQ  Beacons    #Data, #/s  CH  MB    ENC  CIPHER AUTH ESSID

00:09:5B:1C:AA:1D   11  16      10          0    0  11  54.   OPN               NETGEAR
00:14:6C:7A:41:81   34 100      57         14    1   9  11e   WEP  WEP          bigbear
00:14:6C:7E:40:80   32 100     752         73    2   9  54    WPA  TKIP   PSK   teddy

BSSID               STATION          PWR   Rate    Lost  Packets  Probes

00:14:6C:7A:41:81   00:0F:B5:32:31:31  51   36-24     2      14
(not associated)    00:14:A4:3F:8D:13  19    0-0      0       4    mossy
00:14:6C:7A:41:81   00:0C:41:52:D1:D1  -1   36-36     0       5
00:14:6C:7E:40:80   00:0F:B5:FD:FB:C2  35   54-54     0      99    teddy
```

Figure 20-2 Using an open source tool to get a WEP key

- **IEEE 802.11i**   This is the security standard for 802.11. It provides a stronger encryption known as Wi-Fi Protected Access 2 (WPA2). By deploying WPA2 with a strong passphrase, the wireless network is harder to penetrate.

Physical Controls

As noted in Chapter 16, physical security is essential to keeping systems and data secure. Risks associated with physical security, such as theft, data loss, and physical damage, can cause substantial damage to an organization. As part of information assurance, it is important to check an organization's physical security posture for vulnerabilities.

Motion sensors, smoke and fire detectors, closed-circuit television monitors, and sensor alarms are physical detective controls that can be installed to alert information assurance personnel about physical security violations. The following are some of the more common detective physical controls:

- **Closed-circuit television and monitors**   Closed-circuit television (CCTV) is used to monitor computing areas where security personnel may be absent and is useful for detecting suspicious individuals.

- **Motion detectors**   Use motion detectors in unmanned computing facilities. They provide an alert in the event of intrusions. This equipment should be monitored by guards.

- **Sensors and alarms**   Sensors and alarms are used to inspect the environment to verify that air, water, and temperature parameters stay within certain operating ranges. If out of range, an alarm is triggered to call attention to operations and maintenance personnel to correct the situation.

- **Smoke and fire detectors**   Signs of fire can be detected by smoke and fire detectors placed strategically, and testing should be conducted on a regular basis to ensure the detectors are in good working order.

Refer to Chapter 16 for details on physical security and environmental security controls.

Personnel Monitoring Tools

With an increase in the number of employees having access to the Internet and e-mail, there is a need for personnel monitoring to safeguard organizational records and stakeholders' interests. Personnel monitoring is required to maintain information assurance and privacy of organizational records. It protects against internal and external threats to the information assurance or records integrity and protects against unauthorized access or use of records or information. Organizations need to understand the local and international laws pertaining to privacy before implementing monitoring. An employee's consent may be required, and employees should be made aware that such monitoring is in place. Each employee should sign an acknowledgment of monitoring.

Part IV

Network Surveillance

Network surveillance encourages employees to abide by acceptable use policies and limit the personal use of organization resources. Another network surveillance objective is to block spam and viruses that affect personnel productivity. One method of implementing network surveillance is the use of specialized software. The software allows authorized individuals to monitor by accessing their workers' computer systems, remotely view a person's monitor display, and record the keystrokes made on the computer. Network monitoring is also a simple tool to detect ex-filtration (surreptitiously sending information assets to unauthorized individuals) of corporate assets.

E-mail Monitoring

E-mail in today's workplace is the norm. In most cases, the information sent via e-mail across a corporate network is within the boundaries of private communication network. However, while internal e-mail often feels secure and private, e-mail can be retained, read, and disseminated without the knowledge or consent of the sender. Typically, all e-mails are retained in the system even when both parties, sender and receiver, have deleted the messages.

An organization is liable for all communications sent from their network. These e-mails can be retrieved and printed out, and they serve as supporting documents for legal actions. For any inappropriate or illegal communications carried out by an employee, an organization is at risk of facing legal actions. E-mail monitoring is useful in detecting such activities and allows an organization to control and take necessary actions against the culprits.

Employee Privacy and Rights

Employee privacy and rights are the two issues to be considered when deploying a monitoring mechanism. Necessary precautions and steps must be taken to ensure employee privacy and rights are not violated. Ensure monitoring activities are in accordance with applicable laws.

However, as mentioned in Chapter 13, it is becoming a norm for authorities in some countries to monitor personal information. Newly recruited employees are usually required to sign a clause allowing management to monitor whatever information they are managing, including personal information.

The Concept of Continuous Monitoring and Authorization

Chapter 14 discussed the approach for a mature certification and accreditation program. The concept of accreditation as a formalized method of risk acceptance was mentioned. A problem with any assessment technique is time. As time goes on, the value of an assessment diminishes. This is because of changes in the threat environment but also because of changes in the information technology environment. The goal of risk management is to ensure that stakeholders have an informed view of risk to their organization or mission in near real time.

Organizations cannot spend resources continually performing assessment after assessment in the hopes of providing near-real-time risk visibility. The answer lies in leveraging change management and information assurance monitoring tools and methods. Organizations must determine the criticality of controls and the resulting frequency of assessment. Some controls, such as, policies may need to be assessed only annually or even less. Other controls such as network patching and vulnerability assessment may need to be accessed daily, weekly, or monthly.

The results of the assessment need to be combined into a normalized and meaningful dashboard that stakeholders can use to gauge risk to their operations. Stakeholders should be able to access this dashboard at any time to gauge their information assurance–related risk. The dashboard should also provide estimated resources required to eliminate risks and points of contact for specific risks.

Further Reading

- *ACM Computing Curricula Information Technology Volume: Model Curriculum.* ACM, Dec. 12, 2008. http://campus.acm.org/public/comments/it-curriculum-draft-may-2008.pdf.

- Bejtlich, R. *The Tao of Network Security Monitoring: Beyond Intrusion Detection.* Addison-Wesley, 2004.

- Bejtlich, R. *Extrusion Detection: Security Monitoring for Internal Intrusion.* Addison-Wesley, 2005.

- Dittrich, David, and S. Dietrich. "P2P As Botnet Command and Control: A Deeper Insight." Proceedings of the 2008 3rd International Conference on Malicious and Unwanted Software (Malware), October 2008. http://staff.washington.edu/dittrich/misc/malware08-dd-final.pdf.

- Gurgul, P. "Access Control Principles and Objective." securitydocs.com, 2004. www.securitydocs.com/library/2770.

- Honeypot Background. honeyd.org, 2002. www.honeyd.org/background.php.

- Kent, K., and M. Souppaya. *Guide to Computer Security Log Management (Management (SP800-92).* NIST, 2006.

- Nestler, Vincent J. *Computer Security Lab Manual (Information Assurance & Security).* 2005.

- Nichols, R., D. Ryan, and J. Ryan. *Defending Your Digital Assets Against Hackers, Crackers, Spies, and Thieves.* McGraw-Hill Education, 2000.

- Ryan, D., J.C.H. Julie, and C.D. Schou. On Security Education, Training, and Certifications. Information Systems Audit and Control Association, 2004.

- Scarfone, K., and P. Mell. *Guide to Intrusion Detection and Prevention Systems (SP800-94).* NIST, 2007.

- Conklin, Wm. Arthur, *Introduction to Principles of Computer Security: Security+ and Beyond.* McGraw-Hill Education, 2004.

- Schou, Corey D., and D.P. Shoemaker. *Information Assurance for the Enterprise: A Roadmap to Information Security.* McGraw-Hill Education, 2007.

- The Honeynet Project. www.honeynet.org/about.

Part IV

- Tipton, Harold F., and S. Hernandez, ed. *Official (ISC)² Guide to the CISSP CBK 3rd edition.* ((ISC)²) Press, 2012.

- Tipton, Harold F., and M. Krause. *Information Security Management Handbook*, 4th Edition. Auerbach, 2002.

- What Is a Honeynet? SearchSecurity.com, 2007. http://searchsecurity.techtarget.com/definition/honeynet.

Critical Thinking Exercises

1. A CISO decides to deploy a honeypot with a baseline configuration on it into the wild to determine what vulnerabilities exist. What are the advantages and disadvantages to this approach?

2. The CIO of an organization is trying to prioritize the information assurance workload of the organization. The CIO has asked the CISO to take vulnerability scanner output and add it to the organization's dashboard. The CIO then tasks the organization's system owners to correct the most "critical" vulnerabilities first. Is this the most prudent plan to minimize risk in the organization?

CHAPTER 21

Information Assurance Measurements and Metrics

The famous paraphrased statement in Edwards Deming's book *Out of Crisis* notes that "what you cannot measure, you cannot improve." This applies to managing information assurance. The ability to make quantitative judgments and comparisons about information assurance is desirable for continuous improvement. By using the appropriate metrics, an organization will have a basis to determine how and where to allocate its limited resources. Thus, measurements and metrics provide means for an organization to gain a more concrete understanding of the effectiveness of their efforts in securing information.

It is important to establish the difference between measurements and metrics. *Measurement* refers to a specific single point-in-time snapshot of data, whereas *metrics* are derived from comparing predetermined baselines against a series of measurements taken over time. Measurement consists of raw data, whereas metrics are interpretations of the data collected through the measurement process.

This chapter discusses the importance of security measurement and metrics. It provides insights into the processes that organizations use to perform the measurements and to manage an information assurance metric program.

Importance of Information Assurance Measurement

Information assurance measurement helps management make more objective decisions about information assurance and identify noncompliance, and it provides valuable indicators of information assurance performance. With the emergence of legislative and regulatory requirements, organizations need to demonstrate to stakeholders that internal controls have been established and that information systems' assurance posture is adequately managed and monitored.

The use of information assurance measurements makes an organization able to establish the effectiveness of its information assurance controls and processes. Moreover, measurement assists in reporting current and past compliance status to management and forms input for internal audit and management review.

Information Assurance Measurement Process

Foundationally, organizations should base quantifiable information assurance measures on information assurance objectives and policy. Measures should be repeatable and provide a standard process for tracking compliance and performance over time. As illustrated in Figure 21-1, the information assurance measurement process consists of five key steps. The details of the steps are discussed in the next section.

Develop Measurements

The planning stage defines the approach and method for measuring and selecting metrics to support strategy and risk tolerance. Measurement planning includes selecting controls, identifying objectives, creating specifications, establishing data collection, analyzing, and reporting. Planning should identify financial, human, and infrastructure resources required to ensure each task has sufficient resources. You should document planning activities for future reference and to record decisions.

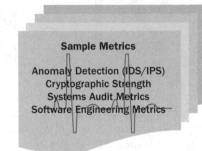

Sample Metrics

Anomaly Detection (IDS/IPS)
Cryptographic Strength
Systems Audit Metrics
Software Engineering Metrics

Collect Data

Using well-planned data collection procedures is the difference between successful and unsuccessful information assurance measurement. Data collection should be designed for establishing baselines followed by continuous monitoring. Design the data structures and analytic techniques before data collection begins. The activities ensure the collected data

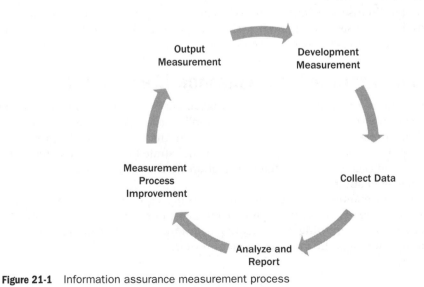

Output
Measurement

Development
Measurement

Collect Data

Analyze and
Report

Measurement
Process
Improvement

Figure 21-1 Information assurance measurement process

can be used to gain an understanding of an information assurance management system and recommend improvement actions.

U.S. NIST uses the approach in Figure 21-2 when determining what data to collect and from which sources.

Analyze and Report

To gain a meaningful understanding of collected data, it has to be analyzed using a predefined measurement method. One of the most common methods of analysis is statistical process control (SPC). Statistical process control uses statistical methods to identify and control processes. SPC is based on the work of Walter A. Shewhart of the Bell Telephone Laboratories in the 1920s and was foundational to Demming's work in measurement and quality control. Since then it has been used in numerous industries to minimize and eliminate waste and inefficiencies. SPC often uses a tool called *control charts* to explain the analysis.

SPC focuses on understanding the relationship of outside events and their impacts on a process and is often used for early detection of events and prevention of problems. SPC works best in environments with consistent output of information and a fairly consistent operation. Networks, training, incidents, and system patching are all processes that typically work well with SPC. Ultimately, SPC focuses on continuous improvement and understanding of inputs and outputs.

Integrate Measurement Output

The output of the measurement activities have many purposes including, but not limited to, providing an indicator about control effectiveness, input to risk assessment, and decision making about information assurance. The output is indicative of compliance

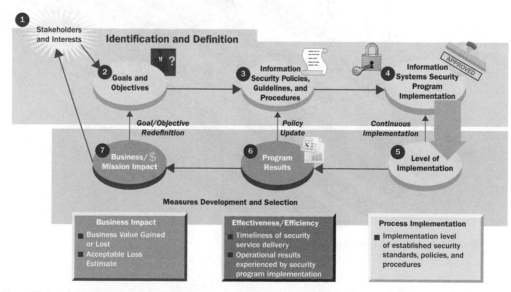

Figure 21-2   U.S. NIST measures development process

with requirements as well as benchmarks among business units or organizations in the same or similar industry sectors.

Improve Measurement Process

Review the measurement process and measurements taken periodically to ensure successful implementation and consistent operation. Improvement is required when new controls are introduced or the current process is incapable of capturing data effectively.

The information assurance team can perform a cost-benefit analysis by comparing the usefulness of the results gathered and the cost spent to obtain the results against the projected measurement objectives. Process improvement should drive measures and metrics maturity. Figure 21-3 from U.S. NIST illustrates the maturing of a metrics and measurement program.

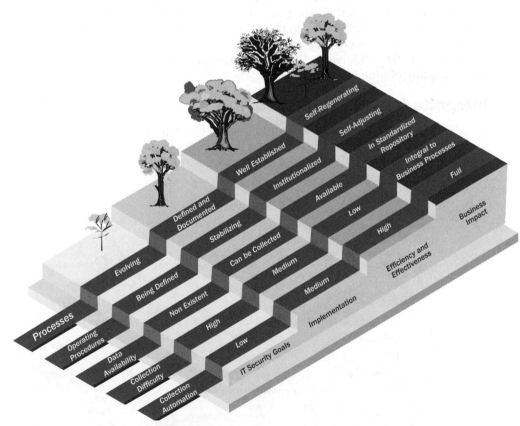

Figure 21-3   U.S. NIST program maturity

Importance of Information Assurance Metrics

Information assurance metrics allow an organization to improve its information assurance performance. The development of an information assurance metrics program allows an organization to monitor the status of measured activities, and corrective actions can be applied based on the observations.

Information assurance metrics provides an organization with both operational and financial benefits. From the operational standpoint, using information assurance metrics allows an organization to gauge the adequacy of the information assurance controls in place. With this information, the organization can make financial decisions about investments in additional information assurance protection or termination of non-productive controls.

Information Assurance Metrics Program

Metrics should yield easily acquired quantifiable information. Initially consider processes that are consistent and repeatable, with ease of data collection. While the easiest-to-collect metrics serve as an initial effort, the organization must determine which metrics are critical for its success.

Unstable processes from which information is hard to retrieve defeat the purpose of having a metrics program in place since it results in unnecessary resource allocation and cost.

Figure 21-4 illustrates the key activities for implementing an information assurance metrics program.

Data Collection Preparation

During the data collection preparation phase, an organization identifies and selects the processes to be included in the information assurance metrics program. This includes defining how the data will be collected, analyzed, and reported. In addition, you should

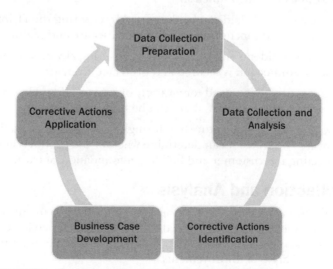

Figure 21-4   Implementation of an information assurance metrics program

define and plan the associated roles and responsibilities since they support the tracking and monitoring of the defined information assurance metrics. Often, metrics are chosen because of a "best practice" or industry standard. Organizations must be cautious when adopting these metrics because they may not align with an organization's key performance indicators (KPIs) or critical success factors.

KPIs are metrics that are critical for an organization's success. They may include metrics that are not specifically related to information assurance such as the following:

- Return on investment
- Return on assets
- Amount of product in a warehouse
- Age of product in a warehouse
- Lead time of manufacturing
- Cost of goods sold
- Days before an accident
- Number of products returned
- Number of new customers

Initially, these metrics may appear to have little to do with information assurance. A knowledgeable information assurance team will quickly point out the following:

- IT investments will fail if not properly secured, and therefore the return on investment will be greatly decreased.
- If assets are leveraged for an Internet attack (such as a company's server is hijacked), the return on the asset may actually be negative if the server can't perform its intended function.
- The cost of goods sold can be decreased by ensuring the IT infrastructure and other overhead functions are running in a secure and mature manner.
- Industrial accidents can be reduced by ensuring any industrial equipment that has a network connection is secured and protected from attackers.
- Products can be returned for a variety of reasons. If an IT product cannot protect the privacy of a customer, there can be backlash.
- New customers can be attracted through trust in an organization's product and services. The IA team can determine whether the products and services are protecting the customer and building a foundation of trust.

Data Collection and Analysis

The data collection and analysis phase develops an insight to the information assurance controls and corrective actions that need to be taken. Data is collected, consolidated, and compared against the predefined target. This comparison identifies the root cause of poor performance and areas of improvements.

Corrective Action Identification

The corrective actions identification phase consists of the preparation of a plan to mitigate the subpar performance and areas of improvements identified previously. The plan identifies corrective actions, prioritizes them, and recommends actions based on the criticality of the performance issue.

Business Case Development

Finally, develop a business case based on the identified corrective actions. The business case analysis compares and contrasts the cost of the remaining *status quo* versus the cost of implementing remedies for corrective actions. This helps an organization justify budget and resource allocation.

Corrective Action Applications

Implement the identified corrective actions for the information assurance controls. This establishes the input for the next iteration of the review cycle.

Further Reading

- NIST. What Are Process Control Techniques? www.itl.nist.gov/div898/handbook/pmc/section1/pmc12.htm.

- NIST. Process or Product Monitoring and Control. www.itl.nist.gov/div898/handbook/toolaids/pff/pmc.pdf.

- Panye, SC. *A Guide to Security Metrics.* SANS Institute, 2006. www.sans.org/reading_room/whitepapers/auditing/55.php.

- Ryan, D., J.C.H. Julie, and C.D. Schou. On Security Education, Training, and Certifications. Information Systems Audit and Control Association, 2004.

- Sademies, S. Process Approach to Information Security Metrics in Finnish Industry and States Institutions. VTT Technical Research Center of Finland, 2004. www.vtt.fi/inf/pdf/publications/2004/p544.pdf.

- Conklin, Wm. Arthur, *Introduction to Principles of Computer Security: Security+ and Beyond.* McGraw-Hill Education, 2004.

- Schou, Corey D., and D.P. Shoemaker. *Information Assurance for the Enterprise: A Roadmap to Information Security.* McGraw-Hill Education, 2007.

- Swanson, M., and B. Guttman. *Generally Accepted Principles and Practices for Securing Information Technology Systems.* NIST, 1996.

- Swanson, M., et al. *Security Metrics Guide for Information Technology Systems (Special Publication 800-55).* U.S. Government Printing Office, 2003.

Part IV

Critical Thinking Exercises

1. An organization is struggling. After years of investing in research and development, a competitor appears to have stolen design documents for the organization's flagship product. The organization's CISO has been asked to give a presentation to the board regarding the best metrics to monitor to prevent information leakage in the future. What information assurance metrics should the CISO propose?

2. A CIO wants to ensure she is investing properly in information assurance. What metrics should her CISO advise her to monitor?

CHAPTER 22

Incident Handling

Incident handling is the first step in an actual recovery process. The activity is undertaken by the organization to manage the consequences of a breach to minimize both tangible and intangible damage. Examples of breaches include intrusion, cybertheft, and denial-of-service and virus attacks. Incident handling is part of information assurance, but it is a reactive control. Some organizations define incident handling as "information security incident handling" or "security incident handling." In all contexts, the functions remain the same regardless of the name.

Incident handling is included sometimes as part of an organization's business continuity plan because it provides the approach to respond quickly and efficiently to unexpected events.

The best way to act on an incident and minimize the chances of a mistake is by establishing predetermined procedures. The procedures should be clear and well documented to ensure that after an incident, the proper steps are followed. Clarity is extremely important to reduce the risk of overlooking actions required by law. An incident-handling plan should be compliant with the applicable laws and regulations. Refer to local civil and criminal laws for guidance. Here are some sample items you would include in your research:

- Evidence management
- Criminal investigations
- Civil investigations
- Administrative investigations
- Response to security incidents
- E-discovery
- Intellectual property

This chapter is an overview of the importance of incident-handling capabilities for an organization and points out the best practices in implementing the incident-handling process.

You should to refer to Chapter 23 for details on computer forensics, which is a component of incident handling.

Importance of Incident Handling

Regardless of the type of organization or size, they all face the risk of being affected by an incident. Incidents may completely disable an organization's operations if not handled properly. Unfortunately, some organizations handle incidents by ignoring them. It is only a matter of time before they realize what ignoring incidents can do to their business. Organizations must react appropriately to incidents not only to limit damage but also to ensure they learn and update their operations to prevent further incidents.

Handling an incident is straightforward if the incident-handling team is well prepared. Even when caught off-guard, planning and preparing for incident handling allows the information assurance team to identify and recover the system and prevent further damage. In conjunction with computer forensics and evidence management, incident handling ensures that digital evidence collected is admissible, authentic, complete, and reliable for legal action (refer also to Chapter 23). Initially, all incidents should be handled as though they have criminal or civil litigation implications. Once an incident has been determined to be criminal or subject to litigation, earlier mistakes or oversight may make information obtained by the information assurance team inadmissible to the courts.

A well-handled incident is good for morale since it allows IT personnel to identify weaknesses, take precautions such as update patches, and sharpen their skills. Therefore, the information assurance posture of the organization improves. Further, during the actual incident-handling process, data collected about threats and vulnerabilities will be useful to the risk analysis process (see also Chapter 11). The data can be analyzed, correlated, and grouped to analyze hackers' attack patterns. Statistics on different types of incidents in the organization may be used to prepare reports about an organization's information assurance posture.

Incident handling tests the communication and teamwork capabilities of an organization. Internally, management must be aware and organized to receive incident updates. If properly communicated, feedback about the incident helps system administrators and system owners improve their systems. Communication between functional groups such as public relations and legal can be strengthened through the development of mature incident response practices. Communication with external parties such as Internet service providers (ISP), vendors, law enforcement agencies, and the press can be developed and refined through the incident response process. When organizations establish working contacts with law enforcement, vendors, and ISP partners, it provides a significant time advantage for future incident response actions.

Incident Reporting

Incident handling revolves around two words: *incident* and *event*. An *incident* refers to actions that result in damage and form substantial threats to the information system. Except for incidents caused by unforeseen natural disasters, IT incidents can be largely avoided by an organization. Events are large or small abnormalities detected in the network or system.

You can prove an *event* has occurred, there is always evidence or we wouldn't be concerned. The event can be a strange message flash on the screen or even a sound. Something that appears in the audit trail or log files may also be an event. Recognizing and recording these events is important. Events become incidents when it is clear measurable damage may occur or an eminent threat exists. Security operations centers and organizational SIEMs are often flooded with events. Some of the larger SIEMs see more than 500,000 events per hour; however, only a few become incidents. One of the most difficult tasks an organization faces is detecting incidents in a large collection of events. Even so, it is important for an organization to gather reliable evidence of incidents since laws are in place to protect organization. These records may be used in a later court case. Be aware that attackers sometimes use tools to alter or delete traces of their activities in log files.

The evidence is more convincing if organizations produce contemporaneous, accurate sources, and records for information. An organization with a timely, accurate, and thorough incident response policy, operational procedures, and standards is far more likely to succeed in prosecution, litigation and recovery. Organizations execute incident response procedures in the way they practice them. Incident response practice and testing should be part of every organization's continuous monitoring approach and risk management strategy.

An important question to ask is, how and when is an event reported? Accurate, thorough, and timely information by witnesses contributes greatly to the success of an incident-handling process. Communicate all events and weaknesses through a robust pre-established event reporting and escalation procedure. Document the procedure in the organization's information assurance policy.

All employees, vendors, and third-party users should know the incident response procedures and should be encouraged to report an event as soon as possible to prevent an escalation to an incident. They should know the channels and procedures for reporting various events and the effect of incidents on a company's assets.

Organizations must establish proper reporting channels such as the use of e-mail, telephone, and reporting forms (remember, an incident may disable all electronic media). Management should use awareness and training to ensure that everyone knows the appropriate channels. Additionally, rules of behavior and contractual agreements should mandate the reporting of events. Everyone must report all identified and suspected information assurance weaknesses in accordance with the event reporting and escalation procedure.

In the United States, the U.S. Computer Emergency Readiness Team (CERT) is part of the United States Department of Homeland Security (DHS) and provides incident response support and incident analysis. There are reporting procedures and reporting templates provided, which organizations may find useful.

Generally, an organizational incident reporting procedure should encompass the following:

- Mechanism for publishing the identified incidents
- Mechanism for reporting and recording information security incidents
- Disciplinary process for those who commit an information security breach or willingly refuse to report a breach
- Relevant instructions such as the need to record incidents promptly

Part IV

Another example is the Danish Centre for Cyber Security (CFCS), which analyzes security incidents, proposes solutions, and warns others of similar incidents while assuring anonymity and confidentiality of all parties. It also coordinates information for foreign response teams and police. The Danish DKCERT is strictly advisory for civilian organization but has authority through its MILCERT component to order changes to the Danish Department of Defense's military IT and communications systems. To support both operations and AT&E, CFCS publishes articles, alerts, advisories, and news regarding vulnerabilities and precautionary measures.

Incident Handling Process

Incident handling centers on preparation; if the organization is not prepared, the process fails. It requires flexibility to manage the processes, procedures, and countermeasures. Flexibility allows the organization to react to different attacks and environments. The process suggested in this illustration is a synthesis of best practices in the industry.

Figure 22-1 shows the process has phases centered on preparation identification, containment, eradication, recovery, and review. The linkage among the phases is a compass or a road map for incident handlers within an organization. The first phase of the process, identification, is inextricably tied to preparation. Together, they are day-to-day practices for incident handlers. Before taking any action about an incident, handlers need to be prepared to identify events that may grow into incidents.

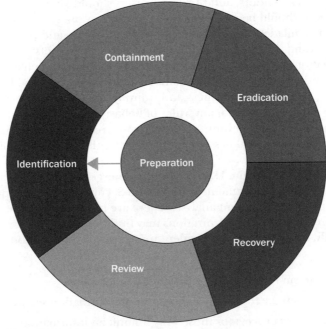

Figure 22-1 Incident handling process

Phase 1: Preparation

Preparation and planning are essential to address any incident effectively. Preparation is a team effort that not only includes internal resources but also those of vendors, contractors, law enforcement, legal counsel, and perhaps national or regional CERT. Budget the most time for preparation and requires the most effort in the preparation process. Preparation is continuous process. Skills and alertness fade over time without AT&E and fresh exercises. Preparation includes defining the incident-handling policy, establishing logging standards and warning banners, setting up the infrastructure and resources, installing the necessary environmental controls, and documenting procedures and baselines.

Every organization should establish an incident-handling policy and warning banners if local laws allow. For example, in the United States, a good practice would be the use of warning banners to inform individuals connecting to the system that access to the system is monitored and recorded to ensure systems are used for authorized purpose only. Unauthorized access, use, or modification is prohibited, and unauthorized users may face charges and criminal or civil penalties if allowed by local law. The policy and banner help define an incident. When legally permissible, users must be required to acknowledge and accept the banner before using an organization's information systems. Other economies may have other requirements or customs.

An incident-handling approach establishes the conditions and responses for an incident. The incident response policy establishes and authorizes the approach to all incident handling organization-wide and requires approval from senior management to ensure a mandate for smooth execution and stimulates employee buy-in.

Once the policy and approach are refined, form the incident-handling team. Draw the members of the team from different backgrounds and discipline such as computer and physical security, system administration, network management, legal, human resources, risk management, and corporate communications. In the event of a serious incident, the technically focused team members will perform onsite investigation, evaluate the situation, and make recommendations. As noted in Chapter 5, incident-handling team leaders should hold professional certifications and credentials validating their expertise, relevant experience, and commitment to continuing professional education. Credentials and certifications applicable to incident handers include, but are not limited to the following:

- International Information Systems Security Certification Consortium (ISC)[2]
  - Certified Information Systems Security Professional (CISSP)
    - Information Systems Security Architecture Professional (CISSP-ISSAP)
    - Information Systems Security Engineering Professional (CISSP-ISSEP)
    - Information Systems Security Management Professional (CISSP-ISSMP)
  - Certified Authorization Professional (CAP)
  - Certified Cyber Forensics Professional (CCFP)
  - Certified Secure Software Lifecycle Professional (CSSLP)

- HealthCare Information Security and Privacy Practitioner (HCISPP)
- SSCP (Systems Security Certified Practitioner (SSCP)
- SysAdmin, Audit, Network, Security (SANS)
  - Certified Incident Handler (GCIH)
  - Certified Intrusion Analyst (GCIA)
  - Certified Forensic Analyst (GCFA)
  - Certified Forensics Examiner (GCFE)
- Information Systems Audit and Control Association (ISACA)
  - Certified Information Systems Auditor (CISA)
  - Certified Information Security Manager (CISM)
  - Certified in Risk and Information Systems Control (CRISK)
- EC-Council
  - Certified Ethical Hacker (CEH)
  - Computer Hacking Forensic Investigator (CHFI)
  - EC-Council Certified Incident Handler (ECIH)

Incident handling requires an emergency/crisis communication plan. This plan is part of business continuity planning (BCP) and should contain a call list for escalation purposes based on severity or criticality of an incident and a call tree to allow all employees to be contacted. This emergency communication plan should be distributed to all personnel in charge and affected users.

Organizations should establish a primary contact point and develop a list of objectives for the incident-handling team. All reporting facilities and mechanisms should be in place to allow employees to report an incident.

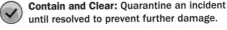 **Contain and Clear:** Quarantine an incident until resolved to prevent further damage.

Organizations must conduct AT&E exercises to ensure an incident-handling team is ready. The

 Watch and Learn: Observe an incident to extract potential training opportunities.

training should be practical rather than theoretical. It should involve rehearsal of potential incident scenarios, use of techniques and tools, forensic evidence handling procedures, administration of various system and hardware, or even games to simulate an incident and the associated activities. "*Capture the flag*" and "*Defense on a Cyber Defense Simulator* (CDS) or *CyberRange*" events offer excellent venues for incident-handling teams to hone their skills.

Phase 2: Detection/Identification

In incident handling, time is crucial. Organizations must take immediate and correct actions after identifying an event or incident. Even if it is later discovered that the event was a false alarm, the incident-handling team gets practice on responding to an event or incident.

To identify events or incidents accurately, team members must be aware of the situation, be updated on the status, and be able to rapidly and accurately integrate the information provided.

During planning, designate an individual as the primary incident handler for the identification phase. The primary incident handler updates the management about the problem within a specific time. Organizations should also determine a line of succession should the primary incident handler be unavailable.

During identification, the incident-handling team performs an initial assessment

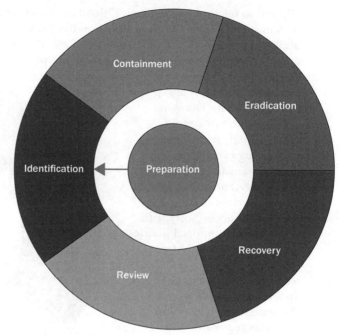

of the validity of an incident. The team assesses the evidence in detail since a single event may be part of an attack chain or lead to litigation.

An incident can be detected by witnesses or through continuous monitoring sensor platforms such as firewalls, audit logs, or intrusion detection systems. Witnesses or systems notify the incident-handling team about suspicious events. Examples are unsuccessful login attempts, unexplained new user accounts, poor system performance, and denial of services.

Some incidents can be detected at the system level. For example, the network perimeter, a network-based intrusion system, firewalls, or routers detect suspicious events. For the host perimeter, the identification is usually detected by a personal firewall, anti-malware system, or IDS. Additionally, file integrity checkers and antivirus software are often monitored for suspicious behavior. Users as witnesses may also detect system-level perimeter intrusions by reporting odd behaviors.

While identifying an incident, the incident-handling team must establish a chain of custody to ensure that all relevant information and evidence is well documented, preserved, and protected. The incident may eventually turn out to be just an event or something that won't be prosecuted; the incident response team can't go back and put a chain of custody on events after the fact. If they do, they may compromise evidence. Incident-handling teams must always remember in many criminal courts the rule is *reasonable doubt*, and, therefore, their actions must be beyond reproach.

Phase 3: Containment

Containment is an immediate act. The organization's incident response plan should focus on mitigating or stopping the damage. As the term implies, the objective of containment is to prevent the incident or situation from escalating. Where possible, an event should not be allowed to become an incident. If that fails, incident escalation and containment reaction may involve a change of passwords for affected systems, blocking of suspicious IPs, or the application of patches to connected systems. To prevent the spread of the problem, take appropriate actions during the containment phase.

As noted in Chapter 18, a structured review is always required before changing a configuration or system. A change made in error or containing errors is almost certain to exacerbate the problem. At any time, members of the incident-handling team must act in accordance with documented standard policies and procedures; otherwise, the integrity of the evidence will be questioned in court later. In addition, failure to use documented policies and practices may cause the incident-handling team to damage the organization's systems further. Backups and validated baseline configurations for the original

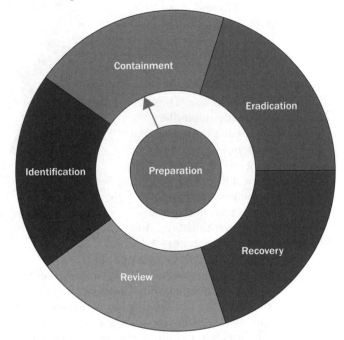

system must be in place for both restoration and forensic purposes. The incident-handling team must always preserve the original copy as evidence and ensure that it remains unchanged. Specific information regarding forensics is covered in Chapter 23.

When dealing with external attacks such as a denial of service (DOS), coordinate closely with the Internet service provider. As noted prior, establishing verified contacts for the ISP with authority to aid the organization is a task that must be performed prior to an event to be most effective. An ISP can provide assistance, especially when there is a large flow of packets flooding an organization's network and services. Most ISPs are experienced in handling network-based exploits and denial of services. Some charge additional fees for services related to DOS attack mitigation. Organizations should decide through a risk assessment if additional protection is worth the price. See Chapter 11 for a discussion of the risk assessment process.

The incident-handling team performs an initial analysis during the containment phase by analyzing a backup copy of the system. The team looks for deviations from the known baseline. If an organization does not have a mature configuration management process as part of its change management process, this task becomes much more difficult. Differences between the baseline configuration and the system under analysis are documented and verified by the incident-handling team. These findings will begin the road map for containment and mitigation.

Organizations may choose to avoid alerting the intruder unnecessarily, by not conducting tracing and mitigation activities or beginning mitigation immediately. This delay decreases the probability of losing a trail to the attacker. If the event impacts mission-critical systems, the organization may have no choice but to begin containment and mitigation. If the organization can withstand the impact of the incident and would gain from understanding more about the attacker, they may want to continue monitoring the attack in a contained environment. Organizations must be cautious when they suspect criminal laws may have been broken. In many countries, individuals are required to report the commission of crimes such as child pornography to authorities immediately upon discovery. Organizations must work with legal counsel to determine what types of events or incidents require immediate law enforcement involvement. Regardless of the path chosen, the organization should then report the status of the analysis (both initial and ongoing) to the senior risk function of the organization. The CISO, CIO, CFO, COO, CEO, or head of the organization is most often briefed about the incident status, depending on severity and area of risk.

After the analysis, the incident-handling team determines the risk of continuing operations. The team should gather logs and diagnostic details from network devices, servers, SEIMs, and end points to determine the severity of the incident and suitable recovery approaches. The team should develop a written recommendation at this point. The recommendation should contain options with associated impacts such as whether to shut down the affected machine or not. These options should be reported to the business or mission owner. If an organization has a C&A process in place, the accreditation official should be updated as well. The CISO, CIO, CFO, COO, CEO, or head of the organization is most often briefed about the incident status and chosen remediation actions, depending on severity and area of risk. In severe incidents, the organization may choose to fail-over to an alternate processing or storage site in accordance with its business continuity plan.

Phase 4: Eradication

Eradication is the most difficult phase for incidents involving malware because malicious codes need to be removed completely and safely. In addition, resolving this phase depends on the severity of an incident and the experience of the incident-handling team.

The eradication phase includes identification and elimination of vulnerabilities that have been exploited.

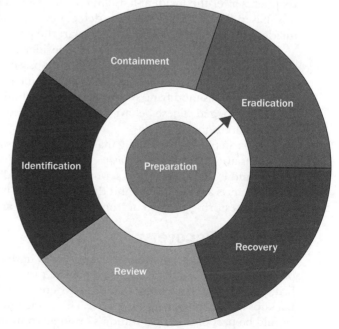

Ideally, the incident-handling team should isolate a system or network to determine how the attack began and, if appropriate, initiate forensic analysis (Chapter 23).

To ensure the attacker does not perform the same attack on other machines within the network, it is wise to perform a vulnerability scan on the network and other systems to identify related vulnerabilities. Additionally, all IDS or IPS systems, host or network based, should be updated with signatures developed from the vulnerability or attack. Additional systems should be prioritized based on value and risk for cleaning, eradication, and re-securing.

These are steps to think about during the eradication phase:

- Even if the incident-handling team was able to successfully stop the malware from executing stubborn forms might reappear the next time a system is started. Where is the problem software located?

- Has the incident-handling team examined locations such as startup files and the registry? How about the BIOS and the master boot sector? These areas are common infection vectors.

- Have programs such as Autoruns been used (http://technet.microsoft.com/en-us/sysinternals/bb963902.aspx)? This displays locations where programs can be set to run automatically in Windows-based systems.

- If the incident-handling team cannot stop the system from running malicious code, rebuild the system from a known good configuration to ensure the vulnerability exploited has been patched. This can be made easier if one has a sound backup policy.

As part of eradication, ensure there is no persistent malware or vulnerability that reappears after the incident-handling team removes it. Properly tuned network and host-based IDSs and IPSs can help detect new infections. If new infections occur, the incident-handling team will have to restart the process and modify the strategy.

The incident-handling team should consider using a malware analysis lab. These solutions are normally appliance- or software-based systems that take suspicious files and execute them in controlled sandboxed environments. During the execution, suspicious behavior such as modifying system files and reaching out to foreign servers across the Internet is logged. These behaviors can then be used to develop signatures for IDSs, IPSs, and malware removal tools.

For particularly challenging malware, specialists may need to be recruited. These specialists are called *reverse malware engineers*. Their job is to analyze malicious code and understand exactly how it works, what it targets, and how best to remove and disable it. These experts are expensive, and the organization must weigh the benefits versus the costs of simply restoring the system from a known good and hardened baseline configuration.

Phase 5: Recovery

Even if the incident-handling team appears to have eradicated all signs of malware and other exploits, organizations should consider rebuilding the system. The recovery phase brings the system back into operation. Systems should be recovered from known good backups and baseline configurations. These documents, configurations, and procedures should be part of the organization's business continuity planning. In severe incidents, the organization may actually need to fail over to an alternate processing and storage site. If the organization is recovering from the alternate site, they will follow the disaster recovery plan. You can find more information about disaster recovery and contingency planning in Chapters 24 and 25.

Once the system is restored, the mission or business owner should verify that the incident handling was a success and the system is back to its normal state. The incident-handling team must always perform tests with assistance and approval from the system owner and system administrator. After obtaining the results and understanding any residual risk, the mission or business line owner will decide whether the system should return to operation. In organizations with a C&A process in place, the accreditation official will make this decision. The incident-handling team's task does not end when the system is restored. Instead, the team must ensure that the organization's continuous monitoring capability is searching for new threats and vulnerabilities constantly.

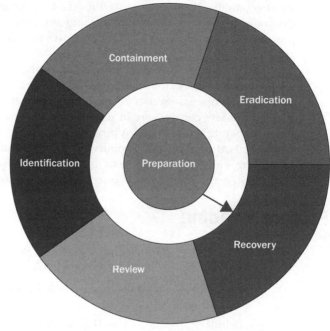

Phase 6: Review

The last phase in the incident-handling process is to prepare a follow-up report and organize a review meeting to allow the incident-handling team to share and learn from the experience. The team should present the report and recommend to management additional countermeasures to prevent recurrence.

Use the review phase to improve incident-handling procedures. The lessons learned

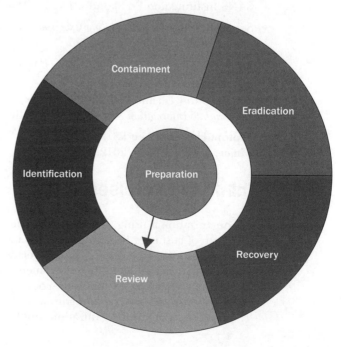

also become feedback to improve the AT&E program for the organization. The AT&E program can be used to develop training and evaluation scenarios for all employees. A positive outcome from an incident improves morale and makes the overall information assurance posture stronger.

Some common follow-on activities from the review are a penetration test and a recertification for systems following a C&A process. The penetration test is often performed as a limited-scope assessment to ensure the same attack cannot happen again and to ensure the appropriate controls are in place to mitigate further attacks of a similar nature. For systems operating under a C&A program and accreditation, they should be re-accessed with a scope focused on vulnerability management, configuration management AT&E program, and any controls identified as deficient in the incident report. Any further deficiencies should be documented and reported to the accreditation official for mitigation or acceptance.

Further Reading

- Jones, K.J., R. Bejtlich, and C.W. Rose. *Real Digital Forensics: Computer Security and Incident Response*. Addison-Wesley, 2005.

- Kruse II, WG, and JG Heiser. *Computer Forensics: Incident Response Essentials*. Addison-Wesley, 2005.

- Nichols, R. *Defending Your Digital Assets Against Hackers, Crackers, Spies, and Thieves*. McGraw-Hill Education, 2000.

- Prosise, C., K. Mandia, and M. Pepe. *Incident Response and Computer Forensics*. McGraw-Hill Education, 2003.

- SANS Institute and Ed Skoudis. *Incident Handling Guidelines*. SANS, 2004.

- Schmidt, Howard A. *Patrolling Cyberspace: Lessons Learned from a Lifetime in Data Security*. Larstan Publishing, 2006.

- Conklin, Wm. Arthur. *Introduction to Principles of Computer Security: Security+ and Beyond*. McGraw-Hill Education, 2004.

- Schou, Corey D., and D.P. Shoemaker. *Information Assurance for the Enterprise: A Roadmap to Information Security*. McGraw-Hill Education, 2007.

- Tipton, Harold. F., and S. Hernandez, ed. *Official (ISC) ^{2} Guide to the CISSP CBK 3rd edition*. ((ISC)^2) Press, 2012.

Critical Thinking Exercises

1. An organization is using a cloud-based system for hosting its sensitive information in the form of customer lists and personally identifiable information. They are using Software as a Service (SaaS) customer relationship management (CRM) platform to manage their sales. Lately, their customers have been complaining about receiving calls from a competitor in another country with detailed information about their purchase histories and relationship with the organization. What is the incident response approach the organization should take?

2. An organization has adopted a *bring-your-own-device* (BYOD) approach for mobile devices such as smartphones and tablets. An employee's tablet has been identified as an unauthorized bridge between the organization's secure network and the public Internet. The organization's incident-handling team is baffled as to how this could happen and attempts to call the employee and retrieve the device. The employee refuses to provide the device and cites their right to privacy and their ownership of the device. The owner states that they have sensitive personal information on the device and under no circumstance will they allow the organization to search the device. What can the organization do in this situation?

CHAPTER 23

Computer Forensics

Computer forensics (digital forensics) is the scientific procedures and accepted set of processes of examining and analyzing allegations of misuse in computer-related incidents. The end-state of digital forensics is to obtain potential legal evidence acceptable to the trier of fact. Forensic analysis uses a range of scientific processes requiring systematic examination and collection of evidence; keeping a legally sufficient set of records and reports; performing experiments; testing hypotheses; describing the process and results; and defending the forensic findings and conclusions. It comes from forensic scientist Edmond Locard's basic exchange principle: "Every contact leaves a trace." There are five steps that should be followed:

1. Gather useful items and items of potential evidentiary interest.
2. Preserve data integrity (chain of evidence).
3. Identify evidentiary artifacts, physical, and critical information.
4. Analyze evidence.
5. Present evidence.

Computer forensics is the scientific bridge between law and computer science that allows digital evidence to be collected in a legally sound manner. Management must realize that every interaction with a digital device leaves a trace. The improper application of computer forensic tools may be dangerous to data and may make forensics collected unacceptable for use by the judicial system.

The computer forensics team should work closely or even be embedded into an incident-handling process (see Chapter 22). The organization may want to engage appropriate digital forensics experts as consultants or work with the appropriate national computer emergency response team (CERT) directly. When an incident occurs, the incident-handling team is often the first to arrive at the scene. Without proper computer forensic procedures in place and reinforced through organizational policy, the evidence may be tampered with or inadvertently contaminated.

The roles, responsibilities and actions performed by internal employees, a law enforcement agency, or external computer forensic experts must be defined before an incident occurs. Management needs to understand the purpose of computer forensics, the requirement to establish a computer forensic function or team if required, the rules and processes of computer forensics, and the consequences of improper handling of evidence. Remember, if the organization is planning to perform forensics, it must be willing to invest in professional training and licensing of multiple tools to cover the widest range of devices and systems and develop a culture that allows proper seizure and preservation techniques. Tools should be validated for proper data acquisition and reporting. To make sure everything works as expected, organizations should practice periodic mock examinations and incident response drills to gain an in-depth understanding of tools and subtleties of use.

Importance of Computer Forensics

It is helpful to view the relationship of computer forensics to information assurance as autopsy is to medicine. If your organization practices computer forensics too often, your information assurance process is failing! Forensic analysis is a post-event response to serious incidents or criminal actions. Computer forensics gathers admissible evidence through a systematic and formal examination procedure for either external use by courts or internal use by the organization. Dr. Rainer Böhme, Assistant Professor of Information Systems and IT Security, University of Münster, developed an ontogeny for forensics. He points out that there is an increased degree of freedom associated with analog forensics, while forge-ability, or what can be counterfeited, decreases on a continuum from computer forensics to analog forensics.

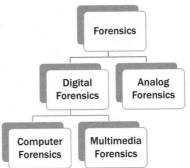

Analog forensics tries to find traces of physical evidence, digital forensics deals with observing patterns that may contain messages, and multimedia forensics focuses on manipulation of multimedia files to either change or embed information.

Cybercrimes involve any unauthorized and unlawful cyber activities. They may range from a simple denial-of-service (DOS) attack to unauthorized use or access of systems. The installation of intrusion detection systems, firewalls, or proxy services may be insufficient to prevent these activities. To successfully discover and prosecute cybercrimes, computer forensic knowledge and skills are essential.

An organization is responsible for protecting client and customer information. Senior managers have been held responsible for failing to exercise *due care*. (See Chapter 27 for specific examples of executives being sued by stakeholders and customers.) By using proper computer forensic personnel procedures and providing forensic tools used by qualified individuals, evidence admissible in a court of law may help organizations preserve their reputation and customers.

Prerequisites of a Computer Forensic Examiner

If an organization needs forensic skills, it typically engages the services of a competent and credentialed forensics examiner. Well-trained computer forensic examiners possess both specialized knowledge and experience. In some economies, such as Australia, examiners may also be called *forensic analysts*. Immature examiners may overlook a trace or destroy evidence. For example, the individual may reboot an attacked system or open files leading to a modification of system properties or erasure of electronic footprints of the criminals.

A strong general IT background is essential. The examiner should be familiar with network topology, architecture and protocols, and hardware functionality and usage, and the examiner should have a clear understanding of how software programs run. Examiners are expected to keep abreast of computer forensic techniques, methodologies, and standards. Many tools are available for computer forensics. An examiner should be familiar with these tools and be able to decide which ones to use during the forensic process.

An examiner must always observe the basic rules of the profession to produce quality forensics in an impartial and objective manner. The examiner must follow formal procedures; otherwise, the findings risk rejection in courts. An examiner should also be able to prepare proper documentation. An ideal examiner has good interpersonal and presentation skills, which help when appearing as a witness in a court case. In addition to a strong foundation in information assurance and technology, the individual must have a lifestyle and personal history that cannot damage their credibility in the eyes of the court or an aggressive defense attorney. A single questionable event from the past can cast a shadow of doubt on an otherwise outstanding individual. Remember, in many courts, the defense needs only to create a reasonable doubt for an acquittal.

Whether outsourced or in-house, the forensic team must understand the nature of the organization and its mission, customers, threats, and operating environment. The examiner will ideally understand the politics of the organization and remain impartial in the analysis. The forensic team must also be able to weather adversity and possible hostility. If a senior executive is under examination, the forensic team may become the target of retaliation. Strong whistleblower policies and anti-retaliation policies can aid in keeping forensic teams focused on collecting evidence instead of being worried about their jobs.

Forensic Skills

Management should seek assistance from individuals with skills and knowledge in the following areas to ensure successful forensic examination. The foremost common forensic skill is the scientific method in which it ensures that the examiner is merely a finder of facts. A second common forensic skill is the ability to deal with dynamic evidence shared across devices.

Antiforensic Techniques and Tools

The underlying principle of antiforensics is that if evidence cannot be found, it cannot be identified, acquired, analyzed, or explored. Merely encrypting evidence is one of the simplest and most effective techniques for hiding it. Attackers are becoming some of the most advanced users of information assurance technologies. An attacker will infiltrate an organization and locate the information they desire. They will then copy the information and encrypt it. The encrypted information is then transferred out of the organization or sometimes held for ransom after the original information is deleted. The forensic examiner should be capable of identifying fully encrypted disks as well as specific files and hidden partitions on the hard drive. Since good encryption is hard to overcome, this technique can overwhelm all but the most skilled and well-equipped examiners.

A related technique for hiding evidence in background noise is steganography. It allows the perpetrator to change selected least significant bits (LSBs) in a file so they can be used to hide a message. For example, in a given 8-bit byte, the rightmost bit is the LSB. In a large string of bits in music MP3s, changing the LSB will have little effect and can actually be used to hide information; however, it creates a difficult problem for the forensics examiner. The examiner must now try to determine how the file is structured, determine whether encryption is being used in conjunction with the LSB, and determine whether MP3 files are the only files affected! Organizations can spend countless hours and resources exhausting possibilities. A superior examiner will know when they have obtained necessary and sufficient information to act on.

Another antiforensic technique involves placing data where it is not expected. For example, data may be placed in the slack space (space not accounted for in the file system since it is between the end of a file and the end of block); unused firmware memory; unused space in the master boot record; or in the host protected area, which is not customarily available to the operating system. Refer to the Further Reading section later in the chapter for where to find more detail on antiforensics as well as the role of the digital investigator.

Forensic Techniques and Tools

Organizations can develop and support a superior forensics team by providing best in class tools that have been certified and well tested. Certified tools are important for evidence to be credible in court. The U.S. National Institute of Standards (NIST) maintains a Computer Forensics Tool Testing (CFTT) program (www.cftt.nist.gov/). Validation by CFTT allows users to make sound decisions about computer forensics tools and encourages developers to improve their tools. CFTT also provides a thorough guidance about mobile device imaging, including requirements, test plans, setup and test procedures, and tool test reports.

As discussed earlier, computer forensics requires expert identification, extraction, preservation, and documentation. To accomplish this, the expert must by supported by forensically sound skills, tools, and methods. One important method is never to conduct any examination on the original media. Creation of validated copies of original data is a keystone principle for forensics examiners. Before any forensics analysis, make sure the team is well trained and has previously used mock tests.

Media and File System Forensics

Successful forensic analysis requires a thorough knowledge of file types and digital media used to store data (one of the three states from the MSR model) and the file structures used on those devices. This analysis may require salvaging deleted data, which may be as simple as changing disc file tables to mark blocks as not deleted. However, this may require file carving techniques to recover data from unallocated space. Tools for this include DataLifter, PhotoRec, and Scalpel.

File forensics becomes more complicated if the media devices are encrypted. In addition, the examiner must be able to find hidden metadata that is frequently included during file creation. A specialized case of data hiding (steganography) was discussed in the "Antiforensic Techniques and Tools" section earlier in this chapter.

Types of Media   Types and capacities of digital storage media devices are constantly evolving. Legacy storage media include media such as punch cards, punched paper tape, floppy disks of all sizes, and a plethora of magnetic gadgets. Typically, digital media have one of two access types: serial and random. Serial media devices store data elements one after another, as they arrive. Since there is no addressing scheme, usually the serial data must be read from the beginning to find a particular block. Random media devices store the data evenly distributed across the storage space and have an addressing scheme to record where the data has been stored. This allows the data to be accessed in the order needed rather than the order in which it arrived. The inherent weakness of random devices comes from the table (index) that stores where the data are and, in some cases, the associated linked lists. If the index fails, the data usually become inaccessible.

Here are some examples of media:

- **Magnetic tape**   A magnetic tape is a serial access medium. This feature makes it an excellent choice for the regular backup of hard disks. Magnetic tape is a strip of plastic coated in a fine magnetic powder bound with polymer glue. Data is stored in frames (usually a byte) across the width of the medium. These frames are grouped into blocks separated by inter record gaps (IRGs). The more data placed in a block, the more efficient the tape.

- **Hard disk drives**   Hard drives are random devices that use a similar magnetic powder as a magnetic tape; however, in the case of a hard drive, the powder is bound to a rigid platter. The disk spins underneath precision magnetic devices (heads) that turn electronic pulses representing data into magnetic fields to write, and the process is reversed to read data. The heads move in small steps over the spinning surface and create concentric tracks. The tracks are broken down into sectors like pieces of pie. The location of data is determined by indexing the location of data on the tracks and sectors. Hard disk drives are subject to physical damage such as drops and also magnetic damage from external electromagnetic sources. Solid state hard drives (SSD) are discussed next in electronic media.

- **Optical Media**   A compact disc (CD), Digital Versatile Disk (DVD), and Blu-Ray are polycarbonate plastic discs with at least one metal layer used to store digital data. They are written and read by reflecting precise laser light from minute pits on the surface. These can be examined by microscopes. Optical media has become a standard medium for backing up or distributing large quantities of data on dependable media. The data is stored on a track like a hard drive; however, the single track of data spirals from the center of the disc to the outside edge. Optical media is highly resistant to magnetic and electronic distortion; however, they are susceptible to damage from ultraviolet light sources, heat, and physical damage by scratching. Optical media is typically liquid resistant but prolonged exposure can break down the metal coating and damage the media.

- **Electronic media**   Electronic media devices are solid-state electronic storage devices. Since they have no moving parts, they are ideally suited for portable devices and those that have to be shock tolerant. There are numerous solid state drives and other electronic media for replacing hard drives and providing storage for almost any device imaginable. They are logically organized like hard drives with sectors. Each sector of flash memory can be erased and written to only a limited number of times.

  Other formats of electronic media that may need to be examined include CompactFlash (CF), Memory Stick (MS), MultiMediaCard (MMC), Secure Digital (SD), SmartMedia (SM), solid-state disks (SSDs), USB drives, and xD-Picture Card (xD). Electronic media are susceptible to electronic pulses, physical damage, and damage from liquid. They also have a finite number of write cycles.

- **Cloud**   Remote network repositories in the Internet cloud, mail/web servers, or FTP sites where another party other than the organization processes, stores, or transmits information on behalf of the organization. Cloud providers present all media risks described above based on their chosen technologies. Additionally, cloud providers may not provide access during a forensic investigation unless the hosted organization provides a legal search warrant or similar court order. Cloud providers often co-locate tenants so several tenants may reside on a single physical hard drive or other media device. Due to this co-location, if a drive is removed for one organization, it may cause a denial of service to another. Organizations must consider the legal costs involved in conducting a forensic investigation with cloud providers.

Sample File Systems   In general, all file systems are designed to provide a standardized method for allocating storage used by systems. These systems are designed to optimize the use and reuse of space as well as the speed of reading and writing. Each type of hardware and operating system addresses this problem differently. Analysts must be familiar and capable of using all modern file systems.

Mobile Devices

As BYOD policies become more permissive, mobile device forensics is increasingly important. BYOD policies are clearly productivity multipliers; however, they potentially expose the organization to new, unmitigated risks. Forensics experts should be able to handle a broad spectrum of devices, protocols, and ISO layer 1 connections.

Devices fall into two main categories: cellular and non-cellular. Cellular devices are functionally radio telephones and may be further divided based on the protocol they use (GSM versus CDMA). All mobile devices have storage (see electronic media in this chapter) that might have to be examined. All have volatile random access memory (RAM) where the programs/applications run. Most have flash ROM, which stores the operating system, user file space, and preloaded applications. SIM cards are used in GSM devices and contain a processor, RAM, and ROM that may contain data of forensic interest.

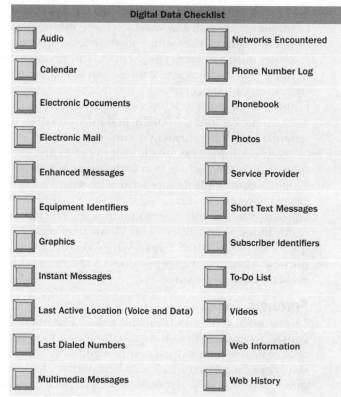

Digital Data Checklist

Audio	Networks Encountered
Calendar	Phone Number Log
Electronic Documents	Phonebook
Electronic Mail	Photos
Enhanced Messages	Service Provider
Equipment Identifiers	Short Text Messages
Graphics	Subscriber Identifiers
Instant Messages	To-Do List
Last Active Location (Voice and Data)	Videos
Last Dialed Numbers	Web Information
Multimedia Messages	Web History

The Netherlands Forensic Institute provides an excellent set of guidelines for preservation of data on mobile devices (www.holmes.nl/MPF/FlowChartForensicMobile PhoneExamination.htm).

Once the data is preserved, the following checklist helps make sure everything is checked.

Multimedia and Content

Although multimedia forensics is different from computer forensics, knowledge of multimedia forensics is important if there is suspicion of systems being used inappropriately. To determine this, the examiner may have to operate with very little knowledge. The examiner may have to infer the characteristics of the sensor, camera, microphone/recorder, or other acquisition device; they can be checked for their presence (identification phase) or consistence (detection phase). Artifacts of previous processing operations can be detected in the manipulation detection phase. For example, you might have concerns if copyright information is stored or distributed through multimedia files that have been manipulated and are inconsistent with others in the same group.

Part IV

Network Forensics

Computer forensic teams usually retrieve information from computer disks or other physical devices; network forensics must also retrieve ephemeral information about network ports used to attack the network. There is one significant difference; network forensic teams have nothing to examine unless precautions were in place (such as packet filters, firewalls, and intrusion detection systems) before the incident occurred.

Network intrusions are difficult to detect and even more difficult to analyze. Port scans are near instantaneous, while a more serious stealth attack on critical systems and their crucial resource may be concealed by a simple innocent port scan. The forensic team should always focus on the classic journalist questions: Who? What? When? Why? Where? How? The purpose of intrusion analysis is to seek answers and evaluate their importance.

Who attacked?

What did they get?

Why did they attack?

Where did they come from?

Where did they go?

When did they do it?

How did they do it?

Forensic Tools

"A craftsman can never blame his tools." This old saying is also true for forensic tools. Of course, forensic analysts can make their own tools but will be better served by using proven tools. The selection of tools may be significant from an evidentiary standpoint since the integrity of the forensic software is important. In Australia, Fixed Disk Image (FDI), developed by Rod McKemmish, is well respected and has been provided to Australian law enforcement at no cost. Others that are broadly recognized for criminal and civil cases in many jurisdictions are Forensic Toolkit (FTK) and EnCase. The following list contains a broad spectrum of forensic tools:

- **AccessData Forensic Toolkit**   This toolkit consists of command-line and GUI utilities used to reconstruct access activities in NT file systems.

- **Guidance Software EnCase**   EnCase is a widely used closed source forensic examination tool. It works on many platforms.

- **Open Source SleuthKit**   Use this to examine a hacked UNIX host, for example. It works on Linux, Mac OS X, Windows (Visual Studio and mingw), CYGWIN, Open and FreeBSD, and Solaris. It supplants the Coroner Toolkit.

- **ForensiX**   This is an all-purpose set of data collection and analysis tools that run primarily on Linux. It's an open source joint project of University of Toronto and Portland State University available on sourcforge.net. For a full discussion of open and closed source tools for forensic analysis, see Daniel Manson's paper "Is the open way a better way? Digital forensics using open source tools."

Virtual System Forensics

There are two problems posed by the use of virtual machines for the forensic analyst. The first problem emerges when a virtual machine (VM) is used to analyze forensic evidence.

Both VMware and Microsoft Hyper-V are common tools to provide VM capability. Initially, a VM is an attractive tool since its configuration is easily modified to match the original system that created the evidence. The operation of VMs is both transitory and ephemeral. They are a level of abstraction beyond normal hardware; the system and data are volatile. Early attempts led to questions about the suitability of the findings obtained as evidence in court since the hypervisor might modify the image. University of Western Sydney Lecturer Derek Bem notes that an image which is known to have changed would be immediately challenged in a court of law as flawed. A computer expert could argue that the changes were not relevant to the evidence being presented; however, it is unlikely that such a line of argument would be accepted by the court ruled by reasonable doubt. The acceptance of VMs has been increasing. Another forensic analysis approach uses a VM as a playback analysis on log files.

Supplemental Forensic Skills

Depending on the engagement, other knowledge and skill areas that may be important to the forensics team are client/server interactions, cloud forensics, social networks, big data paradigm, industrial control systems, critical infrastructure, and virtual/augmented reality. Organizations must consider the circumstances surrounding an incident or crime. While determining forensic skills and experience, organizations must also consider the scope of technologies and systems required to conduct a thorough, accurate, and timely forensic investigation.

Rules of Computer Forensics

To ensure the admissibility, authenticity, completeness, reliability, and integrity of evidence collected, in most jurisdictions, examiners observe these rules:

- **Knowledge level**   Examiners should not attempt to perform an examination that is beyond their knowledge or skill level. They should seek assistance from more experienced examiners.

- **Chain of custody**   Although the rules vary by jurisdiction, examiners should comply with the principle of chain of custody when collecting, handling, and examining evidence to ensure admissibility of the evidence in court. This is discussed in the next section.

- **Evidence preservation**   Examiners avoid degrading the integrity of the evidence and perform examinations only on an image copy of the original. The image copy should be an exact reproduction of the original. Refer also to the "Rules of Evidence" section later in this chapter.

- **Record everything**   Examiners must record every step taken during the examination. Changes may be unavoidable during the computer forensic process. For example, shutting down the server might affect evidence in volatile computer memory. Examiners must document the nature, effect, and reason for any change properly and be prepared to defend their reasoning.

Chain of Custody

In most jurisdictions, chain of custody is a historical view of collecting and analyzing processes, transportation, and preservation of evidence to warrant admissibility as evidence in court. The chain of custody is chronological and is particularly important with electronic evidence because of the possibility of accidental or fraudulent data alteration, deletion, or creation. For evidentiary purposes, detailed chain of custody reports are necessary to establish the physical custody of digital evidence.

When making evidentiary copies, examiners must follow standard procedures to ensure quality and integrity. They must carefully label and preserve all evidence and copies of evidence. For example, media should be write-protected, placed in a container or envelope, labeled, and secured in a fireproof safe. Carefully observe different handling and storing techniques for different types of media.

Computer Forensic Steps

Prior to any examination, the computer forensic team (or information assurance team if forensics is outsourced) should have a standard methodology and procedural documents in place. Despite the different tools and techniques used, a computer forensic methodology should at a minimum consist of the following steps:

- **Identify**   This is the process of identifying evidence to be collected and presented and of identifying the methods, systems, and tools used for recovery and when to involve law enforcement.

- **Acquire**   This is the process of preserving the integrity of the evidence and ensuring the chain of custody is maintained. The tools, processes, and storage space used to safeguard the evidence obtained, as well as the duplicating and preservation methods, must be thoroughly documented.

- **Analyze**   This is the process of examining and assessing the evidence collected. During this process, examiners must avoid using the original evidence collected for assessment.

- **Report**   The forensic analysis should result in a forensics report. The report should contain the results of the analysis, the processes used, and any implications the examiner may determine as relevant to the organization.

Rules of Evidence

There are three basic rules of evidence that computer forensic examiners in most jurisdictions should observe.

- **Authenticity**   This rule describes the relevancy of evidence collected. Examiners should be able to link evidence collected to the incident in a legitimate and logical method.

- **Completeness**   This rule explains the need for completeness of evidence collected. The evidence collected can be used to identify the real attacker and eliminate other suspects.

- **Reliability**   This rule addresses the integrity of evidence collected. The evidence collection and analysis process should ensure authenticity and reality of evidence collected.

Computer Forensics Teams

Although computer forensics has existed for quite some time, there are still limited formal standards, frameworks, certification, and expertise within the field. As technology evolves, more tools and reference materials are available. Dedicated computer forensic teams are an expensive endeavor. They require expensive ongoing training, are often difficult to retain, and fetch some of the highest salaries in the industry. Smaller or midsize organizations may be challenged to justify the need for a permanent computer forensics team. If your organization intends to develop a computer forensic team, consider the information in following sections. If your organization decides it will use consultants, you can still leverage the following sections as a guide to determine what qualifications and capabilities the consultant should have.

Establishing a Computer Forensics Team

When establishing a computer forensics team, management should consider the feasibility of an in-house capability. Management should determine the resources required and the demand. Sometimes engaging an external consultant team is a better alternative. The Certified Forensic Computer Examiner (CFCE) credential by the International Association of Computer Investigative Specialists (IACIS) is narrowly focused on demonstrating computer forensics for Windows-based computers. CFCE requires being in law enforcement. The establishment of broader professional certifications such as the (ISC)² Certified Computer Forensics Professional (CCFP) makes team building more reliable by ensuring individuals know more than how the tools work.

If an organization decides to have an in-house team, consider the size needed. Large organizations and law enforcement organizations require larger teams. Setting up a credible computer forensic team is a formidable process. It is difficult to find skillful and experienced individuals to handle the variety of cases involving digital evidence.

If possible, the computer forensic team should be isolated from regular information technology operations. To ensure integrity and avoid conflict of interest during the evidence collection process, computer forensic duties should not be taken by information technology departments as a part-time activity.

Further Reading

- Alles, E. J., Z.J. Geradts, and C.J. Veenman. "Source Camera Identification for Heavily JPEG Compressed Low Resolution Still Images." *Journal of Forensic Sciences*, 2009. 54(3): 628–638.

- Bem, Derek, and Ewa Huebner. "Computer Forensic Analysis in a Virtual Environment." *International Journal of Digital Evidence*, 2007. 6, no. 2: 1–13.

Part IV

- Böhme, Rainer, et al. "Multimedia Forensics Is Not Computer Forensics." *Computational Forensics*, 2009. pp. 90–103.

- Braid, M. "Collecting Electronic Evidence After a System Compromise." AUSCERT, 2001. www.auscert.org.au/render.html?it=2247.

- Casey, E., and G.J. Stellatos. The Impact of Full Disk Encryption on Digital Forensics. ACM SIGOPS Operating Systems Review, 2008. 42(3), 93–98.

- Cheddad, A., et al. "Digital Image Steganography: Survey and Analysis of Current Methods. Signal Processing, 2010. 90(3), 727–752.

- Garfinkel, Simson. "Anti-forensics: Techniques, Detection, and Countermeasures." *The 2nd International Conference on i-Warfare and Security* (ICIW), 2007. pp. 77–84.

- Jones, KJ, R. Bejtlich, and CW Rose. *Real Digital Forensics: Computer Security and Incident Response*. Addison-Wesley, 2005.

- Karen, R. *We've Had an Incident, Who Do We Get to Investigate*. SANS Institute, 2002. www.sans.org/rr/whitepapers/incident/652.php.

- Kessler, Gary C. "Anti-forensics and the Digital Investigator." Australian Digital Forensics Conference, 2007. p. 1.

- Kirk, P. *Crime Investigation: Physical Evidence and the Police Laboratory*. Interscience Publishers, 1953.

- Kruse II, WG, and JG Heiser. *Computer Forensics: Incident Response Essentials*. Addison-Wesley, 2005.

- Kurosawa, K., K. Kuroki, and N. Akiba. "Individual Camera Identification Using Correlation of Fixed Pattern Noise in Image Sensors." *Journal of Forensic Sciences*, 54(3), 2009. 639–641.

- Manson, Dan, et al. "Is the Open Way a Better Way? Digital Forensics Using Open Source Tools." *System Sciences*, 2007. HICSS 2007. 40th Annual Hawaii International Conference, pp. 266b–266b. IEEE, 2007.

- McKemmish, Rodney. "What Is Forensic Computing?" Australian Institute of Criminology, 1999.

- Mohay, George M., et al. *Computer and Intrusion Forensics*. Artech House, 2003.

- Nestler, Vincent J. *Computer Security Lab Manual (Information Assurance and Security)*. McGraw-Hill Education, 2005.

- Nestler, Vincent J., et al. *Principles of Computer Security CompTIA Security+ and Beyond Lab Manual*. McGraw-Hill Education, 2011.

- Ng, T.T., et al. "Passive-Blind Image Forensics." *Multimedia Security Technologies for Digital Rights*. Academic Press, 2006. pp. 383–412.

- Nichols, R., D. Ryan, and J. Ryan. *Defending Your Digital Assets Against Hackers, Crackers, Spies, and Thieves*. McGraw-Hill Education, 2000.

- Prosise, C., K. Mandia, and M. Pepe. *Incident Response and Computer Forensics*. McGraw-Hill Education, 2003.

- Schmidt, Howard A. *Patrolling Cyberspace: Lessons Learned from a Lifetime in Data Security.* Larstan Publishing, 2006.

- Conklin, Wm. Arthur. *Introduction to Principles of Computer Security: Security+ and Beyond.* McGraw-Hill Education, 2004.

- Schou, Corey D., and D.P. Shoemaker. *Information Assurance for the Enterprise: A Roadmap to Information Security.* McGraw-Hill Education, 2007.

- Yasinsac, Alec, and Y. Manzano. "Policies to Enhance Computer and Network Forensics." Proceedings of the 2001 IEEE Workshop on Information Assurance and Security United States Military Academy. West Point, NY, June 5–6, 2001.

Critical Thinking Exercises

1. A manager suspects an employee may be using an organizational computer to view and download certain illegal materials. The manager has asked the information technology manager for his advice regarding her suspicions about these materials. The IT manager states he can change the password to the user's account, and they can log in together over the weekend while the worker is out and view materials on the workstation. Is this an acceptable approach to determine whether criminal activity is occurring on the organization's computer?

2. An organization is experiencing a loss of information. They find the source of the leak and grow frustrated. While the organization knows who is leaking the information, they are not sure how. The organization has blocked the use of all external media such as USB drives, CDs, and DVDs. It has also developed data loss prevention tools and procedures to prevent information from leaking outside the organization through e-mail. It has also implemented web site filtering so employees cannot use unauthorized web mail or file-sharing services. The only thing in common with the leaked information is that it coincided with new updates to images and pictures on the organization's public web site. What could be causing the leak?

Part IV

24 Business Continuity Management

Maintaining or reconstituting an organizational operation under adverse conditions is something that must be fully thought out. The size of an organization does not change the importance of business continuity management (BCM). Even if an enterprise is run from a garage with records in a shoebox, it must be prepared for disaster. Organizations are exposed to major disruptive events that affect their business processes. Hence, BCM becomes both more important and more critical. BCM is part of continuous risk management. BCM is a planning effort and an operational practice involving reactive, diagnostic, and compensating controls for availability and integrity failures. Refer also to Chapter 11 on information assurance risk management.

BCM is a fundamental part of an organization's recovery process. It is a diagnostic and corrective risk management approach designed to protect an organization's processes, assets, interests, clients, and business objectives. It provides a framework to assess threats, the susceptibility of systems to the threats, and the effects on the organization. A well-designed BCM plan provides fundamental and reliable controls to protect organizations from outages, denial of services, and operational errors. Comprehensive BCM allows the organization to maintain its integrity, availability, sustainability, and industry competitiveness. BCM ensures critical business resource processes, and outputs are secured, protected, and functional in the event of adverse or disastrous conditions.

This chapter describes the importance of BCM and the associated best practices and the types of planning that supports it. Examples are business continuity planning, business unit resumption planning, crisis management planning, disaster recovery planning, and impact analysis.

Importance of Business Continuity Management

BCM ensures that an organization is ready to face and respond to major disruptions that threaten the operation and survival of the organization. Even if an organization has not experienced a disaster, BCM planning defines key functional areas and processes of the organization, as well as the impact of discontinuity. This allows the organization to prepare for the worst-case scenario and to take steps to improve its resilience to the disruption of resources, infrastructure, and support required by these functions and processes.

Despite the size, nature of business, and whether it is in the public or private sector, an organization always needs to answer to the expectations of government, regulators, insurers, business partners, investors, and other key stakeholders. By having BCM as part of the management practice, organizations may fulfill the expectations.

By maintaining continuity, BCM helps minimize financial impact during serious incidents by protecting tangible and intangible assets. Through demonstrating a professional approach to managing adverse situations, reputation is maintained, and chances of negative publicity are mitigated. When an organization ensures its continuity and proves that essential services will remain uninterrupted, customers remain loyal to the organization. From the employee standpoint, BCM also protects information assets and improves job security.

Critical Success Factors for BCM Implementation

The following are critical success factors to ensure the sustainability of a BCM program:

- **Management support**   The most important element in sustaining the BCM program is obtaining management support. This ensures the management will allocate resources for this project. In addition to being the key driver of organizational change, management awareness of the scope of business and overall responsibility steers the program and sets priorities for the success of this initiative.

- **Accountability and responsibility**   The BCM initiative establishes reporting levels and individual responsibilities. All departments should know their role in incorporating BCM in its respective functional areas. To ensure all departments are aware of this role and understand the importance of BCM, a BCM team lead should oversee the overall process development and report to management on obstacles faced.

- **Integral part of information assurance management program**   In some organizations, BCM runs in parallel with the information assurance management program. In others, the information assurance management is subordinate to BCM. Regardless of the model adopted, it is imperative not to separate BCM from the organization's information assurance management program and overall management processes. This allows continuous monitoring and improvement. You should integrate BCM into the total change management process. The rationale for this is to ensure the process remains current, usable, and effective.

Business Continuity Management Processes

The BCM team establishes the objectives and activity scope in conjunction with the chief risk officer. Managing acceptable risk ultimately guides the team. Together, the BCM team develops the continuity planning policy statement for review, approval, and continuous improvement. The team then develops project plans and submits them for the approval by senior management. This approval avoids conflicts and erroneous assumptions. Management must give permission before the program proceeds. The BCM process consists of six stages:

1. Recognize BCP is essential.
2. Identify the business needs.
3. Develop BCM strategies.
4. Develop and implement BCM response.
5. Develop BCM culture.
6. Execute, maintain, and audit.

The phases are illustrated in Figure 24-1.

Stage 1: Recognize BCP Is Essential

Once essential management agrees, establish a BCM program led by the chief risk officer or their designate. The BCM team leader oversees the development and implementation of a BCM program and subcomponents. The BCM team consists of representatives from all functional areas including management, business units, information technology, information assurance, legal, and public relations.

Stage 2: Identify the Business Needs

If an organization does not understand its business and which processes are critical to continued operation, it will not recover from a disaster.

An organization must identify and prioritize critical functional areas and identify minimal acceptable levels of service for each functional area during emergency. The identified functions should meet the objectives stated in the BCM policy. Identify all related supplies,

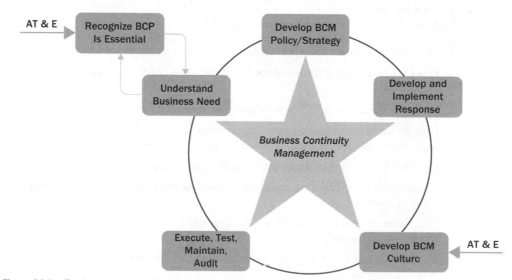

Figure 24-1   Business continuity management life cycle

resources, infrastructure, time required for delivery, and processes demanded by critical functional areas. Establish interdependencies among external parties and clearly outline these relationships.

Alignment to Business Strategy and Operations

Before proceeding with business impact analysis and risk assessment, align business continuity to the overall organization's strategy and operations. By understanding the organization's direction and focus, the business continuity committee will ensure that it is moving in the right direction to develop strategies and recommendations that suit the organization.

The BCM committee has to understand the organization's strategy, short-term, and medium-term plans. First, identify current management information goals, input, detailed business processes, output, and quantified value of activity. Then, document all findings at the end of this exercise. This serves as the referencing guidelines to define the scope for the business impact analysis and the risk assessment. Organizations should also consider any regulations, laws, or rules that apply to them. For example, in the United States, ISO 22301 is the voluntary national standard for providing organizational resilience for private entities.

Business Impact Analysis   The business impact analysis (BIA) is the groundwork of the BCM process with the objective of identifying functional areas that would suffer the most financial or operational loss in the event of a disruption or disaster. From the collected date, document all department functions, inputs, and processes, to develop a business hierarchy of business functions. The hierarchy provides the basis for classifying the criticality of each function. A business impact analysis identifies and classifies measurable and tangible losses of the business after a disruption to the organization's business processes. The business impact analysis report provides critical business information in planning for developing strategies for business continuity.

The following are the steps in conducting a BIA:

1. Management establishes the defined scope and terms of reference.
2. Ensure the information-gathering process is effective; select and identify the best interviewees.
3. Design a customized business impact assessment template.
4. Choose an information-gathering technique that will be used (interviews, workshops, questionnaires, qualitative, and quantitative approaches).
5. Use the data collected and determine the organization's key business functions.
6. Identify the financial, regulatory, and operational impact over time on disruption for each business function.
7. Determine the maximum tolerable outage for these business functions in terms of achieving organizational goals.
8. Execute these business functions and select the key personnel that will be contributing to this initiative.
9. Identify the critical systems, vital records, supply chain, and infrastructure required for the business functions.

10. Estimate the maximum tolerable outage for these critical systems, vital records, supply chain, and infrastructure.

11. Document and present the findings to management.

At the end of the business impact analysis exercise, the BCM committee team should identify all threats to the company and map them to the following characteristics:

- Critical systems, vital data, and records
- Financial considerations
- Image and brand of the organization
- Internal and external relationship for critical functions
- Key personnel for critical functions
- Operational disruption
- Regulatory responsibilities
- Supply chain and infrastructure for critical functions

    In BIA, there are two main recovery periods.

- *Recovery time objective* (RTO) refers to the timeframe during which a recovery should become effective before a disruption prevents the organization from achieving its business objectives and therefore threatens its survival.

- *Recovery point objective* (RPO) is the time in which data should be restored to after a major disruption.

The information obtained in business impact analysis will contribute directly to organizational recovery strategies in terms of determining the recovery priority. You can find more details on RTO and RPO in Chapter 25.

Risk Assessment

Risk is a measure of the potential consequences of a disaster against the likelihood of it occurring.

During the BCM process, the BCM team or an independent assessor will conduct a risk assessment to identify internal or external risks to the performance and probability of disruption to critical organizational functions. A risk assessment identifies, quantifies, and prioritizes risks against criteria and relevant objectives. The criteria would include critical resources, effect of disruptions, allowable outage time, and recovery priorities. The result prioritizes and focuses activities on critical functional areas identified during business impact analysis.

Involve owners of the business resources and processes during a risk assessment process. Remember that not all critical systems use information-processing facilities—some are manual or paper-based; risk assessment should consider all critical business processes. It is important to link all risks to obtain a complete business continuity requirement.

Identify and document all "single points of failure" during a risk assessment process. The committee should record and analyze threats to the organization and its business processes, address and treat all critical risks, and document the acceptance of unaddressed but identified risks. Refer to Chapter 11 for details on information assurance risk management.

Stage 3: Develop BCM Strategies

After identifying all functional areas that are at risk, decide on the best approaches to protect assets and systems. This stage of the BCM process focuses on identifying the alternatives available to reduce loss and assesses effective solutions. This process ensures the business continues to operate key functions from the time of the business disruption until the function is able to recover operational ability. The information provided by business impact analysis suggests appropriate strategies.

Maximum tolerable outage or the RTO determines the point at which the survival of the organization is threatened by disruption. Strategies that cannot meet the RTO are unacceptable. RPO must also be considered, as some organizations cannot afford to lose information. As RPO and RTO decrease, the cost and resources required to implement those increases.

There are three levels of BCM strategies and strategic planning. All three levels depend on one another. The three levels of strategies are

- Organizational strategy
- Process-level strategy
- Resource recovery strategy

Organizational Strategy

The organizational strategy provides structured well-defined policy and procedures. This ensures the continuity of key functional areas, its dependencies, and single points of failure. During the development of process-level and resource recovery strategy, make a reference to the organization's loss reduction strategy.

Process-Level Strategy

A process-level strategy provides a documented framework to support a resource recovery strategy, business continuity plan, and BCM capability prototype.

Based on the findings from the BIA, the process-level strategy examines the interdependencies of all activities, processes, data, infrastructure, and technology. There will be various critical business processes within an organization. Develop separate strategies to handle known processes based on their nature and significance. It is important to develop the process-level strategy within the overall organizational BCM scope and coverage.

The output of the process-level strategy exercise will be a documented strategy. The keys are as follows: Secure agreement and approval by top management. Establish a project plan to execute the agreed strategy. Agree upon and document established relationships and positioning of the critical business functions. Establish the general principles and guidelines for developing resource recovery strategies and business continuity plans. After agreement on the principles and guidelines, develop the corresponding business continuity plan for each of the critical business processes, dependencies, and single points of failure.

Resource Recovery Strategy

A resource recovery strategy coordinates and provides the resources required for the execution of the organizational strategy and process-level strategy of the business continuity plan. Consider employees ratios, priority of business processes, location, and technology requirements to determine the resource recovery strategy as well as the organizational process-level strategy. Figure 24-2 illustrates one example of resource recovery strategy. The amount of resources goes up as more resources are made available to aid in business continuity. This in turn provides superior protection for assets and operations.

Some of the deliverables of a resource recovery strategy are a managerial endorsement document and defined objectives and a predefined collection of recovery resources and services. The resources and services provide the recovery of business processes within an accepted timeframe and required objectives.

There are many strategies that can be implemented. Specific organizational analysis drives strategies. Therefore, the following are nonspecific and simplified:

- **Do nothing**   The loss of some noncritical functions may be acceptable by the top-level/senior management. Hence, no further action is necessary.

- **Change, transfer, or end the process**   Decisions to alter business processes should consider the organization's key objectives and any regulatory and legal implications.

- **Insure**   You can turn to financial compensation or support to shift financial risk, but this option will not be able to cater to all impact losses such as reputation and other nonfinancial impacts.

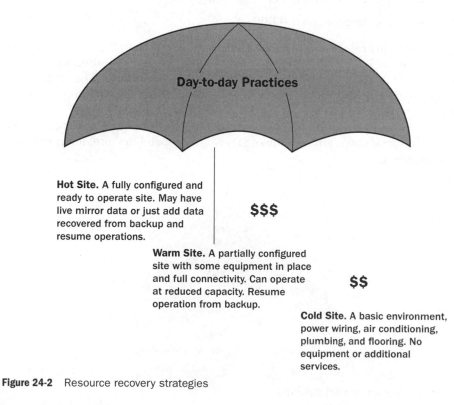

Day-to-day Practices

Hot Site. A fully configured and ready to operate site. May have live mirror data or just add data recovered from backup and resume operations.

$$$

Warm Site. A partially configured site with some equipment in place and full connectivity. Can operate at reduced capacity. Resume operation from backup.

$$

Cold Site. A basic environment, power wiring, air conditioning, plumbing, and flooring. No equipment or additional services.

$

Figure 24-2   Resource recovery strategies

- **Mitigate loss**   Implement some appropriate measures to reduce unacceptable risks within the business.
- **Plan for business continuity**   This is an approach that seeks to improve the organization's continuity capability in case of major disruptions, therefore allowing for the recovery of key business and system processes within predefined objectives.

Stage 4: Developing and Implementing a BCM Response

After defining organization-wide strategies toward business continuity, develop action plans and identify resources needed to support the plans. The steps in the action plans are not the only course of action. In the real world, every event or crisis is different. Procedures based on the revised strategy may require flexibility for exceptional cases.

As already discussed, there are three primary types of BCM plans. They may be divided into a number of subplan items on specific requirements:

- Business continuity plan (BCP)
- Crisis management plan (CMP)
- Disaster recovery plan (DRP)
- Incident response plan (IRP)
- Information system contingency plan (ISCP)
- Occupant emergency plan (OEP)

Figure 24-3 illustrates the crisis management structures for all six BCM plans. For instance, if an event is out of the scope of assumption of a business continuity plan, the event will be escalated to those implementing the crisis management plan. This structure will enable appropriate levels of authority, ownership, control, and response to be determined during various crises.

By developing an effective CMP, management demonstrates to the media, stakeholders, markets, customers, and regulators the organization's capabilities and determinations in crisis management.

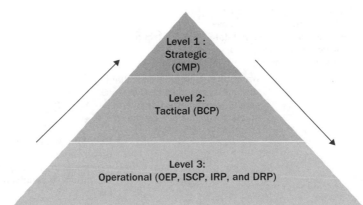

Figure 24-3   Crisis management structure

The deliverables at the end of a crisis management planning exercise include a plan that can aid the crisis management team during an occurrence of a crisis. Since media response falls under a CMP, it is important to construct a crisis communication plan where the plan will incorporate communication management of media and stakeholders. The following six sections describe these subcomponents.

Crisis Management Plan

A crisis management plan is developed by large organizations or small to midsize organizations with critical missions. The CMP addresses the strategic issues of a crisis affecting the organization. This plan is essential for large organizations and ensures the existence of an organized, versatile, and robust crisis response. The procedures or guidelines in a CMP should be able to handle not only natural disasters but also man-made business and industrial crises. Examples of these are financial risks, marketing risks, credit risks, reputation or brand name risks, white-collar criminals, business fraud, environmental pollution, and hostile takeovers. The CMP manages the media that reports any incidents; however, there are other organizations that use BCPs for the same purpose.

Some CMPs also include important individuals and their families as part of the plan. An organization cannot expect employees to favor acting in the interest of the organization over their own families or loved ones in the time of crisis. Organizations must ensure the families and loved ones are accounted for in the plan and actions are in place to ensure their safety and well-being. If critical employees must perform during crisis situations, the organization must ensure they can account for the safety of family and loved ones and provide evidence to the critical employees of their safety. This may involve the identification and acquisition of alternative housing.

The crisis management plan must also recognize the human nature of grief and shock during a disaster. Disasters take a heavy psychological toll on personnel when there has been loss of life or extensive physical destruction. The CMP should address grief counseling and other mental health support options. The Red Cross and numerous international disaster support organizations may offer support in this area, but the organization should ensure in advance it can count on the resource when needed.

Personnel are often most interested in what matters to them. Payroll is high on the list of worries for employees in a disaster situation. The organization must communicate the status of payroll and health benefits. Every effort should be made to ensure payroll and health benefits operations. Because of employee grief and stress, organizations must be prepared for lower productivity during the adjustment period.

Large or critical organizations must ensure they have established relationships with local law enforcement and emergency responders prior to an emergency event. These organizations are often eager to review BCPs and CMPs and provide input in the resources available locally and nationally. Depending on the organization's mission and size, local resources may request the organization participate in joint planning and exercises with local, national, or international counterparts. Smaller organizations should review local emergency response resources such as the Red Cross and local government emergency preparation organizations for further guidance.

Part IV

Business Continuity Plan

As mentioned, the BCP provides procedures for sustaining operations while recovering from disruptions. It addresses organizational mission and business processes at a lower level than the CMP and is more expansive in addressing specific operational plans for information systems and personnel. The BCP activation is determined by the CRO or another designated senior leader.

If the BCP is the pinnacle strategic document for ensuring contingency operations and recovery from disasters, the organization must ensure the crisis management function is included in the BCP. External affairs, public relations, legal, and senior management must be active participants in not only the development of the BCP but also in its testing and ongoing evolution as the organization changes.

The BCP must be updated as part of the change management process. Organizations may grow, shrink, merge, and even dissolve. The BCP and subordinate plans must be updated to ensure changes to the organization are captured and accurately accounted for in contingency and recovery operations. The BCP can quickly become outdated if not comprehensively maintained throughout the change management process. Worse, it may cause further damage during a disaster because it may cause actions based on outdated information and procedures.

Disaster Recovery Plan

A disaster recovery plan is a subset of BCM. Disaster recovery planning minimizes the effect of a disaster and recommends the steps to ensure resources, personnel, and business processes are available. In addition, it ensures that business-critical data is available to resume operation within a predetermined timeframe. A disaster recovery plan focuses on information technology. It references individual information system contingency plans. In contrast, BCM takes a wider approach when dealing with disaster. BCM includes references to occupant emergency plans, incident response plans, and crisis communication plans.

During the process of developing a DRP, the DR team uses information gathered from business impact analysis and risk assessment. Based on the RPO and RTO, a disaster recovery strategy can be determined.

The DRP minimally addresses the following:

- **Data recovery**   The DRP should state the procedures for recovering data from backup storage. The plan should also indicate priorities for data recovery based on the criticality of corresponding business functions. The data recovery sections should reference the ISCPs as necessary.

- **Facility recovery**   The organization needs to decide on the type of offsite facilities that should be acquired, whether a hot site, warm site, or cold site, or whether to engage an external party's facility via reciprocal agreement.

- **Technology and supply recovery**   To restore a business function and process critical business data, the DRP needs to address several matters such as the recovery of network and computer equipment, voice and data communication resources, software, human resources, transportation of equipment and personnel, environmental issues, data and personnel information assurance issues, supplies such as forms and cabling, and documentation on recovery.

Occupant Emergency Plan

The OEP is focused on protecting personnel and ensuring continuity of their functions. Organizations must focus on people, process, and technology if they want to be resilient in adverse times. The OEP provides coordinated procedures for minimizing the loss of life or injury and protecting property damage in response to threats. Personnel and property specific to a facility, not mission or business processes or information systems, drive the OEP. OEPs are best utilized through reference in the BCP or CMP through initiation immediately after an event but prior to DRP or ISCP implementation (the organization will need its staff to enact much of the DRP and ISCP).

The OEP contains information about the facility layout including where emergency supplies are located. These supplies include stable rations, fresh water, batteries, heat sources, sanitation supplies, light sources, emergency communication devices, and in some cases, biohazard suits or breathing filters. The OEP may also contain the locations of alternate information system operating locations and "safe rooms" that may be on standby until an emergency.

OEPs handle personnel safety and evacuation. Routine testing of the OEP should ensure personnel are aware of their physical security and exit procedures. These aspects of the OEP are best practiced during fire drills. The OEP should contain or reference the need to secure office space, workstations, and laptops to prevent vandalism or theft. Of course, personnel security and safety always comes first. The OEP should contain emergency checklists, which can be posted in workspaces that remind employees to take medications, identification, car keys, and other important items if the nature of the incident and time allow.

OEPs often incorporate a "floor warden" or "floor monitor" approach to ensure proper evacuation and accountability for staff. This approach involves ensuring at least two individuals are selected and trained to be responsible for the evacuation of all personnel. If sufficient personnel exist, this responsibility should be rotated throughout the facility to ensure proper training and understanding of emergency procedures.

The OEP should contain procedures for several crisis situations including, but not limited to the following:

- Active shooter
- Bomb threats
- Earthquakes
- Extreme weather such as tornados and hurricanes
- Fires
- Floods
- Hostile employee
- Pandemics
- Prolonged power outages

Organizations should consider filing their OEP with local emergency responders. While localities differ, many local responders will gladly maintain a copy of the OEP on file. This becomes invaluable because the emergency responder will have the exact locations of

Part IV

shelter areas, safe rooms, and evacuation locations for the organization. This single act can mean the difference between life and death in instances such as fires or earthquakes.

Information System Contingency Plan

The information system contingency plan establishes procedures for the assessment and recovery of an information system following a disruptive event. The ISCP is established by the DRP and covers the roles, responsibilities, inventory information, assessment procedures, detailed recovery procedures, and testing of a system.

While the DRP is a higher-level document in the organization, the ISCP is developed for the recovery of the system regardless of site or location. An ISCP can be activated at a system's production site or the alternate site. This is in contrast to the DRP, which is a site-specific plan developed with procedures to move operations of one or more information systems from a damaged or uninhabitable location to a temporary alternate location.

Once a DRP is enacted and has successfully transferred an information system site to an alternate site, each affected system would then use its respective ISCP to restore, recover, and test systems prior to putting them back into operation.

Incident Response Plan

The incident response plan establishes procedures to address cyberattacks against an organization's information systems. The procedures are designed to enable security personnel to identify, mitigate, and recover from malicious computer incidents. The IRP should be referenced in the CMPs, DRPs, BCPs, and ISCPs. You can find more information regarding the incident response process in Chapter 22.

Stage 5: Developing a BCM Culture

Relevant personnel across the organization and dependencies from other organizations must be confident and competent with the BCM program. Even with the best strategy and planning, the system will not be effective without acceptance and commitment from employees.

Since the BCM is integral to the organization's strategic goals as well as day-to-day management, it must be aligned with organizational business objectives. To remain viable during a disaster, organizations must establish a BCM culture and integrate it into daily business operations with the support of the CRO and senior management. Clearly, management must demonstrate their support and commitment in exercising BCM to extend its life span. As with other changes, there will be resistance to BCM plans; use AT&E to help employees understand the importance of BCM to the organization, the structure of the business continuity team, steps taken during the execution of the BCM action plans, and the level of service required during the emergency. You can find more information regarding awareness, education, and training in Chapter 17.

Three techniques are involved in developing and establishing BCM culture within an organization.

- Design and deliver an awareness campaign to create and promote BCM awareness and develop skills, knowledge, and commitment required to ensure a successful BCM practice.

- Ensure the awareness campaign has achieved its goals and monitor BCM awareness for a longer term.

- Perform an assessment on the current BCM awareness level against the management-targeted level.

Stage 6: Execute, Test, Maintain, and Audit

The reliability of the BCM plan is a function of its implementation and effectiveness. Steps of the BCM plan involve the validation of plans by performing simulations of different scenarios by everyone involved. Examine critical systems (such as a UPS) that provide systemic resilience to ensure both reliability and availability. The frequency of exercises depends on the rate of changes made within the organization. Review the result of earlier exercises during the current exercise to ensure identified weaknesses have been addressed.

In addition to ensuring BCM is in order, the organization should keep it current. Changes in specific areas may require more attention. For example, employee turnover, changes in the organization's functions or services, changes to organizational structure, changes to details of suppliers or contractors, changes made to risk assessment, and changes to business objectives and processes may require modified BCM processes.

An audit highlights all key material weaknesses and issues. An internal auditor, external auditor, or external professional BCM practitioner can perform an audit/review of the BCM. Both internal and external reviewers should provide an independent view on the organization's BCM policy, strategies, framework, guidelines, procedures, and standards.

Business Continuity in the Cloud

Cloud computing offers numerous approaches to not only use cloud technologies to enhance existing "on-premise" systems but also systems instantiated on cloud infrastructures. Organizations should be aware of different concerns with various approaches to cloud computing. The most common uses of cloud computing for business continuity include Infrastructure as a Service (IaaS) and Software as a Service (SaaS).

IaaS and SaaS cloud solutions include virtual machines, virtual servers, storage, software, and, in some cases, communication links. As part of overarching business continuity planning, organizations must understand several aspects of the agreement they have with the cloud provider, such as, but not limited to the following:

- Service level agreements
  - Uptime of communications links
  - Uptime of servers or workstations
  - Reliability of data integrity (RPO)
  - Availability of data (RTO)
- Jurisdictional concerns
  - Where are the cloud provider's redundant resources located?
  - Are the alternate or redundant resources subject to the same legal jurisdictions as the primary resources?

- Does the cloud provider outsource the contingency operations with another provider with less stringent controls?
- Costs
  - Do contingency operations enact a separate cost in addition to existing fees?
  - Does the cloud provider charge additional fees for the option to use contingency features of its service?

Further Reading

- DRI International. *Generally Accepted Practices for Business Continuity Practitioners.* Disaster Recovery Journal and DRI International, 2005.
- Good Practice Guidelines. *A Framework for Business Continuity Management.* Business Continuity Institutes (BCI). 2005.
- Mitropoulos, S., et al. "On Incident Handling and Response: A State-of-the-Art Approach." *Computers & Security,* 25, no. 5 (2006): 351–370.
- SAI Global. *Practitioners Guide to Business Continuity Management (HB 292-2006).* SAI, 2006.
- Schou, Corey D., and D.P. Shoemaker. *Information Assurance for the Enterprise: A Roadmap to Information Security.* McGraw-Hill Education, 2007.
- Swanson, M., et al. *Contingency Planning Guide for Information Technology Systems (SP 800-34).* NIST, 2002.
- Tipton, Harold F., and S. Hernandez, ed. *Official (ISC)² Guide to the CISSP CBK 3rd edition.* ((ISC)²) Press, 2012.

Critical Thinking Exercises

1. An organization has begun developing its business continuity plan. The organization is small and manufactures packaging for a variety of cosmetic products. The roles of CIO and the CFO are assigned to the same person who has been nominated to lead the task of business continuity. What are the strengths and weaknesses of this approach?

2. Why should information assurance place such an emphasis on crisis management and business continuity when disaster recovery is an IT function?

Backup and Restoration

When all else fails, the only option available may be to rely on backups. Unfortunately, organizations discover poor management of backups, and untested restoration processes lead to failure. Backups range from enterprise records preserved for legal hold or due diligence to personal files on a personal device with little value. Organizations must use information gleaned from the business impact analysis and risk assessment to determine which information and assets have a requirement for the integrity and availability services that backup solutions provide.

Backup and restoration are important data protection strategies. Backup, as the name suggests, consists of making copies of data for restoration after a disaster. Based on the experience of many organizations, obtaining a reliable backup requires careful planning and consideration. This chapter describes the importance of making backups, alternative solutions available for backup, and best practices one should observe for backup implementation.

Importance of Backup

Why do systems require backup? Backup is protection against data loss and corruption. Organizations without a backup strategy may suffer operational or financial damage after an incident. Losing data means losing business. Backups protect not only critical information but also money, reputation, time, and effort. Information and databases are growing rapidly, and rebuilding them rapidly is not a simple task. Having a reliable backup solution addresses the issues of information loss. Successful data-centric organizations invest significant resources in backup management.

Backup Considerations

Technology advancement provides backup solutions for timely recovery. Choosing the right method or technology is crucial to ensure that the recovery of services is smooth, simple, and cost effective. Consider the following factors to determine the right solution for the organization:

- **Criticality of data**   Backing up all data can be costly. Organizations should consider the criticality of data for backup. A selected range should be determined by considering the allowable downtime for specific services. The maximum allowable downtime is also known as the *recovery time objective* (RTO). The RTO is based on the business impact analysis (BIA) conducted as part of business continuity management. (See Chapter 24 for more information about BIA and business continuity management.) Organizations must prioritize mission-critical information because this information can cause serious financial and reputation damage. When determining requirements for backup, do not ignore less critical services; in these cases, consider a less expensive, and perhaps slower, backup approach.

- **Data size**   An organization should consider the volume of data to be backed up. This requirement should include the total data growth projection for the next three to five years. These requirements will ensure that the implemented solutions will remain adequate. Services with a high volume of data should be categorized appropriately. Such services may require special attention and methods for backups.

- **Databases**   Databases require special attention since they may require high data volume equipment. Selecting the correct backup for such services is critical; maintaining integrity requires high accuracy database backup system. Insufficient data backup capacity may cause loss of extremely valuable information. Determine whether the database requires online backup solutions, which provide real-time backup, especially for mission-critical information.

- **Operating systems**   Determining the operating system is an important task. Backup solutions may support multiple platforms, but some do not. Defining operating systems helps an organization choose a solution that can cater to specific needs. Such consideration should also apply to implementation of new services in the future.

- **Timeframe**   Organizations should determine the allowable timeframe to perform backups. Some organizations, which provide 24/7/365 services, will have low tolerance for performance impact. During the backup process, an organization should anticipate a certain level of service degradation. Services not tolerant of degradation use different methods of backup. They may consider high availability (HA) redundancy solutions and perform offline backup.

Table 25-1 provides examples on how to derive the backup requirements.

Organizations must consider acceptable downtime as part of the BIA process and as part of backup and recovery strategies. As noted, RTO is the time taken to recover the services and data to their original operating status. The data restoration process should not exceed the RTO. Closely linked with RTO is recovery point objective (RPO), which is the amount of data (in a transaction system that is measured in time) that is allowed to be lost at the point of data recovery.

Server Name	Services	OS	Data Size	Data Growth (Yearly)	Application Type	SLA (%)	Maintenance Timeframe
DBMS	Database	Linux	1TB	15 percent	MySQL	99.99	3 a.m. to 4 a.m.
Mailbox	E-mail	Linux	500GB	10 percent	Sendmail	99.8	2 a.m. to 4 a.m.
Tribal	Portal	Linux	100GB	5 percent	Apache	99	2 a.m. to 4 a.m.
Presence	Intranet Portal	Windows	50GB	5 percent	Microsoft IIS	98	9 p.m. to 6 a.m.
Ben Franklin	Print Server	Windows	10GB	2 percent	Microsoft Print Server	98	9 p.m. to 6 a.m.

Table 25-1   Data Categorization Table

An RTO can be derived from SLAs if a BIA is not available; however, RPO must be based on the criticality of services. For instance, a database server that contains financial information is deemed highly critical and has an RPO of an hour. Losing an hour of data from this server may cost $1.5 million. The RPO must reflect accurate impact to the mission or business of the organization.

Thus, if the management determines it is not feasible to incur this monetary loss, it needs to shorten the RPO by providing support and resources. Identifying the RTO and RPO are crucial since they indicate the backup strategy required by the organization. A short RPO demands a more comprehensive (and likely more costly) backup strategy. In some circumstances, the requirement is compounded by a requirement for high availability or short RTO.

Backup Solutions

The following sections describe available technologies and techniques, which can help organizations achieve a good backup and restoration solution.

Media

Some commonly used media are as follows:

- **Blu-ray/CD-RW/DVD-RW** These types of backup media are good for simple data backup. Data backup using this media normally reduces cost because an organization may spend only a few hundred dollars to write all necessary data onto it. The disks have a finite life span that is reduced because of physical damage, exposure to light, and harsh storage conditions.

- **Hard drives** Allocating additional hard drives for backup purposes can be considered another method of backup strategy. Such media can be either external drives or internal drives attached to equipment as an alternative storage media. Use of hard drives with external storage is considered an expensive solution and mostly applicable to network-attached storage (NAS) and storage area network (SAN).

Part IV

- **Redundant mirror** Hard drives can be configured to mirror one another. Thus, should a single drive fail, the other drive will still be operational and continue to function. When a new drive replaces the failed drive, the drives will sync. The obvious drawback to this solution is the cost. This solution may also prove ineffective if both drives suffer a shared power supply failure or controller failure that damages both drives concurrently.

- **Tape media** Tape media is a highly used backup method. Such media came into use in the 1960s. Today, tape media is the single most widely used media, although it is becoming less popular because of the availability of NAS and SAN. Its primary advantage is the flexibility of storing the backup in remote sites. This can eliminate information being lost because of major risks such as flood, fire, and earthquake.

- **Virtual tape library (VTL)** A VTL is a device comprised of a disk or array of disks that mimic a tape library. Data backed up to a VTL can be replicated to other VTLs at remote locations or staged for real tape offloading. The VTL allows organizations to leverage existing backup infrastructure and procedures while employing cheaper and faster technology.

- **Cloud backup** Cloud backup solutions can be tailored to a specific application such as database backup or can be simply Cloud IaaS storage that is utilized to store information. Regardless of application, the cloud provider's information assurance posture must be assessed. Organizations must consider the need for strong encryption when backing up information to a cloud-based backup provider.

Backup Infrastructure

There is a wide range of backup infrastructure ranging from inexpensive to expensive solutions. Normally, an organization opts for a mixture of solutions. Budget is a major constraint in choosing a solution. As noted earlier, prioritization and understanding the criticality of information are key factors in obtaining a backup that works for any organization.

The following list explains some of the more common backup infrastructures available:

- **LAN-based tape backup** This is a classic approach, which is set up by attaching tape media to the central backup and allowing backups via a LAN. This type of backup slows down the network during a backup window; however, it is one of the most frequently used methods. It can be enhanced by implementing iSCSI and Fibre Channel for dedicated servers and critical resources. A robotic external tape loader can be attached to the master backup server so that multiple tapes can be written concurrently.

- **NAS-based backup** Network-attached storage is a collection of hard drives attached to the network. The hardware may range from SATA to iSCSI and may provide several hundred terabytes (TB) of storage. It uses the LAN as the transmission medium; however, unlike LAN-based tape backup, NAS generally provides faster read and write speed compared to tape media.

- **SAN-based backup** SANs are capable of providing high data storage with a full range of data transmission capabilities. SAN is similar to NAS in network connectivity; however, SAN-based backup uses Fibre Channel and high-throughput technologies to transmit data from servers, which is appropriate for high-volume servers such as databases and file storage systems. It is also reliable and durable because of its technology, which supports RAID configurations. Failure of hard drives attached to SAN is largely mitigated because of the RAID configuration and management reporting capabilities.

- **Cloud-based backup**   Cloud backup providers offer a variety of methods to back up information including application programing interfaces and private VLANs for fast WAN transmissions. Organizations need to plan for redundant connectivity to the cloud provider and possible long RTO times depending on the plan selected. Additionally, cloud providers may charge by the month for data storage and also for bandwidth consumed for backups and restoration.

Implementing these solutions can result in highly efficient data storage and backup that is almost unbreakable. However, the cost is expensive. SAN also supports WAN synchronization, which helps in replicating data from primary to secondary locations, which instantly provides backup options. The type used is entirely an organization's choice because it can provide offline or online backup options depending on the amount it is willing to spend.

Backup Software

Backup solutions can be developed in-house or bought off-the-shelf. In evaluating a backup solution, here are some criteria that should be considered:

- **Automatic backup schedules**   The software should also be capable of running unattended schedules and report failures. Such logs can later be retrieved for troubleshooting purposes. Integration into the information assurance management system (IAMS) assists in evaluating overall risk for the organization.

- **Error reporting**   The solution should provide a detailed error report so that troubleshooting will be easier. The clear definition of error makes it easier to identify the actual cause of problems. This will reduce time in troubleshooting and avoid losing valuable data.

- **Multiple device support**   The software should support any media devices regardless of whether they are tape media, NAS, or SAN. Such requirements will be beneficial for an organization, which intends to have mixed backup methods.

- **Multiple level of restoration**   In most cases, restoration should be both full and selective. This is applicable when there is a large amount of information available but an organization requires only certain information to be restored. Examples include restoration of individual mailboxes in an e-mail server.

- **Multiple platform support**   The solution should support multiple operating systems. Generally, backup software is OS dependent. Organizations should analyze the need for multiple platforms. This can also be a contributing factor toward future expansion.

- **Real-time backup**   The software should support backup of open files such as databases. In most cases in which services are provisioned on a 24/7 basis, the

Part IV

application needs to run uninterrupted. Thus, the backup solution should be able to back up as accurately as possible while the application is accessing the file in real time. This type of capability should always be considered for mission-critical systems.

- **Schedules of groups**   Scheduling of backup groups is a compulsory task. Server grouping should be balanced and distributed to avoid long backup windows.

- **Hashing and encryption**   Backup software must support strong encryption features for protecting the confidentiality of information. The software should integrate into an organization's chosen encryption strategy and PKI if used. Key escrow options should be considered as part of software selection, and the strength and validation of encryption modules should be assessed. The software should incorporate hashing functions that ensure the integrity and nonrepudiation of the information being backed up and restored. Organizations should consider validated cryptography such as U.S. NIST FIPS 140-2 validated modules and algorithms.

It is important to recall that if you build backup software internally, it requires extensive test and support to ensure it works in high-stress environments.

Types of Backup

There are three types of commonly used backup solutions. It is important to implement the correct type to control versioning. System failure can occur in several forms because of careless planning, and costly restoration has to be done on the correct versions.

- **Full backup**   This involves copying of the entire system regardless of whether it is a file, system, or database. It is helpful when there is a need to restore the entire system to its original state. However, this technique is space-consuming and time-consuming since its size requires a longer backup window.

- **Incremental backup**   This involves copying only current changes to the system. As such, any files that have been modified since the last backup will be captured and copied to respective media. This technique will reduce time to back up because it concentrates only on changes to systems. Restoring a complete system will require installing the last full backup and then applying all subsequent incremental backups. If, on the other hand, one needs to restore a single file, it is trivial with incremental backup.

- **Differential backup**   This is a cumulative backup that copies files with all changes from the last full backup. The last full backup image is taken as a comparison table with all changes shown by incremental backup. This method keeps track of copied images of incremental backup that are compared against the last full backup. Ultimately, this method provides the most updated version of backup. However, it relies on full backup for complete restoration. The differential backup stores all cumulative chances from the last full backup in a single file. This makes restoration faster than the incremental backup and is less risky since only two files are used. However, backup time increases if there have been many changes since the last full backup.

Scheduling

Scheduling specifies how and when to back up the data. With proper techniques, an organization can optimize the backup window and reduce the risk of service degradation. Use a mixture of backup types to optimize the backup window.

- **Generation**   This technique is widely used. It uses three versions of the backup that resemble a generation: grandparent, parent, and child. The grandparent, as the name suggests, is the oldest version of the backup. This version may be required at some point of restoration because subtle system failures can be difficult to trace and restoration has to be backtracked to the grandparent's version. It helps to provide a contingency plan in the event that the other two versions fail to provide accurate system restoration. The parent backup version is the second oldest, and the child version is the youngest.

- **Incremental**   This technique has only one version, which continues to append to the backup media all changes made by the system. It does not have any generation or version as a contingency plan. If the system fails and the restoration copy fails as well, the organization's fallback plan fails. This method can cause an organization serious damage.

Retention

Retention refers to how long backup media should be kept before it is recycled. Retention is applicable only for the generation technique described earlier because it has three versions of the backup. The incremental technique does not require a retention period because only one version is involved at any one time.

Table 25-2 describes a typical schedule that an organization can adopt for a backup technique. Assume that the retention period of a tape is 14 days and the storage media that stores the information of week 1 is considered as the first-generation data. This is the grandparent's generation. The cycle continues until week 3 when the latest generation is called a child. In week 4, the grandparent will be recycled. The total data retention period for the grandparent is 14 days.

Table 25-3 describes a single set of media being used week after week, without any versioning.

Week	Mon	Tue	Wed	Thu	Fri	Sat	Sun
Week 1	Full backup	Incremental backup	Incremental backup	Differential backup	Incremental backup	Differential backup	Differential backup
Week 2	Full backup	Incremental backup	Incremental backup	Differential backup	Incremental backup	Differential backup	Differential backup
Week 3	Full backup	Incremental backup	Incremental backup	Differential backup	Incremental backup	Differential backup	Differential backup
Week 4	Full backup	Incremental backup	Incremental backup	Differential backup	Incremental backup	Differential backup	Differential backup

Table 25-2   Generation Schedule

Mon	Tue	Wed	Thu	Fri	Sat	Sun
Full backup	Full backup	Full backup	Full backup	Full backup	Full backup	Full backup

Table 25-3 Incremental Schedule

Table 25-3 is an example of an incremental backup schedule. Each backup can stand alone as a full backup for either a full or partial recovery. This is done at the expense of backup time and media storage.

Remember the cost of media is inconsequential compared to the cost of backup failure.

Tape Media

Although more sophisticated media are available for consideration, organizations still use magnetic tape since it is the most convenient backup media and often the most cost effective. Tape media provides a convenient way to store media offsite. Although NAS and SAN hard drives come with plug and play as well as RAID capability, it is not practical to unplug the hard drive for offsite storage. This makes a tape drive a good medium for offsite backup storage while reducing the risk of natural disaster.

Media Care Checklist

☐ All media should be stored in dry, cool, and airtight storage.

☐ All media should be labeled appropriately using physical and electronic labels. Labeling should include data classification.

☐ Media should be handled as gently as possible.

☐ All media has a life-cycle limit before it should be retired. Ensure life-cycle count is not exceeded by use. Verify replacement copies.

☐ When transferring media offsite, use an appropriate transportation container.

Tape media technology has improved tremendously. Tape media provides a storage capability of more than 7TB and yet is still small and lightweight. The organization can easily transport the media offsite.

Using tape as media encourages an organization to adopt the generation technique with tape retention and offsite storing. Assuming that the first generation leaves the tape loader in the second week to internal storage, it eventually reaches maturity as a grandparent and leaves the premises to a remote site. This shows that the presence of the tape at each location (tape loader, internal storage, and offsite) has a retention period of seven days at each location.

Administration

Organizations may have dedicated personnel to administer the backup job. A dedicated administrator focuses on the important needs of backup administration rather than being distracted by other supporting tasks.

In some circumstances, organizations cannot afford to have dedicated personnel, so hiring personnel with normal administration skills to administer backup software in addition is adequate. Backup software requires few specialized skills. Ultimately, a backup and restoration job falls under the system administrator's responsibility.

Examples of tasks performed by a backup administrator include checking of success rates of scheduled daily tasks, checking any backup failure, troubleshooting, changing and rotating the tape schedule, and recycling tapes. Although this sounds simple, the administrator should possess enough skills, training, and understanding of the importance of backup and restoration.

Restoration of Data

Restoration is when the original objective of contingency planning comes into action. The result of this stage is crucial. All the efforts put into planning and implementation should provide an expected result at the restoration stage. There are generally three techniques involved in restoration.

- **Complete restoration**   In this technique, the entire system is restored to its original state. The restoration process may use intelligent agents (software) that are usually highly automated. The destination server should be identified and made accessible by the backup system. This technique reduces the time taken in the restoration process because it does not require rebuilding any server. This technique is usually used if the data on the damaged system is no longer functional. Thus, restoration can be directly targeted to the damaged system.

- **Data restoration**   Organizations employ this technique when data is the only backup that can be restored (that is, not including systems such as the OS). Execute this technique by rebuilding the system to an operating state and restoring the data from backup media. Clearly, this technique requires a longer time to restore the damaged system. However, this technique is preferable when there are not many configuration changes to the system except for an increase in data.

- **Selective restoration**   This technique is employed only if certain sections of the information need to be restored. Restoration should not be done directly onto the damaged system. In fact, a mock-up server should be available for restoration of selective information, and once verified as functional, the information will be transferred to the actual system. This technique is beneficial to organizations in the event of partial data corruption.

From time to time, system administrators must ensure that the backup files can actually be restored. This is a critical testing criterion for any recovery system.

BYOD and Cloud Backups

Understanding where information is stored and transmitted is as important as understanding the criticality of data. If an organization chooses to store information with a third-party cloud provider, it must also ensure appropriate backup strategies are considered

Part IV

as part of the cloud agreement. Many cloud infrastructure, software, and platform providers offer backup, restoration, and continuity options for a fee. The organization must balance the capability and cost of the cloud provider's solutions with the recovery objectives of the organization.

Senior leadership must also set expectations regarding the use of personal devices and personal cloud storage solutions. Employees have an expectation that they can use the same devices, services, and technology in their daily work just like they do in their daily lives. This means they expect they can store sensitive organizational information on their smartphone or in their cloud "drop box" because it is good enough and they are accustomed to working with those tools. This can put the organization in a dangerous position should information need to be restored and the employee is unavailable or unwilling to provide the information. Senior leadership must set the direction of the organization and either accept the risk of not controlling the information or require employees to adhere to a policy of maintaining information on organizationally approved systems and services.

Further Reading

- Little, D.B., and D.A. Chapa. *Implementing Backup and Recovery: The Readiness Guide for the Enterprise.* Wiley, 2003.
- Marlin, S. "Customer Data Losses Blamed on Merchants and Software." *Information Week,* 2005. www.informationweek.com/showArticle.jhtml?articleID=161601930.
- Nichols, R., D. Ryan, and J. Ryan. *Defending Your Digital Assets Against Hackers, Crackers, Spies, and Thieves.* McGraw-Hill Education, 2000.
- Preston, W.C. *Backup & Recovery.* O'Reilly Media, 2007.
- Conklin, Wm. Arthur. *Introduction to Principles of Computer Security: Security+ and Beyond.* McGraw-Hill Education, 2004.
- Schou, Corey D., and D.P. Shoemaker. *Information Assurance for the Enterprise: A Roadmap to Information Security.* McGraw-Hill Education, 2007.
- Toigo, J.W. *Holy Grail of Data Storage Management.* Prentice Hall, 1999.
- Tom, P. *Data Protection and Information Lifecycle.* Prentice Hall, 2006.
- Tipton, Harold F., and S. Hernandez, ed. *Official (ISC)² Guide to the CISSP CBK 3rd edition.* ((ISC)²) Press, 2012.

Critical Thinking Exercises

1. An organization has performed a BIA and discovered 90 percent of its services and data have an RTO of ten days and an RPO of one day. The remaining ten percent of its services and data have an RTO of 30 minutes and an RPO of zero. What is the best strategy for the organization to back up this information?

2. How can organizations ensure their backup information is protected and the integrity of the backup is assured?

Application of Information Assurance to Select Industries

Part V explores the application of information assurance in three selected industries. Healthcare, retail, and industrial control systems will be explored and discussed as examples of applied information assurance. We show the practical application of the MSR information assurance model and other concepts to these industries.

Chapter 26 is based on major issues with healthcare security and privacy. Internationally, healthcare is rapidly changing. For example, in the United States, new legislation has provided requirements and financial incentives for doctors and hospitals to implement and adopt electronic health records. While many have rushed to take advantage of the opportunity, many have also neglected to consider information assurance as part of the people, processes, and technology portion of electronic health record (EHR) implementation.

Chapter 27 explores breaches by major retailers and how modern attacks for retailers differ from other industries. Data flow and the systems used to process, store, and transmit credit card information will be examined as well as practical countermeasures involving technology, policy, and people that retail organizations should consider.

Finally, Chapter 28 addresses industrial control systems. A look at the industrial control environment shows how assumptions about technology and security can have lasting implications for information assurance concerns. As in the healthcare and retail chapters, this chapter will explore common information assurance concerns and provide practical suggestions for using the MSR information assurance model to help understand and mitigate risk.

CHAPTER

26 Healthcare

Internationally, healthcare systems are relying increasingly on technology for improvement in efficiency, safety, patient outcomes, and enhanced communication between patient and practice. Many economies are rapidly adopting electronic health records (EHRs) as a means to streamline operations and keep better operational control over costs and processes. While EHRs can lead to substantial increases in patient satisfaction, health record portability, and cost savings, they can also lead to substantial exposure if not protected properly. Laws in different economies vary. We offer some general advice; however, you should always seek local advice on specifics.

Overview of Information Assurance Approach

As introduced in Chapter 3, the MSR information assurance model involves five *essential* services: confidentiality, integrity, availability, authentication, and nonrepudiation. When applied to the healthcare industry, these overarching concerns become apparent immediately:

- **Confidentiality**   Patients have an expectation not only confidentiality but privacy of their medical records. While privacy is a special case of confidentiality, the requirement of protecting the information from unauthorized disclosure remains. Healthcare organizations and their partners must remember that patients own their information and are legally protected in many nations from disclosing it without permission.

- **Integrity**   Patients must have confidence that their medial record is accurate and timely. Incorrect information in a medical record can lead to prescription errors, dosing errors, surgical mistakes, and worse. The information system handling medical information must ensure records are altered only by authorized personnel or processes and that a function exists to ensure the integrity of the information.

- **Availability**   Especially in urgent or emergency care, the availability of medical information means the difference between life or death. If a healthcare organization is reliant on an EHR as the official system of record for medical files, the records must be available when needed regardless of maintenance, weather, or power outages.

- **Authentication**   To maintain confidentiality, integrity, and nonrepudiation, the EHR must incorporate strong authentication. The authentication must ensure actions can be traced to a unique user or process. Authentication must be logged.

- **Nonrepudiation**   Nonrepudiation ensures actions and changes to the system and records can be traced to a process or individual without dispute. Strong authentication is vital in ensuring accountability. Strong logging and auditing ensures actions are recorded and can be later referenced to individual users. By ensuring EHR users are using the system only as intended in a defensible manner, patients gain confidence in EHR systems when healthcare organizations can prove who accessed their records, for what reason, and what changes were made.

Using the previous information, the next step is to use the MSR framework to analyze the risks present in using EHRs and offer controls to mitigate, transfer, avoid, or accept risk. The approach will involve using the chapters of this book to describe, at a high level, action and controls that healthcare organizations should consider in mitigating risk.

Healthcare-Specific Terminology

The healthcare industry has developed several terms and definitions that define patient health information in electronic forms. The following are commonly used terms as adapted from the National Alliance for Health Information Technology:

- **Electronic medical record (EMR)**   This is the electronic record of health-related information on an individual created, gathered, managed, and consulted by licensed clinicians and staff from a single organization who are involved in the individual's healthcare.

- **Electronic health record (EHR)**   This is the aggregate electronic record of health-related information on an individual that is created and gathered cumulatively across more than one healthcare organization and is managed and consulted by licensed clinicians and staff involved in the individual's healthcare.

- **ePHR**   This is an electronic, cumulative record of health-related information on an individual, drawn from multiple sources, that is created, gathered, and managed by the individual. The integrity of the data in the ePHR and control of access to that data is the responsibility of the individual. Microsoft's HealthVault is an example of an ePHR.

By these definitions, an EHR is an EMR with interoperability (that is, integration to other providers' systems). An ePHR could have interoperability with either EHRs or EMRs. The important distinction between the system types is the interoperability and who controls the patient's information and access to the information.

Information Assurance Management

Information assurance must be a strategic priority established by senior management at the top of the organization. While small organizations may lack the resources to dedicate a full-time information assurance team, senior management must assign responsibility for information assurance throughout the organization. If blended roles are used, senior management must commit to an AT&E program for individuals in information assurance practices and strategies.

Personnel

Healthcare organizations must designate an overarching authority for record security and privacy. This person may be an office manager, a chief information officer, a chief risk officer, or even the head of the practice. Whoever is assigned functional responsibility for security and privacy should possess fundamental information assurance practitioner skills as they are applied to healthcare. Organizations should consider training and credentialing personnel to ensure a minimum level of competence is met. For example, (ISC)^2 offers the Healthcare Certified Information Security and Privacy Practitioner (HCISPP) credential. This credential tests and validates experience over the following domains of knowledge:

- Healthcare industry
- Regulatory environment
- Privacy and security in healthcare
- Information governance and risk management
- Information risk assessment
- Third-party risk management

If senior management decides to outsource information technology, the organization still has a responsibility to ensure the information assurance requirements are met. Including credentialing requirements as part of a contract agreement is a wise move to ensure those who handle sensitive health information understand basic information assurance concepts.

Management Approach

Smaller organizations will most likely default to a bottom-up approach to information assurance management, but must be cautious because some regulatory environments mandate aspects of a top-down approach such as policies, procedures, standards, and guidance delivered from the head of the organization. Regardless of the approach, it should be documented in an information assurance strategy document ideally as part of the organization's work plan or organizational strategy document.

Organizations of any size must determine how to adopt the basic Plan-Do-Check-Act (PDCA) cycle of information assurance management. As technology changes and culture shifts, organizations must have a way to determine the best approach to respond to changing organizational forces. The PDCA encourages a proactive approach to ensuring information assurance is integrated throughout the organization's life cycle.

Part V

Regulations and Legal Requirements

Regulations and legal requirements will vary by location. You can find some of the more common regulations associated with privacy in Appendix F. In addition to privacy laws, some countries, states, and economies have additional laws related specifically to healthcare. For example, the Health Information Portability and Accountability Act of 1996 (HIPAA) in the United States requires healthcare entities and business associates to do the following:

- Report breaches of unsecured personal health information
- Implement the confidentiality provisions of the Patient Safety Rule
- Implement the requirements of the Privacy Rule
- Implement the requirements of the Security Rule

Another example of legal requirements is France. Through the Data Protection Law of January 6th 1978, France requires healthcare professionals to either apply as or work with an accredited medical data host when a third party (like a cloud provider) processes or stores medical information. Accreditation requirements can be quite strict, including appointing a doctor who will oversee the confidentiality and access of the medical data. The organization must understand the explicit requirements imposed by the legal jurisdiction they operate in. Organizations must also be aware of business partnerships, outsourcing arraignments, and cloud computing activities that may trigger certain aspects of legal requirements. We recommend advice from legal counsel in making major decisions in these areas.

Information Assurance Risk Management

 If researched and an acceptable scope is established, the organization should have a good understanding of their operating environment. Senior leaders should be aware of any legal restrictions and should have assigned information assurance responsibilities throughout the organization. The next step is to understand information assurance risk. The MSR information assurance model addresses risk through the use of risk assessments. Risk assessments are based on assets, impacts, likelihood, vulnerabilities, and threats. You can find information regarding the development of risk management systems in Chapter 11.

Assets

The medical records of patients are obviously valuable not only to the business but also to competitors, marketers, identify thieves, and anyone looking to possibly blackmail or smear the reputation of a patient. While medical records rank high on the list of assets, healthcare providers should not neglect other assets such as, but not limited to, the following:

- Prescription pads
- Banking information
- Contract information

- Employee information
- Proprietary procedures
- Research

Remember that not all assets are electronic; manual processes and paper constitute part of the information. These assets present the possibility of theft and therefore should be considered assets as part of an overarching information assurance risk assessment. Remember, assets may be digital or physical. A stack of prescription pads can be used the same way as a digital prescription. A printed medical record has the same information as a digital record. Categorize assets based on impact to the organization.

Some assets, such as medical records, may be "high" impact to the organization, while contract information is deemed "moderate" or even "low." Organizations should consider different aspects of information assurance when categorizing information. For example, a medical record may have a "high" impact if confidentiality is breached but a "moderate" impact if availability is lost. You can find more information regarding threats in Chapter 4.

Threats

Threats in the healthcare industry must be viewed through not only an information technology lens but also a physical lens. For printed medical records, the threat of physical theft is real; Appendix B describes commonly identified threats. The organization should consider each asset and determine which threats apply. Remember, human threats have motivation, means, and opportunity to be successful, while natural threats are based on location, patterns, and environmental conditions. You can find more information about threats in Chapter 4.

Vulnerabilities

Like threats, vulnerabilities must be considered with the operational environment. Digital records are subject to vulnerabilities that hackers could exploit in addition to physical security concerns. Appendix C provides a detailed list of common vulnerabilities organizations should be aware of. Organizations should also incorporate continuous monitoring and vulnerability management programs into their identification of vulnerabilities. You can find more information about continuous monitoring in Chapter 20.

Risk Assessment

As noted in Chapter 11, risk management is the determination of risk by assessing the likelihood of an adverse event (a threat exploiting a vulnerability) and the resulting impact. Each asset must be aligned with relevant threats and vulnerabilities to determine the likelihood and impact to the organization. Remember, threats and vulnerabilities are not simply technical. They may manifest in personnel, procedures, policy, competition, environment, and information technology. The assessment should determine which areas, program systems, or assets of the organization contain the most risk. You can view an example risk analysis table in Appendix E.

Part V

Risk Mitigation

Once risks are identified, mitigation, acceptance, transfer, or acceptance must be identified. This section covers several of the controls mentioned throughout the book in the context of healthcare organizations. You can find more information regarding risk mitigation throughout the book.

Policy, Procedures, Standards, and Guidance

Healthcare organizations of any size must ensure they implement and use policies that memorialize management's information assurance decisions. These policies should be updated and referenced in employee training materials. The policies should provide information about possible disciplinary actions as a result of violations of privacy and unauthorized sharing of personal health information. Policies should include legal or regulatory requirements to show management's commitment for complying with applicable laws and setting the expectation for the rest of the organization.

Procedures and standards work hand-in-hand to provide specific structure around policy expectations. Some of the most common procedures for healthcare providers include, but are not limited to, the following:

- Release of healthcare information
  - To the subject
  - To other parties
- Protection of physical records
  - Destruction of physical records
  - Retention of physical records
- Protection of electronic records
  - E-mail procedures to ensure information is not leaked
  - Proper use of encryption tools when sending or storing health information
  - System testing and upgrading procedures to ensure no leaks occur
  - Proper standards for the secure destruction of ePHI

Standards identify specific technologies or criteria that are necessary to maintain the policy. The following represent some common standards present in healthcare organizations:

- Release of healthcare information
  - Standard forms required
  - Standard for identity proofing
- Protection of physical records
  - Standards of sufficient destruction (tools and technologies)
  - Standard periods for retention

- Protection of electronic records
  - Standard approved encryption technologies approved for use
  - Standards of reporting time for incidents
  - Information system standards for secure configurations

Finally, guidance should be viewed as the glue that holds all three together. While not binding, guidance can be invaluable in providing context around the use of standards, policy, and procedures in specific scenarios.

Human Resources

Healthcare organizations have a duty to hire employees who are trustworthy and who will maintain the confidentiality of patient health information. In addition to background investigations and references as allowed by locality, healthcare organizations should consider whether credentials are necessary for a particular role in the organization. For example, a smaller organization's owner may decide every new hire will obtain the (ISC)² HCISPP credential because they will all be expected to play a part in the decentralized approach to information technology employed at the organization.

Organizations must also be aware of restrictions on hiring. For example, in the United States, a provider that performs services for Medicare patients must ensure their staffs are not on the U.S. Department of Health and Human Services' Office of Inspector General's exclusion list. The individuals and organizations listed have been excluded from the Medicare program and are prohibited from rendering services to and billing for Medicare services.

Certification, Accreditation, and Assurance

Some economics and countries will require healthcare organizations to undergo a form of certification and accreditation. If the healthcare organization is in one of these environments, the requirement will necessarily drive many aspects of their information assurance approach. However, even organizations not subject to mandatory certification and accreditation standards should consider voluntarily adopting them. Not only can certification and accreditation help mature an organization's information assurance processes, it can provide a safe harbor or a position of due care and due diligence. In the U.S., Texas healthcare providers can obtain certain safe harbor provisions for IT security breaches if their system is certified under the HITRUST model.

Information Assurance in System Development and Acquisition

The same information assurance requirements memorialized in the organization's information assurance policy must be incorporated into system development activities and also system acquisition activities. In some countries, third parties such as cloud providers must meet stringent certification and accreditation requirements to process, store, or transmit healthcare information. Senior management must remember their commitment to protect health information extends not only to systems but to the data itself. The requirement for protection follows the data to whatever system or media it may travel.

Part V

Physical and Environmental Security Controls

Healthcare organizations must ensure their offices are physically secure. Most offices contain not only hard copy health information but also expensive medical equipment, prescription drugs, and computer equipment containing electronic health records; both electronic and hardcopy records must be planned for and protected. Healthcare organizations must ensure physical security requirements extend to any business partners or third-party processes, storing or transmitting information on their behalf. Physical security includes monitoring technologies such as cameras and voice recording. Healthcare providers must be careful not to have surveillance in areas where patients may have a legally protected expectation of privacy.

Awareness, Training, and Education

Healthcare organizations must ensure their workforce has continuous information assurance training and awareness. Organizations should require all new hires to complete baselines awareness and training to familiarize themselves with the organization's information assurance policies, procedures, standards, and guidelines. System and sensitive information access should be restricted until the new employee has completed the training.

Annual or even more frequent training and awareness should be incorporated into the organization's information assurance culture. Organizations of any size should consider credentialing information assurance "superusers" with credentials such as the (ISC)² HCISPP and appointing them as "go-to" people when questions surrounding information assurance arise. Successful awareness and training programs add an element of competition in training and awareness completion. Organizations should consider adding training and awareness as a performance element for their employees and contractors.

Of the preventive information assurance tools and techniques available, none carries the significance of proper change management and configuration management. Change management ensures all aspects of the healthcare organization's systems are considered when changes occur. Change management should interact with policy updates, regulatory changes, and changes to information systems to ensure changes do not negatively impact the information assurance posture of the organization.

Configuration management should be implemented to provide a mature and consistent application of technical information assurance controls across the enterprise. When products are vulnerable or updates are required for operating systems, knowing the standard configuration is invaluable in mitigating the risk.

Access Control

Healthcare organizations should strive to adopt multifactor authentication whenever possible. Multifactor authentication requires two different factors for successful authentication. For example, a username provides identification, a password or PIN is something known, and a further element such as a token is something someone has. By requiring additional factors for authentication, healthcare organizations can greatly strengthen not only access control requirements but also nonrepudiation requirements. Access control must be carefully monitored and logged. Successful and unsuccessful authentication attempts should be logged, monitored, and reviewed.

Continuous Monitoring, Incident Response, and Forensics

Much as healthcare organizations care for patients by monitoring vital signs to determine deviation from norms and determining the output from diagnostics, information systems rely on the same rigor to keep a steady read on risk. Most continuous monitoring takes the form of vulnerability monitoring produced through automated vulnerability scanners. Even the smallest of organizations can afford basic vulnerability scanners that will help determine configuration weaknesses of information systems.

Vulnerability information must be relayed to the change management and configuration process for mitigation and patching. Remember, vulnerability is only part of the overall risk equation. If likelihood of a threat exploiting the vulnerability is low, the organization may not want to prioritize the patching or mitigation if it is resource intensive.

Healthcare organizations must engage in incident response. U.S. laws such as HIPAA require timely reporting of information breaches to authorities. Organizations that fail to report a breach face larger fines and sanctions when discovered. Many laws also require organizations to notify patients of the breach and ensure appropriate credit monitoring is in place at the expense of the healthcare organization. Forensics may help a healthcare organization prove due diligence if the forensics process determines sufficient technical controls such as encryption were in place to mitigate the breach.

Business Continuity and Backups

Healthcare organizations must carefully consider the availability requirements of their mission and data. Information needed frequently and without delay should be housed in a hot-site hosting arraignment or similar. Healthcare organizations need to clearly determine business continuity plans and disaster recovery plans to ensure service is available in times of disaster. Healthcare services are often the hardest hit during a disaster because they see increased demand for their services while often operating in a contingency mode themselves.

Further Reading

- American Recovery and Reinvestment Act of 2009 (ARRA). Title XIII, "Health Information Technology for Economic and Clinical Health Act (HITECH)," §13600, 2009. www.gpo.gov/fdsys/pkg/BILLS-111hr1enr/pdf/BILLS-111hr1enr.pdf.

- Center for Democracy and Technology. Health Privacy (web page), 2013. https://www.cdt.org/issue/health-privacy.

- Data Protection Act 1998, Chapter 29. 1998. www.legislation.gov.uk/ukpga/1998/29/data.pdf.

- Hernandez, Steven G. *The Official (ISC)² Guide to the HCISPP CBK.* (ISC)² Press, 2014.

- HIPAA Case Examples and Resolution Agreements. www.hhs.gov/ocr/privacy/hipaa/enforcement/examples/index.html.

- Organization for Economic Co-operation and Development. OECD Guidelines on the Protection of Privacy and Transborder Flows of Personal Data, 1980. www.oecd.org/internet/ieconomy/oecdguidelinesontheprotectionofprivacyandtransborderflowsofpersonaldata.htm.

- Ponemon Institute. Third Annual Survey on Medical Identity Theft. June 2012. www.ponemon.org/local/upload/file/Third_Annual_Survey_on_Medical_Identity_Theft_FINAL.pdf.

- The European Data Protection Directive, 2001. http://eur-lex.europa.eu/LexUriServ/LexUriServ.do?uri=OJ:L:2001:008:0001:0022:en:PDF.

- The Patient Protection and Affordable Care Act of 2010. Pub. L. No. 111-148, § 124 Stat. 119, 2010. www.gpo.gov/fdsys/pkg/PLAW-111publ148/pdf/PLAW-111publ148.pdf.

Critical Thinking Exercises

1. A U.S.-based healthcare clinic consists of an owner who is the head doctor of the practice, a physician's assistant, an office manager, a few nurses, and a couple assistants. Who is responsible for ensuring ePHI security and privacy?

2. Assuming a clinic uses ePHI within the scope of the UK's data protection law, what technical controls should the clinic consider implementing to ensure the confidentiality and privacy of its records?

CHAPTER 27

Retail

Once seemingly immune to information assurance woes, retail organizations are now front-page news for the massive breaches they have experienced. Retail breaches are more complicated than may first appear. While the retailer is certainly part of the breach, there are other parties involved that assume part of the overall risk. The credit card providers, credit card processors, the Payment Card Industry Data Security Standard (PCI-DSS) industry, the customers, and the technology providers all have a hand in ensuring that appropriate information assurance is protecting the business and the customers.

Overview of the Information Assurance Approach

The MSR information assurance model involves five essential services: confidentiality, integrity, availability, authentication, and nonrepudiation. When applied to the retail industry, these overarching concerns become apparent immediately.

- **Confidentiality**   Customers have an expectation of privacy when it comes to their personal information and their credit and debit card information. While many credit cards protect users from fraudulent charges, most debit cards have a limit of exposure and hold the customer liable for losses beyond that amount; in many cases, timely notification of theft or loss is required to mitigate customer losses. In some cases, this amount can be as little as $500. Retailers maintain several types of information that have privacy and confidentiality requirements, such as credit card information, debit card information, bank account information, personally identifiable information, shopping habits (as part of shopping clubs), and surveillance information.

- **Integrity**   Retailers rely on accurate, thorough, and timely information regarding marketing, sales, competition, pricing, and logistics. In increasingly competitive markets, retailers must perform not only in the showroom of the store but also in the marketing department, the shipping department, the pricing department, and the customer satisfaction survey. Inaccurate financial records, shipping records, and even customer records can result in the loss of revenue and customers.

- **Availability**   If a point-of-sale (POS) system is not operational, a sale cannot be made in many of today's high-tech retail operations. With the increased use of credit cards and the decline of cash-based transactions, retailers are relying on a resilient infrastructure now more than ever to ensure transactions can take place in near real time.

- **Authentication**   Authentication has become a hot topic with many retailers because numerous breaches have now been traced to authentication issues related to internal systems and external providers using remote access systems to gain access to a retailer's stock, as well as environmental and sales systems.

- **Nonrepudiation**   In retail, nonrepudiation is critical for staying in business. A retailer must be able to prove when a transaction took place, who was involved in the transaction, and what was traded. Failures of nonrepudiation lead to the retailer giving refunds when no refund is due, not being able to defend itself in court if needed, and not having reliable audit logs when trying to determine whether an insider is stealing from the company.

Now that a basic outline of a retailer has been created, a risk assessment and mitigation approach can be crafted. Retailers are often focused on their core mission of selling products, but they must be willing to understand the risk they have accumulated through the natural progression of technology in retail. Retailers cannot afford to ignore information assurance because the results can be truly catastrophic for their business. The retail industry uses several terms specific to retail business objectives. The following list provides an overview of commonly used terms:

- **POS**   The point-of-sale system is the interface between the cashier (or the self-checkout line) and the numerous back-end systems of the organization. It is typically designed to handle cash, checks, credit card, and social services transactions. Additionally, it is linked to numerous back-office services such as inventory systems and customer information capture systems.

- **Customer information capture systems**   These systems capture information about customers for marketing, promotions, and business intelligence. They are often used with customer loyalty programs and bonus cards.

- **Inventory information capture systems**   Inventory information systems keep track of a retailer's inventory and the amount of supplies on hand at a given moment. They are integrated into the POS system so as inventory is sold, the back-office people know whether they need to start ordering more inventory. Alternatively, if a product is not selling well, the inventory system can display the lead time for inventory turnover, which may prompt a sale or reduction in price.

- **Workforce management systems**   Workforce management systems are designed to provide the basic operational automation for the retailer's workforce such as time and attendance, work schedule, and leave.

- **Supply chain management systems**   These systems are featured at large retailers and serve to model the logistics process for efficient shipping and supplier relationships.

- **Business intelligence**   Business intelligence (BI) is used to find statistical significant events such as triggers or correlations in buyer behavior and business operations. BI typically takes data from throughout the organization to find patterns, trends, and causation.

- **PCI-DSS**   The Payment Card Industry Data Security Standard is an agreement about baseline security among major credit card providers. It is mandatory for retailers who want to accept the most commonly issued credit cards. PCI-DSS mandates operational, managerial, and technical controls. PCI-DSS is often criticized as insufficient for true security. Since it is a baseline, it establishes a minimum starting point from which an organization builds the rest of its security program through the use of effective risk management.

- **EMV**   This stands for Europay, Mastercard, and Visa. This is a global standard for the interoperation of "chip and pin" credit cards. These cards contain a microprocessor that allows for the real-time authentication of a customer through the use of a PIN. It is common outside the United States.

Information Assurance Management

The retail industry has been affected by several high-profile security breaches in the past year. You need only to skim the recent news to understand the retail market is a prime target. Table 27-1 lists selected breaches by retailer with cause and affected individuals based on information from privacyrights.org, a breach reporting clearinghouse.

Date	Retailer	Attack	Approximate Impact	Comments
March 8, 2005	DSW Shoe Warehouse, Retail Ventures Columbus, Ohio	Hacking.	1,400,000 customers' personally identifiable information and credit card information breached.	In addition to credit monitoring costs, DSW was locked in a lengthily dispute with the National Union over insurance coverage.
December 28, 2005	Marriott International Inc. Orlando, Florida	Backup media lost or stolen.	206,000 customers, and employees, personally identifiable information including Social Security numbers and financial information.	N/A

Table 27-1 Overview of Retail Breaches (*continued*)

Part V

Date	Retailer	Attack	Approximate Impact	Comments
January 17, 2007	TJ stores (TJX), including TJMaxx, Marshalls, Winners, HomeSense, AJWright, T.K. Maxx, and possibly Bob's Stores in the United States and Puerto Rico; Winners and HomeGoods stores in Canada; possibly T.K. Maxx stores in the United Kingdom and Ireland.	Hacking.	100,000,000 customer credit card, debit card, check and merchandise return transaction records. Some records may have also contained driver's license numbers, military ID information, and Social Security numbers.	Information obtained in this breach was used fraudulently in an $8 million gift card scheme. Twenty-one U.S. and Canadian lawsuits demanded damages. TJX paid for credit monitoring for 455,000 of the affected. It also reimbursed customers who had to replace identifications as part of the breach. Fifth Third Bancorp was fined $880,000 by Visa for its role in the breach. TJX settled a $9.75 million settlement with 40 states. TJX settled with the Louisiana Municipal Police Employees' Retirement System for $595,000 related to damages caused by legal fees and increased oversight because of the breach. TJX settled with an anonymous party in the amount of $107 million. TJX settled with Mastercard Inc., in which it will pay up to $24 million to banks and other institutions affected by the breach.

Table 27-1   Overview of Retail Breaches (*continued*)

Date	Retailer	Attack	Approximate Impact	Comments
September 28, 2007	Gap Inc. San Francisco, California	Laptop stolen from a third-party vendor supporting HR functions.	800,000 applicants' information, including Social Security numbers.	Gap was engaged in a lengthy legal battle over damages in which it eventually prevailed because the plaintiff could not prove damages.
December 10, 2011	Steam (The Valve Corporation) Bellevue, Washington	Hacking.	35 million customers. Primarily usernames, passwords, and encrypted credit card data.	A judge dismissed a class action lawsuit regarding the breach; the plaintiffs were unable to prove they were in harm or in danger of future harm.
April 27, 2011	Sony, PlayStation Network (PSN), Sony Online Entertainment (SOE) New York, New York	Hacking.	101.6 million (12 million unencrypted credit card numbers)	Sony estimates it will spend $171 million on credit monitoring, welcome-back programs, customer support, network security enhancements, and legal costs associated with the breach. Sony was party to 55 class-action lawsuits and a legal action by its insurer to prevent paying out a $178 million dollar breach coverage fund.

Table 27-1   Overview of Retail Breaches (*continued*)

Part V

Date	Retailer	Attack	Approximate Impact	Comments
December 13, 2013	Target Corp. Minneapolis, Minnesota	Hacking. Custom malware infected the POS systems and transferred information to the attacker. The initial credentials used to gain access to Target's network were obtained from a heating and cooling efficiency contractor.	Up to 110 million customers' payment card information and PINs.	Three class-action lawsuits have been filed. Breach costs are estimated to be up to $3.6 billion. A Target shareholder filed a suit alleging Target's board and executives harmed the company financially by failing to take adequate steps to secure its systems and prevent the attack. Fourteen Target officers and directors were named in the suit.
January 10, 2014	Neiman Marcus Dallas, Texas	Hacking.	1.1 million customers' payment card information.	N/A
February 6, 2014	The Home Depot Atlanta, Georgia	Insider threat. Home Depot employees were arrested for allegedly stealing personal information. They allegedly opened numerous fraudulent accounts with the information.	20,000 employees' and customers' Social Security numbers and birth dates.	N/A

Table 27-1 Overview of Retail Breaches

Clearly, the selected examples in Table 27-1 demonstrate that the retail industry is not immune to the devastating impact of poorly implemented information assurance. Many retailers face the same adversaries and challenges as the retailers in the table. Through the development of an information assurance program with executive sponsorship, organizations can avoid or greatly reduce the impacts of a breach or worse. As noted throughout this book, information assurance management must address several aspects of an organization outside of information technology. Personnel, the management approach, and careful consideration of regulations must all be carefully accounted for in an information assurance program.

Personnel

Retail organizations should consider hiring blended information assurance professionals. An example would be an MBA with an SSCP, CISM, CISSP, or CSSLP certification. This combination of skills is necessary to ensure the person has a working knowledge of business and can apply information assurance controls to the appropriate areas while speaking the language of business impact to the senior executives. While often difficult to find, many educational organizations and professionals have seen this need and developed curriculums around blended information assurance professionals.

Management Approach

Retail organizations should employ a top-down approach for information assurance. Senior leadership must set the tone at the top and inform the entire workforce that information assurance is a priority for the organization and for the organization's customers. A strong information assurance program should be established with clear authority for information system monitoring and incident response. (See Chapters 20 and 22 for more information about incident response and monitoring.)

Management must also ensure their information assurance approach aligns with their IT strategies and encompasses the whole organization, not just traditional IT. Many large retailers maintain full cybersecurity intelligence teams, yet these organizations are the same ones being attacked successfully. In many cases, the reasons revolve around the narrowness of cybersecurity. In Chapter 3, information assurance was compared and contrasted with several related subdisciplines including cybersecurity.

Figure 3-2 helps explain the difference between information assurance and cybersecurity. An organization that focuses only on cybersecurity is vulnerable to a host of serious threats including, but not limited to, equipment theft, third-party credential misuse, shadow IT, cloud computing blind spots, intellectual property theft by employees, and portable media (including paper records) loss.

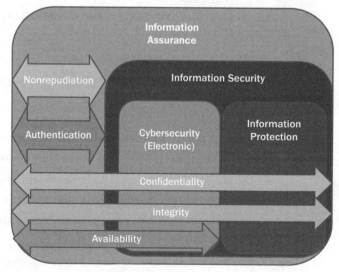

Management should have a vested interest in ensuring the due diligence and due care of the organization. As noted in the Target entry of Table 27-1, the Target board of directors and senior management were named in a lawsuit by a shareholder. Management must understand they can be held accountable for their actions and their lack of action.

Part V

Regulations and Legal Requirements

The most commonly cited regulation surrounding retail operations is the Payment Card Industry Data Security Standard (PCI-DSS). Retail organizations must be aware they are now subject to many more regulations than before due to the growing practices of collecting customers' personally identifiable information and using the information for marketing, business intelligence, and customer loyalty programs. Retailers involved in the medical field including pharmacies must also be aware of medial laws and regulations such as HIPAA in the United States and the Data Protection Act in the United Kingdom. For a list of international privacy laws and regulations retailers must consider, see Appendix F.

PCI-DSS

PCI-DSS is a continuous approach similar to the Plan-Do-Check-Act approach outlined in Chapter 6 of this book. PCI-DSS prescribes an Assess-Remediate-Report life cycle.

- **Assess**   Assessment involves identifying cardholder data, understanding IT assets processing, storing or transmitting cardholder data, and assessing business processes to discover vulnerabilities.

- **Remediate**   Remediation involves fixing and resolving weaknesses discovered during the assessment phase. Not storing cardholder information unless absolutely necessary is a commonly highlighted mitigation.

- **Reporting**   To remain compliant with PCI-DSS, organizations are required to report status to acquiring banks and card brands the merchant chooses to do business with.

PCI-DSS requires mandatory security controls no matter the size of the organization. In summary, PCI-DSS requires the following:

- Install and maintain a firewall and router configuration to protect cardholder data.
- Do not use vendor-supplied defaults for system passwords and other security parameters.
- Protect stored cardholder data.
- Encrypt transmission of cardholder data across open, public networks.
- Use and regularly update antivirus software or programs.
- Develop and maintain secure systems and applications.
- Restrict access to cardholder data by business need to know.
- Assign a unique ID to each person with computer access.
- Restrict physical access to cardholder data.
- Track and monitor all access to network resources and cardholder data.
- Regularly test security systems and processes.
- Maintain a policy that addresses information security for all personnel.

While these 12 areas may seem simple, they are anything but. Entire books have been written on several of the subjects, such as "develop and maintain secure systems and applications." Another area that may seem simple is encryption; however, database encryption, session encryption, and full disk encryption for a laptop are very different from one another but are all required for protecting cardholder information throughout its life cycle.

To be PCI-DSS compliant, organizations must use a qualified security assessor (QSA) to perform their assessment. A QSA is certified by the PCI Security Standards Council to perform compliance verification assessments onsite. The QSA handles the Assess portion of the PCI-DSS cycle. Organizations are responsible for choosing a QSA who has a solid understanding of their business, IT infrastructure, cloud use, and culture. PCI-DSS also requires organizations to use an approved scanning vendor (ASV). These are firms that are certified to determine whether a customer is compliant with the PCI-DSS external vulnerability scanning requirement.

Organizations can greatly reduce their scoping and size of network through the use of network segmentation. Network segmentation isolates cardholder data from the rest of the network through physical and logical controls. For example, common business practice may state that having every service and device on the same network will ease management complexity and allow for greater reuse of common services. However, the entire network is now in scope for assessment and also attack from a practical perspective. This could mean an attacker will leverage a different service on the network such as a heating and ventilation efficiency appliance to steal credentials and then launch an attack against other systems processing or storing cardholder information.

Privacy Laws

As noted previously, Appendix F describes the vast majority of privacy laws available around the world and the majority of states in the United States. In addition to PCI-DSS, retail organizations must be aware of what legal requirements they may be required to fulfill should a breach of customers' personally identifiable information occur. The good news is that many laws have a safe harbor provision for organizations that have conducted due care and due diligence measures such as encrypting cardholder information at rest and in transit.

Most privacy laws require the organization ultimately accountable for the information (the retail organization) to notify the customer of the breach and, in cases of moderate or high risk breaches, offer credit monitoring services for a certain duration. While there is a monetary cost of providing notification and monitoring, the real pinch may come from certain laws that require fines to be paid to regulators such as the U.S. Department of Health and Human Services for HIPAA violations.

Information Assurance Risk Management

The need for information assurance should be crystal clear in the retail space. PCI-DSS provides a good starting point for many organizations but should not be solely relied on as sufficient protection in today's threat environment. In February 2014, South Korea KB Kookmin Bank, Lotte Card, and NH Nonghyup Card were fined ₩6 million and banned from issuing new credit cards for three months because of a data breach. The breach contained information for more than 20 million people (about 40 percent of South Korea's population) that was sold to marketing firms. Allegedly, an IT contractor working for a credit rating firm stole the information. The South Korean Financial Supervisory Commission (FSC) said the three firms ran afoul of due diligence and due care by not preventing leakage of customer information. Several executives resigned or offered to step down over the issue. Managing information assurance risk requires organizations to thoroughly understand their environments, assets, threats, vulnerabilities, and how best to assess their risk.

Assets

Retailers should consider all aspects of customer information and organizational assets to be protected. If the organization collected it, there must be value in keeping it. If not, the organization should determine a secure way to destroy the information. An adversary can't steal or exfiltrate what isn't there. As PCI-DSS notes, the information assurance requirements follow data in all its forms through any system or media.

Assets should be categorized or classified according to their impact to the organization. Credit card information and personally identifiable information should be categorized as moderately or highly important to the organization. The systems that process, transmit, or store sensitive information must be identified and inventoried as part of an asset validation process. Account for all data flows or interconnections. In addition, keep track of which partners are receiving information that your organization has ultimate responsibility for.

Threats

Retailers are mired with numerous threats. In addition to the traditional threats of hackers operating across the wire, retailers must also have a high level of interaction with the public and therefore must prize availability and customer friendliness over other concerns. Recent events have shown retailers suffer most from external hackers gaining access to card information and insider threats that have access to the data and plan on using it for fraud or personal gain.

Hackers find vulnerabilities in information systems and attempt to leverage them to gain control of systems containing sensitive information. However, organizations must understand that all systems are a target. Even if attackers cannot gain access to the target system, they will find other systems connected to it and attempt to compromise those so they can then move "laterally" through the organization.

Insider threats are based on employees and contractors who either intentionally or unintentionally put information and operations at risk through their actions or negligence. An insider threat may be the honest employee who left his laptop in the car and the car got stolen, or it may be the corrupt senior official planning on spending her retirement in a new country with a new identity and a pile of ill-gotten cash.

As if hackers and insider threats were not enough, retail must also worry about natural disasters such as hurricanes, earthquakes, and floods if they are to remain viable. The U.S. Federal Emergency Management Agency (FEMA) estimates that 40 percent of businesses do not reopen after a disaster. Of those that do open, 25 percent fail within one year. Retail operations face formidable threats from several sources; only a robust approach to information assurance with an associated program can help organizations survive. You can find more information regarding threats in Chapter 4.

Vulnerabilities

When retailers talk about vulnerabilities, they are often focused on shrinkage or product loss because of theft or destruction. They may also discuss vulnerabilities in terms of their market and associated strategy to remain relevant in a growing environment of international competition. Retail organizations must pay the same attention to vulnerabilities in their information assurance posture.

Vulnerabilities must always be viewed through the three lenses of people, processes, and technology. All three areas must be assessed to determine where weaknesses actually exist in the enterprise.

Technical vulnerabilities are often the first discussed when the topic of vulnerability management comes up. Many organizations believe if they patch their systems and do a vulnerability scan once a month, they are in good shape. This is a good start but far from sufficient. Technical vulnerabilities can also exist in business partners. Is the information assurance team part of all procurement actions that involves the processing, storing, or transmitting of the organization's information? Is the information assurance team part of all discussions where systems are to be interconnected to share information? Organizations must remember that their requirement to protect cardholder information extends to anywhere that information goes on the organization's behalf. Is the organization aware of the technical vulnerabilities of their partners and what risk they may be accepting and not telling the organization? Organizations need to understand their vulnerably surface extends far beyond "in-house" IT to partners, volunteers, and anyone who holds information the organization is ultimately responsible for.

An organization's processes and operations are just as ripe for exploitation as its IT systems. Consider a billing system that prints out customer information for review during marketing meetings. After the meetings, the administrative assistant collects the information and simply deposits the information into the recycling bin. A resourceful industrial spy comes by the office once a week or so and rifles through the recycling bin and collects substantial information about the organization's performance and customers. Not a single element of IT or technology was involved in this vulnerability. The vulnerability present was completely based on the operating procedures of the organization. If the organization had adopted media-handling protocols that included marking and secure destruction requirements, the information would have been marked sensitive and then been shredded after the meeting.

As pointed out prior, people can be an organization's greatest asset (in fact, they are arguably the only asset an organization has that doesn't always depreciate over time), and they can be one of the greatest risks. Hiring individuals with conflicts of interest, backgrounds that could lead to extortion or blackmail, and those with general trust issues can harm an organization more than any technical breach or operational blunder. A massive fortress is worthless if one of the guards is willing to unlock the door in the middle of the night for an enemy.

Risk Assessment

To handle the combination of threats and vulnerabilities, retail organizations must adopt risk assessment procedures that not only assess risk from a mandatory compliance perspective but also from an organizational risk perspective. The board of directors should consider bringing in outside assessors or auditors to confirm the information assurance program has sufficient authority to provide visibility into risk and mitigate it where possible.

While many retail organizations will be required to use a QSA as part of their PCI-DSS assessment, they should carefully consider the credentials of the organization they choose. Not all assessors understand the business or mission of the organization. While any organization can run a vulnerability scan, an understanding of assets and mission must be present to determine risk to an organization. The impact of a vulnerability changes from one organization to another and sometimes within the same organization. The vulnerability on a test server with no information on it may be low risk, while the same vulnerability on a production server with cardholder information may be high risk. If the assessor doesn't understand the difference between the systems and how they support the organization, the risk assessment will be inherently flawed.

When choosing an assessor, organizations should demand to see past work and also interview the assessor to determine how much about the retail organization they actually know. Additionally, asking the assessor how they plan on gathering initial information about the organization will help understand their assessment approach. Are they simply asking for a network map, a range of IP addresses, and any machines they can't take down? If so, they may not be best suited to give an honest risk assessment. Questions about data flows, business operations, business partners, data interconnections, and business impact assessments should be referred to a more qualified assessor.

Risk Mitigation

Once risk is identified, it must be mitigated, transferred, accepted, or avoided. Retail organizations must attempt to mitigate as much risk as possible through a proactive information assurance program. Information assurance controls implemented during the design and requirements phases of implementation are crucial in preventing information breaches.

Policy, Procedures, Standards, and Guidance

Retail organizations must ensure that sufficient standards, policy, and guidance exist to protect the organization against allegations of negligence and ignorance. Policies should cover the mandatory regulations covering privacy and PCI-DSS compliance in addition to any industry- or economy-specific requirements.

Retail organizations should develop standards for the encryption used to protect cardholder information and sensitive information throughout the organization. In addition to establishing a key escrow policy, standards should specify approved tools and technologies acceptable to process, store, or transmit sensitive information. Only the CISO or other qualified individual should approve deviations from the standard.

Procedures for handling sensitive information must be developed. These should include not only digital information but also physical information such as paper and portable media. The procedures should reference the correct standards for encryption, destruction, and retention. Additionally, incident response procedures should establish clear reporting instructions for any member of the organization to report suspicious activity or confirmed incidents.

Guidance for the organization should include who to contact in the information assurance program when engaging in a data transfer outside of the organization or who to contact when determining procurement requirements for a new system or a new location.

Human Resources

As noted in the February 6 Home Depot breach shown in Table 27-1, insider threats should be a considerable concern in retail. From an attacker's perspective, gaining physical access to the POS system or customer information is the first step in figuring out ways to siphon it out and use it for identity theft or fraudulent actions. While retailers must ensure they control workforce costs, they must also have assurances the workforce is trustworthy.

As part of a mature information assurance program, the retailer's workforce positions should be categorized according to risk and access to information. The information assurance team should assist in determining which positions are deemed critical in terms of trustworthiness. Retail organizations should consider background investigations for individuals who have administrative access to systems (including contractors) and also those who may have access to large amounts of customer data. Separation of duties is also an option for organizations large enough to support splitting tasks and duties among several people to force collusion in the event of fraud. For more information about information assurance integration in human resources, please see Chapter 13.

Some situations, such as the use of seasonal hires, require a different approach. The cost and expense of performing background checks and separation of duties for temporary workforces may not be worth the effort. In these cases, the organization should increase monitoring of information systems and assets. The organization should consider deploying physical controls such as cameras and badging systems to help determine who was accessing a system at a given time; this provides the service of nonrepudiation. Additionally, all workforce members should be required to take the organization's information assurance awareness training and sign a rules of behavior and acceptable use agreement prior to gaining access to any information system.

Certification, Accreditation, and Assurance

While the concept of certification, accreditation, and the associated measures of assurance are foreign to many industries, the retail industry has familiarity with the PCI-DSS compliance standard. While this is a certification, in practice many retail organizations do not attempt to perform accreditation or authorization of information systems, which involves the acceptance of risk to an organization. While this may seem like an optional step, it is done by default in the organization.

Recall that Target's board and senior executives were sued as part of the breach. In addition, the Korean executives of the credit card issues resigned or offered to resign. By default, someone in the organization is accepting risk. The question is whether they realize it or not. Senior leaders benefit from operational risk visibility because ignorance is not a defense for due care or due diligence concerns. By implementing a robust information assurance program that drives a certification and accreditation program, retailers can gain greater visibility in their risk postures. As credit card issues begin to slide liability for fraud to retailers, they will need to adopt defensible positions that can provide proof of due diligence and due care. A mature and documented certification and accreditation program can provide a documented approach for due diligence and due care by showing a systemic risk management approach with consistent reporting and mitigation or acceptance of risk.

Information Assurance: System Development and Acquisition

As detailed in Table 27-1, several breaches have been caused by insecure systems and insecure business partners. As part of their information assurance programs, retailers should include standards for encryption or the adoption of technologies such as chip and pin. Secure system development is also a requirement for PCI-DSS compliance. As systems are developed and moved through their life cycles, the information assurance program should be involved in change management and configuration management to ensure changes to the system do not cause negative impacts to the organization.

To ensure systems are procured and developed with appropriate information assurance, retail organizations should consider integrating an information assurance approval as part of any investment that may process, store, or transmit sensitive information on behalf of the organization. The information assurance program would be responsible for ensuring appropriate controls are in place to protect the organization and the cardholders.

Physical and Environmental Security Controls

Retailers typically employ some of the most advanced technologies in their actual retail spaces but may fail to employ the same level of concern for their information systems. Open network ports, open wireless access points, and POS terminals left unattended and unlocked are all opportunities for attackers to gain access to a system. Often, attackers need only one system to use as a pivot point and then start to attack the rest of the system from inside the organization.

Retail organizations must focus on limiting physical access to their POS terminals, wiring closets, and data centers. In situations where limiting access to wiring closets is not possible, the organization must consider stronger technical controls such as network access control and encryption to help ensure attackers cannot exploit an open closet.

Retailers often use security cameras throughout their retail spaces. Retailers must be aware of any legal obligation they have to notify customers they are under surveillance and ensure the monitoring system is operated in accordance with the law. It should go without saying that people have an expectation of privacy in dressing rooms and bathroom facilities, so cameras are never appropriate in these areas.

Awareness, Training, and Education

All retail employees should take information assurance awareness training as part of their onboarding, and also routinely throughout the year to ensure they are maintaining a basic awareness of the threat environment and the organizational practices required to secure information. Users who refuse to take the awareness training should be counseled and their access limited until they have completed the training.

Specific training should target managers and mid-level management involved in information technology, program management, and procurement. These individuals should be trained by the information assurance program to recognize when the information assurance team needs to be called in to ensure appropriate information assurance processes, standards, technologies, or requirements are implemented as part of ongoing business, changes, new developments, or procurements.

Education should be reserved for senior members of the information assurance team or those in the organization with a substantial role in managing the risk of the organization. Education is an expensive and long-term endeavor that should be focused on the most strategic elements of the organization.

Access Control

Access control is critical for retail operations. Preventing breaches by hacking involves ensuring appropriate access control. As part of an ongoing information assurance assessment program, retail organizations should inventory all administrator-level accounts and determine whether access is still required. Accounts with no owner should be scrutinized and placed under observation. By default, all users of the organization should get only "limited" access accounts to inhibit the installation of malicious software through spear phishing or other methods.

Retail organizations should also consider multifactor authentication for their administrative users and senior executives. Multifactor authentication increases the level of difficulty when brute-force attacks are attempted. Additionally, retail organizations must carefully scrutinize the access they give to outside contractors and vendors. While they should have passed a background investigation or suitability check, they should be given no more access than absolutely required to do their job. Organizations must remember that the third party could lose the credentials to a hacker who could then use them to attack the network and systems of the retailer.

Continuous Monitoring, Incident Response, and Forensics

A mature continuous monitoring program must ensure collection of threat and vulnerability information from the network and systems in addition to information collected from managerial and operational assessments. The continuous monitoring must ensure residual risk is identified and delivered to authorizing or accrediting officials for mitigation, transference, avoidance, or acceptance. Many organizations will cite their SIEM as their continuous monitoring solution; however, the SIEM is only as good as the statistics knowledge and business knowledge of those using it. False alarms and numerous nonevents only lessen the credibility of a security operations or cybersecurity intelligence team.

Business Continuity and Backups

Most retailers are concerned with availability and integrity of their operations when it comes to business continuity and backups. However, losing an unencrypted backup tape can be just as devastating as having an entire system hacked. As part of the retail organization's business continuity and backup strategy, the information assurance program must demand that strong encryption and media-handling procedures are followed. If cloud computing providers are used for business continuity or backups, they must also adhere to the same standards and be subject to audits by the retail organization.

Part V

Further Reading

- Federal Reserve Bank of Atlanta. Into the Breach: Protecting the Integrity of the Payment System, February 10, 2014. http://portalsandrails.frbatlanta.org/emv/.

- Financial Fraud Action UK. Fraud the Facts, 2013. www.financialfraudaction.org .uk/download.asp?file=2772.

- First Data, EMV, and Encryption + Tokenization: A Layered Approach to Security, 2012. www.firstdata.com/downloads/thought-leadership/EMV-Encrypt-Tokenization-WP.PDF.

- Payment Card Industry (PCI) Data Security Standard, November 2013. https:// www.pcisecuritystandards.org/documents/PCI_DSS_v3.pdf.

- Payment Card Industry (PCI). PCI Point-to-Point Encryption: Solution Requirements and Testing Procedures, July 2013. https://www.pcisecuritystandards.org/documents/ P2PE_Hybrid_v1.1.1.pdf.

- Payment Card Industry Data Security Standard. PCI DSS Applicability in an EMV Environment, Version 1, October 2010. https://www.pcisecuritystandards.org/ documents/pci_dss_emv.pdf.

- PCI Security Standards Council. PCI for Small Merchants. https://www .pcisecuritystandards.org/smb/index.html.

- Privacy Rights Clearinghouse. Chronology of Data Breaches 2005 – Present. https:// www.privacyrights.org/data-breach.

- Rosenbush, Steve. Target Warning Shows Limits of Cyber Intelligence. http://blogs .wsj.com/cio/2014/02/14/target-warning-shows-limits-of-cyber-intelligence/.

- Wang, Abigail. Smart Chip Credit Cards Wouldn't Have Saved Target. http:// securitywatch.pcmag.com/internet-crime/320071-smart-chip-credit-cards-wouldn-t-have-saved-target.

Critical Thinking Exercises

1. An executive of a small business is worried about attacks and breaches. He accepts credit cards and has a web presence for ordering and accounting. He currently has all his information systems on a single Internet connection and is worried about hackers. What can the executive do to help mitigate his concerns?

2. A large retailer has just experienced a breach. The CIO has explained to the board of directors that this will never happen again because the credit card issuers are requiring the customers to move to "chip and PIN" technology for their credit cards. Is he right?

Industrial Control Systems

Industrial controls systems (ICSs) is a broad term used to describe several electronic control systems used in industrial manufacturing, power generation, water infrastructures, petroleum industry, and heating, ventilation, and air conditioning systems. Industrial control systems are subject to attack and exploitation because of the nature of how they were originally designed and operated. ICSs are used to control city water supplies, enrich uranium, and deliver oil around nations. ICSs control the valves, pumps, locking systems, doors, and devices of numerous automated systems.

ICS of the past were often designed with a life expectancy of ten years or longer. Where most information technology is designed to depreciate in value to zero over the course of just a few years, investment in industry is often expected to be depreciated and productive over the course of decades. This means information technology designed and implemented ten years ago may still be in operation today. The issue is that most if not all legacy ICSs and most modern ICSs were not designed with robust security in mind.

Many devices were developed with default administrative credentials that cannot be changed or web service portals subject to buffer overflow attacks and cross-site scripting. In addition to these design issues, the ICSs are typically not updated in a timely manner...if they are capable of being updated at all!

Overview of the Information Assurance Approach

The information assurance approach involving industrial control systems focuses largely on ensuring defense in depth by isolating and protecting vulnerable devices with more robust infrastructure. Allowing unfettered ICS connectivity to the open Internet is a recipe for disaster. The information assurance approach must focus on the device function and the need to protect the services the ICS supports. The ICS itself should be analyzed to determine what if any security features are available and if they are configured correctly. From there, securing the ICS is almost totally dependent on ensuring a strong information assurance program, ensuring strong continuous monitoring, ensuring strong information assurance integration into change management and configuration management, and ensuring several layers of managerial, operational, and technical controls exist between the ICS and the outside world.

- **Confidentiality**   Many ICSs function as sensors and provide information about processes and operations to a central reporting hub. The impact of disclosing this information to the public or an adversary must be determined through an impact analysis.

- **Integrity**   Integrity for a vast majority of ICSs is everything. The accuracy of a command or instruction to an ICS cannot be incorrect, and sensor information coming from an ICS must be correct. Information assurance teams reviewing ICSs must pay special attention to integrity impacts.

- **Availability**   Also critically important to the vast majority of ICS is availability. While some ICSs such as SCADA systems are designed to be operated in environments with poor connectivity, the information assurance team must understand through a business impact analysis how much downtime can be tolerated and how much information can be lost.

- **Authentication**   Authentication is becoming more important for ICSs. A decade or more ago, many ICSs did not have any authentication at all or only a rudimentary authentication such as a username. Today, ICSs must be protected as well if not better than network servers and bank accounts. The need to bring aging ICSs and ICSs that were not designed with security in mind into compliance is a real challenge.

- **Nonrepudiation**   ICSs were not originally designed with nonrepudiation in mind. They were developed to ensure information was read or actions were performed. Many systems do not contain the logging and auditing required to provide the nonrepudiation of actions. This is another area the information assurance team will need to review and then determine the best approach to implement compensating nonrepudiation controls if needed.

Industrial Control–Specific Language

As noted earlier, ICS covers several areas of control families.

- **SCADA**   Supervisory control and data acquisition system. SCADA systems are often found in oil, gas, pharmaceutical, and energy applications. They are used when there is a need to utilize poor-quality links such as those with high latency or low bandwidth.

- **DCS**   Distributed control systems. These systems often refer to ICSs designed to operate in industrial settings such as chemical, pharmaceutical, and mining. They gather data and control systems located throughout large physical areas in real time. They are designed to be high-bandwidth and low-latency devices providing near-real-time reporting and action.

- **PLC**   Programmable logic controllers. PLCs largely replaced lattices of relays that formed logic circuits for ICS. PLC is most commonly used for binary operations where speed is critical.

- **Field devices**   ICS devices such as valves and sensor operating away from the central control system.

Information Assurance Management

ICS requires a robust approach for information assurance management. Since ICSs are used for mission-critical operations, it is important the information assurance management team understands the mission of the ICS prior to performing any risk analysis. ICSs are also extremely hard to analyze in their production environment because they are often relied on continuously, and doing any action such as vulnerability scanning that could interfere with their operation is generally more harmful than helpful.

Personnel

Managing information assurance for ICS requires a working knowledge of industrial processes, electronics, pneumatics, physics, and in some cases special industries, such as pharmaceutical manufacturing. When considering information assurance professionals for these areas, organizations should consider those with a CISSP, SSCP, CSSLP, or CISA, with a blended background in industrial systems. These individuals should also be subject to background investigations and reviews, should they be involved in systems considered critical infrastructure.

Management Approach

ICSs mandate a top-down approach to information assurance management. Since ICSs require several compensating controls and defense-in-depth, organizations must ensure senior management has made a commitment to information assurance and provided the authority and resources to protect the mission and services ICSs support. Organizations attempting to manage and protect industrial control systems through a bottom-up approach will be faced with several varieties of implementations and controls throughout the ICS and supporting network infrastructure.

Regulations and Legal Requirements

ICS have little in the way of laws that regulate them directly; however, there are several guidance documents available throughout the world to assist organizations in protecting ICSs. U.S. Executive Order 13636, "Improving Critical Infrastructure Cybersecurity," was issued February 12, 2014. It provides a framework for organizations to adopt that is based on an Identity-Protect-Detect-Respond-Recover framework. Each major section is subdivided into categories, subcategories, and informative references. Figure 28-1 shows an example of the framework.

The framework is designed to be flexible and accommodate all aspects of an organization's existing use of frameworks, such as ISO and CoBit. Organizations must be cautious and ensure they have a strong information assurance team when using the framework because nothing is

Function Unique Identifier	Function	Category Unique Identifier	Category
ID	Identify	ID_AM	Asset Management
		ID_BE	Business Environment
		ID_GV	Governance
		ID.RA	Risk Assessment
		ID.RM	Risk Management Strategy
PR	Protect	PR.AC	Access Control
		PR.AT	Awareness and Training
		PR.DS	Data Security
		PR.IP	Information Protection Processes and Procedures
		PR.MA	Maintenance
		PR.PT	Protective Technology
DE	Detect	DE.AE	Anomalies and Events
		DE.CM	Security Continuous Monitoring
		DE.DP	Detection Processes
RS	Respond	RS.RP	Response Planning
		RS.CO	Communications
		RS.AN	Analysis
		RS.MI	Mitigation
		RS.IM	Improvements
RC	Recover	RC.RP	Recovery Planning
		RC.IM	Improvements
		RC.CO	Communications

Figure 28-1   U.S. cybersecurity framework example

prescribed as a minimum baseline and everything must be developed from existing frameworks to fill in the function areas.

Information Assurance Risk Management

ICS information assurance risk management must focus on understanding the inherent weaknesses found in ICS implementations. ICSs were once isolated systems on dedicated leased lines that have now been migrated to insecure common public networks for costs and efficiency reasons. By connecting ICS to the Internet, these devices are being exposed to attacks and technologies they were never designed to defend against.

Assets

The asset identification for ICS is crucial in determining an appropriate information assurance approach. The information assurance team must be able to identify clearly and accurately the mission or function the ICS serves and the implications of a loss of confidentiality, integrity, availability, nonrepudiation, authentication, or availability. Will people be harmed or die? Will catastrophic explosions occur because of valves not opening to release pressure? Will a city's potable water system become contaminated with coli bacteria because a pump didn't turn on to pump sewage out of a system during a treatment process? The information assurance team must accurately discover not only the ICS assets but also, more importantly, the assets the ICS supports.

The U.S. Department of Defense's Defense Security Service describes the following as attractive targets of espionage and hacking:

The term *trade secret* means all assets such as financial, business, scientific, technical, engineering, or economic information. This includes patterns, plans, compilations, program devices, prototypes, formulas, design, procedures, methods, techniques, codes, processes, or programs—whether tangible or intangible and whether or how stored, compiled or memorialized physically, electronically, graphically, photographically, or in writing if

- the owner has taken reasonable measures to keep such information secret; and
- the information derives independent economic value (actual or potential) from not being generally known to, and not being readily ascertainable through proper means by, the public.
- Such assets may include, but are not limited to,
  - People
    - Government personnel
    - Contractors
    - Military personnel
  - Activities/operations
    - Intelligence collection/analysis
    - Sensitive movement of operations/personnel/property
    - Conduct of sensitive training
    - Communications/networking
    - RDT&E and sensitive technology
    - Production of sensitive technology
    - Protection of nuclear/chemical/biological materials
    - Protection of weapons, explosives, and equipment

- Information
  - Classified
  - Sensitive compartmented information
  - Top secret
  - Secret
  - Confidential
  - Unclassified
  - System designs
  - Intellectual property
  - Patents
  - System capabilities/vulnerabilities
  - Sensitive methods
  - Sensitive financial data
- Facilities
  - Industry sites
  - Headquarters
  - Field offices/administrative buildings
  - Training facilities
  - Contractor facilities
  - Storage facilities
  - Production facilities
  - R&D laboratories
  - Power plants
  - Parking facilities
  - Aircraft hangars
  - Residences
- Equipment/materials
  - Transportation equipment/vehicles
  - Maintenance equipment
  - Operational equipment
  - Communications equipment
  - Security equipment
  - Weapons
  - Automated information systems equipment

The information assurance team should interview line management, middle management, and even operational staff to understand clearly the implications of the ICS. They need to ask questions such as "What if this failed to work?" and "What would happen if the ICS operated at the wrong time with the wrong instructions?" Leading questions can greatly help the information assurance team gather accurate asset and impact information.

Threats

ICSs are targeted by terrorists, extortionists, nation states, organized crime, and black-hat hackers. In perhaps one of the best known stories about ICS hacking, the Stuxnet malware infected versions of PLCs including the Siemens S7, PCS7, and WinCC systems. The malware was designed to specifically target high-frequency drives controlling uranium enrichment in Iran. While the high-frequency drives may have been the target, the malware spread throughout the world, infecting any controller meeting the description programed within but lying dormant until called to action. Large organizations utilizing the targeted controllers have spent tremendous amounts of resources cleaning Stuxnet from their system even though they were not the intended target.

Stuxnet is also innovative in how it spreads. Many ICS owners believe "air gap" measures put in place are sufficient to protect their ICSs. Stuxnet relied on this belief and replicated through USB drives, external hard drives, laptops, and even infected files to get to its target. Reliance on a single protective measure is insufficient to ensure ICS attacks are detected and prevented. You can find more information about threats in Chapter 4.

Vulnerabilities

ICSs are inherently vulnerable because of their design and implementation. When ICSs were designed, the technologies, bandwidth, and attack methodologies of today were not available and therefore were not considered. Because many ICSs have a life span of years or even decades, the companies that supplied them may no longer be in business to support the securing of the ICS, and, in some cases, even if the company does exist, the ICS was not designed to be updated with new features and security patches.

If an organization does not have a mature configuration management, change management, and associated processes, the ability to patch vulnerabilities becomes difficult. Patching on production systems without testing can lead to system failures and possible new vulnerabilities if not properly deployed.

Risk Assessment

ICS-reliant organizations must adopt risk assessment procedures that assess risk not only from an information technology perspective but also from an organizational or mission risk perspective. The senior leadership of ICS organizations should strongly consider bringing in outside assessors or auditors specifically trained in ICS assessment to confirm the organization's information assurance program has the sufficient authority, skills, knowledge, and technical capability to provide visibility into risk and mitigate it where possible. ICS organizations should carefully consider the credentials of the assessor they choose. Not all assessors understand the business or mission of the ICS organization.

Part V

While any organization can run a vulnerability scan, understanding the assets and impacts of ICS environments is critical for understanding risk. The impact of a vulnerability changes from one organization to another and sometimes within the same organization.

When choosing an assessor, organizations should demand to see past work and also interview the assessor to determine how much about ICS and the organization they actually know. Additionally, asking the assessor how they plan on gathering initial information about the organization and its ICS will help understand their assessment approach. Are they simply asking for a network map, a range of IP addresses, and any machines they can't take down? Are they claiming they will do a comprehensive "pen test" and don't need any information about the organization's business? Assessors may not be best suited to give an honest risk assessment if they lack interest in the business of the organization. An assessor asking questions regarding data flows, business operations, business partners, data interconnections, and business impact assessments point to a more qualified assessor.

Risk Mitigation

An ICS requires a layered approach to risk mitigation because typically the ICS can't be upgraded easily and doesn't support many security features. A defense-in-depth approach incorporating people, processes, and technology will provide the best risk management posture for the organization. ICSs often require special segmentation of networks and sometimes physical segmentation or "air gapping" to ensure they are protected against attacks through the network. Even in these extreme situations, organizations must continue their diligence because malware such as Stuxnet can "jump the gap" and find ICSs that are seemingly isolated.

Policy, Procedures, Standards, and Guidance

Organizations working with ICSs have an added burden of ensuring any new technology won't introduce additional risk. The organization should ensure its policy sets senior managers' expectations around the protection of ICSs and protection of the mission they serve. Policies must address any industry, legal, or regulatory requirements the organization may have in ensuring information assets are protected. The organization should consider developing specific information assurance standards for any ICS in operation. The standard should contain hardened configurations, setup specifications, physical security measures, interconnection requirements, scanning requirements, patching requirements, and segmentation requirements.

Procedures should focus on ensuring ICSs are monitored for vulnerabilities and ensure mitigation actions such as patches are deployed in a meaningful time with acceptable disruption to the organization. Guidance should be developed to ensure that new procurements meet the standards and procedures identified prior. Guidance should assist personnel in understanding the unique requirements ICS pose and what resources are available to help ensure they are secured and monitored.

Figure 28-2 from ICS-CERT lists several of the most commonly used ICS standards.

Common Label	Description
AGA 12-1	American Gas Association (AGA) Report 12, "Cryptographic Protection of SCADA Communications Part 1: Background, Policies, and Test Plan," March 2006.
AGA 12-2	AGA Report 12, "Cryptographic Protection of SCADA Communications Part 2: Retrofit Link Encryption for Asynchronous Serial Communications," March 2006.
ANSI/ISA-99.00.01-2007	International Society of Automation (ISA) "Security for Industrial Automation and Control Systems Part 1: Terminology, Concepts, and Models," December 2007.
FIPS 140-2	Federal Information Processing Standards (FIPS) Publication 140-2, "Security Requirements for Cyptographic Modules," May 25, 2001.
Draft FIPS 140-3	FIPS Publication 140-3, "Security Requirements for Cryptographic Modules," to Supersede FIPS PUB 140-2, May 25, 2001. Draft issued July 13, 2007. Still in draft status.
API 1164	American Petroleum Institute (API) STD 1164, "Pipeline SCADA Security" September 1, 2004. API 1164 is currently being updated by API and is going through internal review. The standard is estimated to be available for public use mid-year 2009.
CIDX	(This document was moved from Chemical Industry Data Exchange (CIDX) to the American Chemistry Council in 2006). "Guidance for Addressing Cyber Security in the Chemical Industry," Ver. 3.0, May 2006. This standard will be replaced by ISA 99, "Manufacturing and Control System Security Part 2:" Establishing a Manufacturing and Control System Security Program."
ISO 27001	International Standards Organization (ISO) Publication 27001: 2005 "Information technology-Security techniques–Information security management systems–Requirements. "First edition, October 15, 2005.
ISO 27002	ISO Publication 27002:2005 (replaced ISO 17799), "Information technology–Security techniques–Code of Practice for Information Security Management," renumbered 2007.
IEC 62351	The International Electrotechnical Commission (IEC) publication IEC/TS 62351, Parts 1-6 "Power Systems management and associated information exchange—Data and communications Security," May 15, 2007.
IEEE 1402	Institute of Electrical and Electronics Engineers (IEEE), Document IEEE 1402, "Guide for Electric Power Substation Physical and Electronic Security," January 30, 2000.
ISA 99.00.01-2007	ISA "ANSI/ISA 99.00.01-2007, Security for Industrial Automation and Control Systems Part 1: Terminology, Concepts, and Models, " October 29, 2007.
ISA 99.00.02-2007	ISA "ANSI/ISA 99.00.02-2007, Security for Industrial Automation and Control Part 2: Establishing an Industrial Automation and Control System Security Program," October 29, 2007.
ISA 99.00.03-2007	ISA "ANSI/ISA 99.00.03-2007, Security for Industrial Automation and Control Part 3: Operating an Industrial Automation and Control System Security Program," October 29, 2007.
ISA 99.02.01-2009	ISA "ANSI/ISA 99.02.01-2009, Establishing an Industrial Automation and Control Systems Security Program," February 2009.
NERC CIP	North America Electric Reliability Corporation (NERC) Critical Infrastructure Protection (CIP) standards, CIP-002-CIP 009, standards on security topics, May 2, 2006.
NIST SP 800-40 R2	NIST SP 800-40, Rev 2, "Creating a Patch and Vulnerability Management Program."
NIST SP 800-53	NIST SP 800-53, Rev 3, Recommended Security Controls for Federal Information Systems–Information Security," July 2009.

Figure 28-2 ICS security standards (Source: ICS-CERT)

Certification, Accreditation, and Assurance

Certification can provide a necessary framework for ensuring ICSs meet and maintain the information assurance policies, standards, and procedures developed by the organization. Independent assessors with knowledge in ICS should be consulted to provide thorough assessments of existing ICS and also ICS systems prior to development. Accreditation provides a means to deliver risk information to the business or mission owner to ensure all parties are aware of the risk being accepted by implementing an ICS.

Human Resources

Hiring information assurance professionals to work in ICS environments can be challenging. They should be able to pass a background investigation and also possibly hold a national security clearance if they will be working on classified critical infrastructure projects. As part of the onboarding process, nondisclosure agreements and, if applicable, organizational conflict of interest statements should be completed by new hires.

All new hires regardless of area should be subject to information assurance training including specific training about the ICS. Those involved in the administration or operation of the ICS should receive additional training regarding ICS secure development, deployment, architecture, assessment, incident response, and decommissioning. Ongoing training must be enforced throughout the organization to ensure all employees maintain awareness and those with specialized roles have recurring specialized training for the ICS. Training must specifically include information about potential weaknesses such as bringing USB drives across an "air-gapped" system.

Information Assurance in System Development and Acquisition

ICSs rely almost entirely on their host network and systems. Therefore, ensuring information assurance is included in any procurement policies, standards, procedures, or documents is crucial. As noted in Figure 28-3, from the U.S. Idaho National Laboratory (INL), the ICS should be segmented and protected from the rest of the network environment.

Procurement and acquisition processes must ensure the information assurance team is involved as new technologies such as cloud and mobile devices are being procured. The information assurance team can ensure the technology being procured is supported in the existing security architecture and can give recommendations for products that may meet the security and architecture requirements of the organization.

ICS procurements and development must involve the information assurance team. The information assurance team should ensure security requirements are clearly identified in any ICS development project or procurement action. If enough organizations demand secure ICS, it is only a matter of time before the market provides a hardened ICS system.

Physical and Environmental Security Controls

Because ICSs are notoriously weak in the logical or network sense, you may think they are physically quite strong and robust. Unfortunately, physical access to an ICS should be treated as administrative access to the device. This is extremely challenging because many organizations use ICS in remote or hostile environments where implementing physical protection would be impractical or dangerous. The information assurance team can assist the organization in these situations by assessing locations that provide the highest risk of access. An ICS in the middle of a hostile area controlling a low-value valve does not have the same risk as an ICS server sitting on a factory floor unprotected and running all the robotic controls for an assembly plant. The information assurance team can provide recommendations and a risk management approach to determine the appropriate physical and environmental protection necessary for the ICS.

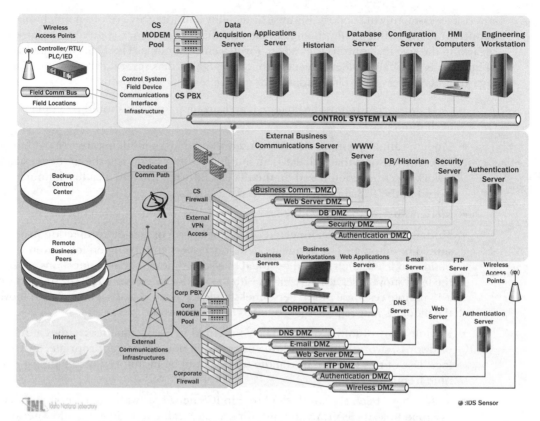

Figure 28-3   INL defense-in-depth network (Source: U.S. Idaho National Laboratory)

Awareness, Training, and Education

Awareness, training, and education should focus on ensuring every member of the organization has a basic understanding about the ICSs supporting the organization and the impact they may have on assets, the mission of the organization, or even human life. In addition to the training and awareness noted in the earlier "Human Resources" section, organizations involved in critical infrastructure may also consider counter-intelligence training. Counter-intelligence training aims to protect an organization and its assets against industrial spies and nation-state hackers. In addition, selected individuals should be afforded the opportunity to participate in Cyber Defense Simulations (CDS) containing ICS components. This will afford them time to gain experience.

Access Control

Access control at the network and infrastructure level is crucial for organizations using ICS. As part of a defense-in-depth approach, organizations should protect vulnerable assets with firewalls, terminal servers, network segmentation, and multifactor authentication inasmuch as a risk assessment will support. Because availability and integrity are often much more important than confidentiality in an ICS, the information assurance team must be careful regarding the specific controls they advise for ICS environments. The U.S. National Institute of Standards and Technology Special Publication 800-82 has several recommendations regarding ICS access control including, but not limited to, the following:

- Default passwords must be changed, and strong passwords should be in place for each modem.

- Modem callback systems should be used when dial-up modems are installed in an ICS. This ensures that a dialer is an authorized user by having the modem establish a working connection based on the dialer's information and a callback number stored in the ICS-approved authorized user list.

- Modems in use should be physically identifiable to control room operators.

- Modems should be disconnected when not in use, or this disconnection process should be automated by having modems disconnect after being on for a given amount of time (if feasible). It should be noted that sometimes modem connections are part of the legal support service agreement with the vendor (for example, 24/7 support with a 15-minute response time). Personnel should be aware that disconnecting/removing the modems may require that contracts be renegotiated.

- Remote control software should be configured to use unique usernames and passwords, strong authentication, encryption if determined appropriate, and audit logs. Use of this software by remote users should be monitored on an almost real-time frequency.

- VLANs have been effectively deployed in ICS networks, with each automation cell assigned to a single VLAN to limit unnecessary traffic flooding and allow network devices on the same VLAN to span multiple switches.

- Wireless access points and data servers for wireless worker devices should be located on an isolated network with documented and minimal (single if possible) connections to the ICS network.

- Wireless access points should be configured to have a unique service set identifier (SSID), disable SSID broadcast, enable MAC filtering, and employ WPA2 encryption with a strong key at a minimum.

- Wireless device communications should be encrypted and integrity-protected. The encryption must not degrade the operational performance of the end device. Encryption at OSI layer 2 should be considered, rather than at layer 3 to reduce encryption latency. The use of hardware accelerators to perform cryptographic functions should also be considered.

- Wireless devices, if being utilized in a Microsoft Windows ICS network, should be configured into a separate organizational unit of the Windows domain.

- Wireless survey should be performed to determine antenna location and strength to minimize exposure of the wireless network prior to installation. The survey should take into account the fact that attackers can use powerful directional antennas, which extend the effective range of a wireless LAN beyond the expected standard range. Faraday cages and other methods are also available to minimize exposure of the wireless network outside of the designated areas.

- Wireless users' access should utilize IEEE 802.1x authentication using a secure authentication protocol (such as Extensible Authentication Protocol [EAP] with TLS [EAP-TLS]) that authenticates users via a user certificate or a Remote Authentication Dial In User Service (RADIUS) server.

Continuous Monitoring, Incident Response, and Forensics

The organization's information assurance team should operate an incident response function that includes continuous monitoring and incident reporting. The incident response team should be trained in the specific ICS the organization uses and should understand the types of data and mission the ICS serves. The incident response team should coordinate with ICS-specific cyber emergency response teams such as the US ICS-CERT. ICS-CERT provides control systems–related security incident and mitigation information. Figure 28-4 provides an overview of a continuous monitoring and incident approach as proposed by the US ICS-CERT.

As part of the continuous monitoring process, organizations should gain an understanding of normal operations. In doing so, they can understand abnormal behavior. The U.S. National Institute of Standards and Technology Special Publication 800-82 advises organizations to be on the lookout for the following:

- An account in use when the user is not at work
- Antivirus or IDS alerts
- Attempted or actual use of administrator-level accounts
- Cleared log files
- Creation of new user accounts
- Disabled antivirus software and other security controls
- Full log files with unusually large number of events
- Locked-out accounts
- Machines connecting to outside IP addresses

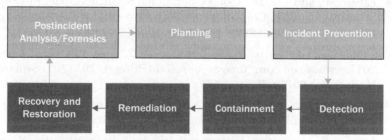

Figure 28-4   Continuous monitoring key elements (Source: ICS-CERT)

- Out of disk space or significantly reduced free disk space
- Requests for information about the system (social engineering attempts)
- Unexpected changes in configuration settings
- Unexpected patch changes
- Unexpected system shutdown
- Unusually heavy network traffic
- Unusually high CPU usage

Business Continuity and Backups

Because ICSs are typically focused on integrity and availability, organizations need to consider the strength and resilience of their network infrastructure. This can conflict with the need to keep an ICS segmented and protected because redundant or load-balanced sites can rapidly direct traffic from one location to another to ensure performance metrics are met. Organizations should ensure networking technologies are properly scoped through a business impact analysis to determine the recovery time objective and recovery point objective for the ICS.

Redundant power systems on separate suppliers, power generation from solar, wind, or thermal, and routine testing should be designed to ensure the ICS can operate in adverse conditions such as natural disasters and possible human-caused outages as well. The networking infrastructure must also be taken into consideration, and in critical applications, diverse connectivity paths should be considered; for example, one path may be via fiber to a local telecommunications company, while a backup link is provided by another company's cellular network or satellite telecom.

Further Reading

- Assante, M.J. Testimony on Securing Critical Infrastructure in the Age of Stuxnet. National Board of Information Security Examiners, November 17, 2010.

- Christensen, Sharon, et al. "An Achilles Heel: Denial of Service Attacks on Australian Critical Information Infrastructures." *Information & Communications Technology Law.* 19, no. 1 (2010): 61–85.

- Fabro, M., and V. Maio. Using Operational Security (OpSec) to Support a Cyber Security Culture in Control System Environment, 2007. http://csrp.inl.gov/Documents/OpSec%20Rec%20Practice.pdf.

- Falliere N., L.O. Murchu, and E. Chien. W32.Stuxnet Dossier. Symantex, February 2011. www.wired.com/images_blogs/threatlevel/2011/02/Symantec-Stuxnet-Update-Feb-2011.pdf.

- IBM Internet Security Systems. A Strategic Approach to Protecting SCADA and Process Control Systems. www.iss.net/documents/whitepapers/SCADA.pdf.

- Interim Report to the Department of Homeland Security. Development of a Baseline Set of Technical Metrics, January 2007.

- Jansen, W. Directions in Security Metrics Research. NIST special publications, April 2009.

- Jelen. G. SSE-CMM Security Metrics, The National Institute of Standards and Technology (NIST) and Computer System Security and Privacy Advisory Board (CSSPAB) Workshop. Washington, D.C., June 13–14, 2000.

- Linden E.V. Focus on Terrorism, Volume 9. Nova Science Publishing, 2007.

- Manadhata, P.K., et al. An Approach to Measuring a System's Attack Surface, CMU-CS-07-146. Carnegie Mellon University, August 2007. http://reports archive .adm.cs.cmu.edu/anon/2007/CMU-CS-07-146.pdf.

- Morris, Thomas H., et al. "Engineering Future Cyber-physical Energy Systems: Challenges, Research Needs, and Roadmap." North American Power Symposium (NAPS). pp. 1–6. IEEE, 2009.

- Morris, Thomas, R. Vaughn, and Y.S. Dandass. "A Testbed for SCADA Control System Cybersecurity Research and Pedagogy." Proceedings of the Seventh Annual Workshop on Cyber Security and Information Intelligence Research., p. 27. ACM, 2011.

- National Cyber Security Research and Development Challenges Related to Economics. Physical Infrastructure and Human Behavior: An Industry, Academic and Government Perspective. The Institute for Information Infrastructure Protection (I3P), 2009.

- Payne, S.C. A Guide to Security Metrics. SANS Security Essentials GSEC Practical Assignment, Version 1.2e. June 19, 2006. www.sans.org/reading_room/whitepapers/ auditing/55.php.

- Savola, Reijo M. Towards a Taxonomy for Information Security Metrics. International Conference on Software Engineering Advances (ICSEA 2007). Cap Esterel, France, August 2007.

- Report to the Department of Homeland Security. INL/EXT-06-12016, Cyber Security Metrics, December 2006.

- Slay, J., and M. Miller. *The Maroochy Water SCADA Breach: Implications of Lessons Learned for Research in Advances for Critical Infrastructure Protection.* Springer, 2007.

- Slay, J., et al. "Process Control System Security and Forensics: A Risk Management Simulation." Proceedings of SIMTECT 09. Adelaide, June 15–19, 2009.

- Swanson, M., et al. *Security Metrics Guide for Information Technology Systems, NIST Special Publication 800-55,* July 2003.

- The CIS Security Metrics Service. The Center for Internet Security (CIS), July 1, 2008. http://securitymetrics.org/content/attach/Metricon3.0/metricon3-kreitner%20 handout.pdf.

- The First National Security Statement to the Australian Parliament. The Prime Minister of Australia the Hon. Kevin Rudd MP, December 4, 2008. http://pmrudd .archive.dpmc.gov.au/sites/default/files/file/documents/20081204_national_ security_statement.pdf.

Part V

- Vaughn, Rayford, Jr., R. Henning, and A. Siraj. Information Assurance Measures and Metrics – State of Practice and Proposed Taxonomy. 30th Hawaii International Conference on System Sciences, Big Island, Hawaii, January 7–10, 2002.

Critical Thinking Exercises

1. The accountants at an energy company have been to a technology presentation about the cloud and Infrastructure as a Service (IaaS). They come into the CIO's office and tell him he can cut his costs by significant margins if they use only IaaSX (the cloud offering from the provider). The CIO is responsible for maintaining a large number of natural gas pipeline control networks in addition to the ICS operating several large refineries. Should he agree with the accountants? Is there another answer he should provide?

2. A heating, ventilation, and air-conditioning company has just installed a state-of-the-art environmental system for an organization. As part of the purchase, the organization is going to receive one year of monitoring and efficiency reporting for free. The vendor requests to have the new equipment connected to the network and be given a domain admin account. The vendor says it needs the admin account so it can access the environmental control servers any time and perform repairs or maintenance. The CISO is discussing the request with the facilities manager. What response should she provide?

Appendixes

In many cases, appendixes are just that, something that is extra. In this book, they contain examples of threats, vulnerabilities, and risks. They provide you with an international compendium of privacy laws and regulations. In addition, they provide sample policies and a sample security checklist.

 Using these appendixes combined with what you have learned from the book, you will be able to transition your career from being a juggler or a one person band.

 During your career, you will lead a small group effectively. Each of your employees will have other jobs; however, this handbook can help them focus on their information assurance roles.

 With more experience you will understand all the basic sounds, notes, combinations, and types of music best performed by specific instruments. It is essential that all of this is done in perfect harmony.

 No matter where you are in your career, this handbook will support you.

APPENDIX

A

Suggestions for Critical Thinking Exercises

Throughout the book, you have been presented with opportunities to challenge yourself with Critical Thinking Exercises. The answers to these questions are not right or wrong; they are intended to stimulate your thinking about information assurance.

Chapter 1

1. An organization is considering developing an encryption policy in its organization. The penetration tester from the team starts documenting specific products and configurations to put into the policy. Should the policy contain these details?

    a. Typically not. A policy is an overarching governance document developed to reflect senior management's position on a topic. While an encryption standard may include specific products and configurations, a policy would merely mention that the organization will follow organizational encryption standards. This helps ensure the policies remain enforceable while allowing the agility to change products or configurations if needed.

2. An organization is considering placing all its policies, procedures, standards, and guidance in a single handbook so executive management has to sign off only once. What are the advantages and disadvantages to this approach?

    a. The sole advantage is found in only needing the senior leadership approval once for the entire handbook. The issue is that as soon as a single part of the handbook is outdated, the entire handbook is outdated. Keeping a comprehensive handbook updated is also challenging because every version changes the entire context of the handbook. A better approach is to use a modular approach with tiered approvals. For example, policies are approved only by senior leadership, but they are scoped and written to last five years or longer. Standards and procedures may be approved by relevant experts such as IT standards by the CIO. Guidance could be developed and approved by almost any line manager throughout the organization. If a cohesive and modular naming framework is designed and implemented, this delegated approach of governance can be quite effective.

Chapter 2

1. An organization's board of directors has recently experienced a substantial change in leadership. The new members of the board have demanded an external audit for internal control and information assurance. What should the president or leader of the organization be prepared to provide to ensure the board is comfortable with the audit results?

   a. The president should understand the organization and the business or mission of the organization and how it relates to information assurance. The audit will most likely focus on internal controls that include regulatory requirements and separation of duties to prevent fraud. The audit will also cover how well the organization has identified its critical assets, services, and vulnerabilities. An organization that has not considered information assurance as part of its core culture and operations will experience a difficult audit.

2. The senior leadership of a large organization has never considered the need for information assurance in the organization's operations. After a series of attacks have crippled similar competitors, senior leadership is now concerned about information assurance. The information technology staff (both in-house and outsourced) has assured senior leadership repeatedly that there is nothing to worry about. Are they right?

   a. The senior leaders of the organization should demand an information assurance function be developed and a permanent information assurance program be established. The information assurance program's primary responsibility will be to enable the mission of the organization while bringing visibility into the risk the organization is assuming. The information assurance program will be authorized to perform risk assessments against both in-house and outsourced IT to provide unbiased risk information to senior leadership and the board of directors if necessary.

Chapter 3

1. What assets or services do you think your organization considers critical for success? What is your organization's responsibility for those assets or services and how are they are currently protected? How do you know an appropriate level of due diligence and due care is being practiced in relation to your organization's use of information systems and data?

   a. Occasionally, organizations overlook the exposure that may come from lax or negligent information assurance practices. Significant fines may be levied on organizations that do not protect sensitive information such as personally identifiable information or sensitive financial information. As information technology is becoming more ambiguous, a material finding in an information system is almost certainly going to relate to an internal control failure in a financial or management system. If your organization has not considered an industry-specific information assurance framework, why not? Consider the laws, regulations, and agreements that govern the work performed and determine whether frameworks exist. These frameworks can provide a starting point for determining the assurance of your organization's use of information technology.

2. A member of your team informs you that the organization can purchase insurance for breaches of personally identifiable information (PII) and financial data such as credit card information. The insurance will cost less than the information assurance program proposed by the CISO. Would you purchase the insurance at the expense of an information assurance program?

   a. If you would purchase the insurance, it is important to understand the insurance will cover only monetary exposure. Often, this covers only the expenses related to credit monitoring or identity theft mitigation. However, this will never cover the loss of reputation, the damage caused to an individual whose identity has been stolen, or business partners who are now sullied by a breach. While cybersecurity or breach insurance can be an important part of any risk management program, it cannot be relied upon to protect your organization in the same manner as an information assurance program can. Additionally, breach insurance providers require a functioning information assurance program before providing coverage.

3. A breach has occurred, and according to the organization's web site privacy policy and terms of service, your customers agreed to whatever level of security the organization deemed sufficient and reasonable. Is the organization protected from retaliation from customers or other entities?

   a. Several legal cases in the past several years have shown courts look at information assurance from a due diligence and due care standpoint. Customers have an expectation of protection and privacy from online retailers and therefore even though they may agree to the terms of service, courts can determine the organization is not meeting a common "reasonable" industry safeguard.

Chapter 4

1. An executive receives an e-mail from a known colleague with an urgent message about the financial state of their organization attached in a PDF. What should the executive do? The executive is unaware of any financial problems with the organization, and the executive didn't request this information.

   a. This may be a spear phishing e-mail. Opening the attachment or following links in the e-mail may lead the executive to compromise their system. Once compromised, that system can be used to launch further attacks against the organization and business partners. The prudent approach is to ensure end-point protection by making sure that your antivirus, anti-malware, and operating system patches are up-to-date. The organization should use security awareness training that includes content related to phishing and spear phishing. Next, the executive should ensure they are logged into their system only with a limited user account. If the executive constantly uses an administrator account, they are opening themselves up for attack because every action performed, including opening the e-mail, is performed at the administrator level of access, which can modify the system. Finally, the executive should call the party with a known good phone number to ensure they did send this information. If they did not, the executive may want to contact local law enforcement and determine whether they can assist in determining who is targeting the organization. The willingness and ability of law enforcement varies greatly by country and district. In almost all cases, the cost of determining who launched the attack greatly exceeds the costs associated with preventing successful spear phishing attacks.

2. An organization has always kept a decentralized information technology infrastructure, which has led to servers under desks, coat closets arbitrarily being turned into wiring closets, and numerous portable hard drives floating around the organization. What could happen if the organization needed to institute a reduction in force because of changing market conditions? What can an organization do to prevent the risk of these changes?

   a. Decentralized IT is often controlled at the whim of whoever possesses it. Therefore, if a rumor is started that a layoff is coming, some employees may be inclined to start copying organizational information to external drives so it can be taken for use at their next job. Worse, employees could start thinking about how to sabotage the organization should they get fired. Any information technology under their control is a possible target. Without understanding the assets of the organization, the controls in place, or how to gracefully remove employees, the organization is at risk of data exfiltration and sabotage. To prevent these actions, the organization should consider centralizing at least the data managed by the organization with tight controls around the access. The organization may also want to ensure any nondisclosure agreements (if any) are enforced during the transition period. Finally, before making any announcements, the organization may want to consider implementing a data loss prevention tool to help reduce the amount of data lost. The best way to avoid loss is to start with an environment that can withstand a layoff. This means a centralized IT infrastructure with tight controls around administrative access and production systems. It also means logging and strong IAAA to ensure accountability for actions. Finally, employees should be screened prior to hire and be required to sign nondisclosure agreements.

3. An organization's web site has been collecting the actions of users for several years now. The web site was a social media overnight success, and the organization never got around to completing a privacy statement or terms of service. The organization has been selling the demographic information to advertisers and market

researchers as part of its core business for more than a year now. The organization receives a legal summons related to privacy concerns of the site. What could have been done in the beginning to prevent the legal exposure?

a. In the United States, the terms of service and a privacy policy are commonly used with web sites such as social media and other sites that collect personally identifiable information (PII). These agreements explain how an organization will use the information and what, if any, expectation of privacy the end user has. While not completely bullet-proof, these documents when used properly can substantially reduce the amount of legal exposure because there is not a perception of deception. In other countries, such as the EU, the Data Protection Directive drives the requirements for collecting and handling PII. Organizations must understand the environments they operate in and the legal jurisdictions they must comply with. A list of privacy laws by state and country is available in Appendix F.

4. What information does your organization use, and what requirements must be met to ensure the confidentiality, integrity, and availability of the information? What drives these requirements for your organization?

a. While some information may seem clear, like PII, other information, such as an executive's calendar, may not. What requirements does the CEO of a business have for his calendar? Is there an expectation of confidentiality, or could it be made public with no recourse? How about the integrity of the calendar? Does it need to be 100 percent correct every time, and is it okay if anyone can make changes to it without permission? What about availability? Can it go down for a week at a time without notice and not have an impact on the organization? This is a simple example of something that may seem trivial (a calendar), but upon further analysis can have a substantial impact on how an organization operates.

5. Your organization has a web site used for advertising your products or services around the world. The site is used only for disseminating information about your organization and its mission. What requirements (if any) should be in place regarding confidentiality, integrity, and availability?

a. Some would say there are no security requirements because "it is just a web site." However, they would be mistaken. What happens if the web site goes down when a large prospective client is searching for information about your products or services? What happens if an attacker defaces your web page or changes information about your products or services pricing and the same prospective client is reviewing the information? Clearly, there are impacts associated with integrity and availability that must be addressed. How about confidentiality? Well, since the entire purpose of the web presence is to spread information, there isn't one in this specific case. Executives and senior leadership must be aware that just because something isn't confidential doesn't mean it doesn't impact the organization and therefore require information assurance.

Part VI

b. The prospective client places a large order over the phone. When the person arrives to deliver the product or service, the client states they never placed the order, and they must have been the victim of identity fraud. They then demand a full refund, and you end up assuming the wasted costs of the order. What could the organization do in the future to help ensure this doesn't happen again?

c. The concept of trust leads organizations to take unwarranted risks that can have lasting impacts. In this scenario, the order process lacked any form of identification and nonrepudiation. Organizations cannot be expected to perform a full background check on every customer, but in this case the organization could have performed more due diligence because of the size of the order. Implementing a nonrepudiation process as part of the process for ordering a certain size or volume would have given the organization a chance to prove the client placed the order and was therefore responsible and accountable to pay for it.

Chapter 5

1. A chief information security officer (CISO) continuously reports issues of risk to senior management even though they continue to deny requests for resources to mitigate the risk. The CISO holds a CISSP. Why is the CISO continuing to report the risk if the board has not done anything about it in the past?

   a. The CISO has an ethical responsibility. In accordance with the ISC^2 ethics, he must "ensure all stakeholders are well-informed on the status of assignments and advise cautiously when required." Additionally, the CISO is bound by the following: "Give prudent advice; avoid raising unnecessary alarm or giving unwarranted comfort. Take care to be truthful, objective, cautious, and within your competence."

2. An organization has decided they need a chief security officer to help determine the best way to implement the information assurance strategy of the organization. What certifications might best determine a strategic information assurance individual?

   a. The $(ISC)^2$ CISSP and the ISACA CISM are the best certifications to review. While the certification is no guarantee of success, it is a statement of accomplishment and minimum knowledge acquired by the individual.

Chapter 6

1. Why is the planning phase extremely important for an organization?

   a. The planning phase will determine control selection, implementation, and ultimately resource costs. Improper planning can lead to substantial rework, which can increase the cost and delay the schedule of implementing effective security for an organization.

2. Should all controls be subject to the ongoing Check phase?

   a. Yes, however they do not need to be subject at the same frequency. Some controls, such as, policy may need to be reviewed only on an annual basis or even longer. Controls such as patch management and IT network inventory should be conducted on a more frequent basis such as daily or weekly. Finally, some controls, such as the network intrusion system, should be monitored in as near real time as possible.

Chapter 7

1. What laws, regulations, or standards does your organization need to comply with?

   a. This is a complex answer since it depends largely on the country, industry, and, in some cases, the local laws of the organization. For example, social media companies have discovered that while they may have started in one country, they are now subject to several differing national and international laws because they have allowed people from those countries to join their services. Senior leaders and exccutives must ensure their information technology activities are consistent with the requirements of international law and local law. Engaging legal counsel early in the process helps ensure compliance.

2. An organization's medical information site is tracking individuals and using information about searches and personal information entered to develop individual profiles for marketing. The web site does not inform visitors they are being tracked and their information is being collected. Which OECD principle has been violated, and what can the organization do to remedy the situation?

   a. The Purpose Specification Principle has been violated. It states the following: "Personal data should be collected for purposes specified not later than at the time of data collection. Subsequent use is limited to the fulfillment of the stated purposes or such others as are not incompatible with those purposes and as are specified on each occasion of change of purpose." The organization should explicitly inform each user how their information will be used and give the user an opportunity to opt in to the process.

Chapter 8

1. An organization has never had a formalized information assurance program. What kind of an approach is most likely currently occurring, and what are the advantages and disadvantages of the approach?

   a. If the organization has not established a top-down approach for information assurance, by default the organization is operating in a bottom-up fashion at best! While there are a few advantages of the bottom-up approach, including lower initial cost, lower organizational friction, and less management involvement, there are also several disadvantages. The disadvantages include little visibility into the risk of operations, unknown spending and performance of security functions, and possible legal exposure because of noncompliance of IT activities. The organization should consider implementing an information assurance program with a top-down approach. Doing so provides an opportunity for greater risk management and visibility while being able to standardize across the organization with tools, techniques, and risk management processes.

2. An organization operates out of the European Union but wants to use a cloud provider based in the United States to store and process healthcare information about people living in the European Union. What laws, regulations, and rules must the organization be aware of?

   a. The organization must first be aware of any EU laws, rules, or regulations related to the proposed activities. Since the organization is somehow connected to healthcare, EU health record and privacy laws should also be considered. Minimally, the EU's Data Protection Directive should be addressed. Finally, because the cloud provider is in the United States, the organization should be aware of the jurisdiction the United States may have over the data and whether federal or even state laws apply to how they are using the cloud in the United States.

3. An organization currently has a web site that processes personally identifiable information (PII) for a client. A network engineer points out a vulnerability in the web site that will cost US$125,000 to mitigate. Currently, the system is operating in the United States, and it would be subject to breach notification laws. What is the best approach to ensure return on investment?

   a. According to the Ponemon Institute, the cost per person for a breach in 2011 was US$194 per an individual. Therefore, from a purely financial perspective, the cost trade-off can be realized at the size of the database. If there are more than 645 individuals ($125,000 / $194 = 645), then it makes good financial sense to implement the change. What about the loss of confidence and trust? What about consumer backlash? What if these records are held as part of a business contract and the organization's actions may tarnish a business partner? These are additional nonfinancial implications that must be addressed prior to understanding the full exposure and full return of the requested investment.

Chapter 9

1. An organization is thinking about moving its core infrastructure into the cloud. It makes extremely good financial sense. What actions must a prudent executive or senior leader take to ensure the financial windfall isn't caused by security shortcomings?

   a. The executive must think about this from several angles. First, there must be a question about the cost of the secure "pipes" needed to connect an organization to its cloud provider. An organization may have had a data center nearby that allowed for fast and secure speeds at low costs. Another question, what visibility into risk does the present operation provide, and what will the cloud provider bring? If currently the organization has insight into server risk, database risk, and workstation risk, will the cloud provider deliver the same insight or less? Finally, what due diligence must the organization conduct to ensure initial security of the provider and ongoing security? What are the costs associated with performing audits or accepting risk for noncompliant activities of the cloud provider?

2. An organization is thinking of collaborating with another to perform some data processing. Your organization has a top-down centralized approach to information assurance while it seems the organization you want to collaborate with has a bottom-up decentralized approach to security. Should you be concerned about this difference in cultures?

   a. The short answer is "yes." The prospective partner may have varying security practices throughout their organization. An answer from one person regarding security may not be the same as another, and getting an authoritative answer about the security posture of the partner may be almost impossible. This could still be a salvageable relationship if the partner can provide information about security around the functions you are interested in and give assurances that your information and processing will never leave the safeguards described.

Chapter 10

1. Within your organization, do you use marking methods to determine sensitive information or information critical to business? If so, what automated means do you have to ensure sensitive information is not leaked?

   a. Organizations use their own style of classification and markings. For example, the terms *confidential, embargoed, close hold,* and *limited official use only* roughly mean the same thing in terms of handling the information. It is important that organizations understand not only what markings they use internally but also what their business partners may use as well. If both parties are not aware of what each other's markings mean in terms of handling and distribution, one party may inadvertently leak sensitive information of the other. Organizations should ensure they have a clear understanding of their own information assurance requirements and those of their business partners. Automation of data leak prevention is complex. Several systems and vendors exist that provide the capability of preventing and detecting data loss and leakage. Most of these systems rely on an extensive training period and ongoing human support to be effective.

2. Consider the sensitive information in your organization and its life cycle. Where does the data reside at rest? On hard drives? In the cloud? Where does the data reside in transit? Over the mobile phone network? Over the open Internet? Over your network? What protections do you know are in place for each of the mediums you identified to protect sensitive information?

Part VI

a. Data at rest is most often referred to data on a hard drive or some form of virtual storage. Data at rest should be encrypted if there are any confidentiality or privacy concerns. In the event the drive is lost, stolen, or accessed by someone without authorization, the information will be much harder to read. Additionally, data in transit should be encrypted. Several protocols and methods exist to ensure data is encrypted over "open" communication lines. The most commonly used is SSL over HTTP (the HTTPS seen in the URL bar of many browsers when accessing secure sites such as banking). IPSec VPN solutions offer a nearly always-on encryption for untrusted links between points. Users concerned about the integrity of data may also want to "hash" and "salt" the data. This process uses complex mathematical operations to determine a single unique operational output for a given file or piece of information. Only the exact file or information can produce that output again.

Chapter 11

1. A CIO has just implemented a new dashboard for the organization. As part of the dashboard, the IT employees and senior management can review the vulnerability status of all IT network assets. Is this dashboard giving a holistic view of risk for the organization?

   a. Probably not unless the only business or mission the organization has is to patch vulnerable systems. Different systems, servers, desktops, and cloud providers support different data and different missions. Therefore, through the categorization process, some information must be deemed more critical than others. This information and the systems processing, storing, or transmitting this information are of higher impact to the organization and therefore should be protected and prioritized above all others. Additionally, numerous quantities of paper and off-network records may exist. Where is the assessment of security for those assets? An IT network monitoring dashboard could be green and then a box of personally identifiable information (PII) could be lost, and the organization will need to recover. Understanding exactly what automated tools are telling the organization and what they are not is critical to understanding risk.

2. An organization has approximately 20,000 workstations and 5,000 servers around the world. A new zero-day vulnerability has been published that affects 90 percent of the systems including servers. Zero-day vulnerabilities are recently discovered, previously unknown system or software weaknesses. How should the organization go about prioritizing mitigation efforts?

   a. It is highly unlikely an organization would be able to push out a patch to all its systems without severely impacting network resources or possibly crippling production systems if pushed without testing. Therefore, a staged rollout would most likely take place. Additionally, the patch should be tested in testing and staging environments to determine whether any possible side effects occur because of the patch. The categorization (classification) process should identify the most critical and valuable assets to the organization, and those should be targeted for remediation first, followed by moderate or sensitive operations and, finally, everything else. If the exposure is severe, the organization may even shut down or isolate some of its network until it can free the resources to patch it.

Chapter 12

1. An organization has had more than a dozen personal health information (PHI) breaches in the past year. The organization has a policy in place that stipulates sensitive information is not to be e-mailed or transmitted outside of the organization. The human resources department has just enabled a new "work from home" telework policy. However, individuals have complained ever since the start of the telework program because they are unable to take information with them to work on at remote locations. How can the organization address this issue with policies, standards, procedures, and guidelines?

    a. The organization can start with a policy that clearly states management's expectations to comply with protecting PHI and clearly identify what PHI is. Next, they can develop standards depicting what technologies are appropriate for processing, storing, transmitting, and protecting PHI. The standards will probably define mandatory encryption requirements for portable media, data in transit, and strong physical protections for printed data. Finally, procedures will be created to explain exactly how a person can use the encryption tools and standards indicated in several different manners such as e-mail, portable media, or locking up a box of PHI in the trunk of a vehicle.

2. An organization has a clear policy creation mechanism, and the organization's information assurance team has ensured every specification and requirement is incorporated into the organization's policy. The organization routinely evaluates the policy every six months to determine whether updates are needed. A breach just occurred, and the encryption policy needs to be updated to include a new standard; however, the next update window won't happen for five months. Additionally, the policy review process is cumbersome and time-consuming because every department in the organization must review and approve of the policies being created. What could the organization do to help streamline this process?

    a. The obvious answers may seem to be speed up the process and cut through the red tape; however, these are often easier said than done because most of the checks and balances put into place in the policy creation process are there for a reason. A more agile approach would be to rewrite the policy at a high level, which would authorize specific information assurance–related standards and procedures. The policy could then delegate the creation and approval of the standards and procedures to the chief information security officer or the chief information officer. In doing so, the standards could be rapidly updated in the event a standard or a procedure changed without the need of updating the entire organization's policy. Additionally, the officers could be granted authority through the policy to issue interim policies by memo in the event of an emergency or if urgent action is required. The key is to ensure interim policies are updated into the organization's final policy.

Chapter 13

1. Consider an organization with several different levels of management and a decentralized information technology infrastructure. Marketing has its own information technology as does manufacturing and finance. What is the best approach when hiring new employees in any area to ensure they understand their information assurance responsibilities?

   a. Much like policies, organizations should have high-level expectations and requirements for information assurance. Each component may then have additional requirements for suitability and access to information. The choice to have a decentralized organization is a choice to accept greater complexity in policy and the resulting implementation of solutions. Therefore, the employee may have one agreement for the organization and another for the specific area they are working in. If an employee is transferred or receives additional responsibilities in another component, they will need to sign additional agreements stating they understand the new security requirements.

2. An EU-based organization operating in the United States has knowingly allowed its employees to use personal information technology to process, store, and transmit organizational information. The organization is now being sued in a U.S. court, and all information of the organization is subject to legal hold. What must be done with the information on employees' personal devices?

   a. In most situations, the personal devices must be imaged in a forensically sound matter to ensure the information on the device is available for discovery. This may bring up personal information on the device that is not owned by the organization but could be interpreted by the courts or counsel to be of value and relevance to the discovery. Organizations should consider carefully if they should allow organizational information onto employees or nonorganizational devices. If they allow the information on personal devices, they should have the employee sign an agreement that states the employee understands the device's full contents may be seized and searched should a discovery action deem it necessary.

3. Recent malware attacks encrypt the storage of computers and devices for ransom. How would an organization handle this situation with information on an employee personal (BYOD) device?

   a. As in the prior example, the first priority must be the protection of the organization's information. The organization should have agreements in place that ensure access and control over the personal device. If these agreements are not in place, the owner of the personal device may refuse to turn the device over for analysis. Once obtained, the device should be analyzed by a qualified mobile device forensic expert. If the information has been backed up off the device, the most straightforward approach may be to initialize the device and restore the information. If the information has not been archived, the organization may need to consider further action. Depending on the value of the information, the organization may decide to re-create the information or attempt to defeat the encryption. Paying the ransom to decrypt the device may not always result in getting the information back. The organization should learn from this incident and evolve to ensure information is replicated or backed up when it is created. Additionally, sufficient controls must be in place to protect these storage locations to ensure they are not subject to encryption malware.

Chapter 14

1. An organization chooses to have its CIO be the accreditation official for all its information systems. What are the strengths and weaknesses of this approach?

    a. The CIO most likely has the best combination of overarching information technology and organizational strategy; this combination makes the CIO an attractive candidate for the role of the accreditation official. However, the CIO is often not the program, mission, or business owner who will be impacted by an information system security failure! The organization may want to consider who really needs to know the risk of an information system. In addition, ask yourself, are the business or mission lines of an organization comfortable with the CIO making security funding and risk management decisions on their behalf? While the CIO may initially sound like an appealing choice for an accreditation official, in many organizations the program manager or the head of a business line is being asked to accredit systems since that person will be held accountable for a system failure.

2. Within an organization, who is best suited to determine the independence of the certifier?

    a. While operational independence should be a minimum requirement of the certifier, the independence should ultimately be decided by the role that must manage and accept the risk. In most cases, this will be the accreditation official. If the accreditation official is comfortable with little separation between the certifier and the system they are reviewing, then the certifier may not need to be independent at all. Organizations must be careful, however, because several industries and standards require independence of the certifier.

Chapter 15

1. A cloud CRM provider verbally promises state-of-the-art security and protection of all organizational information. What can the organization do to ensure the cloud provider is keeping its word? What other concerns should the organization have?

    a. Organizations must look at service providers with even more rigor than internal operations. Many cloud providers have a "take it or leave it" approach with a "one size fits all" approach to services. In these situations, organizations must be willing to accept the terms and the resulting risk to the organization. Cloud providers may try to indemnify themselves against any action to minimize their exposure to their customers' actions and breaches. Organizations should be concerned with where their information will be processed, stored, and transmitted.

Part VI

The geolocation of their systems has far-reaching legal jurisdiction implications. If the information is hosted in a country with weak penalties for theft of intellectual property or breaches, the organization may be at greater risk of compromise. Finally, how much information about the information assurance practices of the provider is available? Has it been independently assessed and evaluated to determine its accuracy? If the accuracy and independence of an assessment are questionable, the organization may be better off seeking another provider.

2. An organization currently allows employees to use their personal devices for organizational work. Because of the openness of this policy, the organization now has almost every modern operating system and every mobile device imaginable operating on its network. Network utilization is extremely high, the help desk is unable to provide effective resolution of support calls because of the variation of platforms, and information assurance incidents are on the rise. What can the organization do to help reign in this environment?

    a. The organization should start by determining what work is critical to the organization and how people are achieving that mission. This can be through interviews, surveys, and system information showing various technologies and approaches to accomplish the work. Once the present landscape is understood, the organization needs to set forth its objectives for changing its operating mode. The organization may desire fewer incidents, higher help-desk resolution, and less bandwidth saturation. Through change management, people need to be informed of these objectives and why they are not only good for the organization but also for the employees in the long term. Once the objectives have been communicated, the organization should plan to standardize configurations. The organization in consultation with the information assurance team should pick the best operating systems, devices, platforms, and services for the organization. Next, they need to map out the level of effort to migrate from the existing situation to the new desired end goal. They need to understand people will need training on new systems and ways of doing business; additionally, processes will need to be updated to ensure the new approved platforms and services can achieve processes currently existing under services which may be phased out. Finally, configuration management should ensure standard baselines are established for all approved services, devices, and platforms. These configurations should be developed in consultation with the information assurance team to ensure security controls are included and maintained.

3. An organization wants to develop a new information system that will process and store personally identifiable information and some health-related information about individuals. The organization works primarily in the United Kingdom and the United States. In a general sense, what requirements should an information assurance team be focusing on during the requirements gathering phase?

    a. The organization should always determine what regulatory or legal obligations they need to fulfill when developing or modifying a system. In this case, personally identifiable information and health information were identified. Additionally, the United States and the United Kingdom were mentioned as potential areas for information processing, storage, and transmission. Therefore, the information assurance team should consider the Health Information Protection and Portability Act (HIPAA) in the United States and the Data Protection Act in the United Kingdom. Both require the organization to perform a variety of notification tasks but also require the implementation of safeguards to protect sensitive information. Encryption would undoubtedly be a requirement for data at rest and data in transit for the system. Additionally, strong policies and procedures for handling the data regardless of its stage in its life cycle will need to be addressed. The information assurance team will need to ensure the requirements are captured, and then ensure that as part of information assurance testing these capabilities are tested to ensure they are operating as intended. Any failure of these controls should be analyzed to determine residual risk and mitigation options.

Chapter 16

1. An organization is renting office space and has noticed several new building maintenance personnel requesting access above and below the organization's server room. An employee thinks she saw one of them plugging a cable into a "box" in the server room when she was in the room trying to get a system to restart. What should the organization do?

   a. The organization may be at great risk of a social engineering attack. An attacker may be impersonating maintenance personnel to gain access to information systems and the organization's valuable information. Additionally, the attacker may be trying to sabotage the information infrastructure of the organization. The solution to this issue has multiple parts. First, the organization's management should confirm with the building's owner and manager that maintenance was indeed ongoing and requested in the area. Additionally, the organization may want to request an authorized roster of maintenance personnel, if possible, and challenge the maintenance personnel when they arrive. The employee who saw them possibly plugging a cable into something in the server room should be interviewed and encouraged to share as much as possible about the event. If there is evidence of an intrusion, local law enforcement should be called and asked to assist. The organization should then consider its physical access control plan and determine whether additional controls are necessary to reduce the likelihood of intrusion. The network and assets should be scanned for vulnerabilities, and any unauthorized or unknown devices found on the network should be located and identified.

2. An organization has just finished implementing its contingency plan. It has a large data center and has installed several generators, fuel tanks, two power supplies from MEGA Power Company, and UPS devices. After installing the new UPS devices, the organization also noted it needed to update its chillers because the UPS systems were generating more heat than the chillers could cool. Once the

chillers were finished being installed, the senior leadership of the organization announced they were prepared for the worst! Are they correct?

a. In the event of an emergency, there are several critical flaws with the approach outlined. First, the dual power supplies are provided by the same company and are likely sourced from the same grid and power generation facilities. In the event one power source failed, the other would likely fail as well. If both power supplies failed, the UPS systems would maintain systems long enough for the generators to power on. The generators would likely provide enough power to power the computer systems, the UPS, and the old HVAC system. Unless the new HVAC's power consumption was considered and the generators were determined to be sufficient, or new generators were acquired, they may not be large enough to power all the equipment and the chillers. In the event of an emergency, this organization would likely need to power down some systems and keep only the most essential ones running. Rigorous and routine testing of contingency plans would help ensure employees understood what to do during emergencies. Additionally, inclusion of the information assurance team during the change management process would have helped catch the changing power and cooling dynamics.

Chapter 17

1. An organization wishes to instill a culture of information assurance throughout its operations. What is the best AT&E level to focus on for all employees?

a. If cultural information assurance excellence is truly a goal for the organization, it will need to focus on the training aspect of the AT&E approach with special attention to ensure the education portion is championed as well. The organization will need to start with awareness and determine how well the existing workforce understands information assurance and the need for risk management in an organization. Once an established awareness foundation is present, the organization needs to focus on rewarding further training and education. This is commonly done with incentive rewards and performance management metrics. For example, if a system administrator successfully completed a relevant information security certification, they would receive a cash award. Education is a much more strategic and lengthy process. Organizations should select individuals who have strategic influence in the organization and allow them to complete higher educational research and degrees related to information assurance and then have them lead the organization in designing, implementing, and testing the organization's training and awareness activities.

2. An organization has spent significant resources on several tools and technologies designed to prevent spear phishing attacks. While the number of successful attacks has certainly decreased, the organization is still unhappy with the number of successful attacks. It seems to take only one attack to take down a significant portion of the network for a day or longer. Worse, when the antiphishing technology is configured for aggressive detection, legitimate business information is falsely

captured and must be manually reviewed before release. The operations manager is suggesting buying more hardware and technology to further inspect e-mail as it comes into the organization, and the CISO is suggesting a targeted awareness and training campaign focused on spear phishing. Which is the best approach?

a. In this situation, if technology is failing, it is time to turn to the people. Remember, information assurance focuses not only on technology but also on people and processes! The CISO's approach of a targeted spear phishing awareness and training campaign is a prudent approach. Technology is often a "cat and mouse" game. Attackers build a sophisticated piece of malware, and security engineers build a sophisticated way to defend against it. The attacker then builds another form of sophisticated malware, and the security engineers counter that. This escalation is constantly occurring in not only technology but in social engineering as well. Organizations need to find the correct balance of people, processes, and technology to manage their risk posture. In this situation, technology is already in place and now needs to be balanced with people and processes. The CISO's approach will provide awareness to people and provide training for secure processes to review e-mail for suspicious attachments. The awareness portion should mention the technologies used to help with phishing, while training should cover how to use the technology most effectively to prevent successful phishing. Finally, to enhance the awareness and training, the CISO may consider how to prevent phishing attacks in the employees' personal lives.

Chapter 18

1. An organization is changing the way it works. For the past ten years, the organization has operated out of a downtown office, and all employees were expected to report onsite for work. Because of the increased costs of real estate, the executive management has identified substantial savings if all employees worked remotely from their homes and the organization maintained only a small office for meetings and executives downtown. The organization has never allowed outside access to its networks and has never allowed equipment off-premises prior to this change. Now, employees are being issued laptops, tablets, and smartphones to do their work. What preventive information assurance controls and tools should the organization be concerned with as part of this change?

a. One of the first areas to consider is the change in physical security. Whereas before, all information was kept in the downtown office location, now the information has the potential to be seen in a home office, kitchen, coffee shop, taxi cab, doctor's office, or just about anywhere an employee can get connectivity. The organization must ensure employees have received sufficient training to understand which information is sensitive and which information may be worked on in a public or pseudo-public location. The organization must also consider the fact that people will have access to its technology and data who did not before. For example, how many employees will allow their children or spouses to use the newly issued tablet for personal use? What about the laptop that was left open and connected to the Internet that a family member used to "just quickly check e-mail?"

Because of the nature of an unsecured environment, additional technical controls such as the time before a system locks may need to be considered. From an information technology perspective, most of the employees will now be working over public and insecure Internet service providers. These service providers often have little interest in providing security service, just uptime and throughput for their customers. Does the organization have a robust VPN solution that can handle the capacity of a full workforce working concurrently? Does the VPN enforce strong certified encryption? Can the VPN solution use multifactor authentication, and will it work for all platforms such as smartphones, tablets, and laptops? The organization may need to consider how its PKI is implemented and how it will integrate into the VPN solution.

IT support is a critical aspect of this proposed change. How will users be serviced by the IT department? If the VPN is down, how will users get serviced? Will they need to bring their systems in? Will the organization allow untrusted and risky desktop control software freely available on the Web? How will the help desk validate an individual when they call in and request a password reset? Will employees be allowed to print information at home? If so, how will the organization ensure the information is stored in accordance with the company's policies?

Finally, how will the organization keep the tablets, smartphones, and laptops patched and up to date? Will the organization trust unsigned updates from any update server on the Internet? Will it require updates be provided through a central trusted patching software server? What if a system has been offline for a long time and is requesting to connect back to the network with months of patches needed and no antivirus updates? Can the organization quarantine the device and determine whether it has not been infected? Seemingly simple culture changes can have a dramatic impact on the information assurance operations and planning of an organization. Information assurance teams must be at the table when changes are being discussed. This is the hallmark of excellent change management.

2. In addition to a near 100 percent remote working situation, the organization decides it is also going to outsource several business functions to cloud Software as a Service (SaaS) providers. One function the organization wants to move first is e-mail. The organization has a statutory requirement to ensure all e-mail is encrypted with a U.S. FIPS 140-2 validated encryption process. What precautions should the organization take prior to committing to an e-mail cloud provider?

   a. As part of system development or acquisition, the organization must fundamentally understand what its information assurance requirements are for the functions and data being entrusted to the cloud provider. The information assurance team should be a critical partner in ensuring any laws, regulations, certifications, and attestations are included in any procurement action. Cloud providers may offer a one-size-fits-all or a take-it-or-leave-it solution. The inflexibility of the cloud provider does not need to kill a move to the cloud, but rather the organization must determine whether it is willing to use a compensating control to achieve the desired result. For example, assume the cloud provider refuses to meet the FIPS requirement for encryption. The organization could choose to implement an e-mail client that will enforce the encryption of e-mail using the organization's existing PKI infrastructure. Therefore, the organization can get the benefits of the cloud e-mail provider while still maintaining the requirement to encrypt all organizational e-mail. This may mean configuration changes for the employees of the organization, and it may also mean they will need training to ensure they understand how the encryption works and what to do if they lose their keys.

Chapter 19

1. An organization has recently acquired a contract that involves processing and storing sensitive information for a government client. The organization uses a decentralized approach to information technology, often letting employees purchase whatever systems they like and connecting them to the organization's network. Given the new contract, what access control changes, if any, should the organization consider?

    a. The organization most likely is following a decentralized access control approach to accommodate the decentralized information technology approach. The organization must consider which employees and functions will be involved in the new contract. Once these employees are identified, they should be either issued new equipment that conforms to mandatory access control or role-based access control. If new equipment is not feasible, the organization should consider strong configuration management to ensure the existing equipment can be configured to support mandatory access control or role-based access control. Information assurance awareness and training programs should be updated to include the new responsibilities of the organization and the expectations of all roles involved in the new contract.

2. Given the cost and resources involved in mandatory access control, why would an organization consider implementing it instead or other less expensive options?

    a. Certain businesses and industries will benefit greatly from mandatory access control. The most common explanations of mandatory access control often discuss military situations with different levels of classified information and compartmentalization. While these scenarios are typical, there are numerous other examples in which mandatory access control makes sense.

    Consider a large law firm working on cases for hundreds of clients. The law firm has an obligation to ensure it does not engage in a conflict of interest between its clients. If all attorneys can see all information or give discretionary access to information, the firm will have a difficult time explaining how it remains impartial. However, if the firm uses mandatory access control and requires all case and client materials to be stored and accessed through a strict permissions program, it will be able to provide confidence that while large, its attorneys are impartial to other work ongoing in the firm.

Another industry that may benefit from mandatory access control is research and development. As in the military, some research projects are divided up or "compartmentalized" so one person is unable to know the entire project completely. Mandatory access control provides a way to ensure only those with "need to know" can access information to do their job. In implementing mandatory access control, the organization now needs to concern itself only with those issuing the access. Tight monitoring of those individuals through auditing, rotation of duties, and forced time off can help ensure a robust approach to control information leakage.

Chapter 20

1. A CISO decides to deploy a honeypot with a baseline configuration on it into the wild to determine what vulnerabilities exist. What are the advantages and disadvantages to this approach?

   a. The primary advantage is the CISO will learn about the attack methods used to attack the configuration and also most likely what vulnerabilities the baseline configuration has. This could save assessment work and also provide a sense of "validation" that the configuration is safe for use. These advantages are typically outweighed by the disadvantages of this approach. By placing the standard configuration in the wild, Internet attackers now can begin to dismantle the configuration's security and weaknesses. Once an attacker discovers the system is a honeypot and contains a standard configuration, they may decide they want to attack the organization further and will have more information to work with. If set up poorly and interconnected with production systems, the honeypot may even be used as a staging ground to compromise the production environment.

2. The CIO of an organization is trying to prioritize the information assurance workload of the organization. The CIO has asked the CISO to take vulnerability scanner output and add it to the organization's dashboard. The CIO then tasks the organization's system owners to correct the most "critical" vulnerabilities first. Is this the most prudent plan to minimize risk in the organization?

   a. If all systems have an identical impact and threat exposure, then the CIO's approach is the best approach. If a single system has a unique impact or threat exposure, then the dashboard will be incorrect. The CIO must be able to direct resources to the highest-risk systems. If only vulnerability information is collected, the CIO is directing resources to the systems with the greatest vulnerability. This could mean directing all resources to a test or low-impact system with a critical vulnerability when a moderate impact system with a moderate vulnerability is more likely to be attacked and harm the organization. To be useful, monitoring tools and methods must be combined with accurate information about threats and impact.

Chapter 21

1. An organization is struggling. After years of investing in research and development, a competitor appears to have stolen design documents for the organization's flagship product. The organization's CISO has been asked to give a presentation to the board regarding the best metrics to monitor to prevent information leakage in the future. What information assurance metrics should the CISO propose?

   a. The CISO should propose information assurance metrics focused on *preventive* and *detective* information assurance controls. For example, the CISO may recommend monitoring:

   - Percentage of research and development (R&D) networks encrypted with US FIPS 140-2 validated encryption

   - Percentage of R&D servers and databases encrypted with US FIPS 140-2 encryption

   - Percentage of R&D employees who have successfully passed information assurance awareness training in the past year

   - Percentage of R&D employees who have a successfully adjudicated background investigation

   - Percentage of R&D functions analyzed for separation of duties and least privilege

   - Percentage of systems successfully implementing mandatory access control

   - Percentage of R&D systems successfully utilizing two factor authentications with nonrepudiation

   - Percentage of R&D systems and networks with functioning intrusion detection/prevention system

2. A CIO wants to ensure she is investing properly in information assurance. What metrics should her CISO advise her to monitor?

   a. The CISO should propose metrics that show a proactive stance in regard to information assurance but also metrics that may indicate information assurance is not being implemented well. Suggested metrics could include the following:

   - Percentage of systems fully integrated into the organization's SIEM

   - Percentage of systems compliant with the organization's continuous monitoring plan

   - Percentage of systems with High or Moderate risks aged beyond 30 days

   - Total estimated monetary exposure for an information system processing financial information or personally identifiable information

   - Number of open incidents and the risk severity of incidents per system, business/mission line, and system owner in the past 30 days

   - Number of detected but failed attacks against the organization's systems

- Percentage of system development and maintenance devoted to information assurance activities

- Estimated cost avoidance based on implementing information assurance controls

Chapter 22

1. An organization is using a cloud-based system for hosting its sensitive information in the form of customer lists and personally identifiable information. They are using Software as a Service (SaaS) customer relationship management (CRM) platform to manage their sales. Lately, their customers have been complaining about receiving calls from a competitor in another country with detailed information about their purchase histories and relationship with the organization. What is the incident response approach the organization should take?

    a. Cloud computing is a perfect example for planning and preparation. If the organization has not explicitly stated its requirements for accessing the cloud provider's information systems, then the provider is not likely to provide any information about vulnerabilities and threats outside of a court order. If the organization has ensured access language and audit or penetration test clauses were included in the contract, they can begin testing to determine whether the cloud provider breached their information. If the organization did an excellent job in preparation, they would ensure any cloud provider system that processed, stored, or transmitted the organization's data would provide system feeds to the organization's SIEM. In any event, the organization certainly has an uphill climb. Instead of working with an internal team of system owners and administrators who all want a resolution to the problem and lessons learned, the organization will likely now be engaging with a cloud provider who wants to protect their reputation and not impact the operations of their systems for other customers. This puts the organization at a great disadvantage in terms of detection, containment, eradication, and reporting. These risks must be clearly identified by the information assurance team and the incident-handling team prior to any engagement with a cloud provider.

2. An organization has adopted a *bring-your-own-device* (BYOD) approach for mobile devices such as smartphones and tablets. An employee's tablet has been identified as an unauthorized bridge between the organization's secure network and the public Internet. The organization's incident-handling team is baffled as to how this could happen and attempts to call the employee and retrieve the device. The employee refuses to provide the device and cites their right to privacy and their ownership of the device. The owner states that they have sensitive personal information on the device and under no circumstance will they allow the organization to search the device. What can the organization do in this situation?

    a. Preparation is again the key! If the organization has a clear BYOD policy and a signed rules of behavior agreement that states any device that processes, stores, or transmits the organization's data is subject to seizure and search, then the organization has reasonable grounds to seize and examine the device. Without the policy and signed agreement, the organization is left largely to the whims of the employee or the expensive and time-consuming route of legal action. Much like the cloud provider, the user may have different motivations for keeping information on the device private. In this situation, the user may have chosen not to participate in the BYOD program if they knew their device would be subject to examination and the organization would not be dealing with this specific incident. This leaves the incident-handling team with little to work with and a possible hostile employee. The incident-handling team will struggle during the containment and eradication phase because it has only a portion of the problem to analyze. The organization will also now need to determine whether other BYOD devices may have been affected in a similar fashion but may be met with the same resistance by every device owner.

Chapter 23

1. A manager suspects an employee may be using an organizational computer to view and download illegal materials. The manager has asked the information technology manager for advice regarding her suspicions about these materials. The IT manager states he can change the password to the user's account, and they can log in together over the weekend while the worker is out and view materials on the workstation. Is this an acceptable approach to determine whether criminal activity is occurring on the organization's computer?

   a. This approach would lead to failure. If the manger believes the employee is committing a crime, they should call in a forensics examiner who can make a forensically sound image of the system suitable as evidence for the criminal system. Additionally, the manager needs to be aware of any legal considerations surrounding the search and seizure of an employee's computer. A consultation with legal counsel is advised. While some legal systems afford no privacy to workers, others require a stringent documented approach before reviewing the computer of an employee. Once the legal requirements have been satisfied, the manager must ensure they have a forensics examiner who is certified and experienced in the technology, industry, and legal system the worker's computer is in. Finally, the examiner must be beyond reproach in credibility and following the rules of evidence. If the examiner can't prove the integrity of the chain of evidence and defend her professional opinions, the evidence may be thrown out or suppressed. The manager should also be aware of any requirements to notify law enforcement. Certain types of crimes against children must be reported immediately to law enforcement in some legal systems.

2. An organization is experiencing a loss of information. They find the source of the leak and grow frustrated. While the organization knows who is leaking the information, they are not sure how. The organization has blocked the use of all external media such as USB drives, CDs, and DVDs. It has also developed data loss

prevention tools and procedures to prevent information from leaking outside the organization through e-mail. It has also implemented web site filtering so employees cannot use unauthorized web mail or file-sharing services. The only thing in common with the leaked information is that it coincided with new updates to images and pictures on the organization's public web site. What could be causing the leak?

    a. Based on the information provided, an attacker was most likely using stenography to hide information in images. These images were then posted on the public web site where those who didn't know wouldn't notice the difference in the images. The attacker would know to download the images and extract the information from them.

Chapter 24

1. An organization has begun developing its business continuity plan. The organization is small and manufactures packaging for a variety of cosmetic products. The roles of CIO and the CFO are assigned to the same person who has been nominated to lead the task of business continuity. What are the strengths and weaknesses of this approach?

    a. Smaller organizations must blend roles and functions to ensure they can meet operational demands while not overspending in personnel. The CIO/CFO choice has many strengths, including knowledge of the financial aspects of the organization and the IT capabilities of the organization. A problem with blending roles is the possibility of conflicts between the roles. For example, a fiscally conservative CFO who is assigned CIO tasks will consider information technology a cost center just like facilities and plumbing. If the CFO is enamored with technology, they may view it as more of a "strategic investment" center and attempt to leverage IT as a core element of the organization's business. Understanding the motivations and limitations of blending roles will greatly assist the senior management of the organization plan for disasters. Without the presence of an impartial risk management function like a CRO or properly defined CISO, the CFO/CIO may not take into account all aspects of the business continuity process. Areas such as facilities, employee protection, and partnering with local emergency responders may be overlooked. The organization may be best served by employing a continuity planning professional to assist the CFO/CIO.

2. Why should information assurance place such an emphasis on crisis management and business continuity when disaster recovery is an IT function?

    a. Information assurance as described by the MSR model is mission focused. Therefore, without an understanding of the mission, directing resources and prioritizing recovery strategies will be misguided and at worse cause more harm than good. Crisis management and business continuity may or may not impact information systems. For example, an active shooter on the campus of an organization may initially appear to have zero impact on information technology, but no employee will be working on their workstation if they know an active shooter is present on campus. Another example is a pandemic. This occurs when a biological incident such as a debilitating strain of the flu incapacitates a large amount of personnel and impacts work. In this situation, IT system functionality such as help desk may need to be redirected to another geographical location not impacted by the illness. Finally, the mission or business of an organization is what ultimately matters. Information technology serves only to advance the business or mission. If the mission or business is not impacted by an IT outage, then no action may be necessary, and on the contrary, the organization may want to review why that information system was operational in the first place.

Chapter 25

1. An organization has performed a BIA and discovered 90 percent of its services and data have an RTO of ten days and an RPO of one day. The remaining ten percent of its services and data have an RTO of 30 minutes and an RPO of zero. What is the best strategy for the organization to back up this information?

    a. The organization has a demanding RTO and RPO for ten percent of its data and services. For this critical data and services, the organization should consider SAN storage with redundant features such as RAID and hot-site mirroring of data. For the remaining 90 percent of data and services, the organization should consider slower but more cost-efficient backup technologies such as tape or even cloud backup. Many cloud providers offer backups for as little as US$0.01 per gigabyte per month, with a recovery time of a few days.

2. How can organizations ensure their backup information is protected and the integrity of the backup is assured?

    a. Organizations must employ backup recovery testing and hashing to meet the requested objectives. Backup recovery testing consists of selectively restoring information to a test system or in some cases a production system and then verifying the restored information is accurate. Some backup software suites have testing modules that compare the integrity of a selected file with the integrity of the backup device or tape. The integrity is confirmed through hashing. Hashing provides proof that the files are identical.

Chapter 26

1. A U.S.-based healthcare clinic consists of an owner who is the head doctor of the practice, a physician's assistant, an office manager, a few nurses, and a couple assistants. Who is responsible for ensuring ePHI security and privacy?

    a. In short, the answer is everyone; however, ultimately the doctor who owns the practice is responsible for what happens to the information collected. Since the practice is in the United States, HIPAA and state data privacy laws apply. A single breach of unencrypted information could spell the end of this small practice if it does not have sufficient cash reserves to pay the fine and possible lawsuits for identity theft.

2. Assuming a clinic uses ePHI within the scope of the UK's data protection law, what technical controls should the clinic consider implementing to ensure the confidentiality and privacy of its records?

   a. Encryption is by far the best solution to help protect sensitive information from confidentiality breaches. Encryption for data at rest should include whole drive or whole device encryption, which protects the information when the device is off or when the wrong authentication is used with the device. Encryption in transit is equally important. Many web pages can use Secure Sockets Layer (SLL) to encrypt information; additionally, the clinic should ensure any transmission of information through insecure means such as standard e-mail is enhanced with the use of compensating controls such as file encryption and session encryption.

Chapter 27

1. An executive of a small business is worried about attacks and breaches. He accepts credit cards and has a web presence for ordering and accounting. He currently has all his information systems on a single Internet connection and is worried about hackers. What can the executive do to help mitigate his concerns?

   a. The executive should start by understanding the basic requirements for information assurance. Simple actions, such as putting the payment system on a separate network connection if possible and implementing more stringent controls on that network should be taken. Additionally, the small business owner may consider reaching out to CISOs in the industry to see whether any are willing to volunteer some time to help understand the basics of information assurance. Some programs exist, such as the CISO-in-residence program based at the Maryland Center for Entrepreneurship. The program allows small organizations to utilize the knowledge and expertise of a CISO as if they were on full time. Additionally, organizations such as (ISC)² require their members to maintain professional experience through training and volunteer service. The executive could reach out and determine whether a CISSP, CSSLP, CISM, or SSCP would be willing to give him an overview of information assurance risks.

2. A large retailer has just experienced a breach. The CIO has explained to the board of directors that this will never happen again because the credit card issues are requiring the customers to move to "chip and PIN" technology for their credit cards. Is he right?

   a. Rarely will a technology solution solve fraud problems. Fraud has always been a challenge for businesses and will remain so. While chip and PIN offers additional protection, the credit card still contains the magnetic strip the customer can use, and the retailer's technology may not be ready to accept chip and PIN.

Additionally, is the retailer ready to turn customers away who forget their PIN instead of swiping the mag stripe? That's not likely; the organization would be better served evaluating their information assurance program to determine where proactive assurance measures such as integrity checks and scanning failed to detect the breach and the attackers. If the attackers were detected, did the information assurance team have the authority to change the system or were they siloed and used only as "advisors?"

Chapter 28

1. The accountants at an energy company have been to a technology presentation about the "cloud" and Infrastructure as a Service (IaaS). They come into the CIO's office and tell him he can cut his costs by significant margins if they use only IaaSX (the cloud offering from the provider). The CIO is responsible for maintaining a large number of natural gas pipeline control networks in addition to the ICS operating several large refineries. Should he agree with the accountants? Is there another answer he should provide?

   a. This scenario is a common situation in organizational risk management. A stakeholder comes to the table with a valid concern or option (such as saving money); however, they may not know the rational for doing things a certain way. Is the IaaS cheaper because of lowered SLAs, increased latency, increased downtime, or by using common carrier communication paths that are not secure or private. The IaaS provider may have a valid solution the CIO could use, but until a full parity analysis has been performed with an assessment by an information assurance team, it is premature to expect to save any money or defray any risk.

2. A heating, ventilation, and air-conditioning company has just installed a state-of-the-art environmental system for an organization. As part of the purchase, the organization is going to receive one year of monitoring and efficiency reporting for free. The vendor requests to have the new equipment connected to the network and be given a domain admin account. The vendor says it needs the admin account so it can access the environmental control servers any time and perform repairs or maintenance. The CISO is discussing the request with the facilities manager. What response should she provide?

   a. The vendor is attempting to connect new devices to the network and also gain domain admin credentials. This combination could spell absolute disaster in many situations. While the vendor employees may be familiar with the configuration and operation of their product, they are most likely not security experts as evidenced by their request. The organization should consider logically or physically separating the vendor's equipment and granting only limited rights to the servers and equipment the vendor is using. If the vendor proposes using web-based services or needs a database, the organization needs to weigh the risk trade-offs between granting the access to a server vs. standing up another server for the environmental systems. The organization must also be aware of the challenges of now maintaining two networks (local or physical) and ensuring both are monitored and protected commensurate with risk. Finally, the organization may want to consider a background investigation for the vendor or any person they propose will have access to the organization's network. Nondisclosure agreements and organizational conflict of interest statements should be signed by the vendor.

B Common Threats

Threats are any potential danger to information or systems, which can range from viruses, malicious code, and worms to natural disasters such as flood and fire. This appendix will explain common types of threats and the impact on information assurance.

NOTE Components of this list are inspired and adapted from the BSI (Bundesamt für Sicherheit in der Informationstechnik) threat list, derived from *Information Security Risk Analysis* by Thomas R. Peltier.

Threat: *Force Majeure*

Force majeure is a French term used in law that you may find in contracts. It means greater (superior) force; it refers to circumstances beyond the control of anyone. A prudent manager will act to reduce the effect of these threats. If not, it may be negligence. In some cultures, these are referred to as acts of God. The following are the different types of threats in this category:

Threat	Description
Drought	Drought may have devastating effects on human, animal, and plant life. There can also be significant effects on businesses that depend on the availability of water for their products or processes. Drought may also affect power availability in areas supplied by hydroelectric systems or facilities that rely on water for cooling.
Dust	IT still relies on mechanical components despite the pervasiveness of electronics. Mechanical systems include disks, hard disk drives, removable hard disks, printers, and scanners. Almost all electronic systems rely on fans for processors and power supplies. In dusty environments, power supplies can also short and fail. Small impurities can cause a device to fail. Control dust associated with repair work on walls, raised floors, or other parts of a building; with hardware upgrades; and when unpacking equipment.

Threat	Description
Environmental catastrophes	The environmental surroundings of an organization may lead to a range of problems from operational difficulties to loss of productivity. Environmental events include technical incidents to political unrest, demonstrations, and riots. An organization's property can be exposed to environmental hazards from traffic (road, rail, air, and water) as well as neighboring business operations. These threats can be fire, explosions, dust, gases, blocking of access, or radiation emissions.
Failure of the IT system	Failure of a single component may cause an entire IT operation to fail and the significance may increase when the component is central to the system, such as a server. Some managers limit their perspective to simple things such as power supply disruption. IT system failures are as likely to result from human error or *force majeure*. If time-critical applications are run on a system, the consequential damage may be extensive unless alternatives are available.
Fire	Fire damage may be accompanied by collateral damage that exceeds the direct damage to IT systems. For example, water damage from firefighting occurs not only at the fire site but spreads due to gravity. Fires may be caused by careless handling of combustible material or improper use or technical of electrical devices. Fires to spread due to the absence of fire detection devices, inadequate fire prevention; failure to observe relevant standards and laws, improper storage of combustible materials, inadequate training, and blocking fire doors open. Soot and fine particulates are as dangerous as dust.
Hazardous/ malicious animals (vermin)	Software bugs are not the only ones we need to worry about. Hazardous/ malicious animals may be common pests (rats, mice, and cockroaches) or other animals (squirrels and snakes). The presence of common pests is a symptom of a dirty, untidy, or messy work environment. This is unpleasant; however, the real threat is that these pests may attack documentation, insulation, and wiring as part of their diet. Other animals may be present because of natural or near-natural environment (similar to their natural habitat). Snakes have been found in the cool area under the raised floor of major computer centers.
Human-sourced incidents	These are conditions surrounding an organization that lead to problems ranging from operational problems to loss of productivity. These conditions include technical incidents to political unrest, demonstrations, riots, terrorism, or acts of war. Exposure to various dangers may come through traffic (road, rail, air, and water) and business operations in the neighborhood or residential areas. These may cause fire, explosions, dusts, gases, blocking of access, radiation, or emissions.

Threat	Description
Incorrect temperature and humidity	Every device has an optimal operating temperature and humidity range. If the temperature is out of range, the result may be a discontinuity of service and failure of devices. In a server room, the equipment heats the room, so if ventilation is insufficient, the operating temperature of the devices may be exceeded, leading to equipment failure. Humidity is important in some instances. It reduces the problems with static electricity; however, if it becomes high, water condenses on the hardware causing damage.
Lightning	Lightning associated with thunderstorms is a threat to IT equipment. A lightning strike causes power spikes that may destroy sensitive electronic devices. The closer the lightning strike is, the greater the damage. Deploy lightning arrestors.
Loss of personnel	Unanticipated personnel loss can have many causes. In addition, regular employment turnover, accompanied by reduced availability because of illness and vacation, may cause problems. Personnel changes become critical if the individual cannot be replaced because of specialized skills. Loss of personnel may cause crucial tasks to be postponed or canceled resulting in disruption of IT operations.
Power failure	Most power fluctuations are for less than a second and may escape notice. Importantly, operations may be disrupted by fluctuations lasting as little as 10ms. Most infrastructure depends directly or indirectly on electric power.
Storms	The effects of a storm or hurricane on external facilities or equipment needed for the operation of the computer center are underestimated. External installations including power lines can be damaged by high winds and flying objects. Critical equipment should be centrally located.
Water	The uncontrolled flow of water into buildings or rooms may come from sprinkler systems, heating systems, disruption of water supply and sewerage systems, rain, burst water pipes, and floods, as well as from water used for firefighting. Independent of how water enters buildings or rooms, there is a probability that it will damage supply facilities or IT components.

Threat: Deliberate Acts

Frequently, deliberate acts by employees and others affect systems. These threat sources range from malicious software to unanticipated personal behavior changes or misconduct. Vigilance is imperative. The following are the different types of threats in this category:

Threat	Description
Call charge fraud	Call charge fraud by hackers involving PBX and VOIP systems has been reported in the press. Existing features of a PBX and VOIP systems can be abused for this purpose. The PBX and VOIP systems should be treated like any other computer system.

Threat	Description
Denial of service (DOS) Distributed denial of service (DDOS)	A denial of service attacks interferes with, prevents, or inhibits the normal use or management of communication, storage, transmission, and processing facilities. A transmission DOS attack may have a specific target; for example, an attacking entity may suppress all messages directed to a particular destination. Another form of denial of service is the disruption of an entire network, either by disabling the network infrastructure component or by overloading it with messages to the point that it cannot respond so as to degrade performance.
Escalation of privileges	An individual may give (or take) access credentials and privileges to someone without privileges. The second individual may proceed to discover access paths to assets for which he has no privilege. In this case, privileges have been escalated.
Forged digital certificates	Digital certificates link a public cryptographic key to an identity (machine or human). The link of a key to the name of a person or unique identifier of a machine is then protected cryptographically using the digital signature of a reliable neutral organization (certifying authority [CA]). These certificates may be used by others to check digital signatures of the person identified in the certificate or to send this person data with the key recorded in the certificate. If a certificate is forged, false signatures will be deemed to be correct when checked and are associated with the person in the certificate, or data is encoded and sent with an insecure key. Forged certificates may be produced in various ways. For example, internal perpetrators at a CA create a certificate with false entries using their own signature key. This certificate will appear to be authentic and verified to be correct when tested.
Hijacking of network connections	Hijacking a connection is more serious than having a connection tapped. Hijacking involves injecting data packets into the network, resulting in in either failure, control, or blocking of the client. Server process may be unable to detect that a different program has now replaced the original client. When an existing connection is taken over in this way after a user has authenticated him, the adversary can perform actions in the name of the authenticated person.
Hoaxes	A hoax may begin with a message containing a warning of a new computer virus or other IT problem. This may induce unwarranted concern or panic among the users. These messages, sent by e-mail, may warn of malware that damages hardware, and it causes infection simply through opening an e-mail (not even an attachment); it cannot be detected by current antivirus software. The warning asks the recipient to forward the message to friends and acquaintances. This results in an e-mail storm.

Threat	Description
Loss of confidentiality of sensitive information	In the case of sensitive information (such as passwords, person-related data, business-related and official information, and research and development data), there is an inherent danger of confidentiality being inadvertently or intentionally compromised. Classified and sensitive information can be obtained from various sources, including the following: • Data communication lines • External storage media (floppy disks, magnetic tapes) • Internal storage media (hard disks) • Printed paper (hard copies, files)
Loss, destruction, disclosure, and falsification of organizational records/information	External and internal perpetrators may try to manipulate or destroy IT equipment, accessories, documents, data, and information. Internal threats are effective since they are harder to detect and may have more complete system knowledge. Effects range from unauthorized inspection and disclosure of sensitive data to destruction of data, media, or complete IT systems. Data or software can be manipulated in various ways: acquisition of wrong data, modification of data, changes to access rights, modification of accounting data or of correspondence, changes to operating system software, or insertion of unauthorized users. The more access rights an individual has, the more serious attacks that can be performed. If these attacks are not detected in time, IT operations may be seriously impaired.
Macro viruses	In the exchange of files (for example, by data media or e-mail), there is a danger that in addition to the actual file, macros or malicious code may be embedded. These macros can be executed only with the specific application software (Word, Excel, or most sophisticated applications). When the document is activated by the user or automatically opens, a contained macro may be executed.
Malicious Software Malicious code (malware)	Malicious code can be divided into two categories: those that require a host program and those that do not. The host-dependent malware code is essentially a fragment of a program that cannot exist independently of some other program. Independent malware is a self-contained program that can be scheduled and run by an operating system. Examples of malware are Trojan horses, viruses, worms, and logic bombs.
Misuse of e-mail services	The misuse of e-mail systems has many sources: at the sending workstation, within an Intranet, on a mail server, or at a receiving workstation. If access to an organization's e-mail system is not protected adequately, unauthorized individuals may misdirect IT systems to generate e-mail or damage through the impersonation of authorized users. Unauthorized persons should be prevented from reading e-mail through end-to-end encryption, and an acceptable use policy should clearly delineate how e-mail is used.

Threat	Description
Misuse of user/ administrator rights/ privileges	Access to resources of a system is a privilege. Misuse of administrative privileges or illicitly possessed superuser (root) privileges are used to harm the system and/or its users.
Sabotage	Sabotage refers to malicious acts to cause damage.
	Computer centers or communication links are attractive targets since a major effect can be achieved at minimum costs.
	External and internal individuals may manipulate the infrastructure of a computer center through targeted attacks on critical components. Additional threat considerations come from inadequately protected central supply points that are not monitored so are easy for outsiders to access.
Social engineering	Social engineering is a human-based thread for obtaining private information. Perpetrators may pose as insiders by using appropriate keywords during conversations and may gain information useful for further attacks. *Sounding* is the use of a telephone call, in which perpetrators pose as the following:
	• Administrator who needs to know the user password to eliminate a system error
	• Supervisor of a secretary needs to urgently complete a task but has forgotten the correct password
	• Telephone engineer who needs to know certain details about communication configuration
Spam	Unsolicited electronic mail or junk newsgroup postings. It wastes time and consumes network resources. Since the Internet is public, there is little that can be done to prevent spam; however, some online services have instituted policies to prevent spammers from addressing their subscribers. Spam is a threat vector for phishing and spear-phishing.
Tampering of mobile phones	The installation of additional electronic circuitry or software is a hardware manipulation. To be carried out, the device to be attacked should be in the possession of the adversary.
	Mobile phones may be used for bugging purposes through changes to the installed control software (firmware). This kind of tampering is more difficult to detect than hardware tampering.
Theft	Theft of IT equipment, accessories, data software, applications, or data information results not only in replacement costs but also in the expense of having to replace equipment or to restore the system to working order. There is a concomitant cost for loss of availability and also in losses resulting from lack of availability. Loss of confidentiality can be damaging and expensive.
	Easy to transport inconspicuously, mobile IT systems are often targeted for theft.

Threat	Description
Trojan horses	A Trojan horse is an otherwise attractive program containing code with a hidden, undocumented function or effect. A user has no influence on the execution of that function. Unlike viruses, self-reproduction need not take place. Any application or system software may be a carrier for Trojan horses. Frequently, scripts like batch files, ASCII control sequences, and Postscript, interpreted by the operating system or by an application, may be misused for harmful purpose. The more privileges are granted to the user, the more effective the harmful effects of a Trojan horse are.
Unauthorized access and use	Without the use of identification and authentication of users, information-processing facilities/operating systems cannot have unauthorized use of IT systems.
	Abuse of the identification and authentication function is possible. It is possible to initiate automatic attempts using a program that systematically tests all conceivable passwords.
	Even for IT systems using identification and authentication mechanisms (user IDs and password verification), there is a risk of unauthorized access from disclosure of credentials.
Unauthorized connection of IT systems to a network	The unauthorized connection of a system to an existing network cannot be ruled out. This threat cannot be prevented with available cable designs, which differ solely in terms of the time and effort required to connect to the cable and compromise data. The unauthorized integration of a computer into a network may be difficult to detect. This unauthorized access allows monitoring of all communications taking place in the affected segment and can facilitate the following activities: • Analysis of message flow • Denial of services • Manipulation of data and software • Manipulation of lines • Masquerading • Monitoring of lines • Replay of messages • Unauthorized access to active network components • Unauthorized execution of network management functions

Threat	Description
Unauthorized entry into buildings	Theft or tampering may be preceded by unauthorized entry into a building. Controls directed at preventing break-ins are also effective against exploits, which depend on a successful prior break-in. If a malefactor can physically contact network components, the devices can be compromised more easily.
	Professional criminals rely on undisturbed access to pursue objectives. The perpetrator may focus on stealing IT components or copying or tampering with systems. Concealed tampering is more harmful than direct acts of destruction.
Unauthorized viewing of incoming fax messages	If fax machines are placed in a publicly accessible area, incoming fax messages can be viewed by any person in the area. Confidential information may be disclosed, lose its value, or be exploited.

Threat: Human Failure

Human failure is where human mistakes are inevitable. Frequently, it is symptomatic of poor training. In the MSR model, training is the foundation of addressing this issue. The following are the different types of threats in this category:

Threat	Description
Hazards posed by cleaning staff or external employees	Hazards posed by cleaning staff and external employees range from improper handling of equipment, attempts to "play" with systems, or theft of IT components.
Improper IT system administration	Improper IT system administration through negligence or ignorance of security controls jeopardizes the system. Improper administration occurs if, for example, network access points (daemon processes) that are not necessary for the regular operation of the IT system or that represent a particularly great threat because of their error-proneness are created or not disabled.
Improper use of the IT system	Improper use of the IT system through negligence or ignorance of information assurance controls jeopardizes the system.
Incompetent personnel	Risks may be posed by employees who have not received adequate on-the-job training; as such, employees may be unable to carry out assigned duties. This is particularly true for knowledge workers who require know-how, spontaneous response, and critical thinking ability, and rarely if ever perform operations without rigid technical controls and processes.

Threat	Description
Loss of data confidentiality/ integrity as a result of IT user error	Through erroneous actions, IT users can cause or allow loss of data confidentiality/integrity. The consequential damage depends on the sensitivity of the data involved. The following are examples of such erroneous actions: Accidental printouts containing personal data are collected by employees from a network printer. Because of incorrectly assigned access rights, an employee can modify data without being able to assess the critical impact of such a violation of integrity. Portable media are dispatched without physical deletion of previously stored data. New software is tested using nonanonymous data. Unauthorized employees thus have access to protected files or confidential information. It is also possible that third parties can have access to this information, for example, if disposal of "test printouts" is not handled correctly.
Loss of data media during transfer	If data media are dispatched without robust packaging (mailing envelopes and so on), damage to the packaging may lead to loss of the data media (particularly portable media, such as a USB drive). The loss can also occur during the mailing process, for example, because of negligence on the part of the mail carrier. If, for example, a USB drive is dispatched with a letter inside a considerably larger envelope, the USB drive may be overlooked and disposed of inadvertently.
Noncompliance with information security controls, standards, and policies	Drawing up rules and procedures does not of itself guarantee the smooth flow of IT operations. All individuals in the organization should be aware of rules and procedures that apply to them. Damage resulting from inadequate knowledge of existing rules and procedures cannot be excused by saying, "I did not know I was responsible for that" or "I didn't know what to do." Here are some examples: If employees are not informed of the procedure for handling incoming portable media and e-mails, there is a danger that a computer virus could be spread throughout the company/agency. The computer center has introduced a new rule that in the event of problems with the intruder detection or fire alarm systems, the security team is to be manned at night as well. The information security guard service, which organizes its own routine, is not informed of this new rule by the information security officer. As a result, the computer center is unprotected for several weeks.

Threat	Description
Sharing of directories, printers, or a clipboard (is a threat if not disabled)	When using the file or print manager, errors are possible when sharing directories, printers, or pages of a clipboard. This can result in resources being shared unintentionally. The necessary password protection may be applied incorrectly or not at all if the user has not been sufficiently informed of the peer-to-peer functions in the operating system. Because shared resources (except for pages of a clipboard) are generally visible to all participants, other participants can detect and abuse this situation. It is possible for confidential data to be read, changed, or deleted without authorization. For instance, if a shared directory has write access without password protection, it would be possible to store files in that directory until the capacity of the hard disk is exhausted.
Software malfunctions/ information security incidents/weaknesses not reported	All employees and contractors should be made aware of procedures for reporting different types of incident (information assurance breach, threat, weakness, or malfunction) that may have an impact on the information assurance of organizational assets. Because of certain reasons such as negligence, incidents may not be reported as quickly as possible to the designated point of contact.

Threat: Technical Failure

Frequently, technical failures result from a disconformity or misunderstanding of training or policy. In many cases, technical failures can be predicted by a statistical process control (SPC) or other means. See Chapter 21 for more information. The following are the different types of threats in this category:

Threat	Description
Cross-talk	Cross-talk is a special form of line interference. The fault is not caused by the environment but by inductive signals on adjacent lines. The intensity of this effect depends on cable structure (shielding, cable capacity, and insulation quality) and on electrical parameters (current, voltage and frequency). This phenomenon is encountered in the (analog) telephone network. There, calls of other network participants can be heard. However, these participants often do not respond to the request to "clear the line" because cross-talk is confined to one direction. Checking one's own lines for coupled-in, other-source signals does not yield any information on whether one's own signals cause cross-talk in other lines and whether these signals can thus be monitored. Exploitable information may be available on other lines because of cross-talk.
Data loss because of exhausted storage medium	Every storage medium has a limited capacity for holding data. When this limit has been reached, the result may be the loss of data and services. Incoming e-mail may be rejected, systems may fail to keep unevaluated audits or audit data, and users may be unable to save additional data.
	The capacity of the storage medium may be exhausted for various reasons, such as application program errors, increased user storage requirements, or a malicious attack specifically intended to reduce existing storage space and thus preventing audit trails from being kept.

Threat	Description
Discovery of software vulnerabilities	Software vulnerabilities are usually unintentional software coding errors not yet identified. This is a risk for the IT system. New weaknesses are repeatedly found in existing (including widely used) or completely new software.
Disruption of power supply	Power failures are a regular occurrence independent of how secure a power supply is. In most cases of power failure, power is down for less than a second and it escapes notice. However, IT operations can be disrupted even by failures lasting as little as 10ms. It is not only direct uses of electric power (PCs, lighting, and so on) that depend on the power supply; all modern infrastructure installations are either directly or indirectly dependent on electric power, including lifts, pneumatic post systems, air conditioning, alarm systems, and telephone private branch exchanges. Even the water supply in high-rise buildings relies on electric power because of the use of pumps to generate pressure in the upper stories.
Failure of a database	If a database fails, for example, because of hardware/software error or an act of sabotage, far-reaching consequences may result, depending on the function and significance of the database. In this case, all applications, which rely on the data in the affected database, are rendered unusable. As a result, users of these applications can no longer perform some or all of the tasks assigned to them, unless these tasks can be carried out manually. If a particular task can be performed only electronically with the help of a database, the following consequences may be seen: • Financial loss • Information security pitfalls that may be severe enough to affect personal well-being (for example, in the case of medical databases) • Partial or complete disruption of operations
Failure of a local area network or wide area network (LAN and WAN)	If time-critical IT applications are run on IT systems connected via wide area networks, the damage and consequential damage arising from a network failure is severe if no controls are implemented (for example, linkage to a second communications network). Customers should therefore inform themselves about the actual quality of this service by requesting detailed information on backup strategies and contingency controls from network providers.
Mobile phone failure	A mobile phone can become unusable for reasons such as the following: • The battery fails because the user forgot to recharge it. • The battery has lost its ability to store a charge. • Components such as the display, keypad, or SIM card are faulty. • The user has forgotten the PIN and cannot use the phone. • If a mobile phone is exposed to harmful environmental conditions, its functional performance can be impaired. Mobile phones can sustain damage through exposure to excessively high or low temperatures, dust, or moisture.

Part VI

Threat	Description
Hardware malfunction	This is the failure of a hardware component to function as intended.
Loss of data in a database	Loss of data in a database can be caused by a wide variety of factors, including inadvertent manipulation of data (for example, through unintentional deletion of data), database crashes, and deliberate intrusions.
	As a result, availability and completeness of data are no longer guaranteed, and the following consequences may arise:
	• Applications that rely on data in the database can no longer be executed or have only partial function.
	• The correlation of data is lost.
	• Considerable time and effort are required to recover lost data.
	Depending on the cause of the data loss, it can be difficult or even impossible to determine precisely which data has been lost. This can lead to further financial losses and information security risks.
Sending a fax message to a wrong recipient	Incorrect linkage in a public telecommunications network or simply incorrect dialing can cause fax information to be transmitted to the wrong recipient. As a result, confidential information can be disclosed to unauthorized parties. The consequential damage depends on the confidentiality of the information. In addition, the initiator will incorrectly assume that a fax message has been sent successfully to the desired addressee. The resulting time delay can prove detrimental.
Software malfunction	This is the failure of a software application to function as intended.
Undocumented functions	Large application programs may contain undocumented functions, such as functions not described in the documentation and that users do not know about. For some operating systems and application programs, there are now books describing a large proportion of previously undocumented functions that have come to light; these books are generally larger than product manuals. Undocumented functions are not, however, confined merely to tools that have useful effects. As long as these functions are not out in the open, the possibility that they can create problems cannot be excluded. In particular, this is a problem when undocumented functions affect IT security mechanisms of the product, such as access control. Such functions often serve as "back doors" during the development or distribution of application programs.

APPENDIX

C

Common Vulnerabilities

Vulnerabilities are flaws that create weaknesses in the overall information assurance of the system or network. This appendix will provide a general overview of types of vulnerabilities and the nature/effect of those vulnerabilities.

NOTE This list is inspired by and adapted from the BSI (*Bundesamt für Sicherheit in der Informationstechnik*) threat list.

Vulnerability: Organizational Shortcomings

An organization that has poor planning and implementation habits introduces vulnerabilities. Throughout the organizational planning process, you should make sure information assurance is kept in the list of high-importance items. The following are the vulnerabilities in this category:

Vulnerability	Description
Inadequate business continuity management	Business continuity management is important to reduce the disruption caused by disasters and information security failures (which may be the result of, for example, natural disasters, accidents, equipment failures, and deliberate actions) to an acceptable level through a combination of preventive and recovery controls.
Inadequate equipment security	There may be undefined equipment sitting and protection plan. Physical security threats and environmental hazards pose the greatest risk to the equipment of the organization. Equipment malfunction may disrupt the conduct of a company's business operations, and the impact of loss varies depending on the criticality of that equipment. The threats may be human and nonhuman. Examples include the following: • Eating, drinking, and smoking in the server room. • Fire and toxic gas introducing chemical effects to equipment. • Inadequate cabling information security. • Inadequate protection from power failure.

Vulnerability	Description
	<ul><li>Insecure disposal and reuse of equipment. Information can be compromised through careless disposal or reuse of equipment.</li><li>Lack of equipment maintenance.</li><li>Unattended printer in a non-air-conditioned room that is exposed to dust.</li></ul>
Inadequate IT documentation	Various forms of documentation may be considered: the product description, the administrator and user documentation required to use the product, and system documentation. If documentation relating to the IT components used is inadequate or lacking, this can have a significant impact both on the selection and decision-making processes regarding a product and in terms of damage occurring during actual operation. If the documentation is inadequate, should a damaging event occur such as hardware failure or malfunctioning of software, error diagnosis and rectification may be delayed considerably or rendered completely impractical. The same applies to documentation of cable paths and wiring within a building's infrastructure. If because of inadequate documentation the precise location of cables is not known, these cables could be damaged during construction work outside or within a building. This may entail prolonged downtime periods, resulting in an emergency situation or even life-threatening hazards, such as electric shock.
Inadequate management of information security	Inadequate management of information security is often a symptom of poor overall organization of the information security process and hence of business operations as a whole. Examples of specific threats that result from inadequate management of IT information security include the following: <ul><li>Lack of personal responsibility. If no information security management team has been set up in an organization or if no information security officer has been appointed and personnel responsibilities for implementing individual controls have not been clearly defined, then it is likely that users will decline to take responsibility for information security, maintaining that it is the responsibility of those above them in the organizational hierarchy. Consequently, controls, which at the outset nearly always require extra work on top of one's normal duties, remain unimplemented.</li><li>Inadequate support from the management. Usually, information security officers are not members of an organization's management team. If the latter does not unambiguously support the information security officers in their work, this can make it difficult to effectively implement necessary controls. In these circumstances, there is no guarantee that the information security management process will be fully implemented.</li></ul>

Vulnerability	Description
	• Insufficient or misdirected investment. If the management of an organization is not kept informed of the information security status of business systems and applications and of existing shortcomings through regular information security reports that lay down clear priorities, it is probable that insufficient resources will be made available for the information security process or that these will be applied in an inappropriate manner. In the latter case, it is possible to have an excessively high level of information security in one subarea and serious deficiencies in another. Another common observation is that expensive technical information security systems are incorrectly used, rendering them ineffective or even transforming them into information security hazards.
	• Insufficient monitoring of information security controls. If information security controls are implemented but not monitored, they are rendered useless. For example, the information security characteristic of logging functions becomes apparent only when logged data is analyzed.
Inadequate mechanisms to quantify and monitor incidents and malfunctions	If appropriate action is not taken in response to an information security incident or system malfunction, considerable damage or loss can occur, or the situation may even develop into a catastrophe. Examples include the following: • Failure to take action when there is evidence that confidential corporate data has been compromised can result in additional confidential information being leaked. • Inconsistencies are found in the log files of a firewall. Unless this is investigated as a hacking attempt, external adversaries can actually penetrate the firewall. • New computer viruses containing damaging functionality at first occur on a sporadic basis but afterward are found on a wide scale. Without appropriate and rapid response, entire organizational units can be put out of action. This is what happened when the Melissa virus appeared. • New information security weaknesses are discovered in the IT systems. If necessary controls are not taken in a timely manner, there is a danger that these information security weaknesses will be misused by either internal or external perpetrators. • The material held on a web server changes inexplicably. If this is not investigated as a possible sign of a hacker attack, further attacks on the server can result in considerable loss of image.

Vulnerability	Description
	• There are signs that corporate data has been manipulated. If the opportunity to follow up the manipulations is overlooked, undetected manipulations can result in extensive consequential damage, such as incorrect stock levels, false book keeping, or unchecked outflow of funds.
Inadequately protected distributors	Electrical distribution points are often freely accessible and kept unlocked in corridors and staircases. Thus, any person can open the distributor boxes, manipulate them, and possibly cause a power failure.
Insecure handling of media	All sorts of media, such as tapes, discs, cassettes, and printed reports, are vulnerable to damage, theft, and unauthorized access. The following are typical mistakes: • No proper information handling procedures; as a result, classified information is not treated with care. • No proper procedure to dispose media that is no longer needed; for example, a project proposal is accidentally disclosed to a competitor because the unused document is not shredded. • Previous contents of reusable media are not erased; as a result, sensitive data is revealed. • System documentation may contain a range of sensitive information, such as descriptions of application processes and data structure. If system documentation is not properly protected, there is a high possibility that the system will be compromised.
Inventory of assets is not maintained and classified	If an inventory of assets is not maintained and classified, it is not held accountable, and appropriate protection for an asset is impossible. Based on varying degrees of sensitivity and criticality of assets, it is necessary to differentiate handling procedures for those assets. A typical mistake made is mishandling documents because of carelessness or ignorance. As a result, sensitive information is disclosed.
Lack of backups, operator logs, and fault logging	No information backup. Information is essential for the survival of most organizations regardless of the business. To ensure the continuity of business operations, information backup is essential. The following are typical threats faced: • Accidental deletion of records • Environmental hazards such as fire and flood • Loss of handheld devices No operator logs. Operator logs are necessary for operational employees to avoid repudiation on activities that have been performed. Also, they help to keep track of changes made to the system, which are thus monitored. No fault loggings. This is relevant to inadequate mechanisms to quantify / monitor incidents/malfunctions.

Vulnerability	Description
Lack of compatible resource, or unsuitable ones	Insufficient provision of resources can disrupt IT-related operations considerably. Insufficient required resources, or failure to provide them in due time, can result in a discontinuity of service. The organization must ensure that consumables (ink, paper, and so on) and spares for repair of systems (power supplies, component backups, and so on) are available as and when required. Similarly, it may happen that unsuitable or even incompatible resources are procured that consequently cannot be used.
Lack of information security in exchange of information and software	There can be a loss of confidentiality and integrity of information if it is not properly protected because of the following: • Inadequate information security of electronic commerce • Inadequate information security of media in transit • Lack of information security for electronic office systems • Undefined information and software exchange agreements • Unprotected publicly available systems
Lack of or inadequate maintenance	Operability of the system used should be ensured on a continuing basis. Regular maintenance can enhance assurance of continuous service. Lack of or insufficient maintenance can result in incalculable damage and late effects.
Lack of user training	Incompetent employees as a result of insufficient user training on the correct use of an IT system may introduce information security risks.
No authorization for removal of property	No mechanism in place to monitor the removal of company property will mean there is a high possibility that insider fraud will take place.
No information security in job definition and resourcing	Lack of information security in job definition and resourcing will usually lead to human error, theft, fraud, or misuse of facilities. This is particularly critical for sensitive jobs. The following are examples: • Fraudulence in an applicant's curriculum vitae and professional qualifications • Neglect of legal responsibilities and rights regarding copyright laws or data protection legislation

Part VI

Vulnerability	Description
Poor adjustment to changes in the use of IT	Rules created for IT applications and the application environment are subject to constant change. This is because of hiring/firing employees, moving employees to different rooms, using new hardware or software, or changing the supply chain. The following examples show that risks may be incurred if the required organizational adjustments are not properly taken into account: • Before electronic documents are transferred, no care is taken to ensure that they have been stored in a format that is readable by the recipient. • Because of alterations to a building, changes are made to previous escape routes. Because of insufficient information provided to the employees, the building cannot be evacuated quickly enough. • An employee forgets to transfer the necessary file access rights to the person who is to take over from him while he is on holiday. This can cause delays in IT operations. • Upon arrival, electronic documents are not scanned automatically for macro viruses because this problem is not known yet or no virus scanning programs are available. • When an IT procedure is modified, a large quantity of printing paper is required. If the procurement unit is not informed, continuity of IT operations and service will be impaired.
Undefined operational procedures and responsibilities	Inadequate operational change controls. Rules created for IT applications and the application environment are subject to constant change. This is because of changes in employees, moving employees to different rooms, using new hardware or software, or changes in the supply chain. Lack of incident management procedures or inadequate procedures. If fault occurrence is not attended to properly, no corrective actions are taken, and therefore the problem persists. No segregation of duties. Segregation of duties is important to ensure that no single employees can misuse the system either accidentally or deliberately. Undefined duties or segregation may result in inefficiency while performing duties. Also, there is a possibility that no one is held responsible in the event of information security breaches and other problems. Undocumented operating procedures. Operating procedures specify the instructions for the detailed execution of each job. Lack of procedures will lead to the mishandling of information and business operations.
Unprotected secure areas	Some organizations possess critical business information-processing facilities and a great deal of sensitive business information. If a company's physical premises are not protected, there is a high possibility that unauthorized access, damage, and interference to business premises and information will take place.

Vulnerability	Description
	Here are some examples: • Doors and windows are left unsecured. • Information-processing facilities are not isolated from delivery and loading areas; as a result, delivery staff can have the opportunity to gain access to the company's information system. • A worker in a secure area is not supervised. As a result, a contractor or temporary employee gains access to the system and steals trade secrets.

Vulnerability: Technical Shortcomings

Technical vulnerabilities are frequently derived from managerial shortcomings. For example, the first vulnerability points to a failure to plan; however, this yields technical vulnerabilities. The following are the vulnerabilities in this category:

Vulnerability	Description
Inadequate system planning and acceptance	Lack of planning in the early stage of system setup may lead to capacity overflow. The following are some examples: • Insufficient bandwidth of a network. The transmission rate in the network is severely restricted for all users. File access in remote IT systems is slowed down considerably, for example, when available network bandwidth has to be shared with other users, initiating a high amount of network traffic (capacity is subject to a high level of utilization by other users), such as when large files are transferred from one IT system to another. • Insufficient route dimensioning. During planning of networks, server rooms, or computer centers, typical mistakes made are defining functionality, capacity, and information security design from the current approach. This approach fails to take into account the fact that the capacities of the network and computers will have to be extended in line with increases in data volumes or the use of new services. • Loss of data in a database caused by a lack of storage space. Also, if acceptance criteria for new information systems, upgrades, and new versions are not defined, it will possibly lead to system malfunctions. Here are some examples: • Performance and computer capacity requirements are undefined. • Recovery procedures and contingency plans are undefined. • There is a lack of training in the operation of new systems.

Vulnerability	Description
Inadequate application access control	Logical access to software and information should be restricted to authorized users. These are some common problems: • Lack of information access restriction • No isolation of sensitive systems
Inadequate information security in application systems	Lack of control for internal processing. Data that has been correctly entered can be corrupted by processing errors or deliberate acts. Lack of output data validation to ensure that processing of stored information is correct and appropriate to the circumstances. No input data validation to detect errors such as out-of-range values, invalid characters in data fields, and missing or incomplete data.
Inadequate network access control	• Information security attributes of network services may be unclear. • Lack of network connection control. Examples of application to which restrictions should be applied are e-mail, one-way file transfer, two-way file transfer, and interactive access. • Lack of network routing control for shared networks that extend across organizational boundaries. • Lack of node authentication for a facility for automatic connection to a remote computer. • Lack of policy regarding use of network services, such as networks and network services that are accessible, authorization procedures for determining who is allowed to access those networks and networked services, and management controls and procedures to protect access to network connections and network services. • Lack of user authentication for external connections may provide potential for unauthorized access to business information, such as access by dial-up methods. • No segregation of network for information systems that are more critical and sensitive than others. • Network routes from the user to the service are not controlled; these may provide opportunities for unauthorized access to business applications or use of information facilities. • Remote maintenance ports are insufficiently protected. Hackers may gain access to the administration port of the IT system. Once they have compromised the system password, they may be able to perform all administrative tasks. The resulting damage can range from a complete system failure, a serious disruption of service/operation continuity, or a loss of the confidentiality of all data stored in the system to a considerable direct financial loss.

Vulnerability	Description
Inadequate operating system access control	IT security facilities at the operating system level should be used to restrict access to computer resources. The following are examples of inadequate operating system access control: • Inadequate terminal logon procedures • No user identification or authentication • No password management system • Use of system utilities is not restricted or tightly controlled • Undefined terminal timeout • Unlimited connection time
Lack of controls against malicious software	To protect the integrity of software and information, protection against malicious software is necessary. Here are examples of ways in which malicious software is introduced: • Inadvertently installing spyware • Lack of maintenance of antivirus software (for example, no update of virus signatures) • Receiving files without checking their origin and reliability

Vulnerability: Procedural Shortcomings

Vulnerabilities are introduced by having poor policies or good policies that do not have sound supporting procedures. Technology will fail if it is not supported by policies, procedures, and people. The following are the vulnerabilities in this category:

Vulnerability	Description
Clear desk and clear screen policy	A clear desk and clear screen policy must be simple and incomprehensible to avoid exposure of the organization's business information to unauthorized access, loss, and damages. Here are some examples of problems: • Classified information is not collected from a network printer immediately after being printed. • Sensitive or critical business information such as a proposal and client information is left on a table.
Inadequate disciplinary policies	If an organization does not have a clear disciplinary process for violating organization information security policies/procedures, employees may be inclined to disregard such policies/procedures.

Vulnerability	Description
Inadequate information security controls for outsourcing	When there is a need to outsource information processing to other organizations, information security needs to be maintained. A typical threat is disclosure of company-sensitive information to unauthorized users. Also, controls need to be in place to ensure confidentiality and integrity of the information released. Some contractors may not be aware of information security responsibilities and may overlook the seriousness of information security compromise.
Inadequate information security controls for third-party access	Where there is a business need for third-party access, controls should be agreed and defined in a contract with the third party. The risks inherent in third party access include the following: • Unauthorized logical access to a company's databases and information systems • Unauthorized physical access to company premises such as computer rooms or filing cabinets
Inadequate software test and release procedures	If new hardware or software is inadequately tested or not tested at all and released without installation instructions, errors in hardware or software may not be identified, or essential installation parameters may not be recognized or considered. Hardware, software, or installation errors resulting from software and release procedures that are inadequate or lacking altogether can result in a considerable threat to business operations. In the confidence that one will be able to install new hardware or software without difficulty, it is often not considered that potential damage is completely out of proportion to the cost of carrying out a proper test-and-release procedure. Software or IT systems that have been inadequately tested and that still contain errors may be integrated into the production environment.
Lack of monitoring of system access and use	Misuse of rights can happen if there is no regular checking and monitoring of system use. Here are some examples: • Lack of event logging. Exceptions and other information security-relevant events are not recorded and kept for an agreed period to assist in future investigations. • Lack of reviews on user access rights and privileges.
Lack of or insufficient policies and policy review	Information security policies serve as a reference guarding the operations of the company. Undocumented policies tend to lead to arguments in cases of dispute. Without information security policies defined, people tend to act according to what they think is correct and find chances to bypass "spoken" rules. Often, existing policies are not modified after changes of a technical, organizational, or personnel nature that have significant impact on information security. Out-of-date policies can impede smooth business operations. Problems can also arise as a result of the fact that policies may be written in a manner that is incomprehensible or without the contextual information needed and so are misunderstood.

Vulnerability	Description
Lack of user access management	Formal procedures should be in place to control allocation of access rights to information systems and services. The procedures should cover all stages in the life cycle of user access, from the initial registration of new users to the final deregistration of users who no longer require access to information systems and services. These are common mistakes: • Improper user registration procedures. • Inadequate privilege management. Inappropriate use of system privileges is often found to be a major contributing factor to the failure of systems that have been breached. • Inadequate password management. Passwords are a common means of validating a user's identity to access an information system or service.
Noncompliance with legal requirements	Design, operation, use, and management of information systems may be subject to statutory, regulatory, and contractual information security requirements. Negligence or lack of knowledge of legal requirements may lead to breaches of any criminal and civil law, including statutory, regulatory, or contractual (gross negligence).
Undefined information security requirements for new systems	Information security requirements and controls should reflect the business value of the information assets involved and potential business damage that may result from a failure or absence of information security.
Undefined management authorization process for new information-processing facilities	A management authorization process for new information-processing facilities should be established. Several adverse effects from not putting controls in new information-processing facilities include the following: • Noncompliance with existing information security policies • Unauthorized use of information-processing facilities • Use of personal information-processing facilities in the workplace may cause new vulnerabilities.
Undefined policies and inadequate controls on mobile computing	Mobile computing introduces new perspectives as well as threats. Because it is mobile, it is more difficult to monitor and control.
Undefined policies and inadequate controls on teleworking	Teleworking uses communication technology to enable employees to work remotely from a fixed location outside of their organization. Possible risks for teleworking include theft of information and equipment, unauthorized disclosure of information, unauthorized remote access to the organization's internal systems, and misuse of facilities.

APPENDIX

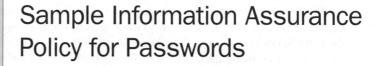

D

Sample Information Assurance Policy for Passwords

This is a sample policy. This password policy is based on one from NASA (www.nccs.nasa .gov/policies/passwd.html).

Password Policy

To remain in compliance with our information assurance policies, passwords on all computing systems must conform to the following standard:

- A password is set to expire every 60 days. You are required, therefore, to change your password at least once every 60 days. (The 60-day period begins each time you change a password.)
- A password must be at least 12 characters in length.
- A password must contain the following:
  - Lowercase characters (*a, b, c,* and so on)
  - Uppercase characters (*A, B, C,* and so on)
  - Numerical characters (1, 2, 3, and so on)
  - Special characters (!, @, #, and so on)

If the password has only one nonalphabetic character, that character must not be the first or last character in the password string.

- A new password cannot be a password that you previously used during the past 24 password changes. (Our computing systems will reject a password previously used during the past 24 password changes.)
- A new password must differ from the old password by at least three characters.

- A new password cannot contain within it a person's name or any word or abbreviation found in a dictionary.

- A password can be changed only once during a 24-hour period.

When you change your password, the new password will automatically be run through a password "cracker" to test the validity of the new password. If the "cracker" determines that your attempted new password is not acceptable, then it will reject this password, and you will need to find a more appropriate password.

We provide password locking services if users want to have their user IDs locked for an extended period of time. Users who want to avail themselves of this service should inform the User Services Group by telephone at (555) 867-5309 of any extended absences when they will not be using their user IDs. This precaution will help ensure the security of your user ID during your absence.

Password Expiration

A password will expire after 60 days. You will automatically be warned by electronic mail (e-mail) 14 and 7 days prior to the expiration of your password. If you fail to change your password before it expires, however, your user ID will automatically be disabled. Once your user ID has been disabled, any attempt to change your password will not succeed.

Any user ID that has been inactive for more than 30 days is disabled. New user IDs that remain unused after 30 days are also disabled. If you enter the wrong password five times in a row when trying to log in, your user ID will be disabled. If your password has expired, if you have forgotten your current password, or if your user ID has been disabled for one of the reasons outlined previously, you will need to contact the User Services Group by telephone at (555) 867-5309 to have a new temporary password issued for your user ID. (It is necessary to contact the User Services Group by telephone because our security policy does not permit the transmission of sensitive information, such as passwords, by fax, e-mail, or voice mail.)

If you want to know when your current password is going to expire, you may contact the User Services Group by telephone at (555) 867-5309.

Choosing an Effective Password

Because of the presence of resourceful hackers, you must be careful in choosing your password. The following are recommendations that should make it much more difficult for a hacker to successfully break in to your user ID.

- Choose a password 12 characters in length. Most operating systems set a maximum of 8 characters for the length of the password. We require a 12-character password because longer passwords are much harder to crack than shorter ones. Any passwords fewer than 12 characters long will be rejected.

- Choose a password that is not a word or abbreviation in any dictionary, including foreign language dictionaries.

- Choose a password with one or more special (in other words, nonalphabetic, non-numeric) characters. If your password has only one nonalphabetic character, that character must not be the first or last character in the password string.
- Choose a password with one or more numeric characters.
- Choose a password with a mixture of uppercase and lowercase characters.
- Avoid simple strategies such as prepending or appending a digit to a word or name. These are some of the easiest passwords to crack.
- Avoid obvious keyboard patterns (such as QWERTY) or numbering schemes (such as 123).
- Avoid passwords that are common to your work such as star identifiers, computer names, and the like.
- Avoid names, especially names of family members, pets, or fictional characters from movies, books, or plays.
- Avoid using personal information (such as. your Social Security number, license plate number, telephone number, and so on) that may be easy to locate.
- Finally, choose a password that you can easily remember. The use of a passphrase may be helpful. (Select a phrase known only by you and use the first or last letter of each word in the phrase as your password.) Be aware that some passphrases may generate a sequence of characters that will match a word or abbreviation in the dictionary. You may have to try several different passphrases to find one that the password "cracker" will accept.

Other Common Precautions to Protect a Password

Here are some other tips:

- Use a different password wherever possible on the different computer systems to which you have access.
- Never give your password to a friend, a coworker, anyone. (This is a violation of our security policy as outlined in the organization's Rules of Behavior. This is also a breach of our information assurance policy and is punishable by law.)
- Do not write down your password. (If, while choosing a new password, you must write the password down, consign it to memory as soon as possible and destroy the materials upon which the password is written.)
- If some of your code or other procedures must contain a password, be careful that this code is itself protected against being read.
- Guard against exposing your password!

Part VI

APPENDIX

E

Sample Risk Analysis Table

Organizations are encouraged to create risk analysis tables. A table should exist for major systems and certainly for all mission-critical processes. This sample focuses on a banking industry analysis.

Description	Probability	Impact
External attack leading to compromise of user workstations by implementing malicious mobile code: This is an attack that could be carried out by users and/or systems connected to the Internet involving the installation of malicious mobile code on the server. This is then downloaded by clients and could result in local damage to the client.	*Medium:* Attack judged to be difficult to carry out.	*High:* Damage to reputation. Probable loss of customers. Possible legal action against the organization.
External attack leading to unauthorized modification of data content: This is an attack that could be carried out by users and/or systems connected to the Internet that leads to a modification of published data. This attack includes the hacking of web pages.	*High:* Available statistics indicate a high level of activity in this area.	*High:* Damage to reputation. Probable loss of customers. Long-term sustained damage to the image of the organization.

Description	Probability	Impact
External attack leading to unauthorized modification of web server software: This is an attack that could be carried out by users and/or systems connected to the Internet leading to some form of reconfiguration of the web server software.	*High:* Available statistics indicate a high level of activity in this area.	*High:* Possible change in behavior of the web server. If publicly visible, this could result in damage to reputation. May facilitate attack on data.
External attack leading to unauthorized modification of system configuration: This is an attack that could be carried out by users and/or systems connected to the Internet that leads to some form of reconfiguration of the OS.	*High:* Available statistics indicate a high level of activity in this area.	*High:* Loss of control of OS configuration. Facilitates attack on web server configuration and data. May be used as a basis for penetrating the internal network.
External attack resulting in denial of service: This is an attack that could be carried out by users and/or systems connected to the Internet that leads to denial of service.	*High:* Available statistics indicate a high level of activity in this area.	*High:* Can result in a serious impact on reputation. Loss of customers and market share. Loss in customer trust and confidence. Limited impact on home-banking clients.
Publication of material violating privacy laws: There is insufficient control, for example, of how information is segregated on the web server, and then this could lead to the leakage of private information from a home-banking system to public web pages. There are other application compromises in this area.	*High:* Because of lack of proper information security management controls being deployed.	*High:* Damage to reputation. Probable loss of customers. Possible legal action against the bank.

Description	Probability	Impact
External attack leading to unauthorized modification of data content: This is an attack that could be carried out by users and/or systems connected to the Internet that leads to a modification of published data. It includes the hacking of web pages.	*High:* Available statistics indicate a high level of activity in this area.	*High:* Damage to reputation. Probable loss of customers. Long-term sustained damage to the image of the organization.
External attack leading to unauthorized modification of web server software: This is an attack that could be carried out by users and/ or systems connected to the Internet leading to some form of reconfiguration of the web server software.	*High:* Available statistics indicate a high level of activity in this area.	*High:* Change in behavior of the web server. If publicly visible, this could result in damage to reputation. May facilitate attack on data.
External attack leading to unauthorized modification of system configuration: This is an attack that could be carried out by users and/or systems connected to the Internet that leads to some form of reconfiguration of the OS.	*High:* Available statistics indicate a high level of activity in this area.	*High:* Loss of control of OS configuration. Facilitates attack on web server configuration and data. May be used as a basis for penetrating the internal network.
External attack leading to compromise of user workstations by implementing malicious mobile code: This is an attack that could be carried out by users and/or systems connected to the Internet involving the installation of malicious mobile code on the server. This is then downloaded by clients and could result in local damage to the client.	*Medium:* Attack judged to be difficult to carry out.	*High:* Damage to reputation. Probable loss of customers. Possible legal action against the organization.

Description	Probability	Impact
External attack resulting in denial of service: This is an attack that could be carried out by users and/or systems connected to the Internet that leads to denial of service.	*High:* Available statistics indicate a high level of activity in this area.	*High:* Can result in a serious impact on reputation. Loss of customers and market share. Loss in customer trust and confidence. Limited impact on home-banking clients.
Publication of material violating privacy laws: There is insufficient control, for example, of how information is segregated on the web server, and then this could lead to the leakage of private information from a home-banking system to public web pages. There are other application compromises in this area.	*High:* Because of lack of proper information security management controls being deployed.	*High:* Damage to reputation. Probable loss of customers. Possible legal action against the bank.

APPENDIX

F

Select Privacy Laws and Regulations by Country/Economy or State

The following tables provide an overview of modern privacy laws and regulations.

Country/State/Economy	Laws and Regulations Related to Privacy
Argentina	Personal Data Protection Act of 2000 (a.k.a. Habeas Data); Data Protection Law N. 25.326: Section 27
Australia	Privacy Act of 1988–Amended in 2000; Federal Privacy Act; Telecommunications Act 1997; Crimes Act 1914; DataMatching Program (Assistance and Tax) Act 1990; Healthcare Identifiers Act 2010 (HI Act); Human Rights Act 2004; Listening Devices Act; Health Records (Privacy and Access) Act 1997
Austria	Federal Act on the Protection of Personal Data 2000; Austrian Civil Code
Belgium	Article 22 of the Belgian Constitution; Law of 8 December 1992 on Privacy Protection in Relation to the Processing of Personal Data
Brazil	Article 5 of the 1988 Constitution; Habeas Data Law 1997; Brazilian Civil Code
Bulgaria	The Bulgarian Personal Data Protection Act; Article 32 of the Bulgarian Constitution
Canada	The Privacy Act–1985; Personal Information Protection and Electronic Data Act (PIPEDA) of 2000 (Bill C-6); Safeguarding Canadians' Personal Information Act
Chile	Law for the Protection of Private Life
Colombia	Law 1266 of 2008
Cyprus	Processing of Personal Data Law of 2001; Part XI of the Banking Law

Country/State/Economy	Laws and Regulations Related to Privacy
Czech Republic	Act on Protection of Personal Data (April 2000) No. 101 1993; Charter of Fundamental Rights and Freedoms; Act 21–1992 on Banks
Denmark	Act on Processing of Personal Data, Act No. 429, May 2000; Danish Constitution (Article 72); § 263 of the Danish Penal Code on Secrecy of Mails
Estonia	Personal Data Protection Act of 2003. June 1996, Consolidated July 2002; Estonian Constitution Article 43; Estonia Data Bases Act
European Union	European Union Data Protection Directive of 1998 (Directive 95/46/EC); EU Internet Privacy Law of 2002 (Directive 2002/58/EC)
Finland	§ 10 of Constitution; Act on the Amendment of the Personal Data Act (986) 2000; Protection of Privacy and Data Security in Telecommunications Act; Protection of Privacy in Working Life; Act on Electronic Services and Communication in the Public Sector
France	Data Protection Act of 1978 (revised in 2004); Article 9 of the French Civil Code; Article 226 of the Criminal Code; French Labor Code; French Penal Code; Prime Ministerial Decree Relating to Access to Personal Information Held by Health Professionals and Institutions under Articles L.1111-7 and L1112-1 of the Code of Public Health
Germany	Article 10 of Basic Law; Federal Data Protection Law (2002); The Act on Employee Data Protection
Greece	The Hellenic Constitution of 1975; Law No. 2472 on the Protection of Individuals with Regard to the Processing of Personal Data, April 1997; Data Protection Authority Decision 115/2001; Data Protection Authority Decision No. 61/2004
Guernsey	Data Protection (Bailiwick of Guernsey) Law of 2001
Hong Kong	Personal Data Ordinance (PDPO); Article 29 of Basic Law
Hungary	Act LXIII of 1992 on the Protection of Personal Data and the Publicity of Data of Public Interests; Act XX of 1949 the Constitution of the Republic of Hungary; Act XLVII of 1997 on the Handling of Medical and Other Related Data
Iceland	Act of Protection of Individual; Processing Personal Data (Jan 2000)
India	Information Technology Act of 2000; Information Technology (Reasonable Security Practices and Procedures and Sensitive Personal Data or Information) Rules, 2011
Indonesia	Law No. 11/2008
Ireland	Data Protection (Amendment) Act, Number 6 of 2003
Isle of Man	Data Protection Act of 2002

Country/State/Economy	Laws and Regulations Related to Privacy
Israel	Section 7 of the Basic Law: Human Dignity and Liberty; Privacy Protection Law of 1981; Privacy Protection (Transfer of Databases Abroad) Regulation of 17 June 2001
Italy	Data Protection Code of 2003; Processing of Personal Data Act, January 1997
Japan	Article 13 of the Japanese Constitution; Personal Information Protection Act (PIPA); Law for the Protection of Computer Processed Data Held by Administrative Organs, December 1988
Latvia	Article 96 of the Latvian Constitution; Personal Data Protection Law, March 23, 2000
Lichtenstein	Data Protection Act 2002; Employment Act 2000
Lithuania	Article 22 and 29 of the constitution; Law on Legal Protection of Personal Data (June 1996)
Luxembourg	Law of 2 August 2002 on the Protection of Persons with Regard to the Processing of Personal Data
Malaysia	Personal Data Protection Act (PDPA) 2010
Malta	Data Protection Act (Act XXVI of 2001), Amended March 22, 2002, November 15, 2002 and July 15, 2003
Mexico	Ley Federal de Protección de Datos Personales en Posesión de los Particulares (Federal Law for the Protection of Personal Data Possessed by Private Persons)
Moldova	Law on State Secrets (1994); Law on Access to Information (2000); Constitution
Monaco	Constitution, Article 22; Act N° 1 165 of 23rd December 1993; Act N° 1 240 of 2nd July 2001; Article 308 of the Criminal Code
Morocco	Data Protection Act
Netherlands	Dutch Personal Data Protection Act 2000 as amended; Constitution
Newfoundland and Labrador	Privacy Act; Personal Health Information Act; Personal Information Protection and Electronic Documents Act (PIPEDA)
New South Wales	Workplace Surveillance Act 2005 No. 47; Privacy and Personal Information Protection Act 1998 No. 133 (NSW) (PPIP Act); National Privacy Principle 9; Section 5B of the Federal Privacy Act
New Zealand	Privacy Act, May 1993; Privacy Amendment Act, 1993; Privacy Amendment Act, 1994; Health Information Privacy Code
Northern Territory	Information Act 2002 No. 62 (NT)
Norway	Personal Data Act; Electronic Communications Act of 2003
Philippines	Data Privacy Act of 2011; Writ of Habeas Data; E-Commerce Law– Republic Act No. 8792
Pakistan	Article 4 of the 1973 Constitution
Peru	Constitution, Article 2.6

Country/State/Economy	Laws and Regulations Related to Privacy
Poland	Act of the Protection of Personal Data (August 1997)
Portugal	Act on the Protection of Personal Data (Law 67/98 of 26 October)
Romania	Law No. 677/2001 for the Protection of Persons Concerning the Processing of Personal Data and the Free Circulation of Such Data
Russia	Federal Law of the Russian Federation of 27 July 2006 No. 152-FZ On Personal Data; Federal Law on the Central Bank of the Russian Federation
Singapore	The E-commerce Code for the Protection of Personal Information and Communications of Consumers of Internet Commerce
Slovak Republic	Act No. 428 of 3 July 2002 on Personal Data Protection
Slovenia	Personal Data Protection Act, RS No. 55/99
South Africa	South African Constitution; Electronic Communications and Transactions Act, 2002
Republic of Korea	Act on Personal Information Protection of Public Agencies Act on Information and Communication Network Usage; Act on the Protection of Personal Data, Law No. 10465; Protection of Communications Secrets Act (1993)
Spain	Organic Law 15/1999 of 13 December on the Protection of Personal Data; Spanish Data Protection Act; Article 8 of the Spanish Constitution; Article 167 of the Penal Code; ROYAL DECREE 994/1999; Act 34/2002; Act 41/2002; Act 32/2003
Sweden	Personal Data Protection Act; Personal Data Ordinance
Switzerland	The Federal Law on Data Protection of 1992; Ordinance of 14 June 1993 to the Federal Act on Data Protection; Section 328 of the Code of Obligations; 1934 Swiss Banking Act; Article 47 of the Federal Act on Banks and Savings Banks
Taiwan	Computer-Processed Personal Data Protection Law 1995; Personal Data Protection Act
Tasmania	Personal Information and Protection Act 2004
Thailand	Official Information Act, B.E. 2540 (1997) for state agencies; Section 37 of Thai Constitution; Financial Institutions Business Act B.E. 2551
Ukraine	Law on Protection of Personal Data; Law on Information; Law on Data Protection in Automatic Systems
United Kingdom	UK Data Protection Act 1998; Privacy and Electronic Communications (EC Directive) Regulations 2003; Regulation of Investigatory Powers ("RIP") Act of 2000; Employment Practices Data Protection Code
Vietnam	Article 38 of the Civil Code 2005; The Law on Electronic Transactions 2008

Country/State/Economy	Laws and Regulations Related to Privacy
Singapore	Singapore Constitution's Bill of Rights
South Africa	South African Constitution; National Credit Act
South Australia	Code of Fair Information Practice
United Arab Emirates	Article 31 of the Constitution; Data Protection Law of 2007; Article 378 & 379 of the Penal Code; Dubai Electronic Transactions and Commerce Law
United States of America (Federal)	The Electronic Communications Privacy Act; Telephone Consumer Protection Act of 1991; Children's Online Privacy Protection Act; Fair Credit Reporting Act; Right to Financial Privacy Act; Taxpayer Browsing Protection Act; Gramm-Leach-Bliley Act; Fair and Accurate Credit Transactions Act; Census Confidentiality Statute of 1954; Freedom of Information Act; Privacy Act of 1974; Computer Security Act of 1987; E-government Act of 2002; Health Insurance Portability and Accountability Act; Administrative Procedure Act; Family Education Rights and Privacy Act; Privacy Protection Act of 1980; Cable Communications Policy Act of 1984; Video Privacy Protection Act of 1988; Employee Polygraph Protection Act of 1988; Driver's Privacy Protection Act of 1994; Controlling the Assault of Non-Solicited Pornography and Marketing Act of 2003; Do-Not-Call Implementation Act of 2003

U.S. State or Territory	Law
Alaska	Alaska Stat. § 45.48.010 *et seq.*
Arizona	Ariz. Rev. Stat. § 44-7501
Arkansas	Ark. Code § 4-110-101 *et seq.*
California	Cal. Civ. Code §§ 1798.29, 1798.80 *et seq.*
Colorado	Colo. Rev. Stat. § 6-1-716
Connecticut	Conn. Gen Stat. § 36a-701b
Delaware	Del. Code tit. 6, § 12B-101 *et seq.*
Florida	Florida Information Protection Act of 2014
Georgia	Ga. Code §§ 10-1-910, -911, -912; § 46-5-214
Hawaii	Haw. Rev. Stat. § 487N-1 *et seq.*
Idaho	Idaho Stat. §§ 28-51-104 to -107
Illinois	815 ILCS §§ 530/1 to 530/25
Indiana	Ind. Code §§ 4-1-11 *et seq.*, 24-4.9 *et seq.*
Iowa	Iowa Code §§ 715C.1, 715C.2
Kansas	Kan. Stat. § 50-7a01 *et seq.*
Louisiana	La. Rev. Stat. § 51:3071 *et seq.*

U.S. State or Territory	Law
Maine	Me. Rev. Stat. tit. 10 § 1347 *et seq.*
Maryland	Md. Code Com. Law §§ 14-3501 *et seq.*, Md. State Govt. Code §§ 10-1301 to -1308
Massachusetts	Mass. Gen. Laws § 93H-1 *et seq.*
Michigan	Mich. Comp. Laws §§ 445.63, 445.72
Minnesota	Minn. Stat. §§ 325E.61, 325E.64
Mississippi	Miss. Code § 75-24-29
Missouri	Mo. Rev. Stat. § 407.1500
Montana	Mont. Code § 2-6-504, 30-14-1701 *et seq.*
Nebraska	Neb. Rev. Stat. §§ 87-801, -802, -803, -804, -805, -806, -807
Nevada	Nev. Rev. Stat. §§ 603A.010 *et seq.*, 242.183
New Hampshire	N.H. Rev. Stat. §§ 359-C:19, -C:20, -C:21
New Jersey	N.J. Stat. § 56:8-163
New York	N.Y. Gen. Bus. Law § 899-aa, N.Y. State Tech. Law 208
North Carolina	N.C. Gen. Stat §§ 75-61, 75-65
North Dakota	N.D. Cent. Code § 51-30-01 *et seq.*
Ohio	Ohio Rev. Code §§ 1347.12, 1349.19, 1349.191, 1349.192
Oklahoma	Okla. Stat. §§ 74-3113.1, 24-161
Oregon	Oregon Rev. Stat. § 646A.600 *et seq.*
Pennsylvania	73 Pa. Stat. § 2301 *et seq.*
Rhode Island	R.I. Gen. Laws § 11-49.2-1 *et seq.*
South Carolina	S.C. Code § 39-1-90, 2013 H.B. 3248
Tennessee	Tenn. Code § 47-18-2107
Texas	Tex. Bus. & Com. Code §§ 521.002, 521.053, Tex. Ed. Code § 37.007(b)(5)
Utah	Utah Code §§ 13-44-101 *et seq.*
Vermont	Vt. Stat. tit. 9 § 2430, 2435
Virginia	Va. Code § 18.2-186.6, § 32.1-127.1:05
Washington	Wash. Rev. Code § 19.255.010, 42.56.590
West Virginia	W.V. Code §§ 46A-2A-101 *et seq.*
Wisconsin	Wis. Stat. § 134.98
Wyoming	Wyo. Stat. § 40-12-501 *et seq.*
District of Columbia	D.C. Code § 28- 3851 *et seq.*
Guam	9 GCA § 48-10 *et seq.*
Puerto Rico	10 Laws of Puerto Rico § 4051 *et seq.*
Virgin Islands	V.I. Code § 2208

G Information System Security Checklist

The following checklist represents a generic approach for a quick assessment of an information system. You can use the checklist for large or small systems and tailor it accordingly.

A. General information

1. A detailed understanding of threats to the organization.

2. A description of threats for individual locations.

3. A list containing phone numbers for all individuals involved in the organizational information assurance.

4. A policy document detailing how the information assurance personnel have access to the IT operations personnel.

5. Documentation on the training of all IT operations personnel.

6. An organization chart and documentation demonstrating the separation of duties to minimize opportunity for collusion.

7. Documentation of an IT operations information assurance group or equivalent. This documentation should include, but not necessarily be limited to, the following:

   a. Names, functions, and phone numbers of all members (for emergency access).

   b. Security specialists, operations specialists, physical security specialists, auditor, facilities engineer, communications security specialists, and others with appropriate skills.

8. Documentation for each area that demonstrates how an effective liaison has been established with local support activities in the following areas:

a. Plant engineering and facilities, construction, electrical, air conditioning, and site preparation

b. Physical security

c. Personnel

d. Safety (safety officer, fire marshal, transportation)

e. Records management

B. General information assurance

1. Documentation that each area has been designated a restricted area in accordance with current organizational policy, if appropriate

2. Documentation of information assurance policies and procedures

3. Documentation of internal audit efforts that determine compliance with information assurance procedures

4. Documentation of a formal risk management program

C. Fire risk and water damage analysis

1. Specific site documentation for fire risk and exposure should contain, but not necessarily be limited to, the following:

a. The construction techniques that demonstrate the fire resistance of the building containing the system. Raised floors and ceilings, curtains, rugs, furniture, and drapes should be from noncombustible materials.

b. The procedures used to manage the paper and other combustible supplies for the computer facilities. In addition, this should document the control of inflammable or dangerous activities in areas surrounding the server room.

c. The storage of portable (magnetic) media outside the server room.

d. The periodic training of operators and administrators in firefighting techniques and assigned responsibilities in case of fire.

2. Documentation that each site has appropriate fire protection.

a. Automated carbon dioxide. If so, do all personnel have training in the use of gas masks and other safety devices?

b. Halogenated agents.

c. Water (either wet pipe or pre-action alarm).

3. Documentation that portable fire extinguishers are spread strategically around the area with markers visible above equipment.

4. Documentation that power shutdown switches are accessible at points of exit. Switches should shut down the air conditioning as well.

5. Documentation on the location of smoke detectors. Are they located in the ceiling, under raised floors, or in air return ducts? It should answer the following questions:

   a. Will air-conditioning systems shut down on detection of smoke?

   b. Who will perform the engineering analysis on the functioning of smoke alarms and how often?

   c. Who tests smoke detection systems, and how often?

   d. Who is responsible for fire drills, and how often should they occur?

6. Documentation of subfloor cleaning and contents, if appropriate. It should include the following:

   a. Water supplies for firefighting

   b. Battery powered emergency/evacuation lighting

   c. Manual alarm systems

7. Documentation of fire alarm systems to include where they ring, who will respond, and how.

8. Documentation of 24-hour attendance and procedures for reporting problems.

9. Documentation of control of potential water damage that includes the following:

   a. The elimination of overhead water and steam pipes except for sprinklers

   b. The existence of subfloor drainage including drainage away from all hardware

   c. The protection of electrical systems from water damage in subfloor area

   d. The water integrity of doors, windows, and roof

   e. The location of sheeting materials for protection of hardware components from water damage

D. Air conditioning

   1. Documentation of the air-conditioning system should include the following:

      a. Unique use of computer air-conditioning system.

      b. The existence of fireproof ducts and filters.

      c. Location of compressor.

      d. Backup air conditioning availability.

      e. Fire protection of cooling tower, if applicable.

      f. Air intake protection with protective screening. Is it above street level?

      g. That the air intakes prevent the uptake of pollutants or debris.

   2. Document the temperature and humidity recording and control.

Part VI

E. Electrical system

1. The electrical system is frequently a weak link in information assurance. Workstations and mobile devices are often overlooked as a source of problems.

2. Document electrical system reliability by showing the following:

   a. That uninterruptible power supplies are available at those locations that require them

   b. That motor generator systems are backed up and that there are lightning arrestors on appropriate circuits

   c. The reliability of the commercial power supply and that it is clean power if the system relies on it

   d. That the physical security system will continue to function even after a power failure

   e. The backup system test frequency and results

F. Natural disasters

1. Document the resistance to natural disaster by showing the following:

   a. The structural soundness and resistance to windstorms, floods, and earthquakes. This would include demonstrating that the buildings are remote from earthquake faults or earthquake proof. Show relationship to geothermal/volcanic areas.

   b. Proper grounding of all electrical equipment for lightning protection.

G. Backup systems

1. Document the existence of backup systems for all critical systems at the site. This should include, but not be limited to, the following:

   a. A fully articulated agreements for backup computers in the following areas:

      1) The same room

      2) Another room in the same building

      3) A separate location including cloud providers

   b. Benchmarks or other indicators that the backup systems can, in fact, handle the intended workload.

   c. Copies of the contract granting access to systems and facilities owned by others.

   d. Quarterly tests, performed to familiarize staff with procedures for using backup system.

   e. A full security review and plan for backup system, if needed.

4. Document a fully written contingency plan covering the following:

   a. Individuals who are responsible for each functional area.

   b. A current "who calls whom" list with alternates. This list should include, but not be limited to, management, emergency crews, selected users, service personnel, facilities personnel, and points of contact at backup sites.

    c. Detailed descriptions of the criteria for determining the duration of disruptions to service.

    d. Individual responsibilities for retaining source documents and/or data files for each application.

    e. Individual responsibilities for the destruction or safeguarding of classified materials in the computer facility in the event the facility must be evacuated.

    f. Individual responsibility for the purchase or lease of new or temporary computer equipment.

    g. Individual responsibility for the acquisition of the following:

        1) Air-conditioning equipment

        2) Computer time/services

        3) Additional manpower

        4) Furnishings, cabinets, and so on

        5) Replacement tapes and disk packs

        6) Alternate sites and their preparation

        7) Travel accommodations for essential personnel

        8) Orderly transportation of computer jobs, personnel, and related materials and appropriate coordination with security

        9) Duplication of backup files

      10) Continuing security in the contingency mode

    h. Document the existence of a contingency training program for all computer personnel

H. Access control

    1. Document the access control that is unique to the computer facilities by showing the following:

      a. That a general guard schedule provides adequate physical security in accordance with the statement of threat and a positive identification system exists for all employees

      b. That the access to computer areas is restricted to selected personnel this would include, but not be limited to, the following:

        1) Unescorted access to the equipment.

        2) Files are segregated so that only specific individuals have access.

      c. That an adequate visitor control procedure exists that includes the following:

        1) Escorts procedures

        2) Proper training of potential escorts about their responsibilities

        3) Personnel trained to challenge improperly identified individuals

      d. That security and operations personnel are briefed on how to react to civil disturbances

e. That a good liaison program exists with local law enforcement agencies and that suitable articulation agreements are in place

f. That all personnel know how to handle telephone bomb threats

2. Document that background checks and rechecks are performed on all employees.

3. Document that policies exist to ensure that computer employees are cross-trained to cover all essential functions.

4. Document the existence of a continuing personnel education program in computer security matters. This should include, but not be limited to, the following:

a. Knowledge of the provisions of organizational security policies and procedures

b. Personnel training of supervisors in human behavior to aid managers in identifying changes in personality and living habits of their people

c. Personnel training of supervisors so that they can identify possibly disgruntled employees

d. Personnel policies that allow for containment or immediate dismissal of employees who may constitute a threat to installation

5. Document that all exterior windows accessible from the ground level are covered with metal grills.

6. Document that no one can gain access to the server area without the knowledge of a guard or another employee.

7. Document that the facilities are manned by at least two appropriately cleared personnel at all times.

8. Document that housekeeping standards for the computer room includes the prevention of accumulation of trash in the computer area and that floors (and associated under floor areas), equipment covers, and work surfaces are cleaned regularly.

9. Document that waste baskets in the computer room are of metal material with closing tops and that they are dumped outside the computer area to minimize dust.

10. Document smoking rules in the facility. If smoking is allowed, document the existence of self-extinguishing ashtrays.

I. System utilization

1. Document that the hardware utilization policy includes, but is not limited to, the following:

a. That systems comply with operations schedules.

b. That techniques exist for matching meter hours to operational hours. This is to ensure that the equipment is not being used for unauthorized purposes during off-duty hours.

   c. That a regular maintenance schedule exists for hardware to ensure reliability and that maintenance personnel have appropriate security clearance.

   d. That batch type jobs are logged and cross-checked against an authorized job list.

   e. That spot checks of output for possible misuse of a system are done and that output distribution systems prevent an unauthorized person from receiving a confidential report.

  2. Document communications control techniques.

  3. Document the existence of emanation security (no RFI detectable outside computer facility).

J. System operation

  1. Document that erasure and declassification procedures include the erasure and overwriting of sensitive data before the contents of that memory can be reused.

  2. Document that the necessary programs, equipment, and procedures exist for declassifying any and all computer equipment used for the processing or storing classified data on site.

  3. Document that policies exist for portable media (tapes, disks, flash drives) that require the following:

   a. Accountability for use and cleaning frequency of portable media

   b. Use by authorized individuals only

   c. The orderly filing of portable media

   d. Portable media storage (vertically and in containers) except when in use

   e. Tape and disk pack utilization records

   f. The frequent cleaning of tape heads to ensure data reliability

   g. Location of the media library in an area secure from explosion or other dangers

   h. The use of magnetic detection equipment to preclude the presence of a magnetic field near the magnetic media

   i. Adequate protection for magnetic media while in transit between locations

  4. Document that media or devices are marked with the following:

   a. Date of creation

   b. Highest classification/categorization level of any information contained on the media

   c. Downgrading or exemption instructions when placed in permanent files

   d. A unique identifier

   e. The classification of the system's environment when the product was produced, if the assigned classification cannot be immediately verified by the customer

f. Special access restrictions

g. Color codes

K. Software

1. Document that software security policy includes the following:

   a. That physical security includes backup file systems at a secondary location for both the programs and the associated documentation. Essential programs, software systems, and associated documentation of programs in the library are located in a locked vault or a secured area.

   b. That access to the essential programs on software systems is restricted to a need-to-know basis in the prime and backup areas.

   c. That a multilevel access control to the data files (read/write/update, block, record, field, and characters) is provided by various levels of security classification.

   d. That periodic checks are made to validate the security software utilities and the tables of access codes.

   e. That techniques are employed that preclude more than one user updating files at any given time, in those areas where remote access to online databases is allowed.

2. Document the following in those areas that allow access by remote terminals:

   a. That keyword or password protection with periodic changes of passwords is employed

   b. That data encryption (either hardware or software) techniques are employed during the transmission of sensitive data

L. Hardware

1. Document that the operating systems are protected from unauthorized activity by the following:

   a. Maintaining built-in protection to prevent the bypassing of security utilities and unauthorized access to databases by a knowledgeable information assurance professional familiar with the system

   b. Demonstrating that memory bounds are tested following maintenance, initial program load, and each restart

   c. Verifying vendor modifications to the operating system before being installed on the system

   d. Verifying all local modifications to the operating system by the information assurance team or personnel designated by it

   e. Maintaining a record of all operating system modifications until at least the next software release

   f. Monitoring software technologists to ensure that they do not circumvent the normal access procedures by the use of special coding

2. Document that application programs are designed to restart using internal recovery procedures.

3. Document that all programming changes and maintenance are well controlled.

4. Document that continuous monitoring is accomplished by showing the following:

    a. That a log of those who access data banks or sensitive files is maintained

    b. That there are software security routines that monitor unauthorized attempts to access portions of the system via online notification of an operator or end-of-day printout

    c. That attempts to misuse the system are followed up in a systematic manner and according to the appropriate rules established by the IT operations leadership and information assurance leadership

5. Document that in-house service personnel are controlled in their access to vital areas. All noncleared individuals should have special escorts while performing their tasks.

6. Document that a list of vendor authorized service and system support personnel is maintained. Positive identification of these individuals is required so that they do not compromise security.

M. Information security

1. Document that online and offline sensitive information is as follows:

    a. Protected by copies being maintained in a separate building from the original

    b. Stored in low fire-hazard containers

    c. Documented in a current inventory of the files

2. Document that system backup dry-runs are attempted on a regular (quarterly) basis and that the backups contain programs currently under development.

3. Document that program changes are controlled and recorded and that changes are made only to a reproduced version of the original program file with the original left intact.

4. Document that computer operations staff review systems documentation on a regular basis to ensure compliance with operational standards.

5. Document that minimum documentation standards are met throughout all operational sections. Documentation should include, but not be limited to, the following:

    a. Detailed production specifications

    b. A comprehensive narrative description of the function of the program

    c. Detailed logic or flowcharts following established industry standards

Part VI

    d. Current program listings

    e. Input and output formats

    f. Output samples

    g. User documentation

    h. Copies of test data used to generate output samples following the procedures in the user documentation

    i. Explanations of codes, tables, calculations, and other details unique to the particular program

    j. Explanations of all error messages and program halts

    k. Procedures for handling rejected records

    l. File sequence descriptions

    m. Control and balancing instructions

6. Document that duplicates of all documentation are stored in low fire-hazard storage equipment in a separate building from the original.

7. Document that the documentation is inventoried at least annually and that the backups are reviewed periodically to ensure that the documentation package is current.

8. Document that changes in programs and documentation are coordinated and approved by the cognizant areas and that these changes are reviewed by the internal auditor.

N. Data standards

1. Document that there is a retention cycle for all data files for all applications. This retention cycle review should include the following:

    a. Certification that the data and documentation retention cycles are coordinated with the data reconstruction procedures

    b. Review by the user for compliance

    c. Certification that the data files are maintained within and under the control of the organization rather than the user

    d. Certification that all files are properly classified in terms of degree of sensitivity and value to the organization

2. Document that the data files are kept in the following locations:

    a. An area other than the computer room

    b. A fire protected area

    c. An access-controlled area

    d. Low fire-hazard storage containers

3. Document dry-runs of the data security system that are performed periodically to ensure compliance with standard procedures.

4. Document that the staff members understand and comply with the legal requirements for file retention and that they understand the relative value of the programs and applications.

5. Document that an overall audit control philosophy relating to computer systems assets exists. This philosophy should include the following:

   a. System usage and production controls

   b. Control of user input to ensure receipt of all data

   c. Monitoring of output to meet established standards

   d. Error reporting and follow-up procedures

   e. Control of program changes

   f. Certification that all program options have been tested

   g. Certification that program conversions provide similar results and do not disrupt production continuity

   h. A policy detailing the separation of duties

   i. Policies for both hardware and software backups

   j. The auditability of the system

   k. A policy of auditor involvement during the development cycle

O. Shared resource (cloud) systems security

   1. Document that for resource sharing systems physical separation exists between tenants. This access may be controlled by one or more of the following:

      a. Locked doors

      b. Posted guards

      c. Other approved restraints

   2. Document that workstations are located such that each user's privacy is ensured.

   3. Document the use of authenticators (passwords, tokens) and the following about them:

      a. That they are tamper-proof

      b. That they are linked to individuals and locations

      c. That they are combined with physical keys

      d. That the ability to change passwords is closely controlled

   4. Document that systems software restricts a given individual to specific data files. This access should control the right to add, delete, or modify files.

5. Document that the system maintains accurate records of all activity against each data file and that security override procedures are closely monitored.

6. Document the procedures used to monitor the changes to the operating and security systems.

H References and Sources of Information

From its inception, the book has been designed so that each of the chapters are self-contained. For your convenience, all recommended readings and resources have been collected in this single location.

- (ISC)². www.isc2.org.

- "Top-Down Approach for Security." *Network Magazine.* Indian Express Newspapers, June 2003. www.networkmagazineindia.com/20030h6/is15.shtml.

- *ACM Computing Curricula Information Technology Volume: Model Curriculum.* ACM, Dec. 12, 2008. http://campus.acm.org/public/comments/it-curriculum-draft-may-2008.pdf.

- AICPA. GAAP Codification. www.aicpa.org/InterestAreas/ BusinessIndustryAndGovernment/Resources/FinancialAccountingReportingTax/ DownloadableDocuments/FASB%20%20accounting%20means%20to%20CFOpdf .pdf.

- Aiello, B. "How to Implement CM and Traceability in a Practical Way." September 2013. www.cmcrossroads.com/article/how-implement-cm-and-traceability-practical-way.

- Alles, E. J., Z.J. Geradts, and C.J. Veenman. "Source Camera Identification for Heavily JPEG Compressed Low Resolution Still Images." *Journal of Forensic Sciences,* 2009. 54(3): 628–638.

- American Recovery and Reinvestment Act of 2009 (ARRA). Title XIII, "Health Information Technology for Economic and Clinical Health Act (HITECH)," § 13600, 2009. www.gpo.gov/fdsys/pkg/BILLS-111hr1enr/pdf/BILLS-111hr1enr.pdf.

- *An Introduction to Computer Security: The NIST Handbook (Special Publication 800-100).* NIST, p. 16.

- *An Introduction to Computer Security: The NIST Handbook (Special Publication 800-12).* NIST, 1996.

- Armistead, E.L. *Information Warfare Separating Hype from Reality*. Potomac Books, 2007.

- Assante, M.J. Testimony on Securing Critical Infrastructure in the Age of Stuxnet. National Board of Information Security Examiners, November 17, 2010.

- Baker, Dixie B. *Assessing Controlled Access Protection*. The National Computer Security Center, Dec. 1, 2006. www.fas.org/irp/nsa/rainbow/tg028.htm.

- BCI. www.thebci.org/about.htm.

- Bejtlich, R. *Extrusion Detection: Security Monitoring for Internal Intrusion*. Addison-Wesley, 2005.

- Bejtlich, R. *The Tao of Network Security Monitoring: Beyond Intrusion Detection*. Addison-Wesley, 2004.

- Bem, Derek, and E. Huebner. "Computer Forensic Analysis in a Virtual Environment." *International Journal of Digital Evidence*, 2007. 6, no. 2: 1–13.

- Böhme, Rainer, et al. "Multimedia Forensics Is Not Computer Forensics." *Computational Forensics*, 2009. pp. 90–103.

- Bottom-up Investing in Investopedia.com. Investopedia ULC, 2007. www.investopedia.com/terms/b/bottomupinvesting.asp.

- Bowen, P., et al. *Information security: A Guide for Managers (Special Publication 800-100)*. NIST, 2006.

- Braid, M. "Collecting Electronic Evidence After a System Compromise." AUSCERT, 2001. www.auscert.org.au/render.html?it=2247.

- Brehmer, B. "The Dynamic OODA Loop: Amalgamating Boyd's OODA Loop and the Cybernetic Approach to Command and Control." 10th International Command and Control Research and Technology Symposium, 2005. pp. 1–15.

- Brooks, Frederick P. *The mythical man-month*. Vol. 1995. Addison-Wesley, 1975.

- Casey, E., and G.J. Stellatos. The Impact of Full Disk Encryption on Digital Forensics. ACM SIGOPS Operating Systems Review, 2008. 42(3), 93–98.

- Catalogue of Threat 2004 in IT-grundschutz Manual 2004, BSI (Bundesamt für Sicherheit in der Informationstechnik) Federal office for Information Security, Germany, 2004. www.bsi.de/english/gshb/manual/download/threat-catalogue.pdf.

- Center for Democracy and Technology. Health Privacy (web page), 2013. https://www.cdt.org/issue/health-privacy.

- CERT-SA, Computer Emergency Response Team: Saudi Arabia, 2008. www.cert.gov.sa/.

- Cheddad, A., et al. "Digital Image Steganography: Survey and Analysis of Current Methods. Signal Processing, 2010. 90(3), 727–752.

- Christensen, Sharon, et al. "An Achilles Heel: Denial of Service Attacks on Australian Critical Information Infrastructures." *Information & Communications Technology Law*. 19, no. 1 (2010): 61–85.

- Cloud Computing Synopsis and Recommendations. U.S. National Institute of Standards and Technology, 2012. http://csrc.nist.gov/publications/nistpubs/800-146/sp800-146.pdf.

- Cloud Security Alliance. Cloud Controls Matrix Version 3, 2014. https://cloudsecurityalliance.org/download/cloud-controls-matrix-v3-0-1/.

- CNSSI-4012, National Information Assurance Training Standard for Senior Systems Managers. June 2004. Supersedes NSTISSI No. 4012, August 1997.

- CNSSI-4013, National Information Assurance Training Standard for System Administrators (SA). March 2004.

- CNSSI-4014, Information Assurance Training Standard for Information Systems Security Officers. April 2004. Supersedes NSTISSI No. 4014, August 1997.

- CNSSI-4016, National Information Assurance Training Standard for Risk Analysts. November 2005.

- Code of Federal Regulations, Part 5 Administrative Personnel, Subpart C—Employees Responsible for the Management or Use of Federal Computer Systems, Section 930.301 through 930.305 (5 C.F.R 930.301-305).

- Conklin, Wm. Arthur, et al. *Introduction to Principles of Computer Security: Security+ and Beyond.* McGraw-Hill Education, March 2004.

- Data classification. HDM Clariza Initiatives, June 16, 2007. www.trehb101.com/index.php?/archives/71-data-classifation.html.

- Data Protection Act 1998, Chapter 29. 1998. www.legislation.gov.uk/ukpga/1998/29/data.pdf.

- DeCew, JW. *In Pursuit of Privacy: Law, Ethics, and the Rise of Technology.* Cornell University Press, 1997.

- Directive Administrative Controls. China Education and Research Network Computer Emergency Response Team (CCERT). https://www.cccure.org/Documents/HISM/015-019.html (Citing (ISC)[2]).

- Dittrich, David, and S. Dietrich. "P2P As Botnet Command and Control: A Deeper Insight." Proceedings of the 2008 3rd International Conference on Malicious and Unwanted Software (Malware), October 2008. http://staff.washington.edu/dittrich/misc/malware08-dd-final.pdf.

- Do's and Don'ts for Effective Configuration Management, TechTarget. http://blogs.pinkelephant.com/images/uploads/pinklink/Dos_Donts_For_Effective_Configuration_Management.pdf.

- Dove, R. "Embedding Agile Security in System Architecture." Insight 12, no. 2 (2009): 14–17.

- DRI International. *Generally Accepted Practices for Business Continuity Practitioners.* Disaster Recovery Journal and DRI International, 2005. DRII. www.drii.org.

- Drucker, Peter F. *The Age of Discontinuity: Guidelines to Our Changing Society.* William Heinemann Ltd., 1969.

- Drucker, Peter F. *Management: Tasks, Responsibilities, Practices.* Harper & Row, 1973.

- Electronic Privacy Information Center. http://epic.org/.

- *Encyclopedia of Applied Ethics.* Academic Press, 1998.

- Fabro, M., and V. Maio. Using Operational Security (OpSec) to Support a Cyber Security Culture in Control System Environment, 2007. http://csrp.inl.gov/Documents/OpSec%20Rec%20Practice.pdf.

- Falliere N., L.O. Murchu, and E. Chien. W32.Stuxnet Dossier. Symantex, February 2011. www.wired.com/images_blogs/threatlevel/2011/02/Symantec-Stuxnet-Update-Feb-2011.pdf.

- Federal Information Security Management Act of 2002 (Public Law 107-347, Title III). December, 2002. http://csrc.nist.gov/drivers/documents/FISMA-final.pdf.

- Federal Reserve Bank of Atlanta. Into the Breach: Protecting the Integrity of the Payment System, February 10, 2014. http://portalsandrails.frbatlanta.org/emv/.

- Financial Accounting Standards Board., GAAP Report. www.fasb.org.

- Financial Fraud Action UK. Fraud the Facts, 2013. www.financialfraudaction.org.uk/download.asp?file=2772.

- *FIPS Publication 199, Standards for Security Categorization of Federal Information and Information Systems.* National Institute of Standards and Technology, 2004. http://csrc.nist.gov/publications/fips/fips199/FIPS-PUB-199-final.pdf.

- First Data, EMV, and Encryption + Tokenization: A Layered Approach to Security, 2012. www.firstdata.com/downloads/thought-leadership/EMV-Encrypt-Tokenization-WP.PDF.

- Friedlob, GT, and FJ Plewa. "An Auditor's Primer on Encryption." *CPA Journal,* 67.11 (1997): 40–46.

- Friedlob, GT, FJ Plewa, T. Schleifer, and C.D. Schou. "An Auditor's Introduction to Encryption." Institute of Internal Auditors, 1998.

- Frost, J.C. Springer, J.M. Springer, and C.D. Schou. Instructor guide and materials to accompany principles of *Introduction to Principles of Computer Security: Security+ and Beyond.* McGraw-Hill Education, 2004.

- Frost, James, and C.D. Schou. "Looking Inward for Competitive Strength in the International Arena." Presented at the Mountain Plains Management Association Meetings. October 1993.

- G Data Development. G Data TechPaper #0271, 2013, G Data, Germany, Patch Management Best Practices, www.cpni.gov.uk/Documents/Publications/2006/2006029-GPG_Patch_management.pdf.

- Garfinkel, Simson. "Anti-forensics: Techniques, Detection, and Countermeasures." *The 2nd International Conference on i-Warfare and Security* (ICIW), 2007. pp. 77–84.

- Good Practice Guide Patch Management. NISCC National Infrastructure Security Co-ordination Center, 2006. www.docstoc.com/docs/7277421/Good-Practice-Guide-Patch-Management.

- Good Practice Guidelines. *A Framework for Business Continuity Management.* Business Continuity Institutes (BCI). 2005.

- Gross, I., and P. Greaves. *Risk Management: A Guide to Good Practice for Higher Education Institutions.* HEFCE, 2001. www.hefce.ac.uk/pubs/ hefce/2001/01_28/01_28.pdf.

- *Guide to CISSP.* Information Security Certification, 2007. www.guidetocissp.com.

- Gurgul, P. "Access Control Principles and Objective." securitydocs.com, 2004. www.securitydocs.com/library/2770.

- Hellman, Martin E. "The Mathematics of Public-Key Cryptography." *Scientific American,* August 1979, pp.146–157.

- Hernandez, Steven G. *The Official (ISC)² Guide to the HCISPP CBK.* (ISC)² Press, 2014.

- Herold, R. *Multi-dimensional Enterprise-wide Security: Corporate Reputation and The Definitive Guide to Security Inside the Perimeter.* Realtime Publishers. http:// searchsecurity.techtarget.com/generic/ 0, 295582, sid14_gci1156151, 00.html.

- Hill, K. "How Target Figured Out A Teen Girl Was Pregnant Before Her Father Did." Forbes, 2014. www.forbes.com/sites/kashmirhill/2012/02/16/how-target-figured-out-a-teen-girl-was-pregnant-before-her-father-did/.

- HIPAA Case Examples and Resolution Agreements. www.hhs.gov/ocr/privacy/ hipaa/enforcement/examples/index.html.

- Holtzman, DH. *Privacy Lost: How Technology Is Endangering Your Privacy.* Jossey-Bass, 2006.

- Homeland Security Presidential Directive 12. Policy for a Common Identification.

- Honeypot Background. honeyd.org, 2002. www.honeyd.org/background.php.

- Howard, M., and S. Lipner. *The Security Development Lifecycle,* Microsoft Press, 2006.

- Hu, Vincent, and K. Scarfone. Interagency Report 7874, "Guidelines for Access Control System Evaluation Metrics." U.S. National Institute of Standards and Technology, September 2012. http://csrc.nist.gov/publications/nistir/ir7874/ nistir7874.pdf.

- Hu, Vincent, D.F. Ferraiolo, and D.R. Kuhn. Interagency Report 7316, "Assessment of Access Control Systems." NIST, September 2006. http://csrc.nist.gov/publications/ nistir/7316/NISTIR-7316.pdf.

- IBM Internet Security Systems. A Strategic Approach to Protecting SCADA and Process Control Systems. www.iss.net/documents/whitepapers/SCADA.pdf.

- Information Government Toolkit. *Information Security Assurance – Social Care Guidance.* National Health Service (NHS). United Kingdom, June 16, 2007. https:// www.igt.connectingforhealth.nhs.uk/guidance/IS_Sc_310_V5%2007-04-27.doc.

Part VI

- Information Security Media Group. "NIST Issues Access-Control Guidance." Bank Info Security, Sept. 23, 2012. www.bankinfosecurity.com/nist-issues-access-control-guidance-a-5134.

- *Information Technology – Security Techniques – Code of Practice for Information Security Management (ISO/IEC 17799)*, ISO/IecIEC.

- Intelligence Community Directive Number 704. "Personnel Security Standards and Procedures Governing Eligibility for Access to Sensitive Compartmented Information and Other Controlled Access Program Information." October 2008.

- Interim Report to the Department of Homeland Security. Development of a Baseline Set of Technical Metrics, January 2007.

- International Organization Standardization and the International Electrotechnical Commission 2005. *Information Technology – Security Techniques – Code of Practice for Information Security Management (ISO/IEC 17799)*. ISO/IecIEC, 2005.

- International Organization Standardization and the International Electrotechnical Commission 2013. *Information Technology – Security Techniques – Code of Practice for Information Security Controls (ISO/IEC 27002)*. ISOIEC. www.iso.org/iso/home/store/catalogue_ics/catalogue_detail_ics.htm?csnumber=54533.

- International Organization Standardization and the International Electrotechnical Commission. *Information Technology – Security Techniques – Information Security Management Systems – Requirements (ISO/IEC 27001)*. International Organization Standardization and the International Electrotechnical Commission, 2005.

- ISACA. www.isaca.org/.

- *ISO 9000:2000 Frequently Asked Questions*. International Standardization for Organization (ISO), 2004. www.iso.org/iso/en/iso9000-14000/explore/transition/faqs.html?printable=true.

- ISO TR 13569. *Banking and Related Financial Services – Information Security Guidelines*.

- ISO/IEC 13335. *Information Technology – Security Techniques – Management of Information and Communications Technology Security*.

- ISO/IEC 27001:2005. *Information Technology – Security Techniques – Information Security Management Systems – Requirements*.

- ISO/IEC 27002:2005. *Information Technology – Security Techniques – Requirements for Bodies Providing Audit and Certification of Information Security Management System*.

- ISO/IEC 27003:2010. *Information Technology – Security Techniques – Information Security Management System Implementation Guidance*.

- ISO/IEC 27004:2009. *Information Technology – Security Techniques – Information Security Management – Measurement*.

- ISO/IEC 27005:2011. *Information Technology – Security Techniques – Information Security Risk Management*.

- ISO/IEC 27006:2011. *Information Technology – Security Techniques – Requirements for Bodies Providing Audit and Certification of Information Security Management Systems*.

- ISO/IEC 27007:2011. *Information Technology – Security Techniques – Guidelines for Information Security Management Systems Auditing.*

- ISO/IEC 27010:2012. *Information Technology – Security Techniques – Information Security Management Guidelines for Inter-sector and Inter-organizational Communications.*

- ISO/IEC 27011:2008. *Information Technology – Security Techniques – Information Security Management Guidelines for Telecommunications Organizations Based on ISO/IEC 27002.*

- ISO/IEC TR 27008:2011. *Information Technology – Security Techniques – Guidelines for Auditors on Information Security Controls.*

- ISSA. www.issa.org/.

- Jansen, W. Directions in Security Metrics Research. NIST special publications, April 2009.

- Jelen. G. SSE-CMM Security Metrics, The National Institute of Standards and Technology (NIST) and Computer System Security and Privacy Advisory Board (CSSPAB) Workshop. Washington, D.C., June 13–14, 2000.

- Jones, K.J., R. Bejtlich, and C.W. Rose. *Real Digital Forensics: Computer Security and Incident Response.* Addison-Wesley, 2005.

- Karen, R. *We've Had an Incident, Who Do We Get to Investigate.* SANS Institute, 2002. www.sans.org/rr/whitepapers/incident/652.php.

- Kent, K., and M. Souppaya. *Guide to Computer Security Log Management (Management (SP800-92).* NIST, 2006.

- Kessler, Gary C. "Anti-forensics and the Digital Investigator." Australian Digital Forensics Conference, 2007. p. 1.

- Kirk, P. *Crime Investigation: Physical Evidence and the Police Laboratory.* Interscience Publishers, 1953.

- Korea Internet Security Agency (KISA). www.kisa.or.kr/eng/main.jsp.

- Kruse II, WG, and JG Heiser. *Computer Forensics: Incident Response Essentials.* Addison-Wesley, 2005.

- Kurosawa, K., K. Kuroki, and N. Akiba. "Individual Camera Identification Using Correlation of Fixed Pattern Noise in Image Sensors." *Journal of Forensic Sciences*, 54(3), 2009. 639–641.

- Linden, E.V. Focus on Terrorism, Volume 9. Nova Science Publishing, 2007.

- *Little Inefficiencies Could Lead to Large Operational Losses/Risks in Hi-Tech Security Solutions*, 004, Technews Publishing Ltd, 2006. www.securitysa.com/news. aspx?pklNewsId=14 4&pklIssueId=60&pklCategoryID=106.

- Little, D.B., and D.A. Chapa. *Implementing Backup and Recovery: The Readiness Guide for the Enterprise.* Wiley, 2003.

- Maconachy, V.C., et al. "A Model for Information Assurance: An Integrated Approach." Proceedings of the 2nd Annual IEEE Systems, Man, and Cybernetics Information Assurance Workshop, West Point, New York. June 5–6, 2001. pp. 306–310.

- Malaysian Public Sector Information Security Risk Assessment Methodology (MyRAM), 2006, Malaysian Administrative Modernisation and Management Planning Unit (MAMPU), Malaysia.

- Manadhata P.K., et al. An Approach to Measuring a System's Attack Surface, CMU-CS-07-146. Carnegie Mellon University, August 2007. http://reports archive .adm.cs.cmu.edu/anon/2007/CMU-CS-07-146.pdf.

- Manson, Dan, et al. "Is the Open Way a Better Way? Digital Forensics Using Open Source Tools." *System Sciences*, 2007. HICSS 2007. 40th Annual Hawaii International Conference, pp. 266b–266b. IEEE, 2007.

- Marlin, S. "Customer Data Losses Blamed on Merchants and Software." *Information Week*, 2005. www.informationweek.com/showArticle.jhtml?articleID=161601930.

- McConnell, P. *A Perfect Storm: Why Are Some Operational Losses Larger Than Others?* Portal Publishing Ltd. www.continuitycentral.com/Perfect_Basel.pdf.

- McKemmish, Rodney. "What Is Forensic Computing?" Australian Institute of Criminology, 1999.

- Mitropoulos, S., et al. "On Incident Handling and Response: A State-of-the-Art Approach." *Computers & Security*, 25, no. 5 (2006): 351–370.

- Mohay, George M., et al. *Computer and Intrusion Forensics*. Artech House, 2003.

- Morris, Thomas H., et al. "Engineering Future Cyber-physical Energy Systems: Challenges, Research Needs, and Roadmap." North American Power Symposium (NAPS). pp. 1–6. IEEE, 2009.

- Morris, Thomas, R. Vaughn, and Y.S. Dandass. "A Testbed for SCADA Control System Cybersecurity Research and Pedagogy." Proceedings of the Seventh Annual Workshop on Cyber Security and Information Intelligence Research. p. 27. ACM, 2011.

- MyCERT, Malaysia Computer Emergency Response Team. 2013. www.mycert.org. my/en/index.html.

- *NASA IT Security Handbook: Access Control.* U.S. National Aeronautics and Space Administration, Dec. 21, 2011. www.nasa.gov/pdf/613762main_ITS-HBK-2810 .15-01_%5BAC%5D.pdf.

- Nash, A., et al. *PKI: Implementing and Managing E-security*. McGraw-Hill Education, 2001.

- National Cyber Security Research and Development Challenges Related to Economics. Physical Infrastructure and Human Behavior: An Industry, Academic and Government Perspective. The Institute for Information Infrastructure Protection (I3P), 2009.

- National Institute of Standards and Technology Federal Information Processing Standard 199, Standards for Security Categorization of Federal Information and Information Systems. February 2004.

- National Institute of Standards and Technology Federal Information Processing Standards Publication 201-1, Personal Identity Verification (PIV) of Federal Employees and Contractors. March 2006.

- National Institute of Standards and Technology. *Special Publication An Introduction to Computer Security: The NIST Handbook* (Special Publication 800-12). 1996.

- National Institute of Standards and Technology. *Special Publication 800-60, Guide for Mapping Types of Information and Information Systems to Security Categories.* NIST, June 2004.

- National Institute of Standards and Technology. *Special Publication 800-18, Revision 1, Guide for Developing Security Plans for Federal Information Systems.* February 2006.

- National Institute of Standards and Technology. *Special Publication 800-30, Revision 1, Guide for Conducting Risk Assessments.* September 2012.

- National Institute of Standards and Technology. *Special Publication 800-37, Revision 1, Guide for Applying the Risk Management Framework to Federal Information Systems: A Security Life Cycle Approach.* February 2010.

- National Institute of Standards and Technology. *Special Publication 800-53, Revision 3, Recommended Security Controls for Federal Information Systems and Organizations.* August 2009.

- National Institute of Standards and Technology. *Special Publication 800-53A, Revision 1, Guide for Assessing the Security Controls in Federal Information Systems and Organizations: Building Effective Security Assessment Plans.* June 2010.

- National Institute of Standards and Technology. *Special Publication 800-137, Initial Public Draft, Information Security Continuous Monitoring for Federal Information Systems and Organizations.* December 2010.

- National Institute of Standards and Technology. *Special Publication 800-37, Revision 1, Guide for Applying the Risk Management Framework to Federal Information Systems: A Security Life Cycle Approach.* February 2010.

- National Institute of Standards and Technology. *Special Publication 800-39, Managing Information Security Risk: Organization, Mission, and Information System View.* March 2011.

- National Institute of Standards and Technology. *Special Publication 800-16, A Role-Based Model for Federal Information Technology/Cyber Security Training.* NIST. http://csrc.nist.gov/publications/drafts/800-16-rev1/draft_sp800_16_rev1_2nd-draft.pdf.

- National Institute of Standards and Technology. *Special Publication 800-100, Information Security Handbook: A Guide for Managers.* October 2006.

- National Institute of Standards and Technology. *Special Publication 800-53, Revision 4, Recommended Security Controls for Federal Information Systems and Organizations.* DOC, April 2013.

- National Institute of Standards and Technology. *Special Publication 800-60, Volume I Revision 1, Guide for Mapping Types of Information and Information Systems to Security Categories.* NIST, 2008. http://csrc.nist.gov/publications/nistpubs/800-60-rev1/SP800-60_Vol1 Rev1.pdf.

- Nestler, Vincent J. *Computer Security Lab Manual (Information Assurance and Security).* McGraw-Hill Education, 2005.

Part VI

- Nestler, Vincent J., et al. *Principles of Computer Security CompTIA Security+ and Beyond Lab Manual.* McGraw-Hill Education, 2011.

- Ng, T.T., et al. "Passive-Blind Image Forensics." *Multimedia Security Technologies for Digital Rights.* Academic Press, 2006. pp. 383–412.

- NIATEC training materials web site. http://niatec.info/pdf.aspx?id=169.

- Nichols, R. *Defending Your Digital Assets Against Hackers, Crackers, Spies, and Thieves.* McGraw-Hill Education, 2000.

- NIST FIPS 140 Series. http://csrc.nist.gov/groups/STM/cmvp/documents/140-1/140val-all.htm.

- NIST FIPS 140-1. http://csrc.nist.gov/publications/fips/fips1401.htm.

- NIST FIPS 140-2. http://csrc.nist.gov/publications/fips/fips140-2/fips1402.pdf.

- *NIST FIPS 199, Standards for Security Categorization of Federal Information and Information Systems.* DOC, February 2004.

- *NIST FIPS 200, Minimum Security Requirements for Federal Information and Information Systems.* DOC, March 2006.

- NIST. Process or Product Monitoring and Control. www.itl.nist.gov/div898/handbook/toolaids/pff/pmc.pdf.

- NIST. What Are Process Control Techniques? www.itl.nist.gov/div898/handbook/pmc/section1/pmc12.htm.

- NSTISSI-4011 National Training Standard for Information Systems Security (INFOSEC) Professionals. CNSS, June 1994.

- NSTISSI-4011, National Training Standard for Information Systems Security (INFOSEC) Professionals. CNSS, 2004. https://www.cnss.gov/CNSS/issuances/Instructions.cfm.

- NSTISSI-4015, National Training Standard for Systems Certifiers. November 2000.

- Office of Management and Budget Memorandum M-01-05, Guidance on Inter-Agency Sharing of Personal Data—Protecting Personal Privacy. December 2000.

- Office of Management and Budget Memorandum M-03-22, OMB Guidance for Implementing the Privacy Provisions of the E-Government Act of 2002. September 2003.

- Office of Management and Budget Memorandum M-04-26, Personal Use Policies and File Sharing Technology. September 2004.

- Office of Management and Budget. Circular A-130, "Appendix III, Transmittal Memorandum #4, Management of Federal Information Resources." November 2000.

- Official Journal of the European Communities, Directive 2002/58/EC of the European Parliament and of the Council of 12 July 2000 concerning the processing of personal data and the protection of privacy in the electronic communications sector (Directive on privacy and electronic communications), www.spamlaws.com/f/docs/ 00 -5 -ec.pdf.

- Organization for Economic Co-operation and Development. OECD Guidelines on the Protection of Privacy and Transborder Flows of Personal Data, 1980. www.oecd .org/internet/ieconomy/oecdguidelinesontheprotectionofprivacyandtransborder flowsofpersonaldata.htm.

- Panye, SC. *A Guide to Security Metrics*. SANS Institute, 2006. www.sans.org/reading_ room/whitepapers/auditing/55.php.

- Pauna, Adrian, and K. Moulinos. "Window of Exposure…A Real Problem for SCADA Systems?" ENISA, December 2013. www.enisa.europa.eu/activities/ Resilience-and-CIIP/critical-infrastructure-and-services/scada-industrial-control-systems/window-of-exposure-a-real-problem-for-scada-systems.

- Payment Card Industry (PCI) Data Security Standard, November 2013. https:// www.pcisecuritystandards.org/documents/PCI_DSS_v3.pdf.

- Payment Card Industry (PCI). PCI Point-to-Point Encryption: Solution Requirements and Testing Procedures, July 2013. https://www.pcisecuritystandards.org/documents/ P2PE_Hybrid_v1.1.1.pdf.

- Payment Card Industry Data Security Standard. PCI DSS Applicability in an EMV Environment, Version 1, October 2010. https://www.pcisecuritystandards.org/ documents/pci_dss_emv.pdf.

- Payne, S.C. A Guide to Security Metrics. SANS Security Essentials GSEC Practical Assignment, Version 1.2e. June 19, 2006. www.sans.org/reading_room/whitepapers/ auditing/55.php.

- PCI Security Standards Council. PCI for Small Merchants. https://www .pcisecuritystandards.org/smb/index.html.

- Physical and Environmental Security Guideline. Information Technology at Emory University, Atlanta. http://it.emory.edu/showdoc.cfm?docid=1860.

- Pipkin, D. *Information Security: Protecting the global enterprise.* Hewlett-Packard, 2000.

- Ponemon Institute. Third Annual Survey on Medical Identity Theft. June 2012. www.ponemon.org/local/upload/file/Third_Annual_Survey_on_Medical_Identity_ Theft_FINAL.pdf.

- Porter, EM. "Competitive Advantage." *Free Press*, 2004. www.12manage.com/ methods_ porter_competitive_advantage.html.

- Prahalad, C.K., and G. Hamel. "The Core Competence of the Corporation." *Harvard Business Review*, May–June 1990.

- Preston, W.C. *Backup & Recovery.* O'Reilly Media, 2007.

- Privacy Act of 1974 (P.L. 93-579).

- Privacy Rights Clearinghouse. Chronology of Data Breaches 2005 – Present. https://www.privacyrights.org/data-breach.

- Prosise, C., K. Mandia, and M. Pepe. *Incident Response and Computer Forensics.* McGraw-Hill Education, 2003.

Part VI

- Rasmussen, GT. *Implementing Information Security: Risks vs. Cost.* 2005. www .gideonrasmussen.com/article-07.html.

- Report to the Department of Homeland Security. INL/EXT-06-12016, Cyber Security Metrics, December 2006.

- Risk Management AS/NZS 4360:1999, 1999. Standards Association of Australia, Australia. www.google.com/search?sourceid=navclient&ie=UTF-8&rlz=1T4GGIH_ enUS242US242&q=AS%2fNZS+4360%3a1999.

- Rosenbush, Steve. Target Warning Shows Limits of Cyber Intelligence. http://blogs .wsj.com/cio/2014/02/14/target-warning-shows-limits-of-cyber-intelligence/.

- Rusell, C. "Security Awareness – Implementing an Effective Strategy." SANS Institute, 2002. www.sansorg/reading_room/whitepapers/awareness/416.php.

- Ryan, D., et al. *On Security Education, Training and Certifications.* Information Systems Audit and Control Association, 2004.

- Ryan, D., J.C.H. Julie, and C.D. Schou. On Security Education, Training, and Certifications. Information Systems Audit and Control Association, 2004.

- Sademies, S. Process Approach to Information Security Metrics in Finnish Industry and States Institutions. VTT Technical Research Center of Finland, 2004. www.vtt .fi/inf/pdf/publications/2004/p544.pdf.

- Sadowsky, G., et.al., *Information Technology Security Handbook, The International Bank for Reconstruction and Development.* www.infodev-security.net/book/.

- SAI Global. *Practitioners Guide to Business Continuity Management (HB 292-2006).* SAI, 2006.

- SANS Institute and Ed Skoudis. *Incident Handling Guidelines.* SANS, 2004.

- SANS Institute. www.sans.org/.

- Savola, Reijo M. Towards a Taxonomy for Information Security Metrics. International Conference on Software Engineering Advances (ICSEA 2007). Cap Esterel, France, August 2007.

- Scarfone, K., and P. Mell. *Guide to Intrusion Detection and Prevention Systems (SP800-94).* NIST, 2007.

- Schmidt, Howard A. *Larstan's The Black Book on Government Security.* Transition Vendor, 2006.

- Schmidt, Howard A. *Patrolling Cyberspace: Lessons Learned from a Lifetime in Data Security.* Larstan Publishing, 2006.

- Schmidt, Howard A. *Larstan's The Black Book on Government Security.* Transition Vendor, 2006.

- Schou, Corey D., and D.P. Shoemaker. *Information Assurance for the Enterprise: A Roadmap to Information Security.* McGraw-Hill Education, 2008.

- Schou, Corey D., et al. "Defining Information Security Education, Training, and Awareness Needs Using Electronic Meeting Space. In Enabling Technologies for

Law Enforcement and Security (pp. 356–367). International Society for Optics and Photonics, January 1999.

- Schou, Corey D., et al. "Business Process Reengineering: Increasing Empowerment And Enablement." Proceedings Federal Software Technology Conference. Salt Lake, Utah. April 1995.

- Schou, Corey D., and K. J. Trimmer. "Information Assurance and Security," *Journal of Organizational and End User Computing*, vol. 16, no. 3, July–September 2004.

- Schou, Corey D., W.V. Maconachy, and J. Frost. *Developing Awareness, Training and Education: A Cost Effective Tool for Maintaining System Integrity.* SEC 1993:53–63.

- Security Standards Council. *PCI SSC Data Security Standards Overview.* https://www.pcisecuritystandards.org/security_standards/.

- Security Tools to Administer Windows Server 2012. Microsoft, October 2012 http://technet.microsoft.com/en-us/library/jj730960.aspx.

- Slay, J., and M. Miller. *The Maroochy Water SCADA Breach: Implications of Lessons Learned for Research in Advances for Critical Infrastructure Protection.* Springer, 2007.

- Slay, J., et al. "Process Control System Security and Forensics: A Risk Management Simulation." *Proceedings of SIMTECT 09.* Adelaide, June 15–19, 2009.

- Stamp, M. *Information Security Principles and Practice.* Wiley-Interscience, 2005.

- Standard for Federal Employees and Contractors. August 2004.

- Sullivan, D. *Balancing the Cost and Benefits of Countermeasures.* RealTime Publishers, 2007. http://search security.techtarget.com/general/0, 295582, sid14_ gci1237327, 00.html.

- Swanson, M., and B. Guttman. *Generally Accepted Principles and Practices for Securing Information Technology Systems.* NIST, 1996.

- Swanson, M., et al. *Contingency Planning Guide for Information Technology Systems (SP 800-34).* NIST, 2002.

- Swanson, M., et al. *Security Metrics Guide for Information Technology Systems (Special Publication 800-55).* U.S. Government Printing Office, 2003.

- The CIS Security Metrics Service. The Center for Internet Security (CIS), July 1, 2008. http://securitymetrics.org/content/attach/Metricon3.0/metricon3-kreitner%20handout.pdf.

- The Common Criteria Evaluation and Validation Scheme. www.niap-ccevs.org/cc-scheme/.

- The European Data Protection Directive, 2001. http://eur-lex.europa.eu/LexUriServ/LexUriServ.do?uri=OJ:L:2001:008:0001:0022:en:PDF.

- The First National Security Statement to the Australian Parliament. The Prime Minister of Australia the Hon. Kevin Rudd MP, December 4, 2008. http://pmrudd.archive.dpmc.gov.au/sites/default/files/file/documents/20081204_national_security_statement.pdf.

- The Honeynet Project. www.honeynet.org/about.

- The Patient Protection and Affordable Care Act of 2010. Pub. L. No. 111-148, § 124 Stat. 119, 2010. www.gpo.gov/fdsys/pkg/PLAW-111publ148/pdf/PLAW-111publ148.pdf.

- Tipton, Harold F., and S. Hernandez, *Official (ISC)² guide to the CISSP CBK 3rd edition.* ((ISC)² Press, 2012.

- Tipton, Harold F., and M. Krause. *Information Security Management Handbook,* 5th edition. Auerbach, 2006.

- Tipton, Harold F., and M. Krause. *Information Security Management Handbook,* 4th Edition. Auerbach, 2002.

- Toigo, J.W. *Holy Grail of Data Storage Management.* Prentice Hall, 1999.

- Tom, P. *Data Protection and Information Lifecycle.* Prentice Hall, 2006.

- Trimmer, K.J., C.D. Schou, and K. Parker. "Enforcing Early Implementation Of Information Assurance Precepts Throughout The Design Phase." *Journal of Informatics Education Research,* 2007.

- U.S CERT. United States Computer Emergency Readiness Team, 2013. www.us-cert.gov/.

- U.S. General Accounting Office. "Report to the Ranking Minority Member, Subcommittee on 21st Century Competitiveness, Committee on Education and the Workforce, House of Representatives, EMPLOYEE PRIVACY – Computer-Use, Monitoring Practices, and Policies of Selected Companies." www.gao.gov/new.items/d02717.pdf. GAO-02-717, 2002.

- United States National Initiative for Cybersecurity Education (NICE). National Cybersecurity Workforce Framework. http://csrc.nist.gov/nice/framework/.

- User's Guide: How to Raise Information Security Awareness. European Network and Information Security Agency, Dec. 1, 2006. www.enisa.europa.eu/doc/pdf/deliverables/enisa_a_users_guide_how_to_raise_IS_awareness.pdf.

- Vaughn, R. Jr., R. Henning, and A. Siraj. Information Assurance Measures and Metrics – State of Practice and Proposed Taxonomy. 30th Hawaii International Conference on System Sciences, Big Island, Hawaii, January 7–10, 2002.

- Verizon. *The 2013 Data Breach Investigations Report.* www.verizonenterprise.com/resources/reports/rp_data-breach-investigations-report-2013_en_xg.pdf.

- Von Lubitz, Dag KJE, et al. "All Hazards Approach to Disaster Management: The Role of Information and Knowledge Management, Boyd's OODA Loop, and Network-Centricity." *Disasters.* 32, no. 4 (2008): 561–585.

- Wang, Abigail. Smart Chip Credit Cards Wouldn't Have Saved Target. http://securitywatch.pcmag.com/internet-crime/320071-smart-chip-credit-cards-wouldn-t-have-saved-target.

- Wen, J., D. Schwieger, and P. Gershuny. "Internet Usage Monitoring in the Workplace: Its Legal Challenges and Implementation Strategies." Information Systems Management Archive, January 2007), Volume 24, Issue 2. pp. 185–196.

- What Is a Honeynet? SearchSecurity.com, 2007. http://searchsecurity.techtarget .com/definition/honeynet.

- Wood, CC. *Information Security Roles & Responsibilities Made Easy.* PentaSafe Security Technologies, 2002.

- Yasinsac, Alec, and Y. Manzano. "Policies to Enhance Computer and Network Forensics." Proceedings of the 2001 IEEE Workshop on Information Assurance and Security United States Military Academy. West Point, NY, June 5–6, 2001.

Part VI

APPENDIX
I
List of Acronyms

The following are common computer security and information assurance acronyms.

$(ISC)^2$	International Information Systems Security Certification Consortium
A&A	Assessment and Authorization
AAC	Advanced Audio Coding
ACK	Acknowledge (a message)
ACL	Access Control List
ACM	Association for Computing Machinery
ADSL	Asymmetric Digital Subscriber Line
AES	Advanced Encryption Standard
ALE	Annualized Loss Expectancy
APT	Advanced Persistent Threat
ARO	Annualized Rate of Occurrence
AT&E	Awareness Training and Education
ATM	(1) Asynchronous Transfer Mode, (2) Automatic Teller Machine (in banking)
AV	Antivirus
B1	Labeled Security Protection, as specified in DoD 5200.28-STD
BCI	Business Continuity Institute
BCM	Business Continuity Management
BCP	Business Continuity Plan
BIA	Business Impact Analysis
BSI	British Standards Institution
BURP	Business Unit Resumption Plan

C&A	Certification and Accreditation
C2	Controlled Access Protection, as specified in DoD 5200.28-STD
CA	Certification Authority
CAP	Certified Authorization Professional, an (ISC)^2 certification
CBCP	Certified Business Continuity Planner
CBK	Common Body of Knowledge
CCB	Change Control Board
CCTV	Closed Circuit Television
CD-RW	Compact Disk Read/Write
CEI	Computer Ethics Institute
CEO	Chief Executive Officer
CERT	Computer Emergency Readiness Team
CFO	Chief Financial Officer
CIA	Confidentiality, Integrity, Availability
CIO	Chief Information Officer
CISA	Certified Information Systems Auditor
CISM	Certified Information Security Manager
CISO	Chief Information Security Officer
CISSP	Certified Information Systems Security Professional, an (ISC)^2 certification
CM	(1) Configuration Management, (2) Change Management
CMP	Crisis Management Plan
COBIT	Control Objectives for Information and related Technology, ISACA
CompTIA	Computing Technology Industry Association
CONOPS	Concept of Operations
COO	Chief Operating Officer
COOP	Continuity of Operations
COTS	Commercial Off-The-Shelf hardware or software
CP	Contingency Plan
CRC	Cyclic Redundancy Check
CRO	Chief Risk Officer
CSO	Chief Security Officer
CSSLP	Certified Secure Software Lifecycle Professional, an (ISC)^2 certification
CVE	Common Vulnerabilities and Exposures
DAC	Discretionary Access Control
DDOS	Distributed Denial of Service
DES	Data Encryption Standard
DMS	Defense Messaging System

DMZ	De-Militarized Zone
DOS	Denial of Service
DR	Disaster Recovery
DRII	Disaster Recovery Institute, International
DRP	Disaster Recovery Plan
DSA	Digital Signature Algorithm
DVD	Digital Versatile Disk
DVD-RW	Digital Versatile Disc (Read Write)
EA	Enterprise Architecture
EEPROM	Electrically Erasable Programmable Read-Only Memory
FFIEC	Federal Financial Institutions Examination Council
FIPS	Federal Information Processing Standards (United States)
FTP	File Transport Protocol
Gb	Gigabits
GB	Gigabytes
GIAC	Global Information Assurance Certification, a SANS certification
GLBA	Gramm-Leach-Bliley Act (United States)
HA	High Availability
HIDS	Host-based Intrusion Detection System
HIPAA	Health Information Portability and Accountability Act (United States)
HTTP	Hypertext Transfer Protocol
HVAC	Heating, Ventilation, and Air Conditioning
IA	Information Assurance
IAAA	Identification, Authentication, Authorization, and Accountability
ICS	Industrial Control System
ICT	Information and Communication Technology
ID	Identification
IDEA	International Data Encryption Algorithm (Block Cipher)
IDS	Intrusion Detection System
IEC	International Electrotechnical Commission
IEEE	Institute of Electrical and Electronics Engineers
IKE	Internet Key Exchange
INFOSEC	Information Security
IP	(1) Internet Protocol, (2) Intellectual Property
IPS	Intrusion Prevention System
IPSec	IP Security
IR	Incident Response

IRP	Incident Response Plan
ISACA	Information Systems Audit and Control Association
ISCP	Information System Contingency Plan
ISMS	Integrated Security Model for SNMP
ISO	International Standardization Organization
ISP	Internet Service Provider
ISSA	Information Systems Security Association
ISSO	Information Systems Security Officer
IT	Information Technology
LAN	Local Area Network
LDAP	Lightweight Directory Access Protocol
MAC	Mandatory Access Control
MD5	Message-Digest Algorithm 5
MLS	Multi-Level Security pertaining to classification levels
MP3	MPEG-1 Audio Layer 3
MPEG-4	Moving Picture Experts Group 4
MS	Microsoft
MS IIS	Microsoft Internet Information Services
MSR	Maconachy, Schou and Ragsdale security model
NAS	Network Area Storage
NDA	Non-Disclosure Agreement
NES	Network Encryption System
NetBIOS	Network Basic Input/Output System (OSI session layer)
NFS	Network File System
NIATEC	National Information Assurance Training and Education Center
NIDS	Network Intrusion Detection System
NIPS	Network Intrusion Prevention System
NIST	National Institute of Standards and Technology (United States)
NNTP	Network News Transport Protocol PEM Privacy
OEP	Occupant Emergency Plan
OS	Operating System
OSI	Open Systems Interconnection Reference Model
PC	Personal Computer
PCI	Payment Card Industry
PDCA	Plan Do Check Act cycle
PEST	Political, Economical, Sociocultural, and Technological
PGP	Pretty Good Privacy, a secure mail protocol

PIA	Privacy Impact Assessment
PII	Personally Identifiable Information
PIN	Personal Identification Number
PKI	Public Key Infrastructure
POA&M	Plan of Actions and Milestones
POP3	Post Office Protocol
PPTP	Point-to-Point Tunneling Protocol
RA	Registration Authority
RAD	Rapid Application Development
RADIUS	Remote Authentication Dial-in User Service
RAID	Redundant Array Of Independent Disks
RAS	Remote Access Service in Windows NT
RBAC	Role-Based Access Control
RCP	Remote Control Protocol
RMF	Risk Management Framework
ROI	Return On Investment
ROSI	Return On Security Investment
RPC	Remote Procedure Call
RPO	Recovery Point Objective
RSA	Rivest Shamir Adelman encryption
RTO	Recovery Time Objective
SAML	Security Assertion Markup Language
SAN	Storage Area Network
SANS	SysAdmin, Audit, Network, Security Institute
SATA	Serial Advance Technology Attachment
SATE	Security Awareness, Training and Education
SBU	Sensitive But Unclassified
SCAP	Security Content Automation Protocol
SCSI	Small Computer System Interface
SD	Secure Digital (storage)
SDLC	System Development Life Cycle
SIEM	Security Information and Event Management
SIM	(1) Security Information Management, (2) Subscriber Identity Module
SLA	Service Level Agreement
SLE	Single Loss Expectancy
SMB	Server Message Block, Small Medium Business
SMS	Short Messaging Service

SMTP	Simple Mail Transport Protocol
SOA	Service-Oriented Architecture
SOAP	Simple Object Access Protocol
SOX	Sarbanes-Oxley Act (United States)
SSCP	Systems Security Certified Practitioner, an (ISC)^2 certification
SSDLC	Secure Software Development Life Cycle
SSL	Secure Sockets Layer
SSO	Single Sign-On
SSP	System Security Plan
ST&E	System Test and Evaluation
STP	Standard Threat Profile
SWOT	Strengths, Weaknesses, Opportunities, Threats
SYN	Synchronize
SYN/ACK	Synchronize/Acknowledge
TACACS	Terminal Access, Controller Access, Control Systems
TB	Terabytes
TCO	Total Cost of Ownership
TCP/IP	Transport Control Protocol/Internet Protocol
TLS	Transport Layer Security
UK	United Kingdom
UPS	Uninterruptible Power Supply
US	United States
USB	Universal Serial Bus
VLAN	Virtual Local Area Network
VPN	Virtual Private Networks
WAN	Wide Area Network
WEP	Wired Equivalent Privacy
WORM	Write Once, Read Many Times
WPA2	Wi-Fi Protected Access, version 2
WWW	World Wide Web

Glossary

The glossary comes from several international sources. It includes terms used in the United States and terms used in other economies, nations, and industries.

access Opportunity to make use of an information system resource.

access control Limiting access to information system resources only to authorized users, programs, processes, or other systems.

access control list (ACL) Mechanism implementing discretionary and/or mandatory access control between subjects and objects. It specifies which subjects are authorized to access a specific object and defines the level of authorization.

access control matrix A representation of subject and object in a tabulated form whereby privileges (of subjects upon objects) are defined at the cell where the intersection of subject and object happens.

Advanced Audio Coding (AAC) A technique for compressing digital audio files. Officially part of the MPEG-4 standard, it is most widely used to create small digital audio files. AAC usually achieves better sound quality than the more popular MP3 format when compared at the same bit rate.

Advanced Encryption Standard (AES) FIPS-approved cryptographic algorithm that is a symmetric block cipher using cryptographic key sizes of 128, 192, and 256 bits to encrypt and decrypt data in blocks of 128 bits. (See NIST FIPS 197)

annualized loss expectancy (ALE) The estimated amount of loss in a year.

annualized rate of occurrence (ARO) Frequency of a particular threat in a year.

application Software program that performs a specific function directly for a user and executed without access to system control, monitoring, or administrative privileges.

asset Any tangible or intangible thing that has value to an organization.

assurance Measure of confidence that the security features, practices, procedures, and architecture of an information system accurately mediates and enforces the security policy.

asymmetric cryptography   A class of algorithm that uses a different key for encryption than for decryption.

audit   Independent review and examination of records and activities to assess the adequacy of system controls, to ensure compliance with established policies and operational procedures, and to recommend necessary changes in controls, policies, or procedures.

authenticate   To verify the identity of a user, user device, or other entity, or the integrity of data stored, transmitted, or otherwise exposed to unauthorized modification in an information system, or to establish the validity of a transmission.

authentication   The process of validating the identity provided by a user.

availability   A condition in which information or processes are reasonably accessible and usable by an authorized party and are timely and critical.

back door   Hidden software or hardware mechanism used to circumvent security controls. This is synonymous with *trap door*.

backup   Creation of a copy of data or software or hardware devices for the purpose of restoration if the masters were to become lost, damaged, or otherwise unavailable for use.

biometrics   Automated methods of authenticating or verifying an individual based upon a physical or behavioral characteristic.

capability table   An authorization table identifying subjects and specifying access rights allowed to those subjects. The rows of tables list the capabilities that subjects can have with respect to all objects.

certificate   Digitally signed document that binds a public key with an identity. The certificate contains, at a minimum, the identity of the issuing certification authority, the user identification information, and the user's public key.

certificate management   Process whereby certificates are generated, stored, protected, transferred, loaded, used, and destroyed.

certification authority (CA)   C&A: Official responsible for performing the comprehensive evaluation of the security features of an information system and determining the degree to which it meets its security requirements. PKI: Trusted entity authorized to create, sign, and issue public key certificates. By digitally signing each certificate issued, the user's identity is certified, and the association of the certified identity with a public key is validated.

change management   A process that ensures all changes to IT infrastructure are assessed, approved, implemented, and reviewed in a controlled manner to reduce or eliminate disruptions to business activities.

checksum   (1) A form of redundancy checks to ensure integrity of information. (2) A value computed on data to detect error or manipulation during transmission. (See *hash*.)

cipher   Any cryptographic system in which arbitrary symbols or groups of symbols represent units of plain text or in which units of plain text are rearranged, or both.

cipher text   Enciphered information.

common criteria   Provides a comprehensive, rigorous method for specifying security function and assurance requirements for products and systems (per International Standard ISO/IEC 5408, Common Criteria for Information Technology Security Evaluation).

computer security   Protection given to an IT system to achieve the purposes of retaining confidentiality, integrity, and availability of information system resources.

confidentiality   Assurance that information is not disclosed to unauthorized individuals, processes, or devices. This is the condition in which sensitive data is protected and disclosed to authorized parties only, such as by using encryption disclosed or other methods.

configuration control   Process of controlling modifications to hardware, firmware, software, and documentation to ensure the information system is protected against improper modifications prior to, during, and after system implementation.

configuration management   (1) A process of controlling changes to device configurations in an IT environment under the control of change management. It involves identifying, recording, and tracking all IT components, including their versions, constituent components, and relationships. (2) Management of security features and assurances through control of changes made to hardware, software, firmware, test, test fixtures, and documentation throughout the life cycle of an information system.

constrained user interface   A way to limit access of subjects to resources or information by presenting them with only the information, function, or access to resources for which they have privileges.

content-dependent access control   A technique to control access to objects based on the content of objects themselves.

continuity of operations plan   Plan for continuing an organization's essential functions at an alternate site and performing those functions for the duration of an event with little or no loss of continuity before returning to normal operations.

control   Measures or safeguards that, when correctly employed, will prevent or reduce the risk of exploitation of vulnerabilities.

copyright   The exclusive legal rights to reproduce, publish, sell, or distribute the matter and form of something (as a literary, musical, or artistic work).

Data Encryption Standard (DES)   Cryptographic algorithm designed for the protection of unclassified data and published by the National Institute of Standards and Technology (NIST) in Federal Information Processing Standard (FIPS) Publication 46.

decree   An authoritative order having the force of law.

defense-in-depth, security-in-depth   Information assurance (IA) strategy integrating people, technology, and operations capabilities to establish variable barriers across multiple layers and dimensions of networks.

degauss   A process that demagnetizes magnetic media so that a low residue of magnetic induction is left on the media. It is used to effectively erase data from media.

demilitarized zone (DMZ)   Perimeter network segment that is logically between internal and external networks. Its purpose is to enforce the internal network's information assurance policy for external information exchange and to provide external, untrusted sources with restricted access to releasable information while shielding the internal networks from outside attacks. A DMZ is also called a *screened subnet.*

denial of service (DOS)   An incident in which a user or organization is deprived of the services of a resource that it would normally expect to have. This could be any action or series of actions that prevents any part of an information system from functioning.

detective controls   Used to identify undesirable events that have occurred.

disaster recovery plan   Provides for the continuity of system operations after a disaster.

discretionary access control (DAC)   (1) An access control model whereby the owner of an object (resource) decides the subject and what privileges that subject can have over the object. (2) Means of restricting access to objects based on the identity and need-to-know of users and/or groups to which the object belongs. Controls are discretionary in the sense that a subject with certain access permission is capable of passing that permission (directly or indirectly) to any other subject. (See *mandatory access control.*)

dual control   Control whereby two or more individuals are required to perform a task at any one time.

e-mail   A message sent or retrieved electronically.

firewall   A hardware or software system used to enforce an access control policy between network segments or zones.

guidelines   General statements of objectives designed to achieve the policy's objective.

hash   A one-way algorithm that maps or translates one set of bits into another (generally smaller) in such a way that the algorithm yields the same hash results every time for the same message, and it is computationally infeasible for a message to be reconstituted from the hash result. Two different messages cannot produce the same hash results.

host   Any computer on a network that is a repository for services available to other computers on the network.

impact   Outcome or consequences of an event.

incident   Assessed occurrence having actual or potentially adverse effects on an information system.

information assurance (IA)   (1) Technical and managerial controls designed to ensure the confidentiality, possession of control, integrity, authenticity, availability, and utility of information and information systems. (2) Measures that protect and defend information and information systems by ensuring their availability, integrity, authentication, confidentiality, and nonrepudiation. These measures include providing for the restoration of information systems by incorporating protection, detection, and reaction capabilities.

information owner   Official with statutory or operational authority for specified information and responsibility for establishing the controls for its generation, collection, processing, dissemination, and disposal.

information system (IS)   Set of information resources organized for the collection, storage, processing, maintenance, use, sharing, dissemination, disposition, display, or transmission of information.

integrity   (1) A condition in which data has not been changed or destroyed in an unauthorized way, such that the current state is identical to the original state. (2) Condition existing when data is unchanged from its source and has not been accidentally or maliciously modified, altered, or destroyed. (3) Quality of an information system reflecting the logical correctness and reliability of the operating system; the logical completeness of the hardware and software implementing the protection mechanisms; and the consistency of the data structures and occurrence of the stored data.

   Note that, in a formal security mode, integrity is interpreted more narrowly to mean protection against unauthorized modification or destruction of information.

Internet   The world's largest collection of networks ranging from those of small organizations to those of large corporations, universities, or governments.

Internet Protocol (IP)   Standard protocol for the transmission of data from source to destinations in packet-switched communications networks and interconnected systems of such networks.

intrusion   Unauthorized act of bypassing the security mechanisms of a system.

intrusion detection   A method or process to detect break-ins or attempts to attack via the use of software systems operating on the system or network. Intrusion detection systems often combine network monitoring with real-time capture and analysis to identify attacks.

Kerberos   A secret key-based service for providing network authentication. Uses tickets and requires time synchronization.

least privilege   Grants users only that access they need to perform their official duties.

likelihood   Probability or frequency.

magnetic remanence Magnetic representation of residual information remaining on a magnetic medium after the medium has been cleared.

malicious applets Small application programs automatically downloaded and executed that perform an unauthorized function on an information system.

malicious code Software or firmware intended to perform an unauthorized process that will have adverse impact on the confidentiality, integrity, or availability of an information system. (See *Trojan horse.*)

malicious logic Hardware, software, or firmware capable of performing an unauthorized function on an information system.

mandatory access control (MAC) (1) An access control model whereby the access policy is controlled by the system, not the owner of the object. (2) Means of restricting access to objects based on the sensitivity of the information contained in the objects and the formal authorization (in other words, clearance, formal access approvals, and need-to-know) of subjects to access information of such sensitivity. (See *discretionary access control.*) (3) Media Access Control address a unique identifier associated with hardware.

message authentication code A short piece of information used to authenticate a message.

mobile code Software modules obtained from remote systems, transferred across a network, and then downloaded and executed on local systems without explicit installation or execution by the recipient.

MSR Refers to a security model adopted by ACM based on an article by Maconachy, Schou, Ragsdale, and Welch.

network intrusion prevention A device (hardware or software) that manages network packets to prevent and defend computers in a network from exploitation.

nonrepudiation A term used for the service that ensures entities are honest in their actions.

object Passive entity containing or receiving information. This access to an object implies access to the information it contains.

OODA Loop Observation-Orientation-Decision-Act A model whereby every person involved in a challenge (business or action loop military) must go through a loop. For example, first observe the conditions of the situation, then become oriented to a position for an action, decide on how to act (some theorists combine the orient-decide step), and finally, act in response to the situation.

password Protected/private string of letters, numbers, and special characters used to authenticate an identity or to authorize access to data.

patch   Software code inserted into a system to temporarily fix a defect. Patches are developed and released by software vendors when vulnerabilities are discovered.

patent   An set of exclusive rights granted by the government to secure exclusive right to make, use, or sell an invention for a set term.

Perimeter Subnet   An isolated network segment between two routers where public accessible computers can be placed.

personal digital assistant (PDA)   A handheld device that combines computing, telephone/fax, Internet, and networking features.

physical information security controls   Procedures put into place to prevent intruders from physically accessing a system or facility.

Plan-Do-Check-Act model   An approach to improvement that emphasizes planning a set of actions, implementing the actions, checking data to assess both the results and the plan, and acting on the data.

policy   A high-level statement of an organization's beliefs, goals, objectives, and the general means for their attainment for a specified subject area.

procedure   Step-by-step guidance or methods for attaining policy objectives.

process   A series of linked steps necessary to accomplish work. A process turns input such as information or raw materials into output such as products, services, and reports.

product accreditation   Formal acceptance of the adequacy of a system's IT security to meet operational requirements within an acceptable risk level. This is an acceptance of risk.

product certification   Evaluation of controls present within a system to ensure compliance with predefined functional and IT security requirements.

proxy server   A mechanism used to offer a computer network service to allow clients to make indirect network connections to other network services through it, thus making the clients invisible to connections from the net.

public key infrastructure (PKI)   A system of digital certificates, certificate authorities, and other registration authorities that verify and authenticate the validity of each party involved in an Internet transaction.

residual risk   The remaining level of risk after risk treatment has been taken.

risk   (1) The chance of something happening that will have impact upon objectives. (2) Possibility that a particular threat will adversely impact an information system by exploiting a particular vulnerability.

risk assessment   Process of analyzing threats to and vulnerabilities of an information system, and the potential impact resulting from the loss of information or capabilities of

Part VI

a system. This analysis is a basis for identifying appropriate and cost-effective security countermeasures.

risk management   (1) The process by which resources are planned, organized, directed, and controlled to ensure risk remains within acceptable bounds at optimal cost. (2) Process of managing risks to an organization's operations (including mission, functions, image, or reputation), assets, or individuals resulting from the operation of an information system. It includes risk assessment; cost-benefit analysis; the selection, implementation, and assessment of security controls; and the formal authorization to operate the system. The process considers effectiveness, efficiency, and constraints because of laws, directives, policies, or regulations.

role-based access control   An access control model that uses a centrally managed set of rules that grants access to objects based on the roles of the subject.

rule-based access control   An access control model that uses simple rules to determine the result of privileges that a subject can have over an object.

screening router   A rule based packet-filtering system to protect the network (administrator controlled).

separation of duties   Division of roles and responsibilities so that a single individual cannot sabotage a critical process.

service-oriented architecture   Architecture whose style of investment looks at the overall current information status of organizations and the immediate controls required.

single loss expectancy (SLE)   The amount of loss incurred in a single threat event.

social engineering   To talk, lie, or play-act to trick legitimate users for secrets of systems such as user lists, user passwords, and network architecture.

spoofing   Unauthorized use of legitimate identification and authentication (I&A) data, however it was obtained, to mimic a subject different from the attacker. Impersonating, masquerading, piggybacking, and mimicking are forms of spoofing.

standard   Mandatory activities, actions, rules, or regulations designed to provide policies with the support structure and specific direction they require to be meaningful and effective.

subject   Generally, an individual, process, or device causing information to flow among objects or change to the system state.

symmetric cryptography   A class of algorithm that uses the same key for both encryption and decryption.

system development life cycle   The overall process of creating, implementing, and retiring information systems through a multistep process from initiation, analysis, design, implementation, and maintenance to disposal.

Telnet   A protocol for connecting to a remote system as a terminal. A potential vulnerability

threat   (1) An event or occurrence that has the potential to compromise the information security of an asset. (2) Any circumstance or event with the potential to adversely impact an information system through unauthorized access, destruction, disclosure, modification of data, and/or denial of service.

trade secret   Proprietary information that is important for its survival and profitability.

trademark   Any distinguishing name, symbol, sound, character, or logo that establishes identity for a product, service, or organization.

Triple DES   Product cipher that, like DES, operates on 64-bit data blocks. There are several forms, each of which uses the DES cipher three times. Some forms use two 56-bit keys; some use three. (See NIST FIPS 46-3.)

Trojan horse   Program containing hidden code allowing the unauthorized collection, falsification, or destruction of information.

uninterruptible power supply   A device that maintains a continuous supply of electric power to connected equipment by supplying power from a separate source when utility power is not available.

USB flash drive   A small, portable flash memory card that plugs into a computer's USB port and functions as a portable hard drive.

validation   Process of applying specialized security test and evaluation procedures, tools, and equipment needed to establish acceptance for the joint usage of an information system by one or more departments or organizations and their contractors.

verification   Process of comparing two levels of an information system specification for proper correspondence (such as a security policy model with top-level specification, top-level specification with source code, or source code with object code).

virtual private network (VPN)   (1) A secure network that uses a public network to connect users to their offices, homes, or organizational networks. (2) Protected information system link utilizing tunneling, security controls (see information assurance), and endpoint address translation giving the impression of a dedicated line.

virus   (1) A code written with malicious intent to modify the way a computer operates, without approval of the user. (2) Self-replicating, malicious code that attaches itself to an application program or other executable system component and leaves no obvious signs of its presence.

vulnerability   (1) A flaw or weakness in procedure, design, implementation, or internal controls that can be exploited and can result in an information security breach or a violation of information security policy. (2) Weakness in an information system, system security procedures, internal controls, or implementation that could be exploited.

web filter   A tool used to control access of end users to the Internet.

zero-day   This term describes a newly discovered vulnerability with no known patch or mitigation.

Index